"Maurus Reinkowski's *The History of Turkey: Grandeur and Grievance* offers a critical retelling of Turkey's triumphs and tragedies, providing an empathic exploration of the country's past over a century. This expertly crafted work illuminates the country's moments of grandeur and delves into its deep-seated grievances. Through an engagement with state-of-the-art research, Reinkowski's keen eye for detail allows him to paint a vivid picture of Turkey's complex history, surpassing standard textbooks. In a time of political crisis, Reinkowski's engaging yet sober book offers a much-needed update to the perhaps overly optimistic scholarship of the last two decades. Impeccably researched and eloquently written, *The History of Turkey: Grandeur and Grievance* is an indispensable resource for scholars, students, and anyone seeking a critical understanding of Turkey's past, present, and future."

— Alp Yenen, Assistant Professor of Modern Turkish History and Culture, Leiden University

"In his thought-provoking introductory chapter, Maurus Reinkowski aptly observes that Turkey is a country that evokes anything but indifference. This rings acutely true in 2023, as Turkey not only faces presidential elections but also gears up to commemorate the centennial anniversary of the founding of the Turkish Republic. *The History of Turkey* provides an invaluable companion to unlock the historical context of these events. Covering a period from 1912 to the present, the book offers a nuanced, meticulously researched and vividly narrated historical overview. It serves as a comprehensive and widely accessible guide to Turkish history and historiography that also features insightful discussions of Turkey's most recent decades. By skillfully embedding key developments within their broader historical and cultural contexts, the rich narrative invites readers to explore the complexity and diversity of Turkish history and allows them to recognize enduring legacies and reverberations of the processes depicted in the book."

— Barbara Henning, professor at Johannes Gutenberg University Mainz, Ottoman and Turkish History

"This work is the culmination of some forty years of diligent language practice, intensive research, meticulous observation, and genuine engagement with the societies of Turkey. The result is a profound piece of scholarship with pages full of intellectually sophisticated analyses and magisterial detail that provide a new interpretation of the land, state, and people. Well-grounded in a wide range of old and new scholarship, it is a highly accessible account of Turkey from both a comparative and global perspective. This book will eloquently but at the same time disturbingly and constantly remind readers how firmly the genesis of state ideology is built on the foundations of the late Ottoman and early Republican period. It is essential reading for introductory and advanced courses on Turkey and the Middle East, and for those who look for a concise, yet authoritative account of the region in order to understand the state, politics, and society in depth. There is no equivalent study of this quality for Turkey; Reinkowski deserves considerable praise for a work that should receive much attention."

— Metin Atmaca, Professor of Ottoman and Middle East History, Social Sciences University of Ankara

"This work of Maurus Reinkowski is an indispensable tool for those aiming to have a profound knowledge on present-day Turkish politics, or to understand this complex society. Having been trained in late Ottoman history and Middle East politics, Reinkowski is a keen observer of political and social developments in contemporary Turkey, also known officially as *Türkiye*. This study is chronologically organized, beginning with the historical roots of modern Turkey, followed by the Kemalist Republic (1923-1950), the period of 1950-1980, and recent Turkish history. What makes this book so appealing is its concentration on contemporary Turkish developments following the military coup of 1980. It discusses structural conditions leading to a crucial break from Kemalism, commenced with the so-called 'Turkish-Islamic Synthesis' ideology of the 1980s, continued by the economic liberalism of Turgut Özal, finally leading to the AKP-era presidential system accompanied by populism and authoritarianism. Reinkowski handles numerous topics, which still bear the quality of actuality, in a precise, informative and balanced manner."

— Selçuk Akşin Somel, Sabancı University, Istanbul

"This mature work combines affection for the subject with detached insight; serious questioning with a positive approach. Drawing on the current state of research, Reinkowski appreciates Turkey's potential and grievances, but also highlights the dead ends of its ultranationalism. Reading his insightful narrative reveals a central challenge: how to build up trust and democratic confidence in the dynamic, but troubled post-Ottoman country that is Republican Turkey? This work differs from many traditional books on modern Turkey that overemphasize Atatürk, while ignoring the late-Ottoman context and new developments of the twenty-first century."

— Hans-Lukas Kieser, Historian, University of Newcastle, Australia, and University of Zurich, Switzerland

The History of Turkey

Grandeur and Grievance

Ottoman and Turkish Studies
Series Editor
Hakan T. Karateke (University of Chicago)

Other Titles in this Series

Crafting History: Essays on the Ottoman World and Beyond in Honor of Cemal Kafadar
Edited by Rachel Goshgarian, Ilham Khuri-Makdisi, and Ali Yaycıoğlu

A History of Ottoman Libraries
İsmail E. Erünsal

Uncoupling Language and Religion: An Exploration into the Margins of Turkish Literature
Laurent Mignon

Excavating Memory: Bilge Karasu's Istanbul and Walter Benjamin's Berlin
Ülker Gökberk

The Ottoman Twilight in the Arab Lands: Turkish Memoirs and Testimonies of the Great War
Selim Deringil

Disliking Others: Loathing, Hostility, and Distrust in Premodern Ottoman Lands
Edited by Hakan T. Karateke, H. Erdem Çıpa, and Helga Anetshofer

Waiting for Müteferrika: Glimpses of Ottoman Print Culture
Orlin Sabev

Investigating Turkey: Detective Fiction and Turkish Nationalism, 1928–1945
David Mason

For more information on this series, please visit:
academicstudiespress.com/ottomanandturkishstudies

The History of Turkey

Grandeur and Grievance

Maurus Reinkowski

Translated from German
by William J. Walsh

BOSTON
2023

Library of Congress Cataloging-in-Publication Data

Names: Reinkowski, Maurus, 1962- author.
Title: The history of Turkey : grandeur and grievance / Maurus Reinkowski ;
  translated by William Walsh.
Other titles: Geschichte der Türkei. English
Description: Boston : Academic Studies Press, 2023. | Series: Ottoman and
  Turkish studies series | Includes bibliographical references and index.
Identifiers: LCCN 2023020658 (print) | LCCN 2023020659 (ebook) | ISBN
  9798887192161 (hardback) | ISBN 9798887192178 (paperback) | ISBN
  9798887192185 (adobe pdf) | ISBN 9798887192192 (epub)
Subjects: LCSH: Turkey--History--1918-1960.
Classification: LCC DR590 .R45513 2023 (print) | LCC DR590 (ebook) | DDC
  956.1/02--dc23/eng/20230503
LC record available at https://lccn.loc.gov/2023020658
LC ebook record available at https://lccn.loc.gov/2023020659

Copyright © 2023, Academic Studies Press. All rights reserved

ISBN 9798887192161 (hardback)
ISBN 9798887192178 (paperback)
ISBN 9798887192185 (adobe pdf)
ISBN 9798887192192 (epub)

Book design by Lapiz Digital Services
Cover by Ivan Grave

Published by Academic Studies Press
1577 Beacon Street
Brookline, MA 02446, USA
press@academicstudiespress.com
www.academicstudiespress.com

Contents

Preface		1
Introduction		4
Chapter 1:	Farewell to the Ottoman Empire	34
Chapter 2:	The Kemalist Republic, 1923–1950	89
Chapter 3:	Precarious Pluralism, 1950–1980	128
Chapter 4:	The Promise of Islamic Conservatism, 1980–2013	174
Chapter 5:	The Road to Another Republic, 2013 to the Present	249
Update on Turkey in the Years 2021–2023		296
Acknowledgements		303
Timeline		305
Abbreviations		312
Bibliography		316
Map: Turkey and its neighbors		354
Index of Names		356
Index of Geographic Names		360

Preface

The Turkish alphabet is admirably clear in its spelling. The consonants are mostly pronounced as in English or German, and the vowels mostly as in Spanish or Italian, with the following unusual letters:

- C/c is pronounced like the j in "jelly"
- Ç/ç is the ch in "church"
- ğ is silent but lengthens the previous vowel
- I/ı is a short, dull sound much like the i in "cousin"
- İ/i is the vowel "i" in Spanish or Italian, that is, like the English ee in "cheese"
- J/j is found mostly in loanwords from French and, like the French j, is pronounced "zh" like the s in "pleasure" or "treasure"
- Ö/ö is pronounced as in German, or the French eu in peu
- Ş/ş is the sh in "ship"
- Ü/ü is pronounced as in German, or the French u in rue

In this book, the spelling of personal and place names follow the spellings current in Turkey today, thus "Erdoğan" and "İstanbul" rather than "Erdogan" and "Istanbul." For the period before the founding of the Turkish Republic, the then current names in European languages are used with the present names appended, for example, Smyrna (İzmir) or Adrianople (Edirne). Constantinople (Kostantiniyye in Ottoman Turkish) became mandatorily replaced by İstanbul only in the Turkish Republic. Nevertheless, we will use İstanbul throughout in the context of either the Ottoman Empire or the Republic of Turkey. For places which are known today under two different names, as for example some cities in Cyprus, both designations are used, for example, Greek/Turkish Famagusta/Gazimağusa.

Abbreviations are used after the first usage of the abbreviated phrase in each chapter. For Turkish institutions and parties, for example, the Republican People's Party (Cumhuriyet Halk Partisi, CHP), only the Turkish abbreviations will be used, as there are no established short forms for these organizations in English or other European languages. For all terms, the translation will be given first, with the Turkish original following parenthetically.

Before the mandatory introduction of surnames on 1 January 1935, Muslims in Turkey only used given names (if often with appended descriptive epithets, conveying, for example, their origin in a city or region). For the period before 1935, we append their later-adopted surname in parenthesis, for example, Ali Fuat (Cebesoy). Because we speak so often of Mustafa Kemal Atatürk, a different rule applies to him: before 1935, he is called Mustafa Kemal, after 1935, Atatürk. Titles like pasha (generals and dignitaries of high standing) are only used, if at all, before 1935. Names from Ottoman times are sometimes spelled slightly differently from the contemporary Turkish norm, for example, (Ottoman) Abdülhamid instead of (Modern Turkish) Abdülhamit, in order to appropriately reflect the Ottoman spelling in the Arabic alphabet. The spelling reform of 1 January 1929, that is, the transition from the Arabic to the Latin alphabet, introduced a number of diacritical marks, like a circumflex on some instances of the vowels a, i, and u, to reflect long vowels in Arabic, as in *Resmî Gazete* (the Official Gazette of the Republic of Turkey) or Millî İstihbarat Teşkilâtı (National Intelligence Organization, i.e., the Turkish secret service). In cases where these institutions still use these old-fashioned spellings today, we adopt them as well. Terms from the religious tradition of Islam, which are almost universally derived from Arabic terms (one of the few exceptions in Turkish is the use of the Persian *namaz* for ritual prayer), appear here as in modern Turkish usage, for example *mezhep* for one of the legal schools of thought in Islamic jurisprudence (instead of the correct standard Arabic transliteration *madhhab*). Islamic religious terms for which there exists a standard English spelling are excepted, like Hajj, Ramadan, or Shari'a.

All references in the footnotes are short form; the complete entries can be found in the bibliography at the end of the book.

The manuscript of this book (its original version was published in German with C. H. Beck) was completed in March 2021. Readers may miss hints to the latest developments and incidents, such as Turkey's position towards Russia's war on the Ukraine since February 2022, but in order to preserve the integrity of the text the 2021 version has been kept unaltered in this book.

Introduction

Turkey is a strong country. It is a member of the G20, the forum of states with most of the world's largest economies. Turkish Airlines (Türk Hava Yolları), which as recently as the 1980s was a carrier with a limited range, today serves more countries in the world than any other airline—by a wide margin. After the Justice and Development Party (Adalet ve Kalkınma Partisi, AKP) assumed power in 2002, the country experienced an impressive economic boom. Turkey fields the second-largest army in NATO; and, with the end of the Cold War in the 1990s, its geostrategic importance has only grown. Turkey is a key player in numerous burning political crises of our day, like how to deal with the collapsing order of the Middle East and with what means Europe should reply to migration pressures from Africa and Asia. The Turkish-descended diaspora is one of the most significant in Europe. Enabled by modern mass media and transportation, these millions of people convey political conditions in Turkey into the heart of Europe—and vice versa. Turkey's land area exceeds that of France, the largest Western European country by territory. Thanks to its dynamic population growth, it currently has well over eighty million inhabitants and has meanwhile surpassed Germany, the most populous country in the European Union.

Turkey is a difficult country. Relations between Turkey and Europe have always been fickle and are burdened on both sides by reservations rooted in the politics of identity. If admitted to the European Union (which is barely imaginable at the moment), Turkey would lay claim to a role commensurate not only with its political but its demographic weight. The immense misgivings which Great Britain, shaped by its imperial past, had about the European Union until its exit in January 2020 would be nothing as compared to those which would be held by Turkey as a member state. Into the early 2010s, Turkey was considered the Islamic country which stood for the compatibility of democracy and Islam in exemplary fashion. Its path to authoritarian rule from the late 2000s has dimmed its reputation as a role model, however. In addition, in light of Turkey's new self-consciousness, relations have become more complicated: on the European side, old certainties of superiority are entangled with new discomfitures; on the Turkish side, new imperial ambitions overlie old anticolonial reflexes.

Turkey is a magnificent country. The geographic and cultural variety of this expansive land is impressive. Turkey encompasses classical Asia Minor, one of the historically and culturally richest regions of the world. It is the successor of the Ottoman Empire, one of the greatest premodern empires, which was destroyed at the end of the First World War, making the creation of a new Turkey, the Republic of Turkey founded in 1923, simultaneously necessary and possible.

The idea, so enthusiastically deployed in European depictions, of Turkey as a bridge between "East" and "West" is not a popular image in Turkey, as in it Turkey appears too much like an object to be used. Today, Turkey prefers to see itself as a "pivotal state." It is a country conjoined with Europe—but not exclusively so. The vitality of Turkish society far exceeds that of the countries of Western Europe. In contrast to many Arab states, whose population growth and surfeit of young people has become a burden to them, Turkey can credit its demographic dynamism, which will continue into the late 2020s, for the development of a large internal market.[1] The restlessness and liveliness of Turkish metropolises is occasionally overwhelming.

Turkey is a torn country. It is not always an advantage to be a bridge between cultures and different regions of the world or even to be a "pivotal state" in a region. Turkey cannot always justify its claim to connect different worlds, even in its own society. Turks point with pride to their history, which reaches back far beyond the Turkish Republic and the Ottoman Empire, but this rich inheritance has also endowed them with difficult legacies, like the

---

1   İçduygu, "Demography," 333. Per UNICEF, *World's Children*, 192, population growth in the decade 2008–2018 averaged 1.5% and will sink to 0.7% in 2018–2030.

animosity, already well-developed in the nineteenth century, between a camp who understand themselves in secular terms and one which sees itself primarily in light of their religious-conservative commitments. Because these camps do not agree on what the history of their own country represents, they have consistently failed to reach an accord on how this history might serve as the foundation of a national self-understanding. Without any such clear idea, relations have consequently been fraught with the large minorities of Alevis and Kurds; to date, the sole solution the country could and has desired to offer is assimilation into the Turkish Sunni majority. The Kurds, who are not Turks, ethnically or linguistically, and the Alevis, who are not Sunnis, have not found this solution attractive, let alone persuasive.

It seemed that features about cosmopolitan İstanbul were on German television almost every night in the early 2010s (such stories always spotlighted a very small part of İstanbul, specifically the city within its borders of around 1900). Nowadays, the authoritarianism of the Turkish government is the hot topic, though without the appeal of the city of İstanbul and the country having entirely given way. Turkey is in any case a country rarely met with indifference, neither in Turkey nor abroad—a sign that it has distinctive qualities of character and is far from the margins of world politics.

Turkey: Territory, Borders, Neighbors

The fundamentals and borders of the Republic of Turkey recognized by international law are found in the Treaty of Lausanne, which was concluded on 24 July 1923 between Turkey and the victors of the First World War, foremost France and Great Britain. The foundation of the Republic of Turkey (Türkiye Cumhuriyeti) followed a few months later on 29 October 1923. Since Lausanne, the borders of Turkey have remained fundamentally the same—with the exception of the region called Hatay around the cities of Antakya and İskenderun which fell to Turkey in 1939. The century-long existence of the Republic of Turkey within the borders of Lausanne supports the conclusion that the state system of the Middle East in the twentieth century, despite its reputation as a region of crises, has been more stable than that of Europe.[2]

Its geographic composition lends Turkey the appearance of a compact unit. With a coastline of 3,371 miles (not including its islands) compared to

---

2   Gelvin, *New Middle East*, 7.

land borders of 1,709 miles, Turkey is a state whose borders are principally maritime. To the north, it's bordered by the Black Sea, to the west by the Aegean, and to the south, the Mediterranean. In addition, the Sea of Marmara communicates with the Aegean through the Straits of the Dardanelles and with the Black Sea through those of the Bosporus. İstanbul sits at the upper end of the Sea of Marmara, that is, at the southern egress of the Bosporus, on one of the most important shipping lanes in the world. The territory of Turkey, encompassing 305,422 square miles, is thereby "a territory of impressive coherence in area and outline, without extreme projections and constrictions of its borders."[3] On the other hand, the west-to-east slope of Turkey catches the eye. West Anatolia was already the core area of the state in late Ottoman times,[4] in the early years of the Republic the eastern regions still seemed like a foreign body. For the Turkish elites living in the West Anatolian big cities, Southeast Anatolia was more than just geographically distant. One would rather roam the great wide world than "through wild Kurdistan." It was—and remains—in parts an area of unpopular probation for doctors, officials, teachers, and security forces.

Only a little more than three percent (9,159 square miles) of the land area of Turkey lies in the region of Thrace west of the straits and therefore "in Europe." The rest lies in Anatolia, also called Asia Minor. The term "Asia Minor" originally was applied only to the western portion of the Asiatic part of Turkey—the peninsula protruding from the Asian land mass between the Black Sea, Sea of Marmara, and Mediterranean. The watershed between the Kızılırmak and Euphrates rivers or, alternatively, a line between the cities İskenderun (on the Mediterranean) and Trabzon (on the Black Sea) divides Asia Minor proper from the regions lying further east. By "Anatolia," the Greeks originally meant the mainland east of the Aegean. In the eleventh and twelfth century, this term was adopted by the Turks, but considerably broadened. This book uses the term "Anatolia" rather than Asia Minor. Keeping with current Turkish usage, Anatolia (Anadolu) connotes the entire Asian region of the Republic of Turkey.

Turkey still belongs to Europe in terms of cultural geography. The lack of large, defined areas of territory rendered uninhabitable by physical or climatic conditions conspicuously differentiates Anatolia from Iran, the Arabian

---

3   Hütteroth, *Türkei*, 18.
4   Per Kreiser, "Kernraum," the density of religious foundations (evkaf) can serve to determine the core Ottoman territories in Western Anatolia and Southeastern Europe.

Peninsula, or Egypt.⁵ The geographic division of Europe from Asia by the two straits is in any case a convention: the Dardanelles and Bosporus are flooded river valleys, and from İstanbul on the European shore, one looks upon the other shore as from Manhattan to Brooklyn.

Due to its geographic position, Turkey might boast a climate comparable to Portugal or southern Italy. The largest part of Turkey, however, lies too high for a subtropical climate. The average elevation of Turkey is 3,707 feet (the Iberian Peninsula, which is in certain respects comparable to Anatolia, has an average elevation of 2,100 feet). A second characteristic of Anatolia is numerous orogenic belts of mountains, almost traversing the entire landscape, which leads to a chambering of the land into massifs and mountain ranges with basins (*ova*) of various orders of magnitude lying between them. Ova, like the southeastern European polje, denotes a flat lowland that is at least partially surrounded by higher terrain. A third characteristic shaping Anatolia is Inner Anatolia's being cut off from the sea by mountain massifs rising immediately behind the coastline, running parallel to the seashore, and in places towering over 10,000 feet. The Pontic Mountains run along the Black Sea coast and the Taurus Mountains along the south coast. Only in the west, on the Aegean coast, is the transition to the Inner Anatolian highland distinctly set back in the interior, and the land falls off less precipitously. A dry continental climate on the Inner Anatolian highland stands in contrast to the subtropical climate along the slender coastlines.⁶ The separation of Inner Anatolia from the coasts and its partial, difficult accessibility in the eastern regions have shaped its economic conditions and political history over centuries.

The regional appellations current in Turkey do not reflect the historical variety of the country. You'll only find ancient territorial names like Lydia (west of İzmir) or Pamphylia (the region around today's Antalya) in cultural travel guides. Cappadocia (Kapadokya), as an important tourist destination, is an established term in Turkey, just like Thrace (Trakya) is a designation for the European territory of Turkey. However, the former Byzantine place-names live on in many city names, above all in Central Anatolia, as in Amasya (Amaseia), Antalya (Attaleia), Bergama (Pergamum), Kayseri (Caesareia), Konya (Iconium), Malatya (Melitene), or Sivas (Sebasteia).⁷ Almost all of the provinces in today's Turkey take their names from their respective

---

5   Hütteroth, *Türkei*, 262.
6   Ibid., 20ff. Hale, *Modern Turkey*, 5, notes incidentally with justification that Inner Anatolia is so mountainous that speaking of one "Inner Anatolian highland" is actually not apposite.
7   See the map in Vryonis, *Decline of Medieval Hellenism*, between pages 14 and 15.

administrative seats. A division into large regions which do not necessarily describe physically or cultural-geographically coherent regions is in wide use, for example in weather reports. These regions are: the Aegean (Ege), Marmara (Marmara), Mediterranean (Akdeniz), Black Sea (Karadeniz), as well as Inner Anatolia (İç Anadolu), East Anatolia (Doğu Anadolu), and Southeast Anatolia (Güneydoğu Anadolu).

Turkey borders eight neighboring countries: Greece, Bulgaria, Georgia, Armenia, Azerbaijan (though only its Nakhchivan exclave), Iran, Iraq, and Syria. These neighbors differ from Turkey with regard to language, ethnicity, and religion—and often all three at once. The two Southeastern European neighbors of Turkey,[8] Bulgaria and Greece, emphasize as the foundation of their national identity their belonging to Orthodox Christendom. Both countries have Turkish minorities. The Turkish minority of Bulgaria comprises about a tenth of the population and is represented by its own party in the Bulgarian parliament. In addition, there are up to a quarter-million Pomaks (Slavic-speaking Muslims), especially in the south Bulgarian Rhodope Mountains. In Greek West Thrace, an area that stretches from about Xanthi to the Greco-Turkish border, there live over a hundred thousand Muslims, with Pomaks and Roma represented alongside Turks, who are the largest individual group.[9] The presence of Turkish minorities in Greece and Bulgaria has repeatedly been the cause of quarrels between Turkey and these countries: because of the Turkish claim to protect them, because of attempts at a national homogenization policy by Bulgaria, and because of the ruling idea in Bulgaria and Greece's public memories that their peoples suffered for centuries under the "Ottoman yoke," that is, oppressive, almost destructive, Ottoman rule.[10] Territorial disputes in the Aegean and the unresolved question of Cyprus additionally burden Greco-Turkish relations.

Turkey's relations with its northeastern neighbors, Georgia and Armenia, both successor states of the Soviet Union, are chilly. Georgia sees itself, as does Armenia, as an island of Christendom in an otherwise majority-Muslim

---

8   In this book, "Southeastern Europe" is used throughout, even when "the Balkans" might be appropriate in places, above all for the areas of Southeastern Europe formerly ruled by the Ottomans. A convincing explication and delineation of the terms "Balkans" and "Southeastern Europe" may be found in Sundhaussen, "Europa balcanica," as well as Sundhaussen, "Balkan."
9   Stieger, *Vergessene Minderheiten*, 115, 151.
10 On this, see Höpken, "Türkische Minderheiten"; Hering, "Osmanenzeit;" Höpken, "Kulturkonflikt und Repression." For the situation after 1990: Gangloff, "Politique balkanique," 350ff.

Caucasus, and its predecessor kingdoms had a fraught history of relations with the Ottoman Empire. It maintains, however, pragmatic contact with Turkey.[11] Turkey, in turn, is forced to rely on Georgia as a land bridge to Azerbaijan, owing to its poor relations with Armenia. To cite just one example, for that reason, the petroleum pipeline that opened in 2006 from Baku to the Turkish Mediterranean port of Ceyhan runs across Georgia. Armenian-Turkish relations remain poisoned to this day. Adding to the burden of the genocide of the Anatolian Armenians during the First World War, is the Armenian-Azerbaijani conflict over the region of Nagorno-Karabakh, in which Turkey has taken Azerbaijan's side.[12] The land border between Armenia and Turkey remains closed to this day. Azerbaijan, linguistically, ethnically, culturally, and politically affiliated with Turkey, possesses no direct land connection to Turkey. There is, however, a narrow corridor to the Nakhchivan (in Azeri: Naxçıvan) Autonomous Republic from the Turkish province of Iğdır immediately north of Mount Ararat. Nakhchivan, an Azerbaijani exclave, is surrounded by Iran, Armenia, and Turkey (albeit only sharing a ten-and-a-half-mile border with Turkey).

While the borders of Turkey were, in general, set at the beginning of the twentieth century, its borders with Persia, today called Iran, were consolidated in the seventeenth century, even when the Ottoman Empire and Persia continued to fight over a multitude of conflicts, principally over control of the areas currently comprising northern Iraq. The Perso-Ottoman, or today's Iranian-Turkish, border was and is barely disputed, because it runs through lightly settled areas and mountain ranges. Iran and Turkey have contradictory hegemonic claims in the broader region, a fact which has emerged clearly, for example, in the Syrian War ongoing since 2011. Despite Sunni-Shi'ite antagonism, the two states are not fundamentally hostile to each other.[13]

The territories of today's Iraq and Syria were under Ottoman rule from the early sixteenth century until 1918. Following their agenda as "Arab national states," Iraqi and Syrian national historiography and politics of public memory

---

11 See Waal, *Caucasus*, 149, 249, on the strong antipathy to Turkey among the Georgian population.
12 Ghaplanyan, *Post-Soviet Armenia*, 152-175. At the beginning of the Armenia-Azerbaijan conflict in 1988, while still under Soviet rule, the status of Nagorno-Karabakh was that of an "autonomous region" within the Soviet Republic of Azerbaijan with a clear Armenian majority population.
13 See for example International Crisis Group, *Turkey and Iran*.

(here resembling those of Greece and Bulgaria) describe the four centuries of Ottoman rule as a time of decline. In addition to this basic perspective, new opportunities for conflict have arisen, like the question of water, which is critical for Iraq and Syria. The eastern parts of Syria receive their water solely from the Euphrates; Iraq is similarly dependent on the water supply of the Tigris and the Euphrates in the entirety of its central and southern areas. Turkey, however, has built a large network of dams on the Tigris (Dicle) and Euphrates (Fırat) which originate in the East Anatolian highland. This policy has been described by its southern neighbors as "water imperialism."[14] Yet another point of conflict is the Syrian claim to the Hatay region lost to Turkey in 1939.

Turkey has no natural friends in its immediate neighborhood. Azerbaijan and the Central Asian states of Kazakhstan, Kyrgyzstan, Turkmenistan, and Uzbekistan are connected to Turkey by the certainty of a common cultural and linguistic history. The languages spoken in these countries, including Turkish, belong to the Turkic language family.[15] Many more languages, predominantly found in Russia and China, belong to this group and are related but often hardly mutually intelligible.[16] Except for Azerbaijan in the Caucasus, the Central Asian Turkic states are thousands of miles distant from Turkey and directly accessible by neither land nor water. In the 1990s, Turkish foreign policy initially indulged in the expectation that, with the collapse of the Soviet Union, Turkey could become a leading state for the Turkic countries of Central Asia. The hope was deceptive, however, because the Central Asian countries did not want to and could not completely free themselves from Russia, given the severe remaking of the region in the Soviet era and the status of Russian as a regional lingua franca. In the meantime, China has ascended alongside Russia as the second decisive actor in Central Asia, thanks to its proximity, its powerful economy, and above all its intention to establish a "new Silk Road," recently more prosaically dubbed the Belt and Road Initiative (BRI).[17]

---

14 Çarkoğlu and Eder, "Water Conflict over the Euphrates-Tigris River Basin": 57.
15 The term "Turkic" refers to all languages of the Turkish language family, whereas "Turkish" is the term reserved for the official language spoken in Turkey.
16 On the variety of the Turkic languages, see Johanson and Csató, *Turkic Languages*; and for the history of the origins of the Turkic peoples, see the compelling depiction in Golden, *Introduction to the History of the Turkic Peoples*.
17 Hillman, *The Emperor's New Road*, offers an introduction.

Who lives in Turkey?

Describing Turkey in its spatial dimensions comes easily. A straightforward portrayal of who lives in Turkey is, by contrast, more difficult. Ethnic groups are not physical givens, rather their description depends on the standpoint of the observer. For example, a group can be interpreted from an outside (etic) perspective or be seen from the inside (emic). Ethnic and religious groups are furthermore complex structures which resist explicit description and classification. Writing about the ethnic diversity of Turkey can easily elicit a reproach for not acknowledging the territorial integrity of the Republic of Turkey or even for wishing to undermine it by consciously placing heterogeneity in the foreground.[18] From the standpoint of an outside observer, however, the ethnic diversity of Turkey is an expression of its historic and cultural richness.[19]

The ethnic diversity of today's Turkey, which rests on the foundation of a very clear Turkish Muslim majority population, is explicable by its Ottoman, indeed even pre-Ottoman, antecedents. The advance of Central Asian Turkic tribal nomads into the central lands of the Muslim world represents a fundamental turning point in Islamic history. On the back of their military strength, these nomads were able to conquer the lands of today's Iran and found the Great Seljuk dynasty there in the eleventh century. The migratory movement of the Turks from Central to West Asia has been compared to a bus ride: during the long trip from East to West, many passengers got off or transferred (e.g., towards Afghanistan or the Indus Valley), but most wanted to keep riding.[20] They arrived in Iran, where around a quarter of the population (primarily in the northwest) is Azeri-speaking. In any case, the following applied: the bus drivers were always changing, the motor had to be replaced repeatedly, and even the chassis was no longer the same.

We know the exact arrival time of this long journey: when Byzantium under Emperor Romanos IV Diogenes attempted to apply a brake to the gradual invasion of his eastern territory by Turkish nomads, a Great Seljuk army, supported by numerous Turkish tribal nomadic confederations, smashed the Byzantine army on 26 August 1071 at Manzikert (today Malazgirt,

---

18   For the exemplar of such careful affirmation, see Andrews, "Introduction," 41.
19   In comparison to Turkey, other countries in the region are incidentally considerably more ethnically diverse or not characterized by a demographically dominant ethnic group. Shi'ite Persian speakers, Iran's main group, comprise only around 60% of the population. Azeri Turks and Kurds are the largest groups in the remaining 40%, comprising 16 and 10%, respectively. See Axworthy, *Iran*, 126.
20   This vivid metaphor is found in Findley, *The Turks in World History*, 5.

north of Lake Van in East Anatolia). Anatolia was laid open to penetration by this new population. From then until the middle of the thirteenth century, approximately a million Turkish tribespeople streamed into Anatolia. These new arrivals in Anatolia belonged to a nomadic tradition that would shape Anatolia into the twentieth century.[21] Over the centuries, the original, formerly predominantly Orthodox populace of Anatolia converted in part to Islam. Also, following the establishment of the Ottoman Empire around 1300 in northwest Anatolia and its later extension across all of Anatolia, the Turkification and Islamization of the country continued—a process which came to a conclusion only in the early twentieth century.

The population of Turkey is cognizant of its diversity, as expressed in the proverb, "There are seventy-two-and-a-half nations in Turkey" (Türkiye'de yetmiş iki buçuk millet var).[22] The situation in today's Turkey pales in comparison, however, to the exceptional ethnic, confessional, and linguistic diversity of the Ottoman era. The Ottoman Empire was—except in the last few decades of its existence—not interested in shaping the population for the purposes of a national culture. The imperial leadership neither wanted nor needed to get involved in the internal organization of many regions and ruling confederations. The Ottoman Empire left Turkey not just the inheritance of its imperial expansion, but also that of its later process of contraction. In the nineteenth and twentieth centuries, millions of Turkish-speaking and/or Muslim refugees from former territories of Ottoman rule streamed into Anatolia; a large portion of them came from Southeastern Europe, which was called Rumelia (Rumeli, "the country of the 'Romans,'" i.e., the Byzantines) by the Ottomans. People in Turkey whose forebears originated in Southeastern Europe still speak today of their origin "from Rumelia" (Rumeli'den). Before and after the First World War, around three million Turks and Muslims had to leave Southeastern Europe for what is today Turkey. The descendants of these displaced persons, who constitute an estimated quarter of the total population of today's Turkey,[23] are a self-evident component of the Turkish Sunni majority.

---

21 On (once) nomadic populations in Turkey, see, e.g., the entries in Andrews, *Ethnic Groups*, 58–62 (Yörük), 63–68 (Türkmen), 68–71 (Tahtacı), 71–73, and 435–438 (Abdal), 472–475 (Karaçadırlı) and 524–537 (Alevisme nomade).
22 Andrews, "Introduction," 18, see also 31, 40, 56. This Turkish proverb is possibly connected to an alleged saying of Prophet Muhammad, transmitted in a hadīth, that the Islamic community will split in seventy-three Muslim sects with only one entering paradise and seventy-two hell.
23 Kentel, "Identité nationale turque," 368. According to Karpat, "Introduction," xvi, between 1856 and 1995 around nine million migrants from Southeastern Europe, the Caucasus,

In addition, there are the descendants of Muslims who fled from or were driven by the Russian expansion in the Caucasus and the northern Black Sea region beginning in the eighteenth century. They include Nogay Tatars (from the steppes north of the Black Sea) and Crimean Tatars who, for the most part, had found a new home in the Ottoman territories of Southeastern Europe when they subsequently had to flee again, this time to Anatolia, along with the Muslims who had always lived in Rumelia. The Circassians deported by Russia from the Caucasus to the Ottoman Empire in 1864 were first settled between Christian and Muslim localities in Rumelia as *Wehrbauern* (defensive peasants). When they were no longer allowed to remain in the European portion of the Ottoman Empire after the conclusion of the Treaty of Berlin (1878), the Ottoman state settled them in, among other places, areas of today's Syria and Jordan.[24] The term "Circassian" covers, in both official and everyday usage in Turkey, almost all ethnic groups who immigrated to Turkey from the North Caucasus beginning in the middle of the nineteenth century—for example, Dagestanis, Ossetes, and Chechens. This genuinely misleading umbrella term goes back to, among other things, the attempt of Circassian associations from the 1950s on to build a union of all Caucasians living in Turkey under the "Circassian" umbrella. The Circassians (here denoting all these North Caucasians) understand themselves to be part of the Sunni Muslim community.[25] All these groups who fled into Turkey on the basis of their Muslim confessional identities were called *Muhacir* (literally, "emigrant") in the late Ottoman era, a term with religious overtones, as it derives from the same Arabic root as the word Hijra, the emigration of the Prophet Muhammad from Mecca to Medina in the year 622 which stands as the beginning date of the Islamic calendar.

A further source of today's ethnic diversity lies in the existence of formerly non-Turkish and non-Muslim ethnicities within today's Turkey which have, over time, become Muslim but which have maintained their ethnic and, in part, their linguistic identities. Among these are the Laz, who live in the eastern Black Sea region (that is, west of Batumi, Georgia). The actual Laz people, who speak a language of the Kartvelian family (like Georgian and Mingrelian),[26] are to be distinguished from the popular styling of all inhabitants of the eastern Black Sea coast as Laz. The cliches about "those"

---

and the Crimea moved into the territory of today's Turkey; their share of the population of today's Turkey is around 40–50%.

24 For the contribution of the Circassians to the economic rise of today's Jordanian capital Amman, see Hamed-Troyansky, "Circassian Refugees."
25 Özbek, "Tscherkessen in der Türkei," 581, 587. On Circassians in the early Republican period, see Yelbaşı, *Circassians of Turkey*.
26 On the Laz, see Benninghaus, "Laz."

Laz widespread in Turkey are comparable to jokes about the East Frisians in Germany—that is, about a breed of people with a strange language and questionable intelligence.

Because state and linguistic borders do not coincide in southeast Anatolia, there is an Arabic-speaking population on Turkish state territory, whose share of the total population is, however, slight.[27] Areas of Arab settlement are in Hatay (the region around Antakya and İskenderun), in Çukurova (the lowlands lying between the Taurus Mountains and the Gulf of İskenderun, including the big cities of Adana and Mersin), and further east in regions bordering Syria and Iraq. The influx of around four million refugees from Syria in the 2010s has naturally altered the perception that Turkey's Arabic-speaking community is gradually dying out (due to its increasing adoption of Turkish).

This historically varied Muslim and today, as a rule, Turkish-speaking population, whose roots often trace back to flight and expulsion in the nineteenth and early twentieth century, now constitutes the clear majority of more than two-thirds of the population in Turkey. Their feeling of belonging rests on two pillars, that is, being both Turkish and Sunni Muslim.[28]

Jews in Turkey are a special bequest of the Ottoman era. The Ottomans not only left Jewish communities in the areas and cities they conquered, but they also welcomed a great number of Jews expelled from the Iberian Peninsula in the late fifteenth century.[29] These new Sephardic (that is, Spanish) Jews made Saloniki into a prominent center of Judaism which was completely annihilated by the German National Socialists in the Holocaust. Since the foundation of the Republic, however, and above all since the establishment of the State of Israel, a constant emigration has taken place. The number of Jews in Turkey has dropped to significantly fewer than twenty thousand. An increasingly open public and state antisemitism and the significant worsening of Turco-Israeli relations since the 2000s have led Turkish Jews to doubt their future in Turkey.

---

27 Procházka, *Die arabischen Dialekte*, 12, estimates the number of Arabic speakers in the major region of Çukurova at seventy thousand people.
28 Per Andrews, *Ethnic Groups*, 73ff., Shi'ites were originally found above all around the East Anatolian cities Kars and Iğdır. According to the US Department of State, *International Religious Freedom Report*, 2, the Shi'ite community of Turkey estimates its share of the population today at 4%, which would be more than three million people—likely a considerable overestimate.
29 Brink-Danan, *Jewish Life in 21st-Century*, sees, also in the case of the five hundredth anniversary celebrations of the acceptance of the Sephardic Jews in the Ottoman Empire, a fundamental contradiction of Jewish existence in contemporary Turkey—between a necessary absolute assimilation into the Turkish majority environment in everyday life and, simultaneously, a politically (occasionally) desirable display of Jewish alterity as an alleged proof of an unbroken continuity of Ottoman-Turkish "tolerance."

Many have consequently taken up the offer of dual citizenship which Spain and Portugal have made to the descendants of Sephardic Jews (without the compulsory military service found in, e.g., Israel).[30]

In the Ottoman Empire, the most important pillars of ethnic and confessional variety—other than the Muslims—were Christian communities. The history of Christians in the territory of today's Turkey reaches back far beyond the Ottoman era. Still, Christian communities, above all the Greek Orthodox flock, can be regarded as a legacy of the Ottoman imperium. Until the beginning of the twentieth century, they were not only tolerated but institutionally recognized as confessional communities, despite the frequent conversions of individuals or entire groups to Islam. Before the First World War, indigenous Christians comprised around a fifth of the population of Anatolia, which has receded to less than 0.1% of the total population of Turkey today. Today the members of the indigenous churches of Anatolia numerically lag behind those Christians who have recently taken up residence in Turkey, for example, Christian spouses of Turkish citizens, economic migrants of Christian confession, or German retirees in Antalya.[31]

The Greeks of Orthodox faith had four core centers of settlement on the territory of modern Turkey during the late Ottoman period: along with the capital İstanbul, there was a large area of settlement on the Aegean coast which was actually strengthened by immigration from Greece in the nineteenth century. A third locus was that of the Karamanlı in Central Anatolia, who distinguished themselves by the use of Turkish in Greek script. The fourth core settlement center lay in the eastern coastal region of the Black Sea and had its origin in the Empire of Trebizond (Trabzon) which fell to the Ottomans in 1461, a few years after the Ottoman conquest of Constantinople in 1453.

Under the terms of the population exchange between Greece and Turkey after World War One, all people of the Orthodox faith had to leave Turkey. Only the Greek Orthodox community in İstanbul and on two islands at the southern entrance to the Dardanelles were exempted from the requirement. While far more than two hundred thousand Orthodox Greeks might have been living

---

30 Côrte-Real Pinto and David, "Choosing Second Citizenship." For the history of the Jewish community in Turkey, see the plethora of publications by Rıfat N. Bali—e.g., Bali, *Model Citizens*.
31 Stoll, "Religion und Laizismus": 41, gives the following figures for the late 1990s: Greek Orthodox, sixteen thousand; Armenians, forty-five thousand; Syriac-Orthodox, fifteen thousand; Chaldeans, two thousand; Catholics, 6,500; other Christian denominations, 9,850.

in İstanbul in 1924, at the beginning of the 2010s, there were only about two thousand, with an average age of sixty-five.³² The infrastructure of the Greek Orthodox community today seems oversized, as the huge building of the Fener Rum Lisesi, the Greek Orthodox high school in the neighborhood of Fener on the Golden Horn, shows, or the seminary for priests on Heybeliada (one of the Princes' Islands off the shore of İstanbul) which the Turkish government closed in 1971 but which is kept ready for use—on principle—by the Greek community. The orphanage of the Greek Orthodox Patriarchate on Büyük Ada, another of the Princes' Islands, closed in 1964 but remains the largest wooden building in Europe, although its final collapse is likely imminent.³³

The Armenians, a significant population before World War One, with a core settlement area in eastern Anatolia, shrunk to only a few tens of thousands due to deaths and flight during the war.³⁴ In the face of continuing repression in the early Republican period, the small Armenian community still present in the eastern Anatolian provinces dissolved; since the 1950s, Turkey's Armenian population has been concentrated in İstanbul.³⁵

The territories of today's states of Iran, Iraq, Syria, and Turkey are the homeland of "Eastern Christians," whose creeds, like the Armenians', emerged from the schisms of the early Christian Church in the fifth century.³⁶ In today's Turkey, and there almost exclusively in southeast Anatolia, the Eastern Christians consist primarily of two groups. The West Syriac Orthodox—also known as Jacobites due to their important reformer, Jacob Baradeus (d. 578)—live in the region of Tur Abdin, the "Mountain of the Servants [of God]," centered around the city of Midyat. They experienced their final demographic decline in the 1970s. From about thirty thousand in Tur Abdin at the end of the 1960s, their numbers have sunk to no more than

---

32 Anastassiadou, *Grecs d'Istanbul*, 372.
33 "Rum Yetimhanesi için 40 Milyon Euro Gerekiyor" (Forty Million Euros Needed for Greek Orphanage), *Hürriyet*, July 30, 2019, http://www.hurriyet.com.tr/kitap-sanat/rum-yetimhanesi-icin-40-milyon-euro-gerekiyor-41287933; Berberakis, "Büyükada Rum Yetimhanesi."
34 According to Bardakci et al., *Religious Minorities*, 135, next to the estimated forty to fifty thousand Armenians with Turkish citizenship, there are more than one hundred thousand illegal immigrants from Armenia working in Turkey.
35 Suciyan, *Armenians in Modern Turkey*, juxtaposes the denial, by state and society, of Armenian suffering during the First World War with the systematic undermining of the guarantees for non-Muslims granted in the Treaty of Lausanne.
36 A clear introduction into the complicated history of the origins of the "Oriental Churches"—despite the antiquated terminology—can be found in Spuler, *Gegenwartslage der Ostkirchen*.

two or three thousand, even if recently there have been tentative attempts at reverse emigration, mostly by people in retirement.[37] The large majority of the West Syriac Orthodox live in a Western European diaspora. The second group, the Eastern Syriac Christians are often called Assyrians and reside in Northern Iraq and, originally, in the furthest southeast of Turkey. They are composed of Nestorians and the so-called Chaldeans who have been in communion with Rome since 1681.[38] In 1918, the Eastern Syriac Christians escaped to the regions of Mesopotamia already conquered by the British. Today they are few and far between in Turkey.

Jews and Christians left an impressive cultural and architectonic legacy in Turkey. They only shape Turkey's present indirectly, though, and they will likely not influence the country's future. At the same time, groups like the Laz, Tatars, and Circassians, and even the Arabic-speaking population of southeastern Anatolia are increasingly not distinguishable from the Muslim Turks of Anatolia due to the influence of modern mass media and powerful country-to-city migration streams. They may retain a consciousness of their particular origins, but at the same time they not only feel like part of the Turkish Sunni majority, but they are perceived and accepted as such. Nevertheless, Turkey cannot justify its claim to be a homogenous national state. The existence of the Kurds and the Alevis clearly refutes it.

The Kurds' main areas of settlement are in western Iran, northern Iraq, northern Syria, and in the southeast of Turkey.[39] The Kurds of Turkey originally lived in a quite compact area of southeast Anatolia. Their above-average rate of emigration to the great metropolises of western Turkey, but also Western Europe, has led to the situation that a purely territorial solution to "the Kurdish problem" in whatever form is no longer imaginable. The Kurds speak different languages from the Western Iranian family; the most important are Kurmanji in Turkey and Sorani in Iraq. In Turkey, Zaza (or Zazaki) is also of significance and is spoken in part among Alevi Turks as well. The Kurds, whose share of the population of the Republic of

---

37 Nestmann, "Ethnische Differenzierung," 571. Per Bardakci et al., *Religious Minorities*, 177-189, public efforts by the Turkish government in the 2000s and early 2010s at improving relations with the West Syriac Orthodox were undermined by everyday repression and incursions in Tur Abdin.
38 Yacoub, *Year of the Sword*, 2, speaks of Western and Eastern Syriac Christians together as an "Assyro-Chaldean-Syriac nation."
39 There are, in addition, smaller Kurdish population groups in the neighboring lands of Armenia, Azerbaijan, Georgia, Jordan, Lebanon, and Turkmenistan, generally as a consequence of flight or forced resettlement.

Turkey may amount to as much as a fifth, differ from the Turkish majority population with regard to language. However, it is the case that many Kurds, due to the decades-long assimilation and language policies of the Turkish state, can only express themselves spottily in their mother tongue (or that of their parents or grandparents).[40] Consequently, most Kurds, not only in Turkey but those living in the European diaspora as well, use Turkish when they want to express their political aspirations. Along with linguistic differences between Turkish and Kurdish, there is a religious difference between the Hanafi Turks and the majority Shafi'i Kurds.[41] This divergent membership in two of the four schools (*mezhep*) of Islamic law has, however, produced no political burden on Kurdish-Turkish relations.[42]

People who have grown up in Turkey can tell on the basis of linguistic quirks if someone comes from the southeast. Except for nowadays rarely worn local costumes, however, Kurds basically cannot be distinguished by outward appearance. Socially, Kurds also do not represent a firmly established population group. If linguistic, religious, cultural, and social factors are not decisive and the Kurds themselves are quite diverse, what then separates the Kurds from the Turks? Many Kurds who have lived for a long time, even for many generations, in the big cities of Anatolia understand themselves as Turks of Kurdish descent. Here, the inherent voluntary principle in the Turkish conception of nationality extends a hand (according to it the will and the readiness to profess one's membership in the Turkish nation and to follow its fundamental prerequisites in language and culture are decisive). A vivid example is the former prime minister and president Turgut Özal (1927–1993), who had Kurdish forebears. At the same time, there is a tendency to simply deny the existence of the Kurds: Kurds in this telling—heard well into the 1990s—are supposedly just "Mountain Turks,"[43] that is,

---

40 According to Behrendt, *Nationalismus in Kurdistan*, 25, the Kurmanji principally spoken in Turkey has largely remained untouched by more recent societal developments, so that Kurmanji and other Kurdish languages "cannot suitably express the sociopolitical realities of modern societal life either in their lexical or their structural range."
41 Kurdish Hanafis may be found in the periphery of Eastern Turkey, e.g., around Arpacay in Kars Province. Nestmann, "Ethnische Differenzierung," 563.
42 Ibid. The other two Sunni schools of jurisprudence, along with the Hanafis and the Shafi'is, are the Malikis and the Hanbalis.
43 Andrews, "Introduction," 36, refers to the Journal of the "Turkish Culture Research Institute" (Türk Kültürünü Araştırma Enstitüsü), in which fifteen articles with this argument appeared in 1982–1984. The 1961 second edition of the work *Doğu İlleri ve Varto Tarihi* (The History of the Eastern Provinces and Varto), in which the author M. Şerif Fırat— himself a Kurd, by the way—contended that the Kurds were of Turkish origin, led to

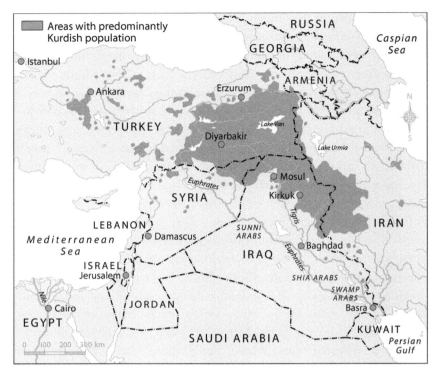

FIGURE 1. Kurdish population areas.

Turks who have become alienated from their Turkish culture and language through long isolation in remote mountainous areas.[44]

What ultimately separates Kurds and Turks is the power of identification of the self and the other. Today, most Kurds do not understand themselves simply as Turks of Kurdish descent, but as Kurds. Kurds who are well integrated in the big cities of western Anatolia and live among the Turkish majority nevertheless view themselves as part of an ethnic group whose civil rights are harmed by the state violence exercised against Kurds in southeast Anatolia. Kurds are understood by Turks simply as Kurds, and in crisis situations are treated as people of lower status, even if many of them are self-evidently part of Turkish society. It is ultimately the power of nationalism which affirms itself by excluding "others" and can only understand compromising with "others" and their concerns as a capitulation.

---

violent protests by Kurds on 8 May 1961, during which 315 Kurdish demonstrators were shot to death and 754 were wounded. McDowall, *Modern History of the Kurds*, 406ff.

44 See the witty suggestion in Massicard, *Alevis in Turkey and Europe*, 104, that given the designation of Kurds as "Mountain Turks," the Alevis could be called "Mountain Sunnis."

The Alevis' share of population in Turkey is presumed to be as much as a fifth, like that of the Kurds. Because some Kurds are simultaneously Alevis and by the same token some Alevis are Kurds, one can't simply add up the numbers of Kurds and Alevis.[45] Alevis do not linguistically diverge from the Turkish majority, unless they are also Kurds or Zaza speakers. The relationship of the Alevis to the state and the majority society in Turkey is far more entangled than that between Kurds and Turks. The original Alevi areas of settlement—before the resettlement measures of the Turkish state in the 1930s and before the migratory movement to the big cities of western Anatolia and Europe beginning in the 1950s—were central and eastern Anatolia, that is the territories of today's provinces of Adıyaman, Bingöl, Elazığ, Erzincan, Malatya, Kahramanmaraş, and Tunceli.[46]

The Alevis are a much less unified and self-contained group than the Kurds. Their religious history separates them from the majority society; at the same time, the question may be asked whether with the term *Alevi* one can really apprehend such a great variety of "heterodox groups with largely differing beliefs and rituals."[47] As in the case of the Kurds, it is true that Alevis see themselves as Alevis, and Alevis are seen by Turkish Sunnis as Alevis. It is perhaps most easily said that Alevis are identified by their distance in religious practice and cultural expression from the Sunni majority population.

The Alevis' existence is due to the imperial competition between the Ottoman Empire and Safavid Persia in the sixteenth century, among other things. Today Iran appears to be the natural center of Shi'ite Islam; however, Iran was converted from Sunnism to Shi'ism from the top down during the Safavid dynasty founded by Shah Isma'il (1487–1524). As the conflict between the Safavids and the Ottomans over the control of eastern Anatolia came to a head in the late fifteenth and early sixteenth century, the local population was faced with the decision whether to take up Sunni or Shi'ite Islam, although they still were in a condition of "metadoxy,"[48] which is to say beyond an understanding of what an "orthodox" religion means.

---

45 Per Bardakci et al., *Religious Minorities*, 99, up to a fifth of Alevis are Kurdish speakers.
46 Alevis have been statistically assessed only once in the history of the Turkish Republic, in 1963 in the "Village Inventory Studies" (Köy Envanter Etüdleri) of the then extant Ministry of Village Affairs. The materials were never published but became known through scholars who were able to inspect them. On this, see Hütteroth, *Türkei*, 277.
47 Hirschler, "Defining the Nation," 157. In addition to large differences in beliefs and rituals, distinctions which are no longer relevant arise, like tribal organization structures (as with, e.g., the Avşar, Çepni, Tahtacı, Türkmen, or Yörük) or occupational specializations as in the case of the Abdal (who were active foremost as musicians and circumcisors) and Tahtacı (woodcutters).
48 Kafadar, *Between Two Worlds*, 76.

The "Redheads" (Kızılbaş),[49] so called after their characteristic headgear, were a political bone of contention. They maintained connections to the Safavid dynasty and were persecuted by the Ottomans due to a lack of loyalty. After the Ottoman-Safavid power struggle was decided in the Ottomans' favor—the victory of Sultan Selim I (r. 1512–1520) at Çaldıran (in the extreme northwest of today's Iran) in 1514 was decisive here—the Kızılbaş withdrew into inaccessible regions of Anatolia. It seems as if the "Kızılbaş—or, as their later self-identification had it, Alevis—first [achieved] their ultimate formation in marginality."[50] Today the difference between Alevi and Kızılbaş is primarily that speakers of the Turkish Sunni majority society can—by using the term *Kızılbaş*—denote more clearly their rejection of the Alevis.[51]

Regarded from an orthodox Sunni standpoint, the Alevis cannot be considered Muslims because they do not observe the Five Pillars of Islam (profession of faith, prayer, fasting, pilgrimage, and almsgiving). One of the fundamental characteristics of the Alevis is that their religious culture shows an aversion both to the state and to clear explanations of their religious practice and identity. So the Alevis, depending on how others see them or they want to see themselves, are Islamic mystics, Shi'ites, Zoroastrians, preservers of shamanistic practices brought out of Central Asia, or even the last representatives of a religious syncretism that has shaped Anatolia since the eleventh century.[52]

Alevism is not a consolidated religion like Orthodoxy, Catholicism, Sunnism or Shi'ism. The Alevis' esoteric tradition shows similarity to that of the Druze (resident in today's Lebanon, Syria, and Israel) and the Alawites (see below) in the sense that the truths of the faith remain reserved for a small circle of initiates. However, this traditionally strict division between the laity and the spiritual authorities and protectors of the faith has softened over time.

The Alawites (also known as the Nusayris) are represented in large numbers among the Arabs of Hatay and Çukurova. Religio-historically, they are not connected to the Anatolian Alevis, even if both Alevis and Alawites naturally trace back to 'Alī (600–661), Muhammad's nephew and son-in-law, who also ranks as first in the line of Shi'ite imams. The Alawites do not have the "meeting house" (*cemevi*) that is of central religious significance for

---

49 For the multifacetedness of this term in Ottoman texts of the sixteenth century, see Baltacıoğlu-Brammer, "One Word, Many Implications."
50 Kehl-Bodrogi, "Alevitentum," 505.
51 Gokalp, "Alevisme nomade," 526.
52 Dressler, "'Heterodoxy' and 'Syncretism'": 251.

the Alevis. The core territory of the Alawites is Syria, although they are also found in Israel, Lebanon, and Turkey. They comprise about a tenth of Syria's population and, under the leadership of the Alawite Hafiz al-Asad (r. 1970–2000) and his son and successor Bashar al-Asad, ascended to the status of the power-holding ethnic group in Syria. In contrast to the Alevis, the Alawites in Syria and Turkey consider themselves Shi'ites today.[53] Among the Alawites in Turkey, as among Arabic-speaking Sunnis, Arabic has been increasingly displaced by Turkish.[54]

Today's Turkey is a territory deeply formed by exodus and in-migration since the nineteenth century. Again and again during the Republican period, Turkey absorbed Turkish and Muslim immigrants, most recently from Bulgaria in the late 1980s and several million Syrians in the 2010s. Since the 1990s, Turkey, following in the Ottoman tradition, increasingly appears to be a country endowed with a colorful variety of immigrants. Much more fundamental for the self-understanding of today's Turkey is that it was and is a place of refuge for millions of Muslim and Turkic refugees and migrants.

Anchor Points of Historiography

In 2023, Turkey is marking with pride the centennial of its founding. Most inside and outside the country will nonetheless share the view that the history of the Republic of Turkey doesn't begin with the day of its proclamation, 29 October 1923. Rather, one must look further back to understand today's Turkey—at least to the War of Independence (İstiklal Savaşı). In this war during the years 1919–1922, the Turkish Muslim population of Anatolia asserted themselves against their opponents, the Armenians in the east and the Greeks in the west—but also against the Entente powers of the First World War who had occupied parts of Anatolia after the defeat of the Ottoman Empire—and were able to found an independent Turkey. On the other hand, to understand the conditions under which this Anatolian national movement successfully conducted its war, one has to look back further than just 1919. The question is how far can and should this looking back reasonably take us?

---

53 Winter, *History of the 'Alawis*, 7, 270. According to Reilly, *Fragile Nation, Shattered Land*, 153, in 1972, Hafiz al-Asad had prominent Lebanese Shi'ite religious jurisprudents attest that the Alawis were Shi'ites and therefore indubitably Muslims.
54 Procházka-Eisl and Procházka, *Plain of Saints and Prophets*, 67, 70.

In May 1789, Sultan Selim III (r. 1789–1807), who had just ascended the throne the month before, summoned an assembly of high officials in order to seek fundamental solutions to the military weakness of the Ottoman Empire. The preceding decades' defeats at the hands of Russia had been too numerous and too devastating to be ascribed to the fickle favor of the fortunes of war. The Ottoman elite had now come to understand that the effectiveness of the Ottoman military had fallen behind that of the European powers categorically. Debates presided over by the sultan led to the proclamation, in 1793, of the New Order (Nizâm-ı Cedîd) including the introduction of new military units of the same name and a dedicated state treasury to maintain these units.[55] The first schools arranged according to a Western model, which served to educate the officer corps in modern sciences and European military technology, date from this period. The Technical University of İstanbul, for example, traces its heritage proudly back to the Engineering School of the Imperial Navy (Mühendishane-i Bahrî-i Hümayun) founded in the late eighteenth century. Sultan Selim III stood for two convictions, namely for the confident insistence that what was old and proven be preserved and what was new and inevitable be dared. His reform endeavors perished in a revolt in the year 1807 which first cost him his throne and shortly thereafter his life.

One could even look back further into the early eighteenth century to the period of the grand vizier Damad İbrahim Pasha (in office 1718–1730), who—under the impact of the unfavorable Treaty of Passarowitz of 1718—tried to obtain an accurate image of Europe by sending delegations to Vienna and Paris.[56] However, the reforms of Selim III in the late eighteenth century represent a profound change of direction in a policy that characterized the entire late Ottoman period: the state took as its foremost task the ability to confront European powers, above all Russia, now its most threatening opponent, through the adoption of Western institutions and innovations. From here, long continuities lead into the early history of the Republic. The measures of the 1920s and 1930s in the young Republic of Turkey can't be understood without the antecedent reform efforts beginning in the late eighteenth century. A history of modern Turkey must unavoidably begin in the eighteenth century as a result.[57] A history of the Republic of Turkey,

---

55 For these reform efforts see, extensively, Shaw, *Between Old and New*.
56 Lewis, *The Emergence of Modern Turkey*, 45.
57 Accordingly, the standard work *Turkey: A Modern History* by Erik Jan Zürcher dedicates more than half of its pages to describing the period before 1923. The two classical

however, shouldn't get lost in late Ottoman history—that would be to succumb to the temptation of overcontextualization.

A look back into the late Ottoman period is indispensable for making sense of the questions being negotiated in today's Turkey and of arguments brought forward about the prehistory of the Republic of Turkey. The chronological presentation in this work begins with the year 1912, thus a good decade before the actual proclamation of the Republic. The years from 1912 on are characterized by sweeping changes which come to a conclusion with the foundation of the Republic in 1923. In the autumn of 1912, Ottoman armies were catastrophically crushed in the First Balkan War by their united opponents, Bulgaria, Greece, Montenegro, and Serbia. The Ottoman Empire lost all of its European possessions up to a narrow strip of territory next to İstanbul. In the Second Balkan War in the summer of 1913, the Ottoman military was able to recapture Adrianople (Edirne) and eastern Thrace as the victors of the First Balkan war turned against each other. In the fall of 1914, Turkey entered the First World War on the side of the Central Powers and on 30 October 1918 had to concede defeat to the Entente powers in the armistice of Mudros. After a short pause, the war of the Anatolian national movement—the War of Independence—ensued during the years 1919–1922. The decade of 1912–1922 was thus not only a period of extremely violent and costly turmoil but was also the period in which today's Turkish identity is fundamentally anchored.

In this context, the question arises: up until what point are we dealing with the Ottoman Empire and from what point the Republic of Turkey? The formal transition from one state to the other took place in the years 1922–1923. On the first of November 1922, the National Assembly in Ankara abolished the sultanate; on 29 October 1923 the Republic of Turkey was proclaimed. In that regard, we can and must speak of an Ottoman Empire at least for the period until 1922. However, there is much to suggest that the Ottoman Empire, as a multiethnic and multiconfessional imperium, ceased to exist in the first couple years of World War One. With the 1918 armistice and the loss of its Arab possessions, the empire lost its imperial character and only preserved a constitutional shell. On the other hand, in the period after 1914, it's not yet easy to speak of Turkey. An Ottoman army still existed in the First World War. To be sure, soldiers of Christian confession were disarmed at the beginning of the war and organized into work details deployed to compulsory

---

depictions by Berkes, *The Development of Secularism*, and Lewis, *The Emergence of Modern Turkey*, also begin in the eighteenth century.

labor duties like railroad construction under the supervision of Muslim troops. The Ottoman army had become a Muslim army by the beginning of the First World War, but to speak of a Turkish army is incongruous, given the great involvement of military contingents from Kurdistan and the Arab provinces. Almost every fifth Ottoman officer came from the Arab lands of the empire.[58] Even the confrontation between the Ottoman government in İstanbul and the newly forming national movement in Ankara in the years 1920–1922 can't be captured in the terminology of Ottoman versus Turkish. The national movement contained more than a few actors who were not Turkish (like, for example, Kurdish notables) but also many others who didn't consider themselves Turks in the first instance, but Muslims. In consequence, for the years between 1914 and 1924, we will speak of Turkey alongside the Ottoman Empire when the self-perception as a specifically Turkish state comes to the fore or when the leadership of the national movement in Ankara is under discussion.

European depictions of the eighteenth and nineteenth centuries contribute to the confusion, in that they mostly did not speak of the Ottoman Empire but rather Turkey. So, for example, the southeastern European possessions of the Ottoman Empire were known as European Turkey. The perspective of that era should not be taken uncritically into today's historiography, because a generic Turkey used for the Ottoman Empire as well as the Turkish Republic obscures the imperial and multiethnic character of the Ottoman Empire and in addition conveys the false impression that there existed a centuries-old core of a Turkish national state. On the other hand it would be, as already noted, unrealistic to hold adamantly and exclusively to the term "Ottoman Empire" for the years 1914–1923.

Alongside the trap of overcontextualization, or losing oneself in late Ottoman history in the search for the correct anchor for understanding modern Turkey, the dangers of undercontextualization lurk as well. There is a remarkable, striking contradiction in the international historiography of the Ottoman Empire and the Republic of Turkey. Today's international Ottomanists (that is those scholars who occupy themselves with Ottoman history, culture, literature, etc.) have tried for several decades to show the interwovenness of the Ottoman Empire in European history. In doing

---

58 Uyar, "Ottoman Arab Officers," 537ff. The share of Kurds was also considerable. Per Bruinessen, *Agha, Shaikh and State*, 381, in 1925 no fewer than half the officers and troops of the Seventh Army stationed in Diyarbakır were Kurdish.

so, they are sometimes inclined to an overzealousness from which they understate the multifarious elements of a direct history of conflict between the Ottoman Empire and its European opponents, as well as those between the Ottoman ruling class and its subjects.[59] Modern Turkish, as well as international, histories of Turkey, by contrast, are conscious indeed of the tight connections between Turkey and Europe and recently also particularly to southern Europe and the Middle East or Central Asia; but they then use the concept of the Turkish national state as the framework of their account. The reasons are apparent: history-writing about premodern empires attempts to work out to what degree they were informed by similar models of rule, while the historiography of the states of the twentieth century can hardly avoid the responsibility to reproduce and retell the defining model of the national state.

And in fact Turkey ultimately stands for only itself. It is conspicuous that no other country offers an immediate comparison.[60] One reason surely lies in the fact that heretofore there has been too little thought and research dedicated to the question of contextualizing Turkey in narrower or wider spheres. It is always easier to treat Turkey as a self-contained unit than to take larger vistas in view.[61] Wishing to regard the former Ottoman possessions in Southeastern Europe and the Arab world as a sustainable interpretive framework comes dangerously close to the neo-Ottoman agenda in Turkish politics over the last twenty years. On the other hand, when attempting to place Turkey in a framework of a broader European history, history-writing and political positioning overlap all too quickly. The question of whether Turkey is seen as part of Europe or not, which can ultimately only be decided on a political level, must not lead to not wanting to discuss the European character of Turkey at all, whether in agreement or rejection. Turkey can't be categorically barred from European history, but at the same time, its belonging to Europe is not obvious without examination. It occupies a completely different position than the neighboring Arab states on the Mediterranean, specifically in that the leading elites of the late Ottoman Empire began to think intensively about their relationship to Europe—beyond war and peace—earlier than any other country in the Islamic world.

---

59 See, e.g., Schmitt, "Introduction," for a critical evaluation of softened international scholarship on the establishment of Ottoman rule in Southeastern Europe.
60 Kirisçi, *Turkey and the West*, 101.
61 See for example Balistreri, "Writer, Rebel, Soldier, Shaykh," 346, on the almost impossible task of wanting to write a comprehensive history of the ethnically, geographically, linguistically, and politically extremely heterogenous Caucasus.

Turkey is therefore far more than a state placed geographically coincidentally near Europe, but rather a country that is a particularly rewarding object of historical study and description due to its historic depth, its many identities, and its complex history of relations with Europe (here it's likely most comparable to Russia). This may well be one of the reasons that have moved some readers to take this book in hand.

Between Grandeur and Grievance

Three fundamental ideas shape the depiction of Turkey in the present volume. First is the contrast between, in the broadest sense, a Kemalist secularist camp and, again in the broadest sense, a conservative camp that ultimately sees its identity in the religion of Islam. Second, the contrast between established urban strata and a population anchored in rural Anatolia which streamed into the big cities by the millions during the huge migratory movement beginning in the 1950s. And third, the charged relationship between grandeur and grievance characteristic of the political-emotional economy of the Republic of Turkey. Let us look first at the former two phenomena which overlap and strengthen each other.

Millions of people's experience of migration from the rural areas of Anatolia into the big cities of Turkey and Western Europe since the 1950s is foundational to today's Turkish society. While the frictions and conflicts which arise from a movement of millions of people are immediately evident, the first contrast named, between secularism and Kemalism versus religiously grounded conservatism, is considerably more difficult to parse solely due to its terminology. Kemalism is in the narrowest sense the political agenda of Mustafa Kemal Atatürk (1881–1939), the decisive, leading personality of the early Republican era. In a broader sense, the quite diversely unrestrained meanings of Kemalism among later generations are intended, all the more because Kemalism never consolidated into a fully developed ideology, neither during Atatürk's lifetime nor after. Nevertheless, one can speak with justification of Kemalism and secularism in the sense of a political disposition, which was supported over decades by an alliance of bureaucrats, officers, professors, journalists, judges, and other leading personalities of Turkish society—the "Kemalist bureaucratic-intellectual-judicial-military complex," as it will be called in this book. "Complex" should not be understood as a highly concentrated ideological class, a sort of central committee of Kemalism, but an interactive structure of people, groups, and currents, which are in many respects contradictory and can even be comprised of political opponents.⁶²

In the second half of the twentieth century, a broad opposition to Kemalism became stronger, reaching from conservative politicians to advocates of an Islamist order. Both the conservative current and the Islamist movement pointed successfully to a mistake in the construction of Kemalism. The Kemalist Republic had pushed religion aside as a relic of the lost Ottoman Empire and as a dangerous competitor, while it simultaneously relied on affiliation with Islam as a foundation of the common national identity. In addition, Kemalism had always exuded a certain alienness and distance towards the people of Anatolia, the supposed beneficiaries of its policies—who did indeed benefit from them, in great part.

For decades, Kemalism nourished its legitimacy from the heroic deliverance of the Turkish nation in the so-called War of Independence of 1919–1922, in which a new Turkey was won against many enemies and all odds. Right-conservatism and Islamism, on the other hand, created their own victim myth, in which the rural Muslim Turkish population of Anatolia supposedly became the largest minority the Kemalist state ever created, by alienating them from their accustomed cultural and religious living environment (which would have come to pass in any case under the conditions of their urban migration). Center-right and Islamist politicians repeated a litany of complaints which became effective over decades, to the effect that the (initially) silent Anatolian majority had been thrust into the status of a lesser majority. The coming to power of the Justice and Development Party Adalet ve Kalkınma Partisi, AKP) in 2002 was therefore of great import because it succeeded as the first Turkish party to combine the support of the two previously divided milieux of the conservative and Islamist electorates on the basis of this myth (which was of course in some respects based in reality).

It must be admitted that the argument here contrasting a secular-Kemalist and a religiously conservative-minded camp is hardly iconoclastic. It might be objected that the dichotomy between a secular attitude versus a religiously grounded conservatism reflects only one snippet of the genuinely multifarious conflicts and antagonisms in the Republic of Turkey. Radical leftists of the 1960s and 1970s, for example, saw only false consciousness in both camps. Kurdish activists stood and placed themselves outside both

---

62 Aytürk, "Bir Defa Daha Post-Post-Kemalizm," 104-106, points forcefully to the dangers of treating Kemalism as an apparently unitary, concrete object and of paying much too little attention to the different currents and fissures within the Kemalist camp.

these camps, which for them were just the two sides of the coin of Turkish nationalism. Some would even go so far as to say that Kemalism and Islamism are merely constructs which actually impede our understanding of the history of Turkey in the twentieth century.[63] For all too long, it is argued, discussion has been oriented around this too-simply formulated contrast. But this is in fact the decisive point: for decades, the vast majority of Turks have wanted to believe in this distinction; political conflicts have been fought along these dividing lines. They were in a certain fashion the most accessible currency in self-definition and identification in Turkish society and politics, and they defined the categories of friend and enemy.

In the Turkish Republic of the twentieth century, thinking in terms of enemies was likely a sign of insecurity and indicative of a low level of interpersonal trust.[64] The experience of migration from the land into the cities and the leaving behind of organized social networks in the village space—a "major cultural dislocation" in conjunction with the loss of village conflict-resolution mechanisms[65]—has shaped the Turkish population for several generations. In addition, we have seen how many emigrants (Muhacir) flooded into the young Republic, people who had arrived in Anatolia only a few decades or even years before and who had not even forgotten the experience of expulsion and flight, much less processed it.

In any case, the conflict between city and countryside has shaped twentieth-century Turkey. It cannot be understood otherwise: without these fundamental social and economic conditions the construction of Kemalist secularist versus religious-conservative camps could never have been so completely executed. The Anatolians, who decades ago came to the cities, have now taken the levers of power, due to their demographic preponderance, but above all thanks to Islam as an honestly unbeatably powerful source of identity far superior to Kemalism. With the developments of the last decades, the two primary fundamental conflicts of the Republic of Turkey, that is, Kemalist secularist versus Islamist conservative and urban- versus rural-origin, have

---

63 According to Lord, *Religious Politics*, 13ff., religion was much more strongly woven into the Turkish state than previously assumed. Therefore, he claims, it is misleading to still speak of a Kemalist state.
64 White, "Turkey in the 1970s," 306. Bora and Can, *Devlet, Ocak, Dergâh*, 38, 50-55, 69 passim, consider feelings of alienation, fear of losing social status, and grudges as the most important factors which drove the youths of Anatolia into the arms of organized right-wing radicalism in the 1970s.
65 Mardin, "Youth and Violence in Turkey," 235.

taken a step back. We may expect that the political future of the country will only partially follow the fault lines of factional camps familiar from past decades. What new lines of conflict will emerge in its place are as of yet only discernible in vague outlines.

One could have assumed that the dissolution of the "classical" conflicts in the Republic of Turkey would have led to an easing of tension in Turkish politics. If we look at the course of recent years, however, the opposite is the case. What specifically is true for the Republic of Turkey of the twentieth and twenty-first century—and here we come to the third defining idea of the book—is the tension between grandeur and grievance, between confidence and anger so characteristic of Turkey. In the history of the Republic of Turkey, the coexistence or the rapid alternation of hero and victim roles, of virility and fragility, is striking.[66] It is obviously difficult for Turks to come to an equanimous posture relative to their country and their own history. The problem is not the excesses of Turkish nationalism but its chasms. So, alongside the confidence that every person (or more exactly: every Sunni Muslim) who wishes to say of themselves that they are a Turk can in fact be one, the exclusion of all others who cannot or do not wish to meet this requirement persists. The geographic and historically based special position of Turkey fills Turks with pride and with the confidence to be able to stand for themselves alone, but by the same token, deep insecurities appear again and again.

Turkey should actually have achieved sufficient stability and strength to be able to cheerfully address the questions which Turkish politics and society pose, namely to understand anew the legacy of Alevism and to find an answer for the question of the status of the Kurds, and so continue the path of development which Turkey has taken since the beginning of the twentieth century. Yet, what makes Turkey, despite all its strengths, so fragile? What causes the alternation of openness and self-imposed isolation, of democratic awakening and authoritarian hardening, of roll-your-sleeves-up confidence and nagging doubts, that is so representative of the political culture of Turkey? This feeling of falling between the cracks shows up on the international stage as well. Being a "bridge" embeds Turkey in a Western context, with a simultaneous

---

66 One of the best-known dicta of Mustafa Kemal Atatürk incorporates the concept of confidence, "Turk, be proud, hard-working, and confident!" (Türk, öğün, çalış, güven!). The concept of rage in the description of Turkish politics is not new. For example, Öktem, *Angry Nation*, takes as a starting point the wrath of people in Turkey at their manipulation by political elites inside and outside of Turkey. Temelkuran, *Euphorie und Wehmut*, 137, 143, 172, 174, sees fury and hatred as corrosive elements in Turkish society.

understanding—not just brought into Turkey from outside—of Turkey as a country that, ultimately, does not belong to Europe. This book operates from the assumption—which you would expect from a historian—that the deeper reasons for this productive but often self-destructive tension lie in ideas about the history of Turkey.

The roots of today's Turkish self-understanding can be found in the decade of change from the multi-ethnic empire of the Ottomans into a Turkish national state. In this highly compressed period of violence and war, which lasted from the beginning of the First Balkan War in autumn 1912 until the end of the War of Independence in summer 1922, heroism and tales of suffering are apparently inextricably interwoven. Herein rests confidence's anchor: in those years, against all expectation and a multitude of enemies, the foundations of a modern Turkey were laid. The War of Independence is one of the main instances of Turkey's grandeur. But the events of the time fuel grievance and rage as well: the devastating defeat in the First Balkan War and the loss of all European territories (save Eastern Thrace); the embitterment that Europe (and today the West in general) has always judged and still judges Turkey with a double standard, for example: the issue of how the Turks proceeded against the Armenians in the First World War was raised to the benchmark of their fitness for being regarded as civilized, while there is barely any awareness in the West of the millions of dead Turks and Muslims in the nineteenth century.

This book does not wish to make the case for a historical miasma, that, in a sense, the fumes of earlier and still-unresolved conflicts are corroding Turkish society and politics. Today's Turkish society can not alter its past, but it can decide to adopt different perspectives on it. Nevertheless, the conflicts of the Ottoman-Turkish threshold period affect not only the present, but are constantly evoked anew in well-practiced forms: the histories of heroism and victimhood are entangled; the mythos of the defeat of the Ottoman Empire is woven into the foundation myth of the Republic of Turkey; the events of the years 1912–1922 are simultaneously sacralized and disclaimed. In this respect, Turkey has remained true to herself in disillusioning fashion under Erdoğan's authoritarian regime since the 2010s. Since Recep Tayyip Erdoğan has been firmly in the saddle, he has not striven to erect an ideal Islamic state intended as a paragon for all Muslims around the world, but rather a state which places the strength and absoluteness of Turkey at the fore, albeit covered in an "Islamic" wrapping.

These theses should not be taken to advocate for a Sonderweg for the Republic of Turkey. The alternation of emotional euphoria and profound discontent may be discerned in the history of many other states. For example, after the Second World War, the foundation of socialist Yugoslavia may be seen as a confident beginning, while the Yugoslav Wars of disintegration of the 1990s were accompanied by justifications for one side's rage against the other's past affronts. The promises of the liberal West in the 1990s are now met in Eastern Europe with disillusion or even open repudiation. The Arab world was carried by a wave of euphoria about decolonization and the promises of Arab nationalism only to sink in the 1970s into the leaden age of Arab autocracies. The Arab Spring of 2011 used up its magic in a few months, to either succumb to the authoritarian regimes' forces of inertia or, as in Yemen, Libya, and Syria, to plunge into the abyss of never-ending war. In Iran, liberal periods were both shorter and of more questionable nature: the Constitutional Revolution of 1905–1911, the time preceding the putsch against Prime minister Mohammad Mossadeq in 1953, and the early phases of the revolution from 1978–1979 before its monopolization by the Shi'ite clerisy under Ruhollah Khomeini (1902–1989). If one places Turkey in this comparative and most obvious context, with Southeastern and Eastern Europe, Russia, the Arab world and Iran, the result comes out more favorably for Turkey. Phases of relative liberality in Turkey often extended over a decade and were not isolated cases in the twentieth century. The history of the Republic of Turkey over the twentieth century cannot in any case be written as a history of decline.

On the occasion of the hundredth anniversary of the Republic, many books will probably appear in Turkish and in other languages. All of them will have their own strengths and weaknesses. In the present work, readers will find certain lacunae, like questions of the gender, literature, culture, or the country's intellectual history. The representation chosen here—that of a political history of the Republic—is due to the predisposition and preference of the author, but also to the conviction that the history of the Republic of Turkey from Atatürk to the present cannot be understood otherwise.

Chapter One

Farewell to the Ottoman Empire

The road from empire to republic was not foreordained, even if the collapse of the Ottoman Empire at the end of the First World War surprised no one. Together with Austria-Hungary and Russia, the Ottoman Empire was one of the three great European territorial empires that had endured for centuries but which could not withstand the dislocations of the Great War. In addition, the Ottoman Empire not only ranked among the losers of World War One, but it had been saved from dismemberment in the nineteenth century solely due to a stalemate in the interests of the European great powers. In 1918, however, no one would have wanted to predict that Turkey, emerging from the ruins of the Ottoman Empire, would be the sole country to succeed in defying the arrangements imposed by the victorious powers, in this case the Treaty of Sèvres of 1920. Through another war in 1919–1922, the nascent Turkish national movement wrested another, new peace treaty from the Europeans, the Treaty of Lausanne (1923), which founded the new Turkey as an internationally recognized sovereign state.

1. Legacy and Burden: The Late Ottoman Era (1876–1912)

Late Ottoman and early Republican history are tightly interwoven. To avoid the danger of losing our account of the Republic of Turkey too greatly in the details of late Ottoman history, this chapter will address three exemplary questions of Ottoman society and politics in the nineteenth century— exemplary in the fashion that they continue to shape the self-understanding of and political debate in Turkey to this day.

The first subchapter is dedicated to the question of how the Ottoman state would frame its relationship to its non-Muslim subjects in the age of nationalism. Ottomanism, a state patriotism ordained from the top, sought an equalization between Muslims and non-Muslims. Today in Turkey, however, the impression prevails that this hand extended by the ruling Muslim elite was humiliatingly rebuffed by the Christian population of the empire— spurred on by the European great powers.

This potential dynamic raises the second question, of how much, if any, room for maneuver the Ottoman Empire still possessed in the face of the overwhelmingly superior power of Europe in the nineteenth century. In contending with European imperialism, the Ottoman elite developed forms of self-justification and asymmetrical diplomacy, which were passed down as cultural techniques to the arsenal of the Republic of Turkey.

A third bequest of the late Ottoman era is the Young Turks, whose rule, beginning in 1908, rested on the unresolved question: If the hitherto attempted paths to renewal had been proven to be errors, what solutions— including radical alterations—remained possible? The answers developed by the Young Turks, and above all the political culture fed thereby, shaped Turkey far into the twentieth century.

Non-Muslims and Ottomanist State Patriotism

On November 3, 1839, Sultan Abdülmecid I (r. 1839–1861) proclaimed the Noble Rescript of the Rose Chamber (Gülhane hatt-ı şerifi). This edict guaranteed life, honor, and property to his subjects, promised a systematic and just collection of taxes, and provided for a comprehensive system of compulsory military service. The subsequent Imperial Decree (hatt-ı hümayun) that Abdülmecid issued on February 18, 1856, affirmed the reform articles of the

1839 edict and, above and beyond that, secured Muslims' and non-Muslims' equality before the law.[67] While some efforts, like a just distribution of the burdens of taxation and of military service, represented intra-Ottoman concerns, the goal of equality before the law for Muslims and non-Muslims was a commitment aimed at the European public.

Confronted with European superiority, weak state and economic productivity, and nationalisms raging across the empire's Southeastern European territories, the Ottoman state elite essayed a new ordering of society. In contrast to previous notions in force for centuries, the idea of "Ottomanism" (*Osmanlılık*), prescribed from above, included a turning away from the concept of 'subject' to that of 'citizen' and, at the same time, the idea of the social equalization of Muslims and non-Muslims. The uniting element was intended to be an imperial patriotism independent of nationality, ethnic background or religion.

A characteristic trait of the Ottoman Empire had always been that a small elite ruled over a large mass of subjects. Despite all the fluctuations in the empire's architecture of rule over the centuries, and many local peculiarities aside, one can say "Ottomans" were not only the members of the Ottoman dynasty, that is, the successors of the first sultan Osman (d. c. 1326), but all those who belonged to the ruling class of the Ottoman Empire. Ottomans mastered the difficult Ottoman language, which is similar to today's Turkish, but written in Arabic script and enriched by an enormous variety of Arabic and Persian loanwords and grammatical elements. Only Muslim men could become Ottomans. Women qualified only by virtue of family membership in the elite, even if, as in the case of the mother of the sultan (the Valide Sultan), they could have, at certain phases of Ottoman history, a direct role in ruling the empire. The scope of this Ottoman elite, which, ethnically speaking, was of a most diverse background, barely registers numerically: out of a population of twenty to thirty million people across the whole empire, "Ottomans" numbered a few ten thousands at most.[68] In addition, there were many shades and gradations. Local elites in many Arabic-speaking areas felt that they belonged to the Ottoman Empire but didn't necessarily have a command of Ottoman and were not regarded as a part of the imperial elite.

---

67 English translations of both reform edicts may be found in Hurewitz, *Diplomacy in the Near and Middle East*, 1:113–116 and 149–153.
68 Toledano, "Social and Economic Change," 263, estimates the size of the Egypto-Ottoman elite in Egypt at the beginning of the nineteenth century at about ten thousand men and women.

The Ottomans differentiated between the flock (*reaya*) to be protected, on the one hand, and the representatives of the military (*askeri*) class and the learned scholars (*ulema*) of religious jurisprudence, on the other. As the flock protected by the rulers, all subjects were alike. Nevertheless, non-Muslims in an Islamic body politic occupied a lower position than followers of Islam. Non-Muslims could remain true to their religions under Islamic rule, insofar as they belonged to one of the recognized "Religions of the Book," that is, religions whose message of salvation was delivered in a scripture. Originally, this class only included Judaism and Christianity. However, Islamic jurisprudents subsequently broadened its definition to include other religions such as Zoroastrianism, Hinduism, and Buddhism. The state and religious authorities of the Ottoman Empire had far greater problems with schismatic Islamic groups like the Alevis or religions completely outside the category, like that of the Yezidis. Still, these religions or religious groupings, which were actually impermissible according to orthodox Islamic interpretation, were halfway tolerated as long as they withdrew to remote areas and didn't show themselves openly.[69]

Jews, Christians, and members of other religions (of the Book) enjoyed the status of "protection" (*zimma*); that is, the exercise of their religion was secured, with recognition of the primacy of Islam, and in principle, no compulsion to convert to Islam was imposed. They were required to furnish a "head tax" (*cizye*) in addition to the levies and taxes common to Muslims as well. They were, however, thereby exempt from compulsory military service (which was also the case for the great majority of the Muslim population until the nineteenth century). The Ottomans expanded zimma status into the form of the so-called *millet*.[70] (This term would eventually come to mean "nation" in modern Turkish.)

Under the "Millet System," Ottoman practice may be understood as consolidating non-Muslim populations into religious groupings which could administer themselves in judicial, charitable, marital, and religious affairs. When referring to the organizational form of the millet, which exercises influence in the societies of many countries of the Middle East to this day, international scholarship does not speak of "religions" but rather

---

69 On Ottoman attempts at enforcing discipline, including forced conversion of Yezidis, in the late nineteenth century, see Deringil, *Well-Protected Domains*, 69–75, and Gölbaşı, "Turning the 'Heretics,'" 2013.
70 At the same time, one must not overtax the term "millet." Braude, "Foundation Myths," 74, sees (perhaps somewhat overemphatically but nevertheless correctly) a "historiographical fetish" in the understanding of millet as an ordering principle valid always and everywhere.

"confessional communities," a choice of words which this book will use preferentially. To speak of something like "the Christian religion" in the Ottoman Empire would not adequately describe the pronounced internal differentiation among Christians in the empire. For countries like Lebanon, whose society and politics are shaped by the coexistence of and friction between numerous religious communities, the term "confessionalism" is key.

The concept of confessionalism in the Middle East has incidentally undergone a notable transformation in the scholarly literature. Into the 1970s, authors still considered proportional democracies, in which the principle of majoritarianism is superseded for the sake of amicable accord, as ideal for confessionally divided states like Lebanon. In the shadow of the Lebanese Civil War (1975–1990), interpretations regarding confessionalism as part of the dark side of modernity came to the fore—with regard to Lebanon at least. In the 2000s, debate arose about "sectarianism," which by then had displaced the more harmless-sounding term "confessionalism," under the influence of the fierce Sunni-Shi'ite conflict in Iraq. In the meantime, attention shifted to the level of the conflict of state interests, here above all Saudi Arabia versus Iran, who were mobilizing the Sunni-Shi'ite antagonism to their own purposes.[71]

Through the reform edicts of the nineteenth century, the intra-Ottoman hierarchy between Muslims and non-Muslims was supposed to be levelled. The first Ottoman Constitution (1876) officially codified the term "Ottomans" for all citizens, thus framing the principle of citizenship. The legal and religious subordination of non-Muslims, which was given expression most clearly through the payment of the head tax, was abolished and replaced by a tax in lieu of conscription (*bedel-i askeri*). Non-Muslims only became subject to mandatory conscription in 1909.[72]

It is often suggested that developments since 1839 led to an over-privileging of non-Muslims, who were able to expand their old privileges (like, for example, the exemption from military service) with new opportunities, like seeking the protection of European powers. Considering this structural preference for Christians, Muslims are said to be the losers in the Ottoman Empire of the nineteenth century.[73] It was, however, more likely a question

---

71 For stages in this development, see for example Lijphart, *Democracy in Plural Societies*; Makdisi, *Culture of Sectarianism*; International Crisis Group, *Next Iraqi War*; Abdo, *New Sectarianism*.
72 On bedel-i askeri, see Shaw, "Ottoman Tax Reforms," 430–432.
73 Zürcher, *Turkey*, 67.

of class. An Armenian peasant in eastern Anatolia, who could not in the least depend upon the state's enforcing the law, was fundamentally disadvantaged relative to arms-bearing Kurds. Christian traders and merchants in the big commercial cities and ports, who in many respects resembled the compradorbourgeoisie of Latin America or East Asia, enjoyed a genuine advantage. From a constitutional point of view, the primacy of the Islamic religion continued; thus, the Constitution of 1876 was understood as a law subordinate to the state religion of Islam.[74]

The prospects for success of the project of Ottoman state patriotism, intended to bridge ethnic, religious, and regional dividing lines, were slim from the beginning—above all faced with Southeastern Europe's Christian populations temptation by the possibility of founding their own national states with the support of the European great powers.[75] The First Balkan War (1912) finally brought about the downfall of the idea of Ottomanism. In place of the conception that the empire had to protect Muslims and non-Muslims alike, a new idea of state structure came to the fore: a community for Muslims alone. In and by means of such a homogenous state, a long-term, fundamental answer to the European challenge might be possible. This option might provide the answer to a further question with which the late Ottoman elite occupied themselves over decades: How can we square the circle of becoming on par with the Europeans without becoming coopted by them?

The "Sick Man's" Attempts at Self-Assertion

For the Ottoman Empire, the nineteenth century was the "longest" and likely the most painful,[76] because in this time period, shaped by a hard-edged struggle for the preservation of the empire, the Ottomans belonged "without a doubt to the world of victims."[77] Ever since the late eighteenth century, Ottoman leadership had to concede the increased military power and

---

74 Feldman, *The Rise and Fall of the Islamic State*, 71.
75 Üngör, *Making of Modern Turkey*, 44, characterizes this feeling of betrayal by their own Christian population as comparable to the German Dolchstoßlegende ("stab-in-the-back myth," misattributing the German Army's WWI defeat to the perfidy of Jews, socialists, and republicans, i.e., in domestic politics).
76 An often-cited work by İlber Ortaylı on the Ottoman nineteenth century is entitled *Its Longest Century* (*En Uzun Yüzyılı*). In fact, it stands to reason to view the period from the 1770s until the First World War as a coherent epoch.
77 Hobsbawm, *Das Imperiale Zeitalter*, 38.

economic performance of Europe, which they initially found inexplicable. In the eighteenth century, the prevailing opinion among Ottoman elites was that reforms would only concern discrete military spheres (like artillery or the navy, which presupposed a greater amount of technical knowledge), and that political reforms would not be necessary, and indeed were to be avoided in order to prevent endangering the equilibrium of Ottoman society.[78] Soon, however, the Ottoman elite were forced to realize that reforms restricted to the realm of the military accomplished little. If one wanted to make use of modern cannon, one needed a knowledge of ballistics. In order to gain deeper insights into the science of ballistics, one could not escape reading for oneself handbooks and textbooks in European languages. Therefore, the knowledge of European foreign languages, especially French, the world language of the nineteenth century, became obligatory. All of this, in turn, was only possible when officers and high administrative officials acquired the corresponding linguistic and intellectual foundations at a young age. Thus, beginning purely with military affairs, the need for reform expanded in ever more far-reaching circles to the most diverse spheres of the apparatus of state and the broader society.

In 1826, Sultan Mahmud II (r. 1808–1839) succeeded in wiping out the Janissaries, the former elite infantry of the Ottoman military. The yeni çeri, the "new army," had long since ceased to be that which they had been in the early centuries of the Ottoman Empire. They were no longer men of Southeastern European Christian origins, drawn from the "boy levy" (devşirme), who were subjected to an exacting education (including conversion to Islam) as elite soldiers of the Ottoman infantry. Rather, they had become part of an urban Muslim "bourgeoisie" and simultaneously a powerful voice of political opposition. With the forcible dissolution of the Janissary Corps as a military formation and political faction, the way to a transformation of the Ottoman military on European organizational lines lay open.

The import of institutions, technologies, and objects from Europe was a minefield, however: the Ottomans adopted elements of contemporary European technical civilization often without an exact understanding of their use—and their choices were arbitrary. Helmuth von Moltke (1800–1891), later chief of the great general staff of the Prussian army, was seconded to the Ottoman army from 1836 to 1839. He saw the Ottomans essaying numerous, little-coordinated reform initiatives, coupled with their wish to not become

---

78   Shaw, *Between Old and New*, 11, 71.

all too dependent on any single European power. This created, according to Moltke, an army along European lines, but "with Russian jackets, French regulations, Belgian rifles, Turkish caps, Hungarian saddles, English sabers, and instructors of every nation."[79]

The 1839 reform policy of "reorganizations" (Tanzimat) announced in the aforementioned Rescript of the Rose Chamber wished to modernize the Ottoman Empire by dint of its own efforts and under its own power, specifically by centralizing and streamlining its administrative apparatus, by strongly expanding its education system, and by enhancing its economic productivity.[80] Abdülhamid II (r. 1876–1909), the last sultan who possessed real power, pushed the Tanzimat and its advocates aside and set out upon a strategy of Islamic self-assertion, reminiscent of a policy of Pan-Islamism. Nevertheless, he still tried to keep pace with European powers by strengthening the empire's infrastructure, military, and economy. The policy of a defensive and simultaneously authoritarian modernization during the Tanzimat period proper (1839–1876) and in the more than three decades of the sultanate of Abdülhamid II did indeed lead to a greater effectiveness of the state. The Ottoman Empire could not, however, make up ground on Europe's impetuous development, but became ever more trapped in dependence on the European great powers.

Both the Ottoman reform decrees of 1839 and 1856 were already closely coupled with the advance of European influence in the empire. The first, of 1839, coincided with British support for a reclamation of the Ottoman provinces in Syria and Palestine. Mehmed Ali Pasha (c. 1770–1849), officially Ottoman governor (*vali*) but de facto independent ruler over Egypt,[81] attempted in the 1830s to conquer the Ottoman Empire from within, with a campaign to Syria and ultimately Anatolia. Only the intervention of Great Britain and Russia kept the Egyptian army from taking İstanbul. The two great powers thus saved the Ottoman dynasty from collapse and forced Egypt into the status of a minor power with limited military forces in the 1841 Treaty of London, sweetened with the concession of allowing them to found their own dynasty, that of the Khedives.[82]

---

79 Moltke, *Unter dem Halbmond*, 352.
80 Findley, "Tanzimat."
81 Toledano, "Egypt's Ottoman Past," penetratingly describes the excision of the country's Ottoman past from the Egyptian historical memory of the twentieth century, by which, among other things, Mehmed Ali, an Ottoman officer from Kavala (in today's Greece), became Muhammad Ali, founder of the modern Egyptian nation.
82 Fahmy, *Mehmed Ali*.

The second reform edict, that of 1856, was issued shortly after the Crimean War (1854–1856), in which the Ottoman Empire ended up on the victors' side, with France and Great Britain. On March 30, 1856, in the Peace of Paris, which governed the results of the Crimean War, the European great powers confirmed the territorial integrity of the Ottoman Empire and assured it would, from then on, "participate in the advantages of the Concert of Europe."[83] At the Congress of Berlin in 1878, however, after a crushing defeat of the empire at the hands of Russia, Bismarck assigned the Ottoman representatives the humiliating role of Europe's villein.[84] Though the European powers had promised in 1856 not to meddle in internal Ottoman affairs and had placed the Ottoman Empire under a kind of guarantee of rights, the territorial losses the Congress of Berlin inflicted on the empire were immense: the empire lost around a third of its territory and over a fifth of its population. Among others, the areas of today's Serbia, Montenegro, Bulgaria, and Romania were severed from the Ottoman Empire and recognized as autonomous entities or even sovereign states (albeit with different borders than today's); Bosnia and Herzegovina were put under Austrian administration. In addition, the European great powers affirmed the right to intervene in Macedonia and demanded reform measures in the so-called Six Provinces (vilâyât-i sitte) in Eastern Anatolia where Armenians represented a large share of the population. These measures were understood here as expanded rights of protection for the local Christian populace.[85]

The Ottomans' desire to protect themselves from being overcome by Europe with European help thus led to the latter's being able to use the situation to pressure them and undermine Ottoman power all the more. The European powers left the Ottoman Empire its core possessions, but its sovereignty was subverted and it was brought into an often humiliating condition of dependency. Two examples should suffice to elucidate the extent of this pressure, infiltration, and penetration.

First is the European policy of protection in favor of the Christian minorities in the Ottoman Empire, which was a legitimate intervention under then-valid European international law. However, due to its amalgamation with

---

83 Protocol of the session of 14 March 1856: the representatives of the participating states (France, Austria, England, Prussia, Russia, and Sardinia) "declare the Sublime Porte admitted to participation in the advantages of the Concert of Europe" (déclarent la Sublime Porte admise à participer aux avantages du concert européen), Testa, Recueil, 5:78.
84 Anderson, Eastern Question, 210.
85 Kreiser and Neumann, Kleine Geschichte der Türkei, 317.

the Europeans' political interests, it discredited the entire legal institution of humanitarian intervention and led to its repudiation in the international law of the twentieth century.[86]

The Eastern question of the nineteenth century also evinced the moral ambiguity of European policy. This concept was meant to express the solicitude of Europeans for the condition of the "Sick Man," though they themselves were the cause for concern. Since the first half of the nineteenth century, the Ottoman Empire had been mortared in as a cornerstone in the international balance of power due to a standoff between the European powers with regard to the question of how a possible liquidation of the Ottoman Empire should proceed. At its core, the Eastern question ultimately meant "how much of the Ottoman Empire, and in what form, absolutely had to be retained in the interest of the European powers."[87]

In reality, the Ottoman Empire should be seen less as a problem child than a kind of excess-pressure relief tank for the European state system, or as an international political bank with virtually unlimited rights of withdrawal for the European great powers. As soon as the Ottoman Empire was finally driven into bankruptcy by the Balkan Wars, Austria-Hungary took over the role of the "Sick Man," and the international system of balance of interests collapsed with the outbreak of the First World War.[88]

The European undermining of Ottoman sovereignty is shown even more clearly in the second example—the so-called capitulations (*imtiyâzât*). Here, the term does not mean "a surrender," but is derived from the "articles" (*capitula*) in which diplomatic concessions were drawn up.[89] Such concessions, or "capitulations," had been granted to European trading nations beginning in the sixteenth century—a time of overwhelming plenitude of power for the Ottomans—as a kind of most-favored-nation provision. With Europe's increasingly superior power from the late eighteenth century on, these privileges,

---

86 Kimminich, *Einführung in das Völkerrecht*, 323. On the European policy of intervention in the Ottoman Empire, see Rodogno, *Against Massacre*.
87 Schölch, "Der arabische Osten," 383. See also Keddie, *Modern Iran*, 34, for a similar stalemate between Great Britain and Russia with regard to Iran, which secured the at least formal independence of the country.
88 Yapp, *Modern Near East*, 90ff. For a prophetic 1875 utterance by the Austro-Hungarian foreign minister Count Gyula Andrássy that the Hapsburg Empire might one day inherit the role of the "Sick Man of Europe," see Haselsteiner, "Haltung der Donaumonarchie," 230n7. In *Sleepwalkers*, Clark approaches Yapp's argument and Andrássy's fear very closely with his concept of a "Balkan Inception Scenario" in which the Entente powers accorded Austria-Hungary no justification for existence.
89 Schmitt, *Levantiner*, 122.

which included, among other things, consular jurisdiction and tax exemption for foreign citizens and Ottoman subjects under foreign protection, were granted to ever more European states and were construed ever more broadly by them. By the nineteenth century, this institution which had been erected under the conditions of Ottoman dominance, had become an instrument of inordinate European influence, especially in the economic realm.[90]

In the nineteenth century, the world outside Europe had only two choices from an economic point of view: either remain outside the globalizing European economic space with the many disadvantages associated therewith, or become increasingly integrated into it—with all the disadvantages resulting therefrom. The Ottoman Empire, because of its proximity to and its economic entanglement with Europe, really only possessed the second option. The economic dependency of the Ottoman Empire was comprehensive. In 1913, four-fifths of the empire-wide production of raw cotton was exported, but ninety percent of its cotton textiles were imported; that is, the Ottoman Empire sent cheap cotton abroad only to have to buy it back again expensively as a finished product. Often—and not at all without justification—one therefore finds arguments on the Turkish side that the Ottoman Empire found itself in a condition of "half-colonization."[91]

Egypt, which was superficially part of the Ottoman Empire until 1914, provides a good example of the different phases of European economic, but also political penetration, which escalated from free-trade imperialism through financial imperialism to colonial imperialism. Egypt had to declare bankruptcy in 1876, on the basis of excessive spending, but above all because of a debt spiral which was catastrophic for Egypt but extremely advantageous for its European creditors. Capitulations were in force here, with disastrous consequences for the Egyptian economy and society, as in the Ottoman central regions. Europeans, free from all taxes and duties, held most capital assets in their hands. Egypt was perhaps the country which "offered the most favorable odds"[92] for financial imperialism worldwide. A year earlier, the same fate had befallen the Ottoman government. Following the sovereign default of 1875 necessitated by an all-too-high interest burden on loans taken

---

90 On this, see Eldem, "Capitulations and Western Trade."
91 Hale, *Modern Turkey*, 37, refers to Conker and Witmeur, *Redressement économique et industralisation de la nouvelle Turquie*, 33; and Karpat, "Transformation of the Ottoman State," 260. See also the frequent and self-evident use of the terms "half-colony" (*yarı sömürge, yarı koloni*) in Aydemir, *İkinci Adam*, 1:235, 292, 328, 338, 483.
92 Mommsen, *Imperialismus in Ägypten*, 40.

out earlier as well as by some drought years, broad sectors of the Ottoman economy were placed in 1881 under the control of an international debt administration. Even today, the massive administrative headquarters of the Administration de la Dette Publique (Düyun-i Umumiye)—presently the İstanbul Lisesi (a German-language high school)—rises prominently above the sea of houses of İstanbul's old city.

Ottoman state officials and intellectuals of the time confronted the question of what possible means might still exist at their disposal, since, despite all efforts, there seemed to remain no prospect of ever being recognized and treated seriously as a legitimate part of Europe. The debates over what the right answer would be entered their next—and final—round.

"Free Radicals": The Young Turks

The politically and ideologically multifarious movement of the Young Turks emerged from the tradition of opposition movements against the autocracy of the Ottoman state and Sultan Abdülhamid II in particular. In the middle of the nineteenth century, a group of intellectuals calling themselves the Young Ottomans[93] (Yeni Osmanlılar) assembled and demanded the introduction of a constitutional order, while simultaneously opposing the excessive political and cultural influence of Europe, making recourse to concepts from Islamic political theology. The criticism the Young Ottomans directed at the Tanzimat and its statesmen was that under them the rule of the state had become increasingly more arbitrary and absolutist than in earlier times, during which institutions like the janissaries could exercise a moderating influence. Therefore it was necessary to return to the original concepts of the Islamic religion, including the principle of consultation incumbent upon the sovereign. Beginning in the 1860s, the label *La jeune Turquie* (the Young Turkey) was applied in political debates to all those who were seriously interested in reforms, and especially for reforms other than those of the Tanzimat.[94]

---

93 When Mustafa Fazıl Pasha (1829–1875), who was descended from the Egyptian khedival dynasty, used the term *jeune Turquie* for the first time in a dispatch to the Belgian daily newspaper *Le Nord*, two of his comrades, Ali Suavi (1839–1878) and Namık Kemal (1840–1888) wanted to find an Ottoman-language equivalent for it and created the term "Young Ottomans." Lewis, *Emergence of Modern Turkey*, 153ff.

94 Lewis, *Emergence of Modern Turkey*, 171–173. Mardin, *Young Ottoman Thought*, 35.

Around 1900, Young Turk intellectuals became decisively more radical, but they were, despite their revolutionary slogans, committed in the first instance to the preservation of the Ottoman Empire. In May 1889, the Committee of Ottoman Union (İttihad-ı Osmani Cemiyeti) was founded at the Imperial Military School of Medicine. Of the seven original founders of this secret society, four came from the Russian Caucasus, one from the Albanian region of Southeastern Europe, and two from Kurdistan. Of them, only Abdullah Cevdet (1869–1932) exercised any lasting effect—a doctor and author of Kurdish descent, he developed into an implacable critic of religion over the following decades. That there were no ethnic Turks among the founding members shows that in the beginning the Young Turks were in no way a faction defined by Turkish nationalism and that the question of a Muslim nation was posed earlier among non-Turkish Muslims than among Turkish Muslims.[95]

In 1894, the Committee of Ottoman Union adopted the name under which it would later become well-known: the Committee for Union and Progress (İttihad ve Terakki Cemiyeti). The CUP first achieved political clout and lasting significance when, in 1908, it entered into an alliance with officers in certain Ottoman garrison cities in Southeastern Europe, so that together they were successful in compelling a resurrection of the constitutional order of 1876. In February 1878, Sultan Abdülhamid II had suspended the Ottoman constitution and prorogued the parliament, and never revived either in the following three decades. The revolt of parts of his own military, which was no longer to be contained, forced the sultan to meet the central demand of the rebels: the revitalization of the constitutional principle and parliament.[96] As a result, in Turkish historiography, the period beginning in 1908 is spoken of as that of the Second Constitution (İkinci Meşrutiyet), that is the phase of a second constitutional government after that of the first in 1876–1878. An attempt at a counterrevolution in the following year (1909) provided the Young Turks with an occasion to depose Abdülhamid II. The two succeeding and final sultans of the Ottoman Empire, Mehmed V Reşad (r. 1909–1918) and Mehmed VI Vahdeddin (r. 1918–1922) were far removed from the plenitude of powers that Abdülhamid had been able to unite in himself.

The Young Turks and the military were not congruent. When, after the Balkan Wars, almost all the leadership positions in the military were reappointed, the promoted officers were not of one mind with the Young Turks

---

95 Zürcher, "Children of the Borderlands," 280.
96 Two standard works on the Young Turks before 1908 are Hanioğlu, *Young Turks in Opposition*, and Hanioğlu, *Preparation for a Revolution*.

across the board. Nevertheless, the officer corps, almost completely a product of the new military educational institutions, considered itself the bearer and tip of the spear of the reform and modernization of the empire. Military doctrines imported from Europe had left a strong impression, like the concept of "the nation in arms" (das Volk in Waffen) (published as a book of the same name in 1883) which Colmar von der Goltz (1843–1916) disseminated as inspector of the Ottoman army schools and later as lecturer at the military academy.[97] In addition, the Ottoman reform measures of the nineteenth century produced undesired consequences. The military academies which were supposed to be the bulwarks of the empire became breeding grounds for political opposition. Instruction in French made the writings of French sociologists and philosophers accessible to the young officers. The curriculum of the military schools featured a significant amount of religious content, but the officers were much more impressed by new European notions, like the crowd psychology of Gustave Le Bon, which foresaw an important role for the military as an indispensable part of the political elite. In addition, the young officers applied the technical approach taught in the military schools to society and thus paved the way for the positivist, vulgar materialist, and Social Darwinist attitudes which would be characteristic of the Young Turks and the founding generation of the Republic of Turkey.[98]

Most of the Young Turks and the members of the Committee for Union and Progress were, in fact, young. At the same time, "young" in contemporary Ottoman usage served to connote opposition to the established powers, a profound desire for change, and the goal of progress. The Young Turks initially spanned the most diverse approaches, liberal and emancipative, but increasingly narrowed their political positions. The Committee for Union and Progress was a particularly militant and resolute group within the Young Turk movement. Liberalism and representative government were watchwords, but their origin laid in a committee of a secret organization modelling itself after underground Russian and Bulgarian revolutionary movements "with an equally suspicious attitude towards the forms of parliamentary democracy."[99] Even after the official removal of its status as a secret organization in 1909, the Young Turks Committee retained its previous method of operating in secret. Its members maintained low profiles but managed to obtain key posts

---

97   Yasamee, "Von der Goltz." Van Ess, "Jubiläum."
98   Hanioğlu, *Atatürk*, 48–53.
99   Mazower, *Salonica*, 279. In addition, the Italian nationalist secret society of the Carbonari is often cited as a model for the Young Turk movement.

in the cabinet. Consequently, the grand vizier was "usually an older and distinguished individual who did not belong directly to the Young Turk party, [but] who naturally had to submit to the dictate of the Committee."[100]

After the successful "revolution" of 1908, there was great excitement across all sections of the population and all confessions of the empire. The bright future of a common Empire and state seemed within reach. In a very short time, however, the horizon darkened. Coldly exploiting the political convulsions in the Ottoman Empire, Bulgaria declared its independence, Austria-Hungary annexed Bosnia-Herzegovina, which it had been administrating since 1878, and Crete announced its unification with Greece. The disaster of the First Balkan War in autumn 1912 finally offered the Young Turks, who saw themselves as increasingly constrained by the requirements of a parliamentary, democratic order, the opportunity to seize power entirely on their own. On 23 January 1913, Enver Bey, a leading member of the Young Turk Committee, undertook a putsch against the government. From 1913 to 1918, the Committee of Union and Progress was directly in power. In these few years, which largely coincided with the First World War, the most visible leaders of the Young Turk Committee were the "Triumvirate" of Cemal, Enver, and Talât.

Cemal was born in 1872 in Mytilini on the island of Lesbos, the scion of an officer family and a graduate of the Military Academy. In 1913, he became military governor of İstanbul and, later, minister of the navy and commander of the Fourth Army in Syria. Within the Triumvirate, he was far and away the weakest politically. Enver, born in İstanbul in 1881, came from humble circumstances, but was nevertheless a graduate of the Military Academy and ranked as a "Hero of Liberty" because he had contributed materially to the success of the Young Turk revolt of 1908. In 1913, he was made a general and minister of war. The third member of the group, Talât (also sometimes found written Talaat) was born into poverty in Edirne in 1874. He did not have a military career, but his position as chief secretary of the Directorate of Post and Telegraph Service in Salonica in 1908 gave him the opportunity to decisively support the Young Turk movement. In the years to come, he held various posts, among which was minister of the interior, in 1909. In 1917, he ascended to the office of Grand Vizier, which he occupied until the end of the war.[101] There are good reasons to regard him as the mastermind of the Young Turks' policies during the First World War.[102]

---

100 Pomiankowski, *Zusammenbruch des Ottomanischen Reiches*, 31.
101 Lewis, *Emergence of Modern Turkey*, 225ff.
102 Thus argues the seminal biography by Kieser, *Talaat Pasha*.

The Young Turks were a passing phenomenon. They only held power directly for a few years, from 1913 until 1918, when they were destroyed along with the Ottoman Empire by the First World War. Why, then, are they so significant—even today? Alongside their responsibility for Ottoman domestic politics and the conduct of the war, their greater significance lies in the fact that a Young Turk-minded elite continued to hold the reins of power directly until at least 1950. "Young Turk-minded" here means a group of actors—officers, intellectuals, politicians—who considered themselves obliged to take state power through political competition or, if this proved impossible, through determination and unscrupulousness. They considered themselves justified in doing so because, as they saw it, they were pursuing the noble goal of saving the nation and the state. In their view of state and society, they were social engineers full of confidence in the fundamentally positive effect of their actions and measures, as long as they weren't frustrated by others. When their ultimate goals were achieved, that is, when the state was made strong and complete societal consensus with this new order had been achieved, then they would happily be ready to step back from their heroic task—or so they said.

The Young Turks wanted to liberate themselves from the paralysis of the autocracy under Abdülhamid II. They believed that they could only counter the dynamic of events—which were only caused in small part by them, most driven from outside—with the most extreme radicalism. The decades under Abdülhamid II may have been leaden years, but after 1913, under the Young Turks, autocracy's lead became a boiling metal which melted away the former edifice of society and state. For the Young Turks, the First World War was both an inducement and opportunity alike.

2. Born from the War (1912–1922)

The Republic of Turkey arose out of the ruins of the Ottoman-Turkish cataclysm of 1912–1922, a period of sweeping and destructive violence.[103] In these ten years—from the two Balkan Wars (1912–1913), through the First World War (1914–1918), to the war of the Anatolian national movement (1919–1922)—the Ottoman Empire founders and the Turkish Republic emerges. By the end of this decade, a multiethnic and multiconfessional

---

103 For an explication of the concept of cataclysm, see Kieser, Öktem, and Reinkowski, "Introduction," 5ff.

empire had given way to a state which saw itself as dedicated to the nation of Turks. The Turks experienced World War I differently than Western Europeans, because in the Ottoman-Turkish context, the Great War was embedded in a succession of wars which began two years before the First World War and only ended four years after it. The years of the First World War, on the other hand, distinguished themselves even among this decade of upheavals by their utmost destructive character. Anatolia was utterly laid waste in the Great War. The loss of human lives, infrastructure, and cultural riches and variety was monstrous. In a few years, Eastern Anatolia lost about a half of its population not because of the war proper but mostly through the epidemics, starvation, and massacres it dragged in its wake.

The Balkan Wars

The decisive experience that suggested that the Ottoman Empire no longer had a future as a multiethnic and multiconfessional imperium was the First Balkan War in autumn 1912.[104] It was immediately precipitated by events on the other end of the Ottoman Empire, in today's Libya. In 1911, Italy had occupied the Ottoman provinces of Tripolitania and Cyrenaica (the western and eastern coastal regions of today's Libya, respectively) on a spurious pretext. In itself, the loss of these North African possessions on the outermost edge of the empire was not particularly significant. After Egypt had fallen under the control of Great Britain in 1882, the Ottoman Empire possessed no connection by land to its possessions in North Africa west of Egypt. Militarily, the Ottomans could only defend themselves with an—in part quite successful—guerilla war. In 1912, they had to acquiesce to Italy's blockade of the Dardanelles and occupation of the Dodecanese (the "twelve islands," Rhodes chief among them) which was meant to put more pressure on their Ottoman opponent. Given the military helplessness of the Ottoman empire, in conjunction with the great powers' indulgence of Italy's violations of international law, Bulgaria, Greece, Montenegro, and Serbia saw an opportunity to wrest away the empire's European possessions. The booty would be big enough to satisfy everyone. As a pretext, the Balkan states claimed that the Ottoman Empire had not implemented the provisions of the Congress of Berlin of 1878 which required reforms in Macedonia.

---

104   For a critical evaluation of this assumption and a plea for seeing the developments after the First Balkan War more candidly, see Öztan, "Point of No Return."

The defeats of the Ottoman army in the first weeks of the war, in October and November 1912, were crushing. Only a few fortresses held out, like Shkodra (in today's northern Albania), Ioannina (in today's northwestern Greece), Monastır (today's Bitola in North Macedonia), and Adrianople (Edirne), but they subsequently had to surrender in the face of the general situation. The Bulgarian army had approached up to the Çatalca Line, the last defensive line before İstanbul, only about sixty kilometers from the city. During the Second Balkan War in June-July 1913, when an argument flared up between Bulgaria and its former allies over the division of conquered territory (which argument Bulgaria quickly lost), the Ottomans were able to reconquer Eastern Thrace and Adrianople (Edirne), which was not defended by the Bulgarians, in July 1913.[105]

The Balkan states' territorial and demographic gains as a result of the First Balkan War were enormous. For example, Greece enlarged its territory by about 70 percent; its population grew from 2.8 to 4.8 million. Serbia's territory nearly doubled, and its population climbed to a million and a half.[106] For the Ottoman elite, on the other hand, the result of losing the war was shattering: inside of a few weeks, all the Southeastern European territories (in terms of today's borders: Albania, Kosovo, North Macedonia, and the northern parts of Greece), among the oldest and richest regions of the Ottoman Empire, were lost.

The territorial and population losses incurred under the framework of the Congress of Berlin of 1878 and the First Balkan War shook the demographic foundations of the empire. In 1912, six and a half million inhabitants, about half Muslim, were lost along with Ottoman Europe. While around the middle of the nineteenth century the total population figures of the Ottoman Empire and Austria-Hungary were comparable, with more than thirty million inhabitants each, the Ottoman population sunk to twenty-six million while Austria-Hungary's grew to 42.5 million. Russia, the greatest threat in the late Ottoman era, already had a population of approximately a hundred and thirty million at the end of the nineteenth century.[107]

With the loss of the large Christian populations in Southeastern Europe, the Ottoman Empire had become a state with a decisively Muslim majority, despite the Christians in Anatolia and the Arab territories of the empire.

---

105 Hall, *Balkan Wars*, recounts the military history of the Balkan Wars. Ginio, *Ottoman Culture of Defeat*, is dedicated to the Ottoman experience of the war. For diplomatic-historical aspects, see Kuneralp and Tokay, *Ottoman Diplomatic Documents*, vol. 7.
106 Clogg, *History of Greece*, 83. Clark, *Sleepwalkers*, 43.
107 Kreiser, *Atatürk*, 71. Zürcher, *Young Turk Legacy*, 64.

52 | The History of Turkey: Grandeur and Grievance

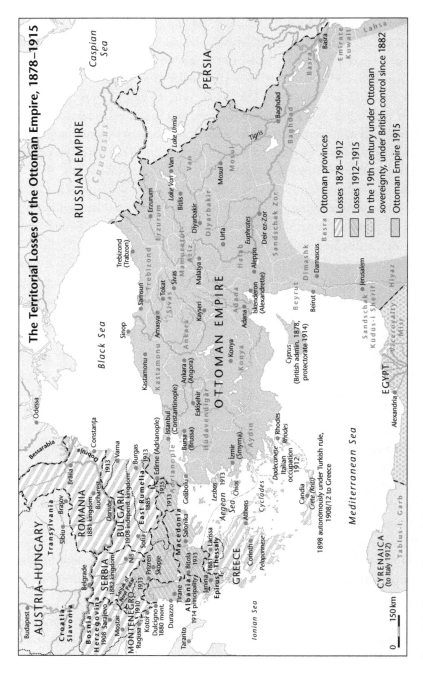

FIGURE 2. Territorial losses of the Ottoman Empire.

The Ottoman elite took from their defeat in the First Balkan War several immediate lessons. The military was radically transformed: conscription, which had previously as a rule had exempted subjects of Christian confession, was reformed and the loophole closed. The officer corps, still largely composed of men trained before the Young Turk revolution of 1908, was, as previously mentioned, dismissed, and a new generation of officers took its place.

The defeat in the First Balkan War cut the Ottomans' self-understanding as a power firmly anchored in Southeastern Europe to the quick and today remains the decisive point of departure for Turkey's desire for military self-assertion.[108] At the same time, the Ottomans' understanding of what the Ottoman Empire should be changed. Ottomanism's idea of a common citizenship, formulated in the nineteenth century, was dead. The earlier openness to non-Muslim populations was withdrawn. The lessons of the Balkan War were that, from now on, they had to concentrate on Anatolia and that the state should serve the Muslims who remained in the empire—albeit under Turkish supremacy. This view would become a cornerstone of the historical perspective of Republican elites. In the 1930s, publicist Falih Rıfkı Atay (1894–1971) wrote up his experiences as an Ottoman officer on the Arab fronts during the First World War and came to the conclusion that Ottoman elites and the Turkish people had misdirected their energies over centuries. The art of empire, he thought, was to make its colonies and nations work for it. The Ottoman Empire, however, as Atay put it in a dramatic image, "lay its huge body on its side and gave its colonies and nations to suckle, until finally they drank its milk mixed with its blood."[109]

The First World War

The Young Turk leadership that had held the government in its grip uncontested since its coup d'état in 1913 was convinced that the Ottoman Empire could not remain without allies in case of a European war. To remain neutral, as they likely correctly feared, would mean that whichever side won would happily divide up the Ottoman Empire among themselves. The Central Powers, led by Germany and Austria-Hungary, were not the first choice of

---

108 For the "siege mentality" of the contemporary Ottoman political elite which arose from the trauma of the Balkan Wars, see Kaya, "Western Interventions," 104, 135–141.
109 Atay, *Zeytındağı*, 41. For similar arguments posed even before the First World War, see Aksakal, *Ottoman Road to War*, 25–28.

the Young Turks, but attempts at approaching the Entente powers of France, Great Britain, and Russia—but also Austria-Hungary—had been tried in the previous months without success. With a victory by the Central Powers, whom they joined, the Young Turk leadership hoped to secure the continued existence and independence of the empire.

On the second of August 1914, a secret German-Ottoman pact was concluded, which provided for the entry of the Ottoman Empire on the side of the Central Powers in case of a war between Russia and the German Empire. In fact, the Ottoman Empire initiated combat operations on 29 October 1914, barely three months after the outbreak of war, by shelling Russian Black Sea ports—without having officially declared war on Russia. Germany formally treated the Ottomans as an equal partner. In August 1914, the information that Germany intended to violate Belgium's neutrality and accept the entry of Great Britain into the war was, however, withheld from the Ottoman side. In addition, Germany had little faith in the military capability of its ally. According to Kaiser Wilhelm II (r. 1888–1918) the state of the Turkish army was "completely dismal—really, so to speak—almost unsalvageable and almost hopeless."[110] Their Ottoman ally served one purpose from the beginning, namely relieving the Western front. To secure the Ottoman front, the Entente powers had to commit at least one and a half million soldiers who might have been otherwise deployed in other theaters of the war.[111] However, the hopes that the German side placed on the "Great Jihad" (Cihad-i Ekber) proclaimed by the Ottomans on 14 November 1914 were not fulfilled.[112]

Germany wanted to support the ally they judged feeble by deploying its own officers and contingents of troops. High German officers were represented in large numbers in the Ottoman army: Friedrich Bronsart von Schellendorf and, after him, Hans von Seeckt on the general staff; Otto Liman von Sanders as chief of the German military mission and, beginning in March 1915, also

---

110 Wallach, *Militärhilfe*, 150, here cites PA-AA (Politisches Archiv, Auswärtiges Amt (Political Archive of the Foreign Office), Türkei 142, vol. 38: Private letter of 3 April 1914 by Wilhelm II from Corfu.

111 Pomiankowski, *Zusammenbruch des Ottomanischen Reiches*, 17. On the Ottoman fronts, Great Britain relied on its colonial resources in particular. Four-fifths of the Indian soldiers deployed by the British Empire served in the Arab theaters of the war. The largest contingent of them, comprising 590,000 men, fought in Mesopotamia. Rogan, *Fall of the Ottomans*, 71.

112 On this, see Hagen, "German Heralds of Holy War," and Lüdke, *Jihad Made in Germany*. For an example of the all too confident assumptions of Germany's potential successes, see the Denkschrift of Max van Oppenheim in Epkenhans, "Geld darf keine Rolle spielen."

commander of the Fifth Army which defended the Dardanelles; Colmar von der Goltz as military advisor to the sultan and, beginning in October 1915, commander of the Sixth Army in Mesopotamia; Erich von Falkenhayn as commander of the Army Group "Lightning" (Yıldırım) in Palestine beginning in mid-1917; and Friedrich Kreß von Kressenstein on the Sinai Front. Even in the Ministry of War, important posts were occupied by Germans.[113]

Germany wanted to use the war to lay the foundations of a long-term domination of the Ottoman Empire, or to achieve—in the German turn of phrase of the day—an "Egyptification of Turkey" (Ägyptisierung der Türkei),[114] that is, achieving a position in the Ottoman Empire commensurate with that of the British in Egypt since the 1880s. The Young Turk Committee had its own goals in turn. Under the protective shield of the great European war, it shook off unloved obligations within the European state system. As early as 2 August 1914, the Ottoman government suspended its debt payments. When it announced on 9 September the abrogation of the capitulations takin effect on 1 October, a festive mood reigned in İstanbul the next day—ships and buildings were illuminated.[115] The Young Turks assumed with justification that during the war their allies' limits of tolerance would be elastic.

No one foresaw that the war would last four years. Nor had anyone believed that the Ottoman army could survive as long as it did, especially given its catastrophic state in the first months of the war. In December 1914 and in January 1915, an overly ambitious foray under the personal command of the Minister of War Enver Pasha on the Russian front at Sarıkamış (southwest of Kars in East Anatolia) failed abysmally. Ottoman troops, however, proved themselves in their most important task. The primary goal of the Entente powers in the Ottoman theaters of war was to take the southern straits of the Dardanelles in hand and "decapitate" the Ottoman Empire by occupying İstanbul. In March 1915, naval task groups of the Entente failed to break through the Dardanelles. The second attempt to overpower the Ottomans by landing massive formations on the Gallipoli (Gelibolu) peninsula west of the Dardanelles also failed. At the beginning of 1916, the expeditionary forces of the Entente withdrew entirely.

In spring 1916, a British expeditionary corps was surrounded by the Ottoman army at Kut al-Amara in Mesopotamia and, on 26 April, had

---

113 Tunçay, "Siyasal Tarih," 46.
114 Pomiankowski, *Zusammenbruch des Ottomanischen Reiches*, 183.
115 Ahmad, "Ottoman Perceptions of the Capitulations," 18.

to surrender. These successes coupled with Germany's victories on the Eastern Front in the summer of 1915 seemed to be a favorable development for the Central Powers. The withdrawal of Russia from the war after the Revolution in November 1917 was a particular gift. The demands which Germany could impose upon Russia in the Treaty of Brest-Litovsk on 3 March 1918 were tremendous.[116] By comparison, the Ottoman Empire's spoils were very modest: Russia evacuated the three East Anatolian provinces of Ardahan, Batumi, and Kars which it had received from the Ottoman Empire within the framework of the Congress of Berlin of 1878.

The fundamental superiority of the Entente powers to the Ottoman Empire in logistics, military technology, and troop strength became ever more clear on the two British-Ottoman fronts in Mesopotamia and Sinai-Palestine. At the end of the war, the British had pushed the Mesopotamian front far into the north, almost to Mosul. After two German-Ottoman advances (in January-February 1915 and in the high summer of 1916) failed at the Suez Canal[117], which was extravagantly defended by the British military, the British began to work their way through the Sinai Peninsula in the direction of Palestine in the second half of 1916. On 9 December 1917, the British Army took Jerusalem; in summer 1918, the Ottoman front in northern Palestine collapsed.

The Ottoman government recognized the hopelessness of their situation and, on 30 October 1918, several days before the German capitulation, signed an armistice on the British ship HMS Agamemnon, anchored at the port of Mudros on the island of Lemnos. The armistice provided for the occupation of the straits by the Allies, among other things. In addition, the Entente powers reserved the right to occupy any strategic point in the Ottoman Empire in the case of a threatening situation. On 2 November 1918, a German torpedo boat brought the leading members of the Young Turk Committee to Sevastopol, which was still under German occupation. Cemal, Enver, and Talât never set foot in Turkey again.[118]

---

116 Herbert, *Geschichte Deutschlands*, 158. Russia lost "a third of its population, railway network, and agricultural cropland, more than half of its industry, and almost 90% of its coal deposits."
117 See the military-historical account in Erickson, *Palestine*, for the two Suez offensives.
118 See Yenen, *Young Turk Aftermath*, for a comprehensive history of the Young Turk exile after the First World War.

Destruction and Denial: Assyrians and Armenians

Over the course of the war, 2.8 million men served in the Ottoman army, around twelve percent of the contemporary population of twenty-three million. At no point, however, did the strength of Ottoman manpower exceed eight hundred thousand men under arms. The loss of life in the Ottoman military was very considerable. Of the almost three million soldiers mobilized during the war, 771,844 were killed or went missing in action, 763,753 were wounded, and around five hundred thousand men deserted. Of the one hundred thousand soldiers of the Third Army who engaged in the aforementioned Battle of Sarıkamış over December 1914 and January 1915, only eighteen thousand returned. The majority were not killed in combat, but froze or died of their wounds or exhaustion. At the Battle of the Dardanelles alone, the losses on the Ottoman side to death, sickness, and wounds amounted to half of the five hundred thousand soldiers deployed on that front.[119]

In contrast to the Franco-German front, but thoroughly comparable to other theaters, like Serbia for example, losses among the civilian population were higher than among the troops. In the Arab territories of the Ottoman Empire (with an estimated population of 3–4.5 million), around a half million people died during the war due to a famine partially caused by a 1915 plague of locusts. For Eastern Anatolia, however, the war years were even more horrific. There the front meandered back and forth between Russia and the Ottoman Empire until 1917; however, only a small portion of the human losses were directly caused by military actions. Muslims and non-Muslims were affected by war and death equally. All suffered from hunger and disease. At least a million people died in an epidemic of spotted typhus which arose in Eastern Anatolia. In total, during the First World War, over all of Anatolia, around two and a half million Muslims, three hundred thousand Greeks, and up to a million and a half Armenians lost their lives.[120]

At the same time, these figures can deceive, as death did not reap these souls purely indiscriminately. Deliberate violence against civilians made the war in Anatolia much more iniquitous by far than it was already. The Young Turk Committee wanted to use the circumstances of the war to establish the

---

119 Rogan, *Fall of the Ottomans*, 56; Erickson, *Ordered to Die*, 211; Pomiankowski, *Zusammenbruch des Osmanischen Reiches*, 144.
120 Foster, "1915 Locust Attack," 370; Pomiankowski, *Zusammenbruch des Osmanischen Reiches*, 165; Zürcher, *Turkey*, 163ff.

Muslim population's unassailable supremacy in Anatolia after the war. At least a quarter million Assyrians died, only a few in combat; the majority were murdered in massacres.

Reports from the consuls and missionaries stationed in the region are an important source for our contemporary understanding of the genocide of the Armenians. In the case of the Assyrians, we don't have such reports, so we only have fragmentary knowledge of their fate during the First World War. Their areas of settlement lay in remote mountainous regions in today's Iran-Iraq-Turkey triangle. As early as 1914, Talât, as minister of the interior, directed the governor of Van to deport the Eastern Syriac Christians of the province of Hakkâri (where they comprised more than a third of the population) to the interior of the country. In the vilayet of Diyarbekir (Diyarbakır), the Assyrians were included in the extermination of the Armenians. In Urmia, in western Iran, the converse was true; there, when the Ottoman army conquered the city in 1917, the Armenians were wiped out in the obliteration of the large Assyrian community.[121]

The massacres of the Assyrians are a particularly clear indication of the plans of the Young Turk elite to rid themselves of the Christian population of Anatolia once and for all. The East Syriac Christians—unlike the Armenians—had no national ambitions, a fact recognized by the Young Turk government itself. The Armenians were thus in no way the only ones who were affected by a policy of genocide; instead, the intention of creating irreversible demographic changes culminated in the annihilation of the Armenians of Anatolia.[122]

The beginning of this ethnic cleansing on the night of 24–25 April 1915, when the Young Turk government had two hundred thirty-five leading individuals in the Armenian community of İstanbul imprisoned, was likely precipitated by the imminent landing of the Entente powers on the Gallipoli peninsula (which started on 25 April), but there must have been plans laid in the months before.[123] In May 1915, the forced migrations, abductions, and extermination of the Armenians in East Anatolia began. Regular military units were not deployed in these actions, but rather local police augmented by irregular units (*çete*) under the leadership of a secret Young Turk paramilitary

---

121 Morris and Ze'evi, *Thirty-Year Genocide*, 373–380.
122 Ibid., 373, 488, 496. In the last twenty years, the literature on the Armenian genocide has grown rapidly. Three standard works should be mentioned here as examples, alongside those already introduced in this account: Bloxham, *Great Game of Genocide*; Kévorkian, *Génocide des Arméniens*; Suny, *They Can Live in the Desert*.
123 Morris and Ze'evi, *Thirty-Year Genocide*, 244–253.

force, the Teşkilat-ı Mahsusa (Special Organization). The irregular units, which likely numbered in the tens of thousands of men, consisted of the local Turkish and Kurdish population, released prisoners, and Muslim refugees, primarily Circassians and Chechens. The inhabitants of Armenian settlements were informed of their imminent deportations only a short time, sometimes only a few hours, in advance. The deportations could have led in the direction of Western Anatolia, given their alleged goal of preventing possible collaboration between the Armenians and the Russian army. Their final destination, however, was the Euphrates Valley, lying far in the Syrian desert, in which large masses of people had little prospect of survival.

Armenian men of military age were initially taken aside and murdered. On their long deportation treks, Armenian civilians were repeatedly robbed, kidnapped, abused, and raped, by their guards but also by local populations. The death of prisoners through hunger, disease, cold, or heat, was consciously accepted or even sought. Countless Armenian women and children were robbed and forcibly Islamized.[124] This was not a singular spasm of violence. The massacres of early summer 1915 continued into the summer of 1916 at the deportations' destinations in the Euphrates Valley. The central figure in the organization of the Armenian genocide was Talât, serving as interior minister. He used a two-pronged modus operandi. Official orders, according to which attacks against deportees were to be avoided, were simultaneously contradicted and replaced by secret, mostly oral orders with contrary content. One may—and must—speak of a genocide, because the goal was unambiguous: to end the existence of Armenians in Anatolia forever.

There was not a unitary line in contemporary German policy with regard to the genocide, except perhaps to avoid a break with their Ottoman allies. One can hardly imagine an appeal from German officers would have been pointless from the outset, given the numerous senior officers like Friedrich Bronsart von Schellendorf, Otto von Feldmann, Hans Humann, and Otto von Lossow who had close personal relationships with the Young Turks.[125] An energetic German intervention against the extermination of the

---

124 In 2004, the human rights attorney Fethiye Çetin published the book *Anneannem: Anı* (My Grandmother: Her Memories), in which her grandmother relates her Armenian heritage shortly before her death. Altınay and Çetin, *Grandchildren*, contains a collection of memoirs of Muslims about their Armenian grandmothers.

125 Gencer, "Armenische Frage," 199. Trumpener, *Germany and the Ottoman Empire*, 21, 28ff., 69ff. 72, 75, 96, 108, 112, 126–130, 134, 204ff., 269, 349ff., 367–370, comes to the (from today's perspective) generous judgment that the German side fundamentally had

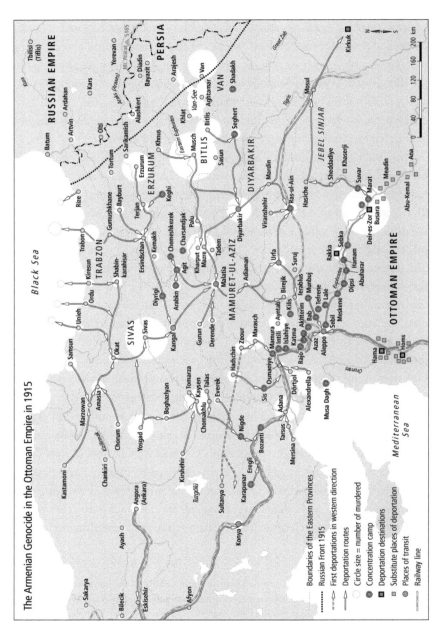

FIGURE 3. Armenian genocide.

Armenians was ruled out, however, by the fact that individuals like Bronsart von Schellendorf and Humann were themselves militantly anti-Armenian.[126] Reichskanzler Theobald von Bethmann Hollweg informed the German ambassador Paul von Wolff-Metternich, who had recommended officially condemning the Ottoman policy in December 1915, "The proposed public condemnation of an ally during an on-going war would be a measure unprecedented in history. Our sole goal is to keep Turkey at our side until the end of the war, irrespective of whether Armenians perish or not. In a war of long duration, we will still need the Turks very much."[127] In addition, German diplomats and officers were too caught up in their own views and goals. On 22 November 1915, on his way to the Army of Mesopotamia which had been placed under his command, von der Goltz, otherwise an open-minded person, wrote to his wife from Aleppo (Haleb) with a mix of sympathy, displaced responsibility, and imputations of guilt against Great Britain. The unbounded misery of the Armenians, who were subjected to a "dreadful national tragedy," was on display on the north Syrian plain. "One must feel pity in the depth of one's soul and simply cannot help. What tragedies this malign war has already occasioned—and how many it will still bring about—are hardly calculable. If one remembers that it really only came about out of the miserable gluttony of England, then one comes to fully appreciate the guilt of that country."[128]

The massacres of the First World War are embedded in a long prehistory of forced migration and violence. In the decades before World War One, millions of Muslims were driven out of the Caucasus and Southeastern Europe and found refuge in Anatolia. The traumatic loss of European possessions, the experience of displacement and flight, nationalist radicalization, and the existential threat in the years of the First World War led to an ideological mélange by which the Turkish state leadership saw itself as justified in going to extremes. Often such observations of the circumstances of the time are connected with the more or less openly stated argument that the history of Muslim expulsions and flight in the nineteenth and early twentieth century to some extent inevitably had to "invite" violence against the

---

little influence and conceded nearly all contested questions because it considered the Ottoman Empire an indispensable ally.
126 Ihrig, *Justifying Genocide*, 114, 136.
127 Kaiser, "Deutsche Diplomatie," 213, quotes from a note of Bethmann Hollweg, Berlin, 17 December 1915, in answer to a message from Metternich to Bethmann Hollweg of 7 December 1915, A 36184, PA-AA (Politisches Archiv, Auswärtiges Amt—Political Archive, Foreign Office), Türkei 183/40, no. 711.
128 Goltz, *Denkwürdigkeiten*, 428.

Christians of Anatolia.[129] This Turkish defense against possible responsibility for the genocide of the Christians of Eastern Anatolia (the massacres of the Greek Orthodox populations who largely lived in Western Anatolia were ignored in any case) was constructed astonishingly early and continues today fundamentally unchanged: "We were victims ourselves and never planned anything evil."

As the military commander and governor-general of Syria, Cemal Pasha was not one of those principally responsible for the genocidal policy of the Young Turk Committee in Eastern Anatolia. Nevertheless, in his memoirs which appeared in German in 1922, all the stances of downplaying, defensiveness, and guilt reversal which would dominate later Turkish politics of memory and suppression are already fully formed. Cemal portrayed himself as unwitting and uninvolved, despite his holding a prominent position in the Young Turk leadership. He claimed that after being given command in the Arab provinces he learned no more about the situation in Eastern Anatolia, "nor on what grounds the Government saw itself called upon to deport all Armenians." The argument positing an Ottoman "multiculturalism," so popular in Turkish historiography in later decades, is preempted by Cemal. The Armenians, in his telling, were completely acculturated with regard to Ottoman culture and the Turkish language. "The result was that for five hundred years there was no sort of conflict between the two people, and there was not a single Armenian who had not made the Turkish tongue and custom his own." In this sense, he argued, the Ottoman Empire had had minority rights for centuries, which Europe was only able to bring itself to realize in modernity. "Were not these rights, granted by a great Turkish sultan in the fifteenth century, the highest application of those principles of the 'Rights of Minorities' which President Wilson has endeavored to get recognized by the civilized world?" Only the instrumentalization of the Armenians on the part of the European great powers, foremost among them Russia, since the nineteenth century fundamentally altered the situation. Turks and Kurds now "naturally regarded Armenia, so to speak, as a snake let loose by Russia against them." All too promiscuously had Armenian nationalists taken up this alliance which in wartime "endangered the rear of our army in the Caucasus and which might under circumstance have completely annihilated it." Cemal's reference, correct in itself, to the murder of Anatolian Muslims by Armenian military units and to the suffering of the Muslim Turkish population flows into his attempt at reversing guilt.

---

129 For such an argument, McCarthy, *Death and Exile*, will serve as an example.

"But does anyone know how many Kurdish and Turkish inhabitants of the vilayets of Trebizond, Erzerum [sic], Van, and Bitlis were done to death in circumstances of the greatest cruelty by the Armenians when the Russians marched into these provinces? Then let it be stated that the number of Turks and Kurds killed on this occasion far exceeded one and a half millions. If the Turks are to be made responsible for the Armenian massacres, why not the Armenians for the massacres of Turks?"[130]

The meaning of "Armenian events" (Ermeni olayları) in official Turkish usage has changed very little over the course of the century. Only the numbers have become more concrete. The arguments appear in a more scholarly fashion and are formulated with knowledge of the positions of international historiography. Yusuf Halaçoğlu (b. 1949) could speak with particular authority on the Armenian question in a book from the 2000s, because from 1992 to 2008 he served as the president of the government-adjacent Turkish Historical Society (Türk Tarih Kurumu). According to Halaçoğlu, the responsibility for the Turkish-Armenian conflict during the war years lies with Armenian nationalist organizations who allowed themselves to be spurred on by the great powers. Given the cooperation of Armenian nationalists with the Russian army and the massacres committed by Armenians against the Muslim population during the war, the authorities, he argues, had no choice but to prevent these actions directed at the Ottoman state and to resettle the Armenian civilian population on a large scale. To judge by the Ottoman documents, apparently around fifty thousand Armenians lost their lives during the resettlement operations due to logistical difficulties, disease, and above all, attacks from local bandits. All the other Armenians, around four hundred thousand people, are said to have reached the resettlement locales in today's Syria selected by the government. In general, according to Halaçoğlu, "the largest relocation of people carried out by a state in the twentieth century was conducted in a rather disciplined manner." By contrast, one must proceed on the assumption that the number of the Muslims killed by Armenian nationalists must run "presumably into the hundreds of thousands."[131]

The grounds for such Turkish concealment and dissimulation are obvious. Many people in Eastern Anatolia enriched themselves through the annihilation of the Armenians, as well as through the seizure of tens of thousands

---

130 Djemal Pascha, *Erinnerungen*, 314ff., 318, 354, 357–359.
131 Halaçoğlu, *Armenierfrage*, 85, 95.

of Armenian women and children.[132] What was and is downplayed by the Ottoman and, later, Turkish side as the Armenian Question[133] bears the hallmarks of a bureaucratically planned and supervised mass murder and has, for this reason, world-historical significance.[134] For Germany, the chief ally of the Ottoman Empire at the time, this moral burden weighs heavily not least because direct lines lead from the Armenian genocide to the Holocaust.[135]

Leading personalities of the Young Turk Committee fled İstanbul at the end of the war. Beyond Cemal, Enver, and Talât, individuals like Arif Cemil (Denker, 1887–1945), Dr. Bahaeddin Şakir (1817–1922), Cemal Azmi (1868–1922), and Dr. Nazım Bey (1870-1926) were materially involved in the genocide against the Armenians and therefore had every reason to remove themselves from İstanbul before the arrival of the Entente powers. Most of them found refuge in Germany, where a network of sympathizers was helpful to them. Bahaeddin Şakir and Cemal Azmi both fell victim to revenge murders by the Armenian national movement, whose most important target was Talât, who was shot to death on 15 March 1921 by the assassin Soghomon Tehlirian, acting as part of an Armenian clandestine cell's "Operation Nemesis."[136] Whether Cemal Pasha was murdered by Armenian nationalists or at Moscow's order in Tbilisi on 21 July 1921 is disputed to this day. Enver Pasha, on the other hand, died on 4 August 1922 in an engagement with Soviet troops during his attempt to erect a caliphate in Central Asia.

Must the dark chapter of the Armenian genocide appear in a book about the Republic of Turkey at all? The principal perpetrators fled the country at the beginning of November 1918, several years before the foundation of the Turkish Republic. But it must, because the recognition of the Armenian

---

132 See Gerlach, *Extremely Violent Societies*, 92–102, for state and personal profiteering amid the Armenian genocide. According to Keyder, "Exchange of Populations," 45, thanks to the abundance of Armenian Christian property available for plunder, the liberal economic order of the late Ottoman period reverted, in the early Republic of Turkey, to a classic patrimonial-style state which reliably distributed land and benefactions to its clients.

133 Alongside Djemal Pascha, *Erinnerungen*, in which the chapter on the Armenians is named "The Armenian Question," see also as just one further example, Öke, *Ermeni Meselesi*; its English translation is correspondingly entitled *The Armenian Question*. Öke places the Armenian question in the context of international power politics and ascribes its origin to the manipulative policies of the great powers.

134 The Polish Jewish jurist and peace researcher Raphael Lemkin coined the term "genocide" based on his insight into the fashion in which the Armenians were exterminated in Anatolia without any sanction in international law. Power, *A Problem from Hell*, 17–20.

135 On this, Ihrig, *Justifying Genocide*, is fundamental.

136 Hosfeld, *Operation Nemesis*.

genocide is so difficult for many Turks today, not only because it would be connected with an admission of guilt or the possibility that it might even result in material demands from the Armenian side. There is an intuitive fear that a sober recounting of the events could place the origins of the Turkish national state in question. Seen from outside, this does not have to be the case. An honest look at the Ottoman-Turkish cataclysm does not mean that therefore the existential justification of the Republic of Turkey is placed into question. The unremittingly maintained defensive posture shows, however, that there is a lot of fragility beneath the heroics of the foundation of the Republic of Turkey.[137]

The War of the Anatolian National Movement

Every schoolchild in Turkey knows the date on which a certain Mustafa Kemal landed in Samsun on the Black Sea coast from a ship sailing from İstanbul. It was the nineteenth of May 1919. Mustafa Kemal, who had served in the First World War as, among other things, divisional commander at the Battle of the Dardanelles, was sent by the sultan's government as an inspector to demobilize the remaining Ottoman troops in Inner Anatolia and confiscate their weapons and munitions. Mustafa Kemal, however, pursued an end completely at odds with his assignment: he wanted to take part in the construction of a resistance movement in order to prevent a potential partitioning of Anatolia among the Entente powers, as well as the Armenians, Greeks, and Kurds. The nineteenth of May 1919 is considered the beginning of the War of Independence (İstiklal Savaşı) which lasted until 1922, and Mustafa Kemal is considered its indispensable hero—even if its success was due to many others in addition to him, and the circumstances of the Anatolian national movement were less clear by far than they were portrayed in the later, official history of the founding of modern Turkey.

In the first months after the armistice, the Ottomans' disappointment over the lost war was great. The leading Young Turks had fled, so power—or, rather, what was left of it—reverted to the court of Sultan Mehmed VI Vahdeddin (r. 1918–1922). The sultan and his entourage worked closely with the Entente powers. Their expectation was to obtain a more favorable result

---

[137] For an earlier formulation of the line of argumentation in this chapter, see Kramer and Reinkowski, *Türkei und Europa*, 93–99. On the centrality of this question for Turkish self-understanding well into the very recent past, see Bayraktar, *Politik und Erinnerung*.

from the peace negotiations in Paris by being accommodating. Among the signs of the Ottomans' compliance was the establishment of a special military court for the sentencing of those responsible for the Armenian genocide.[138] The Ottoman government in İstanbul's propitiation and circumspection with regard to the Entente powers, however, weakened its position relative to the Anatolian national movement.

This movement was additionally fueled by the landing of Greek troops in Smyrna (İzmir) on 15 May 1919. Under British pressure, the Entente powers had accepted Greece's proposal to enforce in advance the terms imposed on the Ottoman military with the help of Greek troops. Greece, driven by its irredentist Great Idea (Megali Idea) of uniting all Greeks in a common nation-state, actually had a much more wide-ranging plan: the parts of Western Anatolia in which Greeks lived, or in which they had lived before their expulsion, would be integrated into a new Greater Greek Empire. In fact, the Entente powers had only set aside the area around Ayvali (Ayvalık) and Smyrna (İzmir) for the Greek occupation zone; however, in October 1919, they acceded to a vastly larger occupation area, the eastern border of which ran along a line connecting the Western Anatolian cities of Menderes, Salihi, Akhisar, and Edremit.[139] The Entente powers again acquiesced in the Greek troops' crossing of this extended line as well. For centuries, the Greek Orthodox population in Anatolia had been a minority. During the war years, but even in the years preceding the conflict, many Greeks had fled Western Anatolia for the territory of Greece because of violence directed at them; now they returned in part under the protection of the Greek military. With the aim of restoring a Greek majority in Western Anatolia, Greek troops now undertook a policy of ethnic cleansing in a region in which Greeks probably only still comprised about a seventh of the population.[140]

The harshness of the terms of the Treaty of Sèvres played into the hands of the Anatolian national movement. Signed on 10 August 1920, it was the last of the Treaties of Paris submitted to the defeated parties in different suburbs of the city, with Germany (at Versailles, June 1919), Austria (Saint-Germain-en-Laye, September 1919), Bulgaria (Neuilly-sur-Seine, November 1919), and Hungary (Trianon, June 1920). The terms of the treaty were so severe that the sultan had to recall the first Ottoman delegation because they refused

---

138 On the few verdicts enacted by this special court martial and its early end, see Akçam, *Armenien und der Völkermord*.
139 Zürcher, *Turkey*, 147ff.
140 Plaggenborg, *Ordnung und Gewalt*, 223.

to sign it. The Treaty of Sèvres defined a Turkey drastically pruned of rights and resources. The two straits would be under Allied control. An independent Armenian state would be created in Eastern Anatolia, which would have comprised the majority of today's northeastern Turkey. In Southeast Anatolia, a Kurdish autonomous region was intended—far more vaguely than the project of the Armenian state—which, at some later time and under certain circumstances, would be converted into its own Kurdish state. The Greeks were guaranteed control over Eastern Thrace and the areas around Smyrna (İzmir). The region of Smyrna would remain under Greek administration for five years; subsequently the population would decide the affiliation of the region in a plebiscite. A separate treaty stipulated to France and Italy zones of "particular interest" in Anatolia. France's zone of influence would reach far into eastern Central Anatolia, extending from the mandate region promised to it in Syria. Italy would receive a zone of interest in Southwestern Anatolia.[141]

The Treaty of Sèvres was the result of conflicting interests and ambitions among the Entente powers. The still unbroken imperialist self-conceptions and senses of mission of France and Great Britain stood in contrast to the impulse for self-determination of "nations" proceeding from then-US president Woodrow Wilson (in office 1913–1921). In the case of the Ottoman Empire, these contradictory motivations were overlaid with identity-political aims, specifically the wish to drive "the Turks" "out of Europe" for good and to restrict the area owed to them. For example, the territorial claims granted to Greece in Western Anatolia can be understood as a very one-sided application of the principle of national self-determination and simultaneously as an attempt, in connection with the idea of philhellenism, to transplant the primacy of Western Civilization—an intention David Lloyd George (British prime minister 1916–1922) openly championed.[142]

To the surprise of the Entente powers, indeed to that of the whole world, Turkey—alone among the countries subjected to the Treaties of Paris—managed to reduce the Treaty of Sèvres to so much wastepaper. Thus, in Turkish eyes,

---

141 Oran, "Peace Treaty of Sèvres," 66. A complete English-language version of the treaty is at https://wwi.lib.byu.edu/index.php/Peace_Treaty_of_Sèvres, accessed 20 April 2023. An abridgment appears in Hurewitz, *Diplomacy in the Near and Middle East*, 2:87–89.
142 On 11 January 1917, the Entente powers informed the US government that the Ottoman Empire would be driven out of Europe because it "has proved itself so radically alien to Western civilization." Toynbee, *Western Question in Greece and Turkey*, 328. See also Barr, *Line in the Sand*, 64, and MacMillan, *Paris 1919*, 437, for Lloyd George's powerful antipathy to "the Turks."

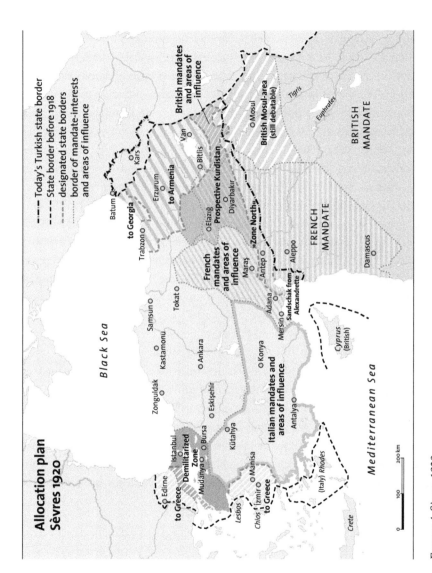

Figure 4. Sèvres, 1920.

the War of Independence is better called the War of Liberation (Kurtuluş Savaşı). At the time, its leaders chose the more moderate expression, "the national struggle" (Millî Mücadele). Can we then speak of the War of Independence, as Anatolia was never a colony and the armistice of October 1918 did not fundamentally abolish the sovereignty of the Ottoman Empire? Surely, had the Treaty of Sèvres become reality, Turkey's future would have become uncertain. Hungary, however, survived the punishing terms of the Treaty of Trianon, according to which it lost two-thirds of its previous territory and three million Hungarians had to live outside their own country from then on.[143]

In any case, the years 1919–1922 were a time of struggle for independence and sovereignty, borne by a national movement in all of Anatolia. The goals of Mustafa Kemal and his allies were to not allow the territorial demands of the Greeks and Armenians to be realized and to drive out the troops of foreign states deployed in Anatolia—a herculean-appearing task given the balance of forces. In May 1919, there were thirty-five thousand troops of the old Ottoman army that had not yet been demobilized. Of them, only the barely twenty thousand soldiers of the Fifteenth Army Corps in Eastern Anatolia under Kâzım (Karabekir) could be considered an organized military unit. In contrast, there were almost two hundred thousand regulars of the Entente powers stationed in Anatolia in April 1920.[144] Even into 1920, the national movement boasted only very weak individual formations which were primarily composed of irregular units. The leaders of the national movement felt besieged and threatened, because internal revolts had brought all Anatolia into turmoil.[145] One mainstay was secret societies like the previously mentioned Special Organization (Teşkilat-ı Mahsusa) and the Sentinel Association (Karakol Cemiyeti) which had already been armed for a future guerrilla war by the Young Turk Committee during the First World War. Furthermore, many employees of the Ottoman government supported the national movement in secret.

The first national congress in Erzurum of 23 July–7 August 1919 followed a meeting of the leaders of the national movement in Amasya on 19 June 1919. The congress ended with a declaration of the indivisibility of the territory under Ottoman control at the moment of the Ottoman surrender on 30 October 1918 and a call for all Muslims to defend themselves against

---

143 Leonhard, *Der überforderte Frieden*, 1077.
144 Kreiser, *Atatürk*, 157, gives the following figures: thirty-eight thousand British, fifty-nine thousand Frenchmen, seventeen thousand Italians, and ninety thousand Greeks.
145 Aydemir, *İkinci Adam*, 1:139, 153, 155.

Greek and Armenian separatism. At the second congress, in Sivas over 4–11 November 1919, the local resistance movements merged into the Association for the Defense of the National Rights of Anatolia and Rumelia (Anadolu Rumeli Müdafaa-ı Hukuk-ı Milli Cemiyeti).[146] The congress proclaimed the foundation of a national government in Anatolia, in open opposition to the Ottoman government in İstanbul. Almost all the comrades-in-arms of the Anatolian national movement still assumed at this point that, after a successful war, a sultan, free of the patronage of the Entente powers, would again be the sovereign ruler in İstanbul (and personally unite the offices of sultan and caliph). The congress of Sivas reasserted the geographic borders of a common state for the Muslims of Anatolia which was still to be achieved. All of the areas that were not occupied by Entente troops on the day of the armistice would belong to the Muslims of Anatolia. This decision gave rise to later Turkish claims on northern Syria and the region around Mosul (today in northern Iraq), which British troops first occupied a few days after the armistice.

In October 1919, the Ottoman government in İstanbul and the Anatolian national movement agreed upon a compromise: the sultanic government in İstanbul would recognize the Association for the Defense of the National Rights of Anatolia and Rumelia just as a provisional authority in Anatolia. By contrast, adherents of the defensive association would run in the December 1919 elections to the Ottoman parliament, in which they won a large majority.[147] In spring 1920, however, a final quarrel split İstanbul and the national movement, which had in the meantime chosen Ankara as its central base.

The choice of Ankara as a capital on 27 December 1919 rested above all on military-strategic considerations. After the loss of European territories in the First Balkan War, İstanbul lay at the extreme western edge of the empire. Consequently, as early as 1913–1914, German military advisers had given serious consideration to moving the capital to Konya or even Damascus.[148] The capital of the national movement could not be too far from İstanbul and had to be connected to the extant railroad network; at the same time, it had to

---

146 For a detailed account of the local and regional predecessor organizations, see Tunçay, "Siyasal Tarih," 60–68.
147 Hanioğlu, *Atatürk*, 99–101.
148 In 1897, von der Goltz suggested that the Ottoman Empire should transform itself into a Turkish-Arab empire, instead of remaining a weak Byzantium one. In this context, he suggested relocating the capital to Konya or Kayseri or even to Damascus, Mosul, or Baghdad. Colmar Freiherr von der Goltz, "Stärke und Schwäche des türkischen Reiches," Deutsche Rundschau 24.93 (1897), 95–119. Statement following Yenen, "Envisioning Turco-Arab Co-Existence," 8ff.

be shielded from possible attacks by the Entente powers. Ankara was thus a natural choice, even if the city had little to offer otherwise. Ankara was finally declared the capital on 13 October 1923.[149]

According to Turkish national historiography, on 17 February 1920, the Ottoman Parliament performed one last great service to the nation: it concluded the so-called National Pact (Misak-ı Millî), with two main resolutions: (1) All regions which were not occupied on 30 October 1918, the day of the Armistice of Mudros, were the homeland of Anatolian Muslims; and (2) the future of the occupied Arab territories, the former Russian provinces of Ardahan, Batumi, and Kars, as well as Western Thrace were to be decided by popular referenda.

The Entente powers saw the danger of the national movement's seizure of power in İstanbul and officially occupied the city, in which Entente troops had been stationed since 1918, on 16 March 1920. Sultan Mehmed Vahdeddin dissolved parliament on 11 April 1920. Ninety-two members of the Ottoman parliament made their way to Ankara as a result. There, they, along with two hundred and thirty-two representatives chosen by the local chapters of the defensive association, formed the Grand National Assembly (Büyük Millet Meclisi), which convened for the first time on 23 April 1920.[150]

In its early phase (into 1920), the military arm of the Anatolian national movement—with one exception in Eastern Anatolia—consisted of irregular formations which fought intrinsically superior units of the Entente powers. A strength of the national movement was its broad social basis. In recognition of their merits in the fight against French occupation, the cities of Antep, Maraş, and Urfa were given honorifics and were extolled as Gaziantep ("Antep, Warrior for the Faith [or Nation]"), Kahramanmaraş ("Heroic Maraş"), and Şanlıurfa ("Glorious Urfa"). The movement bore a common, explicitly Muslim nationalism, so that Kurds and religious jurisprudents (ulema) joined the movement without hesitation. In the first National Assembly of 1920, eighty-five of 403 representatives had a traditional religious education, and Kurds were represented in approximate proportion to their share of the population, with seventy-two of 437 representatives.[151] Had the Anatolian national movement failed in 1920 or 1921, for example, through a decision by the Entente powers to throw their total military weight on the balance, it would probably "have gone down in history as an attempt to reconstruct

---

149 Tunçay, "Siyasal Tarih," 81.
150 Zürcher, *Turkey*, 138ff., 151.
151 Kreiser, *Atatürk*, 230ff.

a powerful Ottoman-Islamic state with slightly nationalistic undertones."[152] For this reason, it is much more appropriate by far to speak of it as a Muslim Anatolian than a Turkish national movement. Only when the national movement had achieved its goals, did Mustafa Kemal and his closest comrades admit a Turkish-nationalist agenda.

The Entente powers had neither the means nor the will to proceed against such a surprisingly successful national movement. In addition, Mustafa Kemal succeeded with skilled diplomacy in narrowing the fight, initially conducted against multiple opponents, to war with Greece exclusively. In autumn 1920, Armenian units in Eastern Anatolia were crushed devastatingly. The Treaty of Alexandropol (today's Gyumri, Armenia) of 2 December 1920 embodied a diktat of the Anatolian national movement, demanding that Armenia declare the Treaty of Sèvres void on its part. In 1921, Italy and France sought an agreement with the national movement. The rapprochement with the Bolshevik leadership promoted by Mustafa Kemal led to two Soviet-Turkish treaties. On 16 March 1921, a Soviet-Turkish treaty of friendship was signed in Moscow. On 13 October 1921, a treaty was concluded in Kars, declaring friendship between Turkey and Armenia, Azerbaijan, and Georgia, all three already under Soviet control. The Soviet-Turkish accord and the military and financial support from Moscow which followed were extremely helpful in the battle against Greece, whose further advance in the direction of Central Anatolia was life-threatening to the national movement.[153]

In two battles, in January and again in March–April 1921, troops of the national movement succeeded in stopping the Greek advance, for the time being, at the İnönü River (near Eskişehir). Faced with a renewed offensive of the Greek army in summer 1921, the Turkish forces withdrew to the Sakarya River, less than sixty miles from Ankara. After a battle of several weeks, the Turkish side managed, on 13 September 1921, to finally break the Greek forward advance. Had the Greeks succeeded in breaking through, their strength would probably have been sufficient to occupy Ankara. In that case, the Entente powers would likely have come to a different assessment of the situation in Anatolia.[154]

---

152 Behrendt, *Nationalismus in Kurdistan*, 395.
153 Hanioğlu, *Atatürk*, 119–123. Tellal, "Relations with the Soviets," 97. An English translation of the Turco-Soviet treaty of March 1921 may be found in Dmytryshyn and Cox, *The Soviet Union and the Middle East*, 473–480.
154 Aydemir, *İkinci Adam*, 1:187.

In summer 1922, the Turkish side went on the offensive and was able to destroy five of the eight divisions of the Greek army deployed at Dumlupınar, near Afyonkarahisar, on 30 August. The first Turkish units moved into Smyrna (İzmir) on 9 September 1922. The Greek campaign in Western Anatolia and the Turkish countermovement ended in a débâcle. The chaotic evacuation of the non-Muslim population from Smyrna, massacres of the civilian population, and, on 13 September 1922, the inferno very probably set by the Turkish invaders ended the city's life as a center of the Levantine world. Smyrna became İzmir.[155]

On 11 October 1922, Great Britain, which had hitherto occupied the zone around the two straits, signed an armistice with the Ankara government at Mudanya (on the east coast of the Sea of Marmara) and recognized that government as a coequal counterpart. The way to the Treaty of Lausanne, with which the Treaty of Sèvres was abrogated and the Republic of Turkey was internationally recognized, had been paved.

3. Paths diverge (1922–1925)

The Ottoman Empire had been a large communications space, even if in its last few decades its fundamental structure was not particularly stable and different parts of Ottoman society had come to believe that they had little to say to each other. It had been a common empire for all those who had attended the officers' academies in İstanbul and who had taken military commands in the most varied parts of the empire; for all of those who had the same access to the religious and normative texts of Islam in Arabic as religious jurisprudents; for all those who conducted trade with each other and who shared at least one of the plethora of languages spoken in the empire; for the great majority of the people in the Ottoman Empire who, despite all the conflicts, saw coexistence grown from the common realm of experience as an obvious component of their homeland.

The Ottomans' loss of their Southeastern European possessions after the First Balkan War shows how formerly century-long connections can seemingly vanish overnight. Though reference to their origins in the Balkans remained among Muslims who had fled to Anatolia, the severance was

---

155 For the place of Smyrna in the greater context of the expulsions of Greeks from Anatolia, see Morris and Ze'evi, *Thirty-Year Genocide*, 381ff.

immediately effective. One reason for it was the complete change in elites in countries like Bulgaria, Greece, Montenegro, and Serbia. Another was that the concepts of nationalism and nation-states now offered the opportunity of being able to say, apparently authoritatively, where someone belonged and where not. In any case, it is striking how little—or not at all—Turkish public opinion occupied itself with Southeastern Europe in the twentieth century. Only the Bosnian War of the 1990s returned Southeastern Europe back into the emotional center of Turkish society.

The Arab provinces' break with their Ottoman past was less decisive and above all less rapid. The loyalty of the Arab population to the Ottoman state and sultan was very strongly strained during the war, but it was never completely broken.[156] From today's perspective of nation-states, that at the end of the war the paths they'd trodden together since the sixteenth century would diverge seems obvious—but this only came about thanks to decades of school education and state history policy. All the new Arab states who understood themselves more or less convincingly as nation-states sought their self-affirmation in their distancing themselves from the Ottoman period. So in the Arab-nationalist historiography of the twentieth century, it was considered a self-evident fact that "the Turks" had continued to oversee the Arab lands' decline that had already begun in 1258 with the Mongol conquest of Baghdad, and thereby laid the groundwork for the underdevelopment and helplessness of the Arab world before Western imperialism.[157] Turkish-nationalist historiography, on the other hand, advanced the proposition that the Arabs had turned treacherously against the common Ottoman Empire conceived for all Muslims.[158]

The End of the Levant and the Creation of the Middle East

The carcass of the Ottoman Empire, one of the last representatives of the dying species of premodern imperia, was laid out to be carved up after the First World War. There was even more to carve up than originally foreseen. In spring 1915, France and Britain had assented to prospective Russian control over İstanbul and the straits. Now after the Bolsheviks had withdrawn themselves from the war, Russia was no longer included.

---

156   Rogan, *Frontiers of the State*, 220ff. Yenen, "Envisioning Turco-Arab Co-Existence." But see the more reserved perspective in Tamari, *Year of the Locust*, 14.
157   On this, see Abou-el-Haj, "Social Uses of the Past," and Barbir, "Memory."
158   See for example Kürkçüoğlu, *Arap Bağımsızlık Hareketi*, 249–252.

The Anatolian national movement and the mutual mistrust between allies France and Great Britain threw a monkey wrench in the works. Indeed, Great Britain could not long dominate the new arrangement in the Middle East, which it had materially erected, with France partly as a partner, partly as an opponent, because it would be displaced as the leading power in the region by the United States in the second half of the twentieth century. Nevertheless, the new order brought about by Great Britain was the most dramatic break in centuries in the history of the region we now know as the Middle East.

This new order was the result of a confusing succession of collusions, bargains, and deals between France and Great Britain. They extended from the informal division of the Arab territories of the Ottoman Empire before the war, through mutual promises and accords during the war years, to the concluding settlements in the early 1920s, above all at the Conference of San Remo in April 1920, which finally determined the outlines of the League of Nations mandate for France (today's Lebanon and Syria) and Great Britain (today's Israel, Palestine, Jordan, and Iraq).[159]

As an overarching designation for this new order, the expression "the Sykes-Picot order" is often used. In November 1915, the French diplomat François Georges-Picot and his British negotiating partner Mark Sykes agreed that in the case of a victory by the Entente powers, areas of Ottoman rule in the eastern Arab world would be divided up between France and Great Britain. This plan for partition was sealed with a secret Franco-British agreement in May 1916.[160] Nevertheless, "the Sykes-Picot order" can only function as shorthand for a much more involved history. The agreement was never implemented in its original form because of later developments, above all because of the dropping out of their Russian ally, who had been taken into account in the treaty.[161]

With the breakdown of the once-common Ottoman communications space, subcultures which were suited to it also fell apart, like that of the Levantines. In the Levant, that is, on the shores of the Eastern Mediterranean, over the centuries a "supranational group, the prototype of an ethnically

---

159 On the informal division of the region before World War One, see Khalidi, "Economic Partition." Fromkin, *Peace to End All Peace*, 401, gives an exhaustive recounting of the agreements among the Entente powers.
160 For the text of the agreement, see Hurewitz, *Diplomacy in the Near and Middle East*, 2:18–22.
161 For an earlier version of the argument, see Reinkowski, "Ein neuer Naher Osten?," 95ff.

mixed community," had found a particular niche.[162] To be a Levantine stood for a certain way of life, namely to live in Muslim-majority community, having originally emigrated from Europe as a "Frank," and to possess connections in the European-Christian world.[163] No one understood how to use the interstices between imperial and state power structures like the Levantines. The nineteenth century, under the protection of the omnipresent European great powers, was likely the golden age of the Levantines. This way of life might appear today as a variety of a desirable cosmopolitanism, but for the Ottomans, the Levantines were unprincipled and disloyal, and for European observers of the day, they stood for moral degeneracy and rootlessness.[164]

After the First World War, İstanbul briefly saw a flash of cosmopolitanism, flaring up out of necessity. In November 1920 alone, one hundred and thirty-five thousand adherents of the White movement (the opponents of the Bolsheviks in the Russian Civil War of 1919–1922) and others who didn't wish to live in a Bolshevik Russia fled via the Russian Black Sea ports to İstanbul. The living conditions in İstanbul were difficult for them and most saw the city only as a springboard to the way further west.[165]

With the intention of putting the land and economy in the hands of their own people, the Republic of Turkey embarked on a development which would only begin in the other lands of the Middle East decades later. The Levantines and the Jews of Egypt lost their basis of existence with the putsch of the "Free Officers" in 1952 or, at the latest, with the Suez Crisis of 1956.[166] The Beirut of today may recall the Levantine world of the nineteenth and early twentieth century in certain respects, but the unremitting trials of Lebanon, beginning with the civil war in the 1970s and 1980s over its absorption of an overwhelmingly large number of Syrian refugees to its present deep economic crisis, leave the today's Lebanese with little time or space for nostalgia.

The provincialization and encapsulation of Turkey and the Middle East in general after the First World War is reflected in the economic conditions of

---

162 Schmitt, *Levantiner*, 15.
163 Sweepingly dubbing all Christian Europeans "Franks" presumably goes back to the time of the Crusades. Lewis, *The Muslim Discovery of Europe*, 22.
164 Schmitt, *Levantiner*, 73. The condescension, indeed downright contempt, of European observers for the Levantines is very similar to European interpretations of "the Balkans," as part of oneself that is simultaneously disconcerting. Todorova, *Imagining the Balkans*, is fundamental here.
165 Criss, *Istanbul during the Allied Occupation*, 30. Deleon, *White Russians*.
166 Pink, *Geschichte Ägyptens*, 211, 219ff.

the interwar years. From the beginning of the First World War into the late 1940s, formerly Ottoman-ruled territories became de-globalized. The disappearance of the Greek and Armenian populations of Anatolia pertains to this phenomenon. Many of the export-oriented and commercially successful farmers of Western Anatolia and the eastern Black Sea Coast, not to mention craftsmen, money changers, and traders, who had linked the rural areas of Anatolia with the port cities and European trading companies, were no longer alive, or at least no longer in Turkey.

The economies which had to develop within the new national borders only recovered very slowly from the aftermath of the First World War. Egypt, for example, recorded no increase at all in per-capita income between 1913 and 1940. The extremely low growth figures for the economy in the first decades of the Republic of Turkey are thus no idiosyncrasy; nevertheless, the figures are shockingly low. Per-capita productivity in Turkish agriculture only reached pre-war levels in the early 1930s. At the end of the 1940s, per capita productivity was in total only a quarter higher than on the eve of World War One. The average growth rate from the 1920s into the late 1940s lagged at only 0.6%.[167] From a Turkish perspective, this was not too high a price to pay for having achieved the establishment of an (apparently) homogenous nation-state, economic independence, and sovereignty. The Treaty of Lausanne (1923) represents the most important milestone for the international recognition of an independent, sovereign Turkey.

The Treaty of Lausanne

In the last two years of the First World War and in the first years thereafter, numerous, mostly very short-lived republics sprouted up in West Asia and North Africa. Republics were declared in Azerbaijan, Bashkiria, Bukhara, on the Crimea, in Gilan (in Iran), in Morocco's Rif Mountains, in the South Caucasus, and Tripolitania (in Libya). The revitalized Soviet Union soon incorporated all the republics in the Caucasus and Central Asia. In North Africa they were quashed by the European colonial powers.[168] The Anatolian national movement stands out among this large number of evanescent

---

167 Owen and Pamuk, *Middle East Economies*, 7, 11, 22–24, 27.
168 Reichmuth, "Die muslimischen Republiken der Nachkriegszeit."

Muslim republics by its assertiveness and its transformation into a sovereign and internationally recognized state.

Even today, Turkey reads the 1923 peace treaty of Lausanne as an outstanding agreement which stands on its own. Seen in a larger context, however, it is the concluding point of the Treaties of Paris, however late, and consequently part of the reordering of the Middle East resulting from them. The Treaty of Lausanne fixed the existential conditions for the new Republic of Turkey, which simultaneously became, in a certain sense, an associate member of the reordering of the Middle East.

On 13 November 1922, the Entente powers issued invitations to a peace conference in Lausanne in order to speak "about the affairs of the Near Orient."[169] Mustafa Kemal assigned his confidant İsmet (İnönü), whom he had already named foreign minister on 26 October 1922, with the leadership of the Turkish delegation for the pending peace negotiations. İsmet (İnönü) had distinguished himself by his services in the War of Independence; his later surname was derived from the defensive battles successfully won by him on the İnönü River in January and March–April 1921.

The Turkish delegation faced several groups of states: France, Great Britain, Italy and Japan had called the conference; furthermore participated—in various parts of the proceedings—Albania, Belgium, Bulgaria, Greece, the Kingdom of the Serbs, Croats, and Slovenes, Portugal, Rumania, the United States (though the US took part in the negotiations as an observer), and a Bolshevik delegation from Russia.[170]

The Turkish delegation came to Lausanne with maximalist territorial demands. They demanded, in addition to the Sanjak of Alexandretta (today the Turkish province of Hatay), more territories in the north of today's Syria, the province of Mosul, the Aegean islands off the Turkish mainland, Cyprus, and a plebiscite in Western Thrace (part of Greek territory). In addition, the Turkish delegation had received the instruction to not concede two points under any circumstances: they were to prevent the establishment of an Armenian state in Eastern Anatolia and the reintroduction of capitulations. The negotiations, which began on 20 November 1922, were freighted with great tensions, not only between the Turkish delegation and their counterparts, but also between İsmet (İnönü) and the parliament in Ankara. The parliamentary opposition reproached the delegation's leader for not pressing

---

169 Kreiser, *Atatürk*, 174.
170 Payk, *Frieden durch Recht*, 479f; Oran, "Peace Treaty of Lausanne," 127.

home the demands of the National Pact, that is, establishing the borders of the Republic of Turkey congruently with the area under the control of Ottoman troops at the armistice of October 1918.[171]

Because the two parties could not find agreement on several points (abolition of capitulations, economic and financial questions including the disposition of Ottoman state debts, the question of the straits), the negotiations were broken off on 4 February but restarted on 23 April 1923. Finally, on 24 July 1923, the Treaty of Lausanne was signed.[172] The war of the Anatolian national movement was a brilliant military achievement for the young Turkey, and the Treaty of Lausanne its diplomatic equal—even if the Turkish side had to agree to compromises on many points.[173] The recognition of Turkey as sovereign within internationally acknowledged borders was central. In this regard, from this point, "sovereignty belongs unconditionally to the nation" (Egemenlik kayıtsız şartsız milletindir),[174] as the dictum of Mustafa Kemal states, which stands today as a guiding principal on the front wall of the parliamentary chamber of the Great National Assembly of Turkey (Türkiye Büyük Millet Meclisi).

If one regards Turkey's environment at the time, its acquisition of unlimited sovereignty was the exception. In Egypt, for example, Great Britain, faced with violent protests and unrest, felt forced to rescind its protectorate, declared in 1914, and grant the country independence on 1 February 1922. Simultaneously, however, Britain stipulated that it retain control of British lines of communication through Egypt, responsibility for the country's defense, and rights of protection over foreign interests as well as the Anglo-Egyptian Sudan.[175] Applied to Turkey, such standards would have meant that complete control over the straits and, partially, the military defense of Anatolia would have rested in someone else's hands.

---

171 Zürcher, *Turkey*, 161. Tunçay, "Siyasal Tarih," 80. See also the collection of telegraphic correspondence between Lausanne and Ankara in Şimşir, *Lozan Telegrafları*.

172 The totality of the protocols of the negotiations—from the perspective of the Entente powers—is found in The *Lausanne Conference on Near Eastern Affairs, 1922–3: Records of Proceedings and Draft Terms of Peace* (London: HMSO, 1923). A complete English-language version of the treaty is at https://wwi.lib.byu.edu/index.php/Treaty_of_Lausanne, accessed 20 April 2023. Excerpts from the treaty are in Hurewitz, *Diplomacy in the Near and Middle East*, 2:119–127.

173 Oran, "Peace Treaty of Lausanne," 129.

174 The contemporary Ottoman-language formulation was Hakimiyet bila kaydü şart milletindir, also found in the first article of the Constitution of 1921 (the Teşkilat-ı Esasiye Kanunu, or Law on Fundamental Organization).

175 Pink, *Geschichte Ägyptens*, 189.

The abolition of capitulations, along with the repeal of the free-trade treaties concluded in the nineteenth century, was perhaps not quite the "Magna Carta of the new country,"[176] but nevertheless the humiliating economic penetration of the country had come to an end. Turkey could also escape the liquidation costs of the perished Ottoman Empire in part. Turkey did not, in fact, have to pay any reparations to the Entente powers, and the loans that the Ottoman Empire had made from Germany were written off. Yet Turkey had to assume two-thirds of the Ottoman state debt which was determined at the negotiations to be 129.4 million Turkish gold lira or about 118 million British pounds (the remaining third of the Ottoman state debt was assigned to the Mandate regions in the eastern Arab world). Shortly after the payment of the first installment (which was only due in 1929), Turkey discontinued payments. New negotiations finally led to a reduction of more than half of the agreed-upon sum.[177] A bitter pill for the Turkish side was that the established customs tariffs were only allowed to be changed beginning in 1929, and that it only regained the monopoly on alcohol, salt, and tobacco held by the international debt administration (Administration de la Dette Publique) beginning in 1927. By the same token, the validity of the foreign concessions of the day remained in force—the last French railroad concession expired in 1947.[178]

At least as significant as the liberation from the torture implements of the European commercial imperialism of the nineteenth century was that Turkey could establish its conception of what constituted "minorities" in the country. The sole criterion considered in the Treaty of Lausanne for the recognition of minority groups was religious membership—a clear narrowing of the term relative to the provisions found after the First World War. Their foundations were the clauses on minorities in the treaty between Poland and the Entente powers of 28 July 1919 in Versailles. The goal was to settle the minority questions in the new international post-war order to encourage the loyalty of minorities to their particular states and to thereby dry up irredentist movements. The minority rights supported by League of Nations and to be protected foundered on their subversion by individual countries and on the incapability of the international community to punish offenses against minority rights.[179]

---

176 Jäschke, "Ismet Inönü," 3.
177 Hale, *Modern Turkey*, 39. Owen and Pamuk, *Middle East Economies*, 13, 17.
178 Deringil, *Turkish Foreign Policy*, 14.
179 Bayar, "In Pursuit of Homogeneity," 112.

In the European legal texts of the time, the term "minority" was valid for members of religious and linguistic communities. Aided by Lausanne's definition of a minority in purely religious terms, the Turkish side could take the position that the Muslim population in Turkey manifested no distinctions. Presumably, the religiously bound concept of "minorities" advocated by the Turkish negotiators was not only rooted in the Ottoman imprint on their thinking[180] but also involved a considerable amount of manipulation. We have seen that the Ottoman state elite had, at least in part, already left behind the concept of Ottoman citizenship based on confessional classifications. In addition, the Turkish national idea gives great weight to belonging to Islam, but is chiefly based on the idea of one state for all Turks. The Turkish negotiating position was clever in so far as it fed the "orientalizing" ideas on the European side. Obviously—or so the Entente negotiators likely thought—the Turkish side was still trapped in an Ottoman mentality because their conception of minorities seemed to rest entirely on confessional groups (millet). But because non-Muslim minorities in Anatolia had become insignificant in the meantime, a confessionally defined regulation of minorities was necessarily meaningless ab initio. Also arguing for this interpretation is the fact that Turkish law recognizes "the term minority only in the context of the minority clause of the Treaty of Lausanne,"[181] so it was obviously formulated solely for this purpose.

The provisions for minority protection in Articles 37–44 of the Treaty of Lausanne secured all "non-Muslims" a status guaranteed under international law. In the practice of the Turkish state, these rights of protection are reserved for Armenians, the Greek Orthodox, and Jews.[182] With the limitation to a purely confessional definition of minorities, the Kurds, who had still been accorded the vague option of their own state by the Treaty of Sèvres, dropped out of the legal framework entirely. The Alevis, who actually should have been considered a religious minority, were also calculatedly excluded completely from the protection clauses by the Turkish side.[183]

---

180   Per the interpretation of Rumpf, "Minderheiten in der Türkei," 465.
181   Ibid., 459.
182   The official and rather crude pretense is that other religions groups like, for example, the "oriental Christians" had voluntarily relinquished their right of protection. Oran, "Peace of Lausanne," 135. In any case, the three confessional communities privileged by Lausanne were forced several years later to produce a declaration of waiver—invalid under international law. Pekesen, *Ende der jüdischen Gemeinden*, 153ff.
183   Rıza (Nur, 1879–1942), after İsmet (İnönü) the number two in the Turkish delegation openly stated in his memoirs that "the Kızılbaş [that is, the Alevis], who are genuine

Confessional membership did not only become the determining rule in the treaty itself. In the framework of the negotiations in Lausanne, a comprehensive population exchange between Greece and Turkey was agreed upon. Already during the war years, up to a half million Orthodox Greeks had fled or been driven out of Anatolia; hundreds of thousands more died, or were murdered, between 1914 and 1922. Between 1919 and 1923, that is, still before the official population exchange, hundreds of thousands more Greeks were expelled, with a high death rate among them. Consequently, the number of Orthodox Greeks who left Turkey between 1923 and 1926 amounted to barely two hundred thousand. In contrast, three hundred thirty-five thousand Muslims, most of them Turkish-speaking, left Greece.[184] Only the Greek Orthodox inhabitants of İstanbul and Turkish islands of Imvros (Gökçeada) and Tenedos (Bozcaada) situated south of the Dardanelles and the Muslim, Turkish-speaking population of Greek Western Thrace were exempted from the population exchange.

Along with the technocratic harshness of the population exchange—which was in no way a repatriation for the affected people, but a deportation to a strange land—the absurdities resulting from the purely confessional classification catch the eye. The Pontic Greeks (that is, those living on the Black Sea coast), many of whom had temporarily moved to the Russian side of the Black Sea in the nineteenth century, spoke a Greek that was barely comprehensible to Greeks from other places.[185] Greeks from Central Anatolia, the so-called Karamanlı, only spoke Turkish, while the Muslims on Crete and around Ioannina only had command of Greek.

The foundation of the agreement on a population exchange between the Greek and Turkish sides, with the encouragement and support of the Entente powers, was the creation of nationally homogenous states. This is a further indication of the Treaty of Lausanne's belonging to the system of the Treaties of Paris, because the concept of a population exchange was an "intrinsic element of the principles enunciated at Paris."[186]

As a founding document of modern Turkey, Lausanne exercised a long-running effect. In the following years, there were only a few supplements

---

Turks and who number two million," could in no way be regarded as a religious minority because "otherwise, they [the Entente powers] would have jumbled us up higgledy-piggledy." Nur, *Hayat ve Hatıratım*, 3:1044ff.
184   Morris and Ze'evi, *Thirty-Year Genocide*, 385, 393, 467–472, 474, 487.
185   Lewis, *The Emergence of Modern Turkey*, 355. Clogg, *History of Greece*, 49.
186   Weitz, "From Vienna to the Paris System," 1334.

and modifications to the international status of the Republic of Turkey. In December 1925, the League of Nations in Geneva and the International Court of Justice in The Hague—also influenced by the violent measures against the Kurds in the young Republic of Turkey—came to the final determination that Mosul would not pass to Turkey. In June 1926, Turkey finally accepted this decision.[187] At Lausanne, Turkey hadn't been able to put through its demand for the Sanjak of Alexandretta, today the Turkish region of Hatay. In 1924, however, France, which had administratively split up its mandate region (in today's Lebanon and Syria) from the beginning, set up a separate administrative region of Alexandretta in order to have a possible "future bargaining chip" in its relations with Turkey.[188] In 1926, France granted the sanjak local self-administration. In 1937, the League of Nations, with French consent, granted the territory autonomy under nominal French control. The majority-Turkish parliament in the sanjak voted for annexation to Turkey, confirmed by a Franco-Turkish treaty of 23 June 1939. In August 1926, Turkish troops could reoccupy the straits, but it was stipulated in the Treaty of Lausanne that the waterways were to be supervised by an international control commission. A treaty signed in Montreux in 1936 and still valid today finally established Turkey's complete governmental and military sovereignty over the Bosporus and Dardanelles.[189]

A Break Between Comrades-in-Arms

At the beginning of the 1920s, hopes were great in the former Arab provinces of the Ottoman Empire that the new national government in Ankara would support them in their own aspirations for independence from the newly established British and French mandates. The leaders of the revolts in Syria saw the Anatolian national movement as their model; some even hoped to become the "Mustafa Kemal of Syria." The loyalty of the Arab officer class to the Ottoman Empire was unbroken during the First World War. After war's end, former Ottoman officers of Arab origin saw no difference between themselves and the leaders of the Anatolian national movement, and some even

---

187 On the international and regional context of this settlement, see Tejel, "Making Borders from Below."
188 Provence, *Last Ottoman Generation*, 91.
189 Özersay, "Montreux Straits Convention." The text of the Treaty of Montreux is found in Hurewitz, *Diplomacy in the Near and Middle East*, 2:197–203.

participated in the war in Anatolia. Fifteen percent of the officers who fought in the Anatolian War of Independence came from the former Arab territories of the Ottoman Empire.[190] Like the leaders of the Anatolian national movement, most of them were born in the 1880s and had passed through Ottoman military academies.

In October 1921, France came to an agreement with the government in Ankara to give up its "zone of influence" in Anatolia. In turn, Ankara pledged not to destabilize the French mandatory territory in Syria. For that reason, potential cooperation between the Anatolian and Syrian national movements was doomed, even if the Arab side refused to believe it at first. The government in Ankara prioritized its own victory in Anatolia instead of wanting to lead the revolts in the Arab territories on the basis of a brittle Muslim Ottoman identity.

As the Anatolian national movement distanced itself from its allies in the eastern Arab world, Mustafa Kemal also began to separate himself from most of his own companions. The Anatolian national movement was led by officers of a single generation. The closeness of the birth years of its leading personalities is striking, for example, Fevzi (Çakmak, 1876–1950), Ali Fethi (Okyar, 1880–1943), İbrahim Refet (Bele, 1881–1963), Hüseyin Rauf (Orbay, 1881–1964), Mustafa Kemal (Atatürk, 1881–1938), Kâzım (Karabekir, 1882–1948), Ali Fuat (Cebesoy, 1883–1968), and İsmet (İnönü, 1884–1973). This group resembles each other not only with regard to their ages, but also in their common education at the higher Ottoman military academies, their experience of the war years, and their orientation towards the fundamental convictions of the Young Turk movement. The ascendancy of this generational cohort was the consequence of the massive purge of the officer corps after the First Balkan War, the dynamics of the First World War, and the flight of the core Young Turk leadership in November 1918. On 19 June 1919, a few weeks after his arrival in Samsun, Mustafa Kemal conferred with a group of important officers in Amasya. With a single exception, Cemal (Mersinli, 1873–1941), all the participants at this meeting would, a few years later, belong to the political opposition in the early Republic of Turkey, including such prominent individuals as Ali Fuat, İbrahim Refet, Hüseyin Rauf, and Kâzım Pasha (who took part in the meeting by telegraph).[191]

---

190 Provence, *Last Ottoman Generation*, 103, 166.
191 Kreiser, *Atatürk*, 141.

What were the reasons that Mustafa Kemal wanted to and could divest himself of his former companions? Very early on, even during the Anatolian national movement's war, the heroic fight under the leadership of Mustafa Kemal was acclaimed. In September 1921, the National Assembly bestowed the rank of marshal (*müşir*) on him and—even more prestigiously—the title of *gazi* for his victory over the Greek army on the Sakarya River in the same month. With the victories of September 1921 and again in summer 1922, Mustafa Kemal had become untouchable, as Halâskar Gazi, "Saviour and Conqueror."[192] But with those honors, per the general understanding, did not come the right to have the politics of the country and its elite at his arbitrary disposal. Mustafa Kemal succeeded, however, in disempowering his former comrades-in-arms who did not now back his clearly emerging authoritarian one-man rule and his accelerated policy of a comprehensive westernization. The leading party under Mustafa Kemal's control emerged directly out of the War of Independence. In 1921, the Association for the Defense of the National Rights of Anatolia and Rumelia (Anadolu ve Rumeli Müdafaa-ı Hukuk-ı Milli Cemiyeti) became the First Group (Birinci Grup) in Parliament in Ankara, and thereby for all intents and purposes a party which could be based on the extant infrastructure of the Defense Association. The parliamentary elections of June 1923 produced a strong majority for the First Group, which renamed itself the Republican People's Party (Cumhuriyet Halk Fırkası, and from the early 1930s, Cumhuriyet Halk Partisi, CHP) in August 1923.

This electoral success alone would not have sufficed for achieving undisputed precedence. In 1925, however, Mustafa Kemal used revolts in Eastern Anatolia as a pretext to stifle the opposition. He delivered the final blow a year later. An assassination attempt ostensibly planned against him in İzmir and uncovered on 15 June 1926 served as a pretense to haul leading figures of the opposition into court and sentence some of them to death. Among those executed, for example, was Mehmed Cavit, who had served as finance minister in the Young Turk period. Heroes of the War of Independence like Kâzım, Ali Fuat, Refet, and Cafer Tayyar (Eğilmez, 1878–1958) were not condemned to death, but, completely discredited, had no political future. The reasons for these purges were not only ideological. Mustafa Kemal knew very well how to distinguish between loyal followers who were always ready to subordinate themselves, and others who were of the view that the national movement had been the collective endeavor of a group of like-minded equals. From March

---

192 Tunçay, "Siyasal Tarih," 75. Zürcher, *Turkey*, 159.

1925 on, the government of Turkey can be described as an authoritarian regime, or indeed as a dictatorship.[193]

The Kurds get nothing

The war won by the national movement brought together that which more or less belonged together; it also, however, divided much that had previously belonged together. The most important parting of ways was that the Turks of Anatolia had achieved their goals to a great extent while the political ambitions and aspirations of the Kurds, on the other hand, came to nought. Initially, the extermination of the Armenians in the First World War had opened the prospect of a state for the Kurds, who had largely shared the same settled territories as the Armenians.[194] In the years 1914–1922, the Kurds and Turks were alliance partners. After their defense against the common threat, however, the two lacked a common enemy and once again confronted each other as opponents.[195]

The Kurdish side could do as good as nothing against the resolution of the consolidating Turkish state. A Kurdish nationalism only developed very late in the day. The first efforts by members of the Kurdish upper class in İstanbul at founding Kurdish national associations were interrupted by the First World War. In 1918, the Society for the Rise of Kurdistan (Kürdistan Teali Cemiyeti) was founded anew, followed in 1923 by the Society for Freedom (Azadi) which was led by the officers of Kurdish militias. Azadi members comprised a considerable share of the opposition coalition under the leadership of Shaykh Said. He hailed from Palu (in today's Elazığ Province) and was a shaykh of the Nakşbendi Sufi brotherhood. Islamic mystical brotherhoods like the Nakşbendi were and are today groups which seek religious enlightenment and at the same time can espouse political ambitions.

---

193 Hale, *Turkish Politics and the Military*, 68ff. Balistreri, "Turkey's Forgotten Political Opposition," 179. Zürcher, *Turkey*, 174, 176.
194 Bruinessen, *Agha, Shaikh and State*, 360.
195 Üngör, *Making of Modern Turkey*, 118, shows for certain, with reference to a document in the main Ottoman archive (Cumhurbaşkanlığı Devlet Arşivleri Başkanlığı—Osmanlı Arşivi, DH.ŞFR, İAMM, message from Konya on 28 June 1915), that already in June 1915, the "Directorate for the Settlement of Tribes and Immigrants" (İskan-ı Aşair ve Muhacirin Müdüriyeti) had directed that the Kurds were to be settled scattershot across Anatolia in order to extinguish their language and national traditions as soon as possible.

In February 1925, a rebellion led by Shaykh Said broke out, in which all kind of motives were joined: religiously motivated antipathy to the government in Ankara, the prospect of plunder, Kurdish nationalism, and resistance to an ever more severe, centralized power. It was already put down by the end of March. Shaykh Said came from a Zaza-speaking Kurdish tribe; consequently, he found no support from the Alevi populace in the region and little support among Kurmanji-speaking Kurds. In April 1925, Shaykh Said was captured; he was condemned on 28 June and hanged with forty-six of his adherents in Diyarbakır on the following day. The retaliation of the Turkish state was brutal. Hundreds of Kurdish villages were destroyed, thousands of innocent bystanders killed. The populations of entire districts were deported to Western Anatolia.[196]

The Shaykh Said Rebellion exacerbated the domestic political situation. On 21 February 1925, martial law was imposed on Eastern Anatolia. On 2 March, prime minister Fethi (Okyar) received a vote of no-confidence supported by Mustafa Kemal, and İsmet (İnönü) took over his office. On 4 March, parliament passed the Law on Strengthening the Public Peace (Takrir-i Sükun Kanunu). On the same day, the "Independence Courts" (İstiklal Mahkemeleri) initially established in 1920 for the control of revolts were reactivated. One was established in Ankara, another dispatched to Eastern Anatolia. From this point on, the "existence of a separate Kurdish identity was officially denied" in the Republic of Turkey.[197] The Shaykh Said Rebellion was only one in a whole series of Kurdish rebellions in the 1920s and 1930s. It failed because it, like all the preceding and subsequent revolts, remained local and only possessed the support of part of the Kurdish population. The logic of tribal society obviously led to a situation where Kurdish leaders could only take action in accordance with the simple proposition, "the enemy of my enemy is my friend."[198]

The end point of this series of Kurdish rebellions and at the same time the "darkest chapter of Kemalism"[199] was the massive 1937–1938 repression of a rebellion of mostly Zaza-speaking Kurdish Alevis in the unruly region of Dersim in eastern Central Anatolia. In the 1930s, disarmament, deportation,

---

196 Bruinessen, *Agha, Shaikh and State*, 353–405, comprehensively depicts the background and the course of the revolt.
197 Zürcher, *Turkey*, 172. According to Mango, *Atatürk*, 428, after the founding of the republic, Mustafa Kemal never uttered the word "Kurd" in any of his speeches.
198 Bruinessen, *Agha, Shaikh and State*, 75.
199 Plaggenborg, *Ordnung und Gewalt*, 145.

and forced resettlements were imposed on the region. Dersim was made into a province and given the new name Tunceli. A law of 25 December 1935 provided for direct military rule over the province, followed by a street- and bridge-building program. Beginning in 1936, the region was in a state of siege. A rebellion under the leadership of Seyit Riza (1862–1937) against the increased role of the state and its accompanying policy of assimilation broke out at the end of March 1937 and raged until it was put down in September 1938. The state employed all means at its disposal, including the air force. Sabiha Gökçen, the namesake of the second-largest public airport in İstanbul and an adoptive daughter of Atatürk, took part in the bombardments as a combat pilot.[200] Up to forty thousand people died. With the suppression of the rebellion in Dersim, the curtain descended for decades on the Kurdish question in Turkey.[201]

If one takes the dictatorship in the Soviet Union as a yardstick, the repressive measures of the young Republic could be regarded as moderate and begotten of a "Kemalist self-restraint."[202] Nevertheless, it is simultaneously true that the exclusion and partial demonization of groups confessionally or ethnically different from the Muslim Turkish norm is characteristic of the Turkish Republic even today. At the same time, not only the genocide during the First World War, but the whole history of violence of the 1910s through 1930s in Anatolia was concealed over the following decades. The War of Independence, a mandatory object of study in schools and universities, had to outshine everything else in its heroism.

---

200 See Altınay, *Myth of the Military Nation*, 33–58, on Sabiha Gökçen as a symbolic figure for the Turkish military. On the supposition, first raised in the İstanbul-based Armenian newspaper *Agos* in 2004, that Sabiha Gökçen was an Armenian orphan, see Ulgen, *Sabiha Gökçen's Secret*.

201 On the Turkish state's systematic policy of denying these events and on the wrestling of posterity with the psychological consequences and those of the politics of memory, see Törne, *Dersim*.

202 Plaggenborg, *Ordnung und Gewalt*, 263. However, see also the alternative argument of McDowall, *Modern History of the Kurds*, 210, that the Turkish state wished to exterminate the Kurds but failed due to "the sheer size of the task."

Chapter Two

The Kemalist Republic, 1923–1950

This chapter's speaking of a Kemalist republic only up until mid-century may elicit objections, because it may be argued without exaggeration that a Kemalist republic existed up until the beginning of the twenty-first century. But to treat the Republic of Turkey into the early 2010s under a Kemalist rubric narrows its history too greatly to a single question, namely that of the dominance of Kemalism. However, for the Republic of the 1920s to the 1950s, it is absolutely the case that the power of a Kemalist governmental elite was not only undisputed but almost all-encompassing. In addition, in this period of just under thirty years, one may speak of a Kemalist republic in the sense that it is then that the foundations were laid of a Kemalist paradigm for governance and interpretation which only began to break down at the beginning of the twenty-first century.

1. Atatürk and Kemalism (1923–1938)

After the war decade of 1912–1922, the Republic of Turkey could—and in many respects had to—begin with a blank slate. The population of the Ottoman Empire in the territories that would later become Turkey was around seventeen million before the First World War. By 1924, it had fallen to around thirteen million. The share of Christians in the population had also shrunk dramatically. While almost every fifth person living in the territory of today's Turkey was a Christian in 1913, ten years later, it was only one in forty.[1]

Mustafa Kemal was smart enough to keep his distance from the Young Turk leadership which had been discredited in defeat, though he simultaneously had the good fortune to have been pushed to the margins by them. He was involved in the Young Turk movement very early and shared their ideas. The record of Atatürk's lifetime of achievement must include the fact that many deeds and actions which gave him free rein were anticipated by others.

Mustafa Kemal Atatürk

The decisive figure in the history of the early Republic is Mustafa Kemal Atatürk. Without him, there would have been a chance to successfully prosecute a war against the mandates of the Treaty of Sèvres, and without him perhaps an independent state could have come into being. However, without Mustafa Kemal, *the* Republic of Turkey as we knew it in the twentieth century would never have come about. Mustafa Kemal did not determine state ideology and praxis in detail, but he established its underpinnings and anchored them so deeply that they lived on after his death in 1938.

Even his surname was policy. On 21 June 1934, a law obligated all Turkish citizens to adopt a family name by 1 January 1935. The name *Atatürk* (Father of the Turks) which parliament bestowed on Mustafa Kemal on 24 November 1934, has remained reserved for the founder of the Republic.[2] Because family names had to be concocted de novo, most Turks have more or less descriptive surnames like "Cotton" (Orhan *Pamuk*, novelist and winner of the Nobel Prize for Literature), "South" (Yılmaz *Güney*, director), "Son of the Sword-Bearer" (Kemal *Kılıçdaroğlu*, chairman of the largest opposition party), or "Real Iron" (Cem *Özdemir*, German Green party politician of Turkish descent). However, it's not always possible to

---

1   Pamuk, "Economic Change," 275. Keyder, "Exchange of Populations," 43. Other authors come up with a lower Christian portion of the population before the First World War. McCarthy, *Muslims and Minorities*, cites 16.5% as the 1911–12 share of population of Christians on the territory of the future Turkish Republic. Karpat, *Ottoman Population*, 188ff., cites 17.6% for the territory of the whole Ottoman Empire in 1914.

2   After his adopting a surname, Mustafa Kemal only signed himself "K. Atatürk." Mango, *Atatürk*, 498.

read Turkish surnames unambiguously. For example, *Erdoğan*, the family name of the current Turkish president can be read as "male falcon," "born early," or "born a soldier." While the Hapsburg bureaucracy maliciously assigned discriminatory family names in their eighteenth-century introduction of surnames for Jews, the Kemalist bureaucracy did not succumb to this temptation. The law on names not only forbade referring to tribes, foreign ethnic groups, or nationalities, but also forbade choosing offensive or ridiculous names. The law on names was, however, repressive in the sense that members of ethnic minorities had to adopt Turkish names or at least adapt them phonetically to Turkish orthography.[3]

The term "Atatürkism" (*Atatürkçülük*) is rarely used in European languages to refer to Atatürk's political agenda and legacy. The term "Kemalism" (*Kemalizm*), derived from the latter of his given names, is the established term. In Turkish, *Atatürkçülük* may be favored in respectful speech and in remembrances of Atatürk, while *Kemalizm* focuses on the ideological aspect and can have a pejorative connotation—also because *Kemalizm* is a loanword, from the French *Kémalisme*.[4]

Mustafa Kemal was born in 1881 in Saloniki (Selanik), today's Thessaloniki, then an important Ottoman port and industrial city on the Eastern Mediterranean. Outside of his Turkish-speaking family, whose ancestries are not precisely known,[5] the environment in which Mustafa Kemal grew up could not have been further removed from what one might consider a homogenous Turkish nation-state. Saloniki had a population diverse even by the standards of the Ottoman Empire. At that time, it was very difficult to tell—outside of the generally clear lines between religions—who would be considered an Albanian, a Bulgar, a Greek, or a Macedonian. Language and ethnicity did not always coincide. Of all Ottoman cities, Saloniki had admitted the greatest number of Sephardic Jews who had fled the Iberian Peninsula in the late fifteenth century to avoid forced conversions and persecution. In the Ottoman Empire's first modern census in 1831, Saloniki had the smallest percentage of Muslims of all large Ottoman cities.[6]

---

3   Vocelka, *Glanz und Untergang*, 382. Türköz, *Naming and Nation-Building*, 108–113, 143–160.
4   Jenkins, *Political Islam*, 102, points out that "Kemalism" first became an established term in the 1936 work *Kemalizm* by Munis Tekinalp (1883–1961).
5   Mango, *Atatürk*, 28, refers to Albanian and Slavic forebears. According to Hanioğlu *Atatürk*, 24, the family saw itself as descendants of the conquerors from Anatolia.
6   Mazower, *Salonica*, 35ff.

In the seventeenth century, the Sabbateans (Turkish *Dönme*) broke away from the larger Jewish community of Saloniki. Followers of the "false Messiah" Sabbatai Zevi (1626–1676) nominally converted to Islam, the Sabbateans were far removed from Halakhic Judaism in the nineteenth century. Although the Sabbateans never comprised more than a few thousand people, they are highlighted here for two reasons. The Sabbateans played an outsized role in the conspiracy theories of the Republican era, and with their high levels of education and economic success as merchants, they contributed significantly to the fact that by the end of the nineteenth century, Saloniki was regarded as "the most liberal, progressive, and revolutionary city in the empire."[7] Without doubt, this cosmopolitan Saloniki formatively shaped the young Mustafa Kemal.

Mustafa Kemal decided on a military career early, apparently by his own choice. In January 1896, after graduating from the military preparatory school in Salonica, he enrolled himself in the military school in Monastır (today Bitola in the Republic of North Macedonia). In 1899, Mustafa Kemal was accepted to the military academy (Erkân-i Mekteb-i Harbiye) in İstanbul. In 1902, he graduated eighth in his class of 459 cadets and was therefore able to undertake instruction as a general staff officer from 1902 to 1905. Until the outbreak of the First World War, his career was not superlative. He took part in the defense of Tripolitania and Cyrenaica as well as the Balkan Wars. Engaged as a military attaché in Sofia at the beginning of World War I, he returned to active duty at his own pressing request in 1915 and became commander of the Nineteenth Division in Tekirdağ in Thrace. Mustafa Kemal played an important role on the Dardanelles Front with this division, only recently having been put together. In August 1916, he was able to take back the cities of Bitlis and Muş in Eastern Anatolia which had been intermittently occupied by Russian troops.[8] Mustafa Kemal, who had begun the war as a lieutenant colonel, finished it as a brigadier general and honorary aide-de-camp, thus having achieved the rank of pasha (general).[9]

---

7   Ibid., 74. On the Sabbateans in general, see Baer, *Dönme*. Baer's "An Enemy Old and New" describes the origin of a conspiracy theory about an alleged Jewish Sabbatean Zionist Freemason Young Turk plot that circulated for decades in Islamist and extreme-right circles and was taken up in the 2000s even by authors who understood themselves to be on the Left, like Yalçın Küçük, Ergün Poyraz, and Soner Yalçın, and was carried forward with great success in published works.
8   Lewis, *Emergence of Modern Turkey*, 243–245.
9   Hanioğlu, *Atatürk*, 83. Kreiser, *Atatürk*, 14.

Mustafa Kemal's ascent during the war was limited by his willful character and his critical stance with regard to his country's ally, Germany. Mustafa Kemal did not shy away from confrontations with Erich von Falkenhayn, the German commander of Army Group "Lightning" (Yıldırım) from February 1917. For example, Falkenhayn was adamant that his orders be translated into Ottoman by orientalists educated in Berlin. These translations, however, were incomprehensible to Ottoman officers because of the orientalists' scant familiarity with everyday language.[10] Mustafa Kemal's displeasure with his German allies and the top German officers in the Ottoman Army went beyond questions of conduct and military tactics. In a long memorandum of September 1917 which Mustafa Kemal submitted to the Grand Vizier, he warned of an outsized dominance of German officers and of the danger "that the Ottoman Empire risked becoming a German colony if the present situation continued and the Central Powers won the war."[11]

The day after the German military mission to the Ottoman Empire came to an end with the Armistice of Mudros on 30 October 1918, Mustafa Kemal was named commander of all Ottoman troops on the Syrian front. The defining turning point in his life was, however, the inspectorate in Inner Anatolia assigned to him in May 1919, which Mustafa Kemal turned decisively to his own ends. When the Ottoman government recognized that its general was not complying with his assignment demobilizing the Ottoman army, but was rather building up a national resistance movement and therefore summoned him back to İstanbul, he submitted his resignation on 8 July 1919 and thereby placed himself in open opposition to the Ottoman government. For a short time, Mustafa Kemal was thus no more than a private citizen. His leading position in the national movement was never contested by his comrades, though. In August 1921, Mustafa Kemal was named provisory supreme commander by the national movement. Beginning in July 1922, he held this position without the temporal restriction. Immediately after the founding of the Republic on 29 October 1923, the National Assembly elected Mustafa Kemal president. He held that office until his death.

As previously related, the relationship between the leadership of the national movement in Ankara and the sultanic government in İstanbul was complicated. Many of Mustafa Kemal's early comrades held the belief that

---

10 Strauss, "Disintegration of Ottoman Rule," 311.
11 Hanioğlu, *Atatürk*, 81, here draws on the original source of 20 September 1917 in *Atatürk'ün Bütün Eserleri* (The Complete Works of Atatürk), 2:1915–1919 (İstanbul: Kaynak Yayınları, 1999), 120–125.

the success of their movement would lead to the restoration of a sovereign sultanate and caliphate. In the Ottoman Empire, the sultanate was always the decisive office, the caliphate more an accessory. A component of the comprehensive titulature of the Ottoman sultan since the sixteenth century, the caliphate experienced an appreciation in value at the end of the eighteenth century when the Russian Empress Catherine II ("the Great," r. 1762–1796) laid claim to the right of protection over Ottoman subjects of Orthodox faith and in return the Ottomans claimed legal rights as the caliph of all Muslims, including those in Russia.[12] Sultan Abdülhamid II emphasized his role as caliph and put into effect pan-Islamic-inspired projects like the Hijaz Railway connecting Damascus and Medina, built in 1900–1908 and facilitating the annual journey of pilgrims on the Hajj.

The dissolution of the sultanate on 2 November 1922 and subsequently the caliphate on 3 March 1924 removed a competing center of power in İstanbul. The immediate pretext for the abolition of the sultanate was that the Entente powers had invited the sultanic government to the peace negotiations in Lausanne alongside the government in Ankara. The suggestion of the Ottoman government to dispatch a combined delegation under the leadership of Grand Vizier Ahmet Tevfik (Okday, 1845–1936) to the negotiations in Lausanne led to an uproar (desired by Mustafa Kemal) in the nationalist parliament in Ankara, which ended with the decision to abolish the sultanate. On 17 November, Sultan Mehmed VI Vahdeddin left the country on a British ship. Abdülmecid II (1868–1944) succeeded him as caliph with largely ceremonial duties because power now unambiguously resided in Ankara. A long term of office was not granted to the last of the Ottoman caliphs, however.

The abolition of the caliphate two years later was far riskier than the dissolution of the sultanate, because it injured the religious sensitivities of many people, including some among the leaders of the national movement. As a pretext, Mustafa Kemal once again took a request coming from the outside. The Aga Khan III (Sir Sultan Mahomed Shah, 1877–1957), whose tomb sits prominently on the upper left bank of the Nile in Aswan, and Syed Ameer Ali (1849–1928), two of the most important personages among the Muslims of South Asia, called for the preservation of the caliphate in a letter to Prime Minister İsmet (İnönü), which was reprinted in three İstanbul daily newspapers on 24 November 1923.[13] With this external intervention, Mustafa Kemal

---

12 Kreiser and Neumann, *Kleine Geschichte der Türkei*, 380ff.
13 Lewis, *Emergence of Modern Turkey*, 263.

had an excuse to be able to discredit the caliphate as a dangerous competitor to the national government in Ankara, as a gateway for foreign influence, and as an institution already completely obsolete. In early 1924, after Mustafa Kemal had ensured himself of the backing of military leadership, the party he led proposed the abolition of the caliphate to parliament on 2 March 1924. Parliament adopted this proposal on the following day.[14]

The abolition of the caliphate left an open wound in the Islamic world, because in its conception of an ideal world, all Muslims are supposed to come together in a single community (*ümmet*) under a religiously legitimated leader, the caliph. This striving for a restoration of the caliphate has repeatedly led to hopeless attempts at refounding it, like for example, the proclamation of Cemaleddin Kaplan (1926–1995) as "Caliph of Cologne" in 1994, or of Abu Bakr al-Baghdadi (1971–2019) as caliph of the Islamic State in Mosul in 2014.[15]

What distinguished Mustafa Kemal among his allies and opponents, allowing him to ascend to the status of undisputed leader of modern Turkey? One of his strengths was that, in contrast to his comrades in the War of Independence, he pursued an intrinsically coherent agenda of what was to be done after the victory. He wanted to transform Turkey into a progressive nation-state both independent of and simultaneously recognized by the West. The radicalism and clarity of his political goals provided him with tactical advantages and let him recognize who could and who had to be his ally at any given point. Faced with important decisions, Mustafa Kemal operated in the certainty that the officer corps supported him. The opposition, on the other hand, came up short with their approach of trying to rein Mustafa Kemal without deposing him. Mustafa Kemal succeeded thanks to his extraordinary personality and a "unique combination of tactical mastery, ruthlessness, realism, and sense of purpose" to concentrate absolute power in his hands.[16]

Like many other intellectually engaged officers in his circle, Mustafa Kemal was exposed to the writings of French intellectuals, which were immediately accessible to him thanks to his knowledge of French—the window to the world in the late Ottoman era. He unambiguously belonged to the educated class of his generation which, however, had an all-too mechanistic

---

14   For the historical context, see Nafi, "Abolition of the Caliphate."
15   For these two aspirants to the caliphate, see Schiffauer, *Gottesmänner*, and Gerges, *ISIS*, 129–143. Two days after the dissolution of the caliphate in Turkey, Husayn ibn Ali (1853/56–1931), Sharif of Mecca and King of the Hijaz 1916–1924, declared himself caliph. Feldman, *The Fall and Rise of the Islamic State*, 95.
16   Zürcher, *Turkey*, 184.

understanding of science and "saw in the doctrine of vulgar materialism an indispensable manual for constructing a prosperous, rational, and irreligious modern society."[17]

As clear as Mustafa Kemal was in his political goals, he nevertheless followed no firm ideological program and never had a problem with adopting the necessary political camouflage for any given occasion. For example, in the early phase of the national movement, he conveyed the image of a "Muslim communist" in order to win the support of the Bolshevik regime in Moscow. Mustafa Kemal's obligatory references to Islamic tradition and religion were even more indebted to political tactics and were thrown overboard as soon as he had secured power.[18]

On the other hand, Mustafa Kemal's attitude to the "West" (which, from a late Ottoman perspective still substantially coincided with Europe) was absolutely clear: there was no other way forward than to follow the successful path of European science and culture and simultaneously to confront the European countries as an independent power.[19]

Mustafa Kemal's experiences may have contributed to his decisions, like often-encountered slights of Muslims (albeit against a background of the Ottomans' centuries-long belief in and practice of Muslim supremacy). So, for example, the ban on the fez in the early Republic could have been nourished by a personal experience—on a trip to the empire's Libyan provinces, Mustafa Kemal was mocked by street urchins for his Ottoman headgear during a short stop in Sicily.[20] Mustafa Kemal's attitude regarding the West may thus be described as a kind of "anti-Western Westernism": a dedicated pursuit of the modernization of Turkish society along Western lines was coupled with a vehement rejection of economic penetration and political interventions by Western powers.

The Kemalist Reforms of the 1920s and 1930s

A fundamental and conspicuous aspect of Kemalism was the "reform" policy of the 1920s and 1930s instigated by Atatürk. As radical as the changes in the legal system, state structure, religion, and culture of the young Turkish

---

17 Hanioğlu, *Atatürk*, 50.
18 Ibid., 50, 105, 108ff.
19 On the fundamentally problematic construct of "the West," see, e.g., Osterhammel, *Flughöhe der Adler*, 101–114.
20 Jenkins, *Political Islam*, 95.

Republic were, however, they built upon the late Ottoman and Young Turk modernization agenda of the preceding decades.

It is correct to speak of "modernization" in this context, because the actors themselves were convinced they had a mandate to modernize their society.[21] The Young Turks were already in uncharted territory with some of their activities. In 1915, the Ministry of Justice placed all courts under its control and nationalized the pious endowments (*evkaf*)—an intrusion into two areas which were previously under the sole administration of religious jurisprudents (ulema). In 1917, marriage was declared a contract binding on all persons, thereby no longer consisting of a covenant solely resting on a confessional basis and concluded under the supervision of the respective religious authorities.[22] The Young Turk reforms, however, never reached the dimensions of the earth-shattering changes which were demanded of society, the legal system, and religious culture in the early Republican period.[23]

A first clue to the radically new character of the Kemalist reforms was the different conditions under which the actions were taken: the Ottoman and Young Turk reforms were meant to promote the survival of the empire and only fulfilled their commission imperfectly. The Kemalist reforms took the opposite tack: only when the international position of Turkey had been completely stabilized and Mustafa Kemal had become the uncontested leader were the reforms implemented with full force.

On 20 January 1921,[24] the parliament in Ankara enacted the Law of Fundamental Order, comprising twenty-three articles, which was organized around the principle of national sovereignty and in which the State of Turkey (Türkiye Devleti) was first invoked. When, on 20 April 1924, Parliament replaced this predecessor charter with a regular constitution of the same name (i.e., Teşkilat-ı Esasiye Kanunu), thereby superseding the Constitution

---

21 For this, see a programmatic document by Ziya Gökalp with the title "Turkification, Islamification, Modernization." Gökalp, *Türkleşmek, İslamlaşmak, Muasırlaşmak*, which contains articles by Gökalp previously appearing in a variety of places, was first published in book form in 1918 under this title.
22 Hale, *Turkish Politics and the Military*, 53.
23 Hanioğlu, "Second Constitutional Period," 105, points out that the Young Turk intellectual Kılıçzade Hakkı (1872-1960) had already listed all the reforms that would later be adopted by Mustafa Kemal in the programmatic article "Pek Uyanık bir Uyku" (A Very Wakeful Sleep), *İctihad*, February 21, 1912.
24 The dates given for the individual steps of reform are not always consistent in the literature. In this chapter, all dates are taken from the reliable works of Jäschke, *Geschichtskalender*, 1927–1929, 1930, 1931, 1933, 1935. On Gotthard Jäschke himself, see Kreiser, "Jäschke."

of 1876 which was still officially in force, Articles 2 and 26 declared that Islam was the established religion of the state and that Parliament was responsible for the enforcement of Shari'a, the legal corpus of religious and secular obligations and regulations based on the Islamic religion.[25] This obligation, "little more than lip service to assuage conservative circles,"[26] can be seen as an early concession before the final securing of power in the middle of the 1920s. Only a few years later, in a resolution of Parliament of 10 April 1928, the passage about the Parliament as the organ of Shari'a and Islam as the religion of the Turkish state was abrogated. In any case, the Constitution of 1924 was not revolutionary, unlike the individual laws and regulations which followed it and which may be grouped into four categories: (1) the introduction of legal codes derived from European prototypes; (2) regulations which reached especially deeply into everyday life; (3) regulations on language and writing; and (4) regulations directly addressing the question of religion.

The civil law code adopted on 17 February 1926 belongs to the first group. It was adopted almost word-for-word from the Swiss civil code: the civil-procedure code was based on that of the Swiss canton of Neuchâtel. The civil code contained clauses on the free choice of religion and consequently lifted the ban on apostasy (the absolute prohibition against Muslims' converting to other religions), on recognition of civil marriage as a legally binding form of matrimony, on the prohibition of polygamy, on the execution of divorces solely by courts (and not simply the declaration of intent by the husband), on the abolition of the prohibition against Muslim women's marrying non-Muslim men, and on the equality of men and women in inheritance law. The hierarchical differentiation between men and women and between Muslims and non-Muslims established in Islamic law was thereby a thing of the past. A new criminal code based on the Italian criminal code of 1889 was adopted on 1 March 1926 (and was effective as of 1 July 1926). A new commercial code derived from German and Italian models followed on 29 May 1926.

This borrowing of different legal codes, which was surely not always thought out systematically, recalls in certain respects the eclectic reforms of the nineteenth century. The new rulers of Turkey adopted legal systems from abroad "which seemed appropriate" and answered the question of how

---

25 For the Turkish text of the Constitutions of 1921 and 1924, see https://www.anayasa.gov.tr/tr/mevzuat/onceki-anayasalar/1924-anayasasi/, accessed 30 August 2020.
26 Hanioğlu, *Atatürk*, 157.

the emerging state reforms were to be classified "with the slogan '*Biz bize benzeriz*,' that is, 'We resemble ourselves.'"[27]

With respect to the second group of regulations, those on remaking everyday life, their chronological order may have been shaped by certain contingencies, but their content was most certainly not. An example of such regulations is the law adopted on 26 December 1925 (entering into force on 1 January 1926) on the introduction of the Gregorian calendar and the twenty-four-hour day on the European model (in the Islamic, and incidentally Jewish, tradition, the new day begins at sundown). On 24 May 1928, the adoption of internationally used numerals was enacted, as was the introduction of metric weights and measures on 1 April 1931. As already mentioned, on 1 January 1935, all Turks were obliged to adopt a surname.

The third group of measures comprised the alphabet reform and the language reform which followed it. The alphabet reform was introduced at an appearance by Mustafa Kemal in Gülhane Park in İstanbul on 9 August 1928. The parliamentary act of 3 November 1928 on the introduction of the Latin alphabet (which was to be effective on 1 January 1929) was likely viable without too much resistance because in the late 1920s, an estimated 85 percent of the population was illiterate.[28] In the space of a few months, all publications, guidelines, and official correspondence had to be converted from the Arabic to the Latin alphabet. While the alphabet reform was a clear and decisive step, the language reform which followed it—the replacement of as many lexical and grammatical elements of Arabic and Persian origin as possible by Turkish neologisms—got out of hand.

The language reform was so profound and such a "catastrophic success"[29] that the original text of the great speech (*nutuk*) delivered by Mustafa Kemal to the second congress of his Republican People's Party (Cumhuriyet Halk Fırkası) over 15–20 October 1927, lasting thirty-six hours in total, is no longer comprehensible, even for an educated readership. For decades, one could discern the political preferences of a person from his lexical choices. Kemalists attempted, as much as possible, to speak a "pure Turkish" (*Öz Türkçe*), a Turkish which of course was hardly authentic, filled as it was with creative neologisms. The proponents of a conservative Islamic way of

---

27   Hirsch, *Land Atatürks*, 265.
28   Jenkins, *Political Islam*, 99.
29   According to the subtitle of Geoffrey Lewis's *Turkish Language Reform*. See also the comprehensive work in three volumes by Steuerwald, *Untersuchungen zur türkischen Sprache*.

thinking continued to express themselves "Ottomanizingly," that is, cultivating a style and vocabulary that recalled the Ottoman language with its vast numbers of Arabic and Persian loanwords.

The attempt to provide the language and alphabet reform with solid underpinnings led to a confused aggregate theory. Having cut the cord of the Arabo-Perso-Islamic language, script, and scholarly tradition, Turkish intellectuals believed it necessary to find a new, self-sufficient foundation for a modern Turkey and modern Turkish. The Turkish History Thesis (Türk Tarih Tezi) goes back to the 1920s, but it was officially enacted at the first Turkish History Congress, which took place in Ankara from the second to the eleventh of July 1932.[30] According to this doctrine, the Turks, a white, Aryan people, settled originally in Central Asia. They had to seek new homesteads because of continuous drought and, along their way, founded all the high cultures of antiquity, including those of the Sumerians and Hittites.[31]

According to the even more ambitious Sun Language Theory, an *Ur*-Turkish was actually the original language of humanity. According to this theory, Turkish had always been spoken in Anatolia. These eccentric theories of Turkish history and linguistics became less important after the death of Atatürk, likely less because they'd been made up out of thin air than because they hadn't caught the public's fancy. Mustafa Kemal and others in the national political leadership seem to have seriously championed these opinions, apparently driven by the search for a secure anchor for national pride.[32] The language and writing reforms succeeded in their goal of taking Turkey out of the centuries-old communication space shared with the Arabic and Persianate worlds, and in doing so, it contained an implicit antireligious agenda.

A whole bundle of measures, however, were aimed directly at religion, and here we come to the fourth group of reforms. The Hat Law (Şapka Kanunu) of 25 November 1925, which required men to wear a European-style hat in public, was a measure that was still more indirect. The hat reform aimed to put an end to the traditional plethora of Ottoman headgear, many of which carried religious significance. In a society which had prescribed strict sumptuary norms for centuries, for a man to wear a European hat bordered on a renunciation of belief. The hat was incompatible with the rites of Islamic prayer,

---

30 Aligned with the Turkish Historical Society (Türk Tarihi Tetkik Cemiyeti, later Türk Tarih Kurumu) founded in 1931 and still extant today. For its current activities, see https://www.ttk.gov.tr/, accessed 20 April 2023.
31 Lewis, *Emergence of Modern Turkey*, 359.
32 Hanioğlu, *Atatürk*, 195. Zürcher, *Turkey*, 191. Laut, *Das Türkische als Ursprache*.

because the brim hindered the mandatory touching of the forehead to the ground. The hat reform may have provoked more resistance than the abolition of the caliphate. Consequently, the people in the countryside—in a form of covert resistance—switched to a flat cap (*kasket*) which only fell out of fashion as the dominant headgear of the male population of Anatolia in the 1980s.

Mustafa Kemal and his comrades now believed themselves powerful enough to directly attack the place of religion in society and government with numerous measures and laws. On 3 March 1924, the day of the abolition of the caliphate, the Presidium for Religious Affairs (Diyanet İşleri Reisliği, later Diyanet İşleri Başkanlığı, Ministry of Religious Affairs) and the General Directorate for Pious Endowments (Evkaf Umum Müdürlüğü) were established. The Diyanet replaced the Ministry of Religious Law and Pious Endowments (Şeriye ve Evkaf Vekaleti) which had itself replaced the office of the Şeyhülislam, the supreme religious jurisprudent in the Ottoman Empire. The establishment of this directorate clearly shows that Kemalism did not have a separation of Church and state in mind, but the control of religion by the state. At bottom, the Kemalist state continued the Ottoman model of established religion and "state secularity," only with the innovation that the religious class no longer possessed veto power over its own affairs.[33]

The 30 November 1925 Law Concerning Closure of Dervish Lodges, Convents, and Mausoleums and the Prohibition and Abolition of Mausoleum Keepers and Certain Titles (Tekke ve Zaviyeler ile Türbelerin Seddine ve Türbedarlar ile Bazı Unvanların Men ve İlgasına Dair Kanun) distinguished itself in its particular hostility towards religion, and not in merely symbolic fashion. Many people's deep connections to dervish fraternities and the shaykhs of those orders appeared simultaneously objectionable and dangerous to the Kemalist state. That the ringleader of the East Anatolian revolt in Spring 1925 had himself been a sheikh of the Nakşbendi dervish order contributed to the severity of the law.

The Independence Courts (İstiklal Mahkemeleri) active from 1925 to 1929 repeatedly issued death sentences for people who agitated against the particularly visible and radical reforms in the Hat Law and the prohibition of dervish orders. Under the provisions of the Law on Strengthening the Public Peace (Takrir-i Sükun Kanunu), passed in March 1925 and in force

---

33 On the mutual penetration of established Islam and state secularism typical of the Ottoman Empire, see Mardin, "Turkish Islamic Exceptionalism": 148ff.

until 1929, the state showed its full severity to those who offered resistance—resistance to the reforms was considered high treason.[34]

In October 1932, the call to prayer in some mosques in İstanbul could be heard in Turkish for the first time (complete with the replacement of the Arabic word for God, *Allah*, with the Turkish *Tanrı*). In the 1930s, the garlands of electric lights (*mahya*) which even today are draped between minarets in Ramadan no longer bore joyful messages like, "Welcome, blessed Ramadan!" (Hoş geldin mübarek Ramazan), but political slogans like "Buy Turkish goods" (Türk malı al).[35] On 27 November 1934, the National Assembly abolished all nonmilitary titles of honor, including religious honorifics like *hacı* (someone who had completed the pilgrimage to Mecca), *hafız* (someone who had memorized the Koran), and *molla* (someone who had completed an education as a religious jurisprudent). On 27 May 1935, a law making January first a holiday and Sunday the weekend day off was passed.

Mustafa Kemal had already distanced himself far from religion before the First World War. His attitude did not differ from the radical, scientistic positions of many late Ottoman intellectuals, as expressed in a dictum of Abdullah Cevdet, "Religion is the science of the masses, whereas science is the religion of the elite."[36] Unlike, for example, the express radicalism of the language reform, Mustafa Kemal stopped short of a campaign for atheism. His decidedly antireligious frame of mind and his simultaneous readiness to take religious sensibilities into consideration is not necessarily a contradiction. "We see Mustafa Kemal as a staunch agnostic who was simultaneously able to perceive the deep roots of religion in Turkish society as a social reality in the Durkheimian sense."[37]

In contrast to Reza Shah in Iran (r. 1925–1941), Atatürk did not succumb to the temptation to officially forbid the veiling of women.[38] In addition, while the measures Mustafa Kemal introduced in the realm of religion were indeed

---

34 According to Jenkins, *Political Islam*, 95ff., in consequence of the furor against the Hat Law at least thirty-six demonstrators were executed and several hundred received prison sentences.
35 Georgeon, "Religion, Politics and Society," 177, 187.
36 Abdullah Cevdet, "Şehzade Mecid Efendi Hazretleri'yle Mülâkat," *İctihad* 57 (20 March 1913): 1257, quoted in Hanioğlu, *Atatürk*, 56.
37 Kreiser, *Atatürk*, 237.
38 When some radical supporters wanted to ban the veil in 1935, Atatürk did not support the proposal. Hanioğlu, *Atatürk*, 208ff. Reza Shah decreed a ban on the veil in January 1936 under the influence of a visit to Turkey in June–July 1934. Marashi, "Performing the Nation."

radical, they were embedded in the longer history of Ottoman established religion and state secularism. In contrast to Turkey, in countries like Iran and Afghanistan, such measures appeared as if out of nowhere and greatly upset not only the general public, but also the local political elites. The dramatic gesture of the Afghan king Amanullah (r. 1919–1929, as emir 1919–1926, as king 1926–1929) of permitting his wife Soraya to cast off the veil in 1928 contributed to his having to abdicate a year later.[39]

The realm of religion shows the Kemalists' radicalness, but also their readiness, when necessary, to retreat. Religious institutions which could be a potential source of competing power were razed. Where a compromise was possible and caution before popular fury's potentially boiling over seemed necessary, as in the case of the veil, compromises were made. Mustafa Kemal's 1932 inspiration that imams should give the Friday sermon (*hutbe*) in a tailcoat and bareheaded was not implemented, nor was the requirement that Turkish would become the language of prayer.[40]

Despite such instances of circumspection, by around 1930 the entire legal system had been freed from religious ties. Additionally, the secularization of the state, education, and law was linked with an attack on religious symbols and "popular Islam."[41] With the repression of the forms of demotic faith, like the visiting of saints' shrines, the Kemalist elite severed an important bond of loyalty between themselves and the mass of the population. An oppositional structure between "secular" and "Islamic" camps, which had already loomed in the nineteenth century became firmly established and would not only affect the Republic of Turkey but collectively "would strongly shape the history of the Islamic world in the twentieth century."[42]

The New Ankara, A Project of German Architects

The contradiction between the gray reality in Turkey and its elites' claim to modernity may never have been as great as in the first couple decades of the Republic. The Turkey of that time was a bitterly poor country in which only the smallest part of the population wanted to or could locate themselves

---

39 Schulze, *Geschichte der islamischen Welt*, 133.
40 Hanioğlu, *Atatürk*, 155ff.
41 See Kriss and Kriss-Heinrich, *Volksglaube im Bereich des Islams*, on the rich, but today all but completely lost traditional survivals of a "folk Islam."
42 Schulze, *Geschichte der islamischen Welt*, 16.

within the categories of a modern nation-state. The new capital of Ankara uniquely epitomized the project of Kemalist modernism. Ankara became a modern city in the 1930s, but modern in a different fashion than cities like London, New York, or even Alexandria. As late as the 1980s, Ankara still recalled a Soviet planned city more than the capitals of Europe. Early panorama photos from the 1920s and 1930s show a very small city, on whose periphery new government buildings stood, lost in the Anatolian steppe landscape. The Ankara of that time stood more for the aspiration to than the reality of a modern city. Can we speak then of a Kemalist high modernism? If we understand "high modernity" as the state elite's self-imposed task of improving living conditions and imposing a rationalized order onto all aspects of social life by deploying the total power of the modern state, then the Kemalist project of a modern capital in Ankara is almost a prototypical experiment of high modernism.[43]

In 1915, two-thirds of the city of Ankara was destroyed by a fire. Consequently, the new capital offered a clean slate for building up and out. The architect and city planner Hermann Jansen (1869–1945) laid out a zoning plan for the city in 1928 and a master plan in 1929. Ankara was intended to be a garden city with elements of modern urban planning, with a population of at most three hundred thousand people. The plans were quickly overtaken by reality; that population threshold was passed by 1950.[44]

The architectonic reshaping of Ankara begun in the 1920s coincided with the immigration of hundreds of Germans and Austrians, many of them Jewish by faith or heritage, who were fleeing Nazi Germany. In the years after Hitler's seizure of power on 30 January 1933, almost a third of the faculty of German universities were let go.[45] Those who were dismissed and those who were persecuted flooded out of the country, but "in no other land did the immigration of hundreds of highly qualified specialists likely have such clear consequences, reaching into the present day, as in Turkey."[46]

Not just anyone could immigrate into Turkey. One's usefulness to the Turkish state had to be shown. But the need was great and extended to the most diverse fields of knowledge and disciplines.[47] The Austrian pathologist

---

[43] Scott, *Seeing like a State*, 88ff. On a slightly different formulation of the term "high modernism," see Herbert, "Europe in High Modernity."
[44] Duru, "Ankara'nın İmarı," 109, 114–121.
[45] Herbert, *Geschichte Deutschlands*, 365.
[46] Dogramaci, *Kulturtransfer*, 17.
[47] Representatives of humanities and social sciences may serve as examples here: Assyriology, Benno Landsberger (1890–1968); German Studies, Traugott Fuchs (1906–1997);

Philipp Schwartz (1894–1977) led negotiations with the Turkish government, brokering scientists to Turkey in the name of the Emergency Committee of German Scientists Abroad (Notgemeinschaft deutscher Wissenschaftler im Ausland).[48] Some, like Ernst Reuter (1889–1953) who had been active in politics in Germany, sought new areas of activity, as he did in urban planning. A considerable portion of these emigrants did not return to Germany after the war, but moved on to the United States. A few succeeded in making the move to a new country even before the end of the war, like the economist Wilhelm Röpke (1899–1966) who moved to Geneva in 1937, or the Romanist Leo Spitzer (1887–1960), who was offered a professorship in the US in 1936. The composer Paul Hindemith (1895–1963) repeatedly came to Turkey in 1935–1938, before he—thanks to his wife—found a new home in Switzerland in 1938 and eventually moved to the US in 1940. Still, during his few stays in Turkey, Hindemith influenced the Turkish Five (Türk Beşleri), the first generation of professional composers of classical music in Turkey. Some émigré scholars, like Erich Auerbach (1892–1957) composed their greatest works in Turkey.[49] A few of the Central European emigrants, like the Germanist Traugott Fuchs (1906–1997) and the Ottomanist Robert Anhegger (1911–2001) remained in Turkey all their lives.[50]

None of the refugees from National Socialism left behind such a clearly visible legacy as the city planners and architects of Ankara. Among the migrants were politically active individuals such as the aforementioned Ernst Reuter or the married architects Margarete Schütte-Lihotzky (1897–2000) and Wilhelm Schütte (1900–1968), who had spent several years in the Soviet Union before their time in Turkey. Schütte-Lihotzky returned to Vienna in December 1940 as a political activist. After her imprisonment by the Gestapo in January 1941, she fortunately survived the National Socialist era.

Hittitology, Hans Gustav Güterbock (1908–2000); Indology, Walter Ruben (1899–1982); Classical Philology, Georg Rohde (1899–1960); Law, Ernst Eduard Hirsch (1902–1985); Romance Studies, Erich Auerbach (1892–1957); Sinology, Wolfram Eberhard (1909–1989); Urban Planning, Gustav Oelsner (1879–1956); Economics, Wilhelm Röpke (1899–1966).

48 A contemporary program of the Alexander von Humboldt Foundation for the support of endangered scholars financed by the German Foreign Office is named after Philipp Schwartz. See https://www.humboldt-foundation.de/en/apply/sponsorship-programmes/philipp-schwartz-initiative, accessed 20 April 2023.

49 On Auerbach in Turkey, see Konuk, *East West Mimesis*, and Bormuth, *Auerbach*.

50 The Germans' exile in Turkey has described extensively. See, for e.g., Widmann, *Exil und Bildungshilfe*; Cremer and Przytulla, *Exil Türkei*; Hillebrecht, *Haymatloz*.

Even those who were not particularly interested in politics could not really escape partisanship. The orientalist Helmut Ritter (1892–1971) had lived in Turkey since 1926, after he was prosecuted for his homosexuality in Germany and had lost his professorship in Hamburg. Although Ritter was originally salaried by Germany, he did not cast his lot with the German community loyal to Hitler.[51]

Some, like the Austrian architects Ernst Egli (1893–1974) and Clemens Holzmeister (1886–1983) were already active in Ankara in the 1920s and were largely unpolitical. Egli was able to move to Switzerland, his Jewish wife's homeland, in 1940, after he had worked in Turkey for thirteen years, helping lay the foundations of a functional, modernist-oriented architectural style in Turkey. Clemens Holzmeister, on the other hand, enjoyed a leading position as an architect close to the state in the Austrofascist years, that is 1933–1938 under Engelbert Dollfuss and Kurt Schuschnigg, alongside his work in Turkey. As an emphatic opponent of the *Anschluss* of Austria to Germany, he went into exile in Turkey in 1938. Holzmeister himself was politically conservative but his residence and atelier in Tarabya (on the European side of the northern Bosporus) seems to have been a meeting place for the German-speaking opposition to Hitler. Holzmeister planned and built a large part of the new government quarter in Ankara; he designed a new monumental style for government buildings that was close to the architecture of Fascist Italy.[52] His best-known edifice is the parliament building of the Grand National Assembly of Turkey (Türkiye Büyük Millet Meclisi), which was not finished until 1963 due to delays.

All of Ankara's city planners and architects understood themselves to be modernists, but they had differing perspectives on the substance of modernism. Bruno Taut (1880–1938) did not enjoy the *kübik* (*cubique*) style developed by his predecessors. Although he only lived in Turkey for two years between his arrival in 1936 and his premature death in 1938, he designed the building of the Faculty of Languages, History, and Geography of Ankara University and was one of the founders of the "Second National Style," which would replace cubic architecture in Turkey after 1938. The "First National Style" which dominated state architecture from 1908 into the 1920s was created by foreigners (like the Italians Giulio Mongeri and Raimondo d'Aronco, the Frenchman Alexandre Valaury, and the German August Jasmund) and

---

51 Lier, "Ritter." Van Ess, *Im Halbschatten*.
52 Nicolai, *Moderne und Exil*, 12, 20, 42ff. Dogramaci, *Kulturtransfer*, 32ff.

Turkish architects such as Mimar Kemaleddin (1870–1927) and Vedat Tek (1873–1942). A similar combination produced the Second National Style, with Turkish architects like Sedat Hakkı Eldem (1908–1988) and the German Paul Bonatz (1877–1956) playing key roles. Bonatz first came to Turkey after the Nazi regime stopped giving him commissions in the later war years, but he taught as a professor at the Technical University of İstanbul from 1946 until his departure in 1954. Even more than Holzmeister, Bonatz gave Turkish state architecture a monumental-triumphalist direction, which culminated in the magnum opus of the Second National Style, the Atatürk Mausoleum (Anıtkabir) finished in 1953, for which the architects Emin Onat (1910–1962) and Orhan Arda (1911–2003) were responsible.[53]

Even the statues erected on central-city plazas represented a claim to a modern, Western society. The monuments, which were at first dedicated almost solely to Mustafa Kemal, placed him—immovably, as it were—in the public space. A first statute of Mustafa Kemal, molded by the Austrian sculptor Heinrich Krippel (1983–1945), was ceremoniously made accessible to the public on the spit of land beneath the Topkapı Palace in İstanbul on 3 October 1926. The statue turns its back on the seraglio of the Ottoman sultans and looks in the direction of Anatolia. With this portrayal, Krippel, who executed commissions from Turkey in his Vienna studio from 1925 to 1938, created the model for many future Atatürk statues. They show Atatürk as general, diplomat, politician, and commander alike.[54] Atatürk gazes proudly upon the country and its people, but in a certain sense, wasn't he looking *past* both of them at something else?

Affiliation, Cooptation, Exclusion: The Creation of the Turkish Nation

The ambitious nationalist attempt to anchor the Turks in Anatolia long before the eleventh century led to the contortions of the Turkish History Thesis and Sun Language Theory of the 1930s, but the prosaic and realistic sides of Kemalist nationalism are also visible in its basic tenet that the homeland of the Turks is Anatolia. Irredentism played no relevant role in Kemalism, neither with regard to "bringing home" other Turkic peoples into a hypothetical

---

53 Nicolai, *Moderne und Exil*, 148.
54 Dogramaci, *Kulturtransfer*, 268.

Greater Turkish Empire led by the Republic of Turkey, nor with regard to the potential reestablishment of the former Ottoman territories of rule in Southeastern Europe, the Caucasus, or the Arab world.[55] At the same time, Turkey's limitation to Anatolia was coupled with an absolute insistence on the inviolability of the borders guaranteed by the Treaty of Lausanne. The unity of the state was virtually sacralized: "The tenet of the indivisible unity of the nation's territory and people is as important to the centralized, unitary state of Turkey as the principal of federalism is to the Federal Republic of Germany."[56] The Turkish "Sèvres Syndrome," that is, the fear that Turkey could be divided up as had been allegedly planned in the 1920 Treaty of Sèvres, is real on the one hand, on the other, it served and serves as a strategic defense against all other claims, in the first instance against those of the Kurdish population for the solution of *their* national question.

Every nation-state in the world has emerged from a heterogenous population. Even "natural"-seeming nation-states like France took centuries for this process to produce a "nation," and even today they remain faced with reservations about the project by parts of their population (one thinks for example of the Bretons). At the same time, it is hardly unusual when the absorption of diverse population groups into the "nation-state" runs into limits; new rifts may even come to light, as in Spanish Catalonia. When it comes to the construction of a nation-state, the Republic of Turkey shows substantial consolidation but also considerable gaps in the process of amalgamation. As we have already seen, in the nineteenth and early twentieth century, immigrant Muslim populations who were only partially Turkish-speaking integrated themselves quickly into the Sunni-Turkish majority society. The ecumenical nature of Islam and the integrative aspects of the Turkish national idea have created a stable collective identity for Muslim Turks.

Seen formally, the Turkish definition of nationhood is based on territory and citizenship: Article 88 of the Constitution of 1924 stated that all

---

55 Some caveats have to be made: the "reclamation" of the Aegean Islands situated immediately across from the Turkish mainland was always a concern in late Ottoman and later Turkish policy. See Trumpener, *Germany and the Ottoman Empire*, 28ff., on the time of the First World War. Mango, *Atatürk*, 378, on the negotiations in Lausanne. Following Önder, *Die türkische Außenpolitik im Zweiten Weltkrieg*, 190, there are indications in the archive of the German Foreign Office that Turkey demanded the Aegean Islands situated immediately across from the Turkish mainland in return for a possible accession to the Axis Powers, in addition to Cyprus and the control of the crude oil pipeline extending from Mosul to Tripoli (Lebanon) via Palmyra.

56 Rumpf, "Minderheiten in der Türkei," 472.

inhabitants of Turkey are to be regarded as Turks, regardless of confession and ethnicity. Yet in contradiction to the formal concept of *ius soli* (the "right of soil," or birthright citizenship), the actual Turkish understanding of nation—albeit not explicitly stated in constitutional texts—makes a double affiliation with Turkdom and Islam a prerequisite for completely valid membership in the nation. In its official self-definition the Turkish nation-state model emphasizes a voluntary understanding, following the French model. Atatürk's famous dictum, "Ne mutlu Türküm diyene" (How happy the one who says, "I am a Turk") may therefore be understood not in a cynical fashion as exclusionary and nationalistic, but as meant primarily as affiliative: thus a Kurd can pursue a great career in politics or business, provided he or she refers to his or her Kurdish background as an ancestral heritage, much as many Turks can point to their roots in Rumelia (the formerly Ottoman territories in Southeastern Europe) without anyone desiring to or being able to create an identity conflict out of it. The Turkish definition of citizenship has an integrative character, but at the same time, it possesses exclusionary characteristics, in that all those who don't conform to the hard and double core identity of Turkishness and being Muslim are excluded. This tension between an assimilating and an exclusionary understanding of citizenship remains characteristic of the Turkish nation-state today.

Exclusions of "improper" Turks are legion in the early Republican era. The Law on Officials (Memurin Kanunu) of March 1926 established that government officials must be ethnic Turks. In the Law on Settlement (İskan Kanunu) of 1934, which regulated questions of immigration and settlement, the right to settle was restricted for those who could not be regarded as part of the "Turkish race" or "attached to Turkish culture."[57]

It is noteworthy, however, that in the basic Turkish conception of national affiliation, the dividing line between being Turkish and not being Turkish is more permeable than that between being Muslim and not being Muslim. Non-Muslims are left with merely minority status—guaranteed! Articles 37 to 44 of the Treaty of Lausanne, which guarantee non-Muslims protection and equality before the law, were taken up in Articles 69 and 88 of the Constitution of 1924, but down to the present day, the Turkish state makes a fundamental distinction between Muslims and non-Muslims. The Turkish negotiations in Lausanne and all later state policy bespoke a deep mistrust of the Christian population as a potential fifth column of the West. Thus mandatory military

---

57   Jenkins, *Political Islam*, 104ff.

service for non-Muslims was not just a question of equality, it was intended to limit non-Muslims' potential economic advantages.

One can invoke the historical experience—more or less backed up by reality—of Christians collaborating with European powers in the late Ottoman Era to explain these reservations with regards to Christians. But in the young Republic of Turkey, there existed reservations with regard to its Jewish population as well, who could not conceivably have been thought of as the cat's paw of a foreign power until at least the foundation of Israel in 1948. At the beginning of the Republican era, the Ankara government classified the Jews as "harmless."[58] However, the goal of reparatory economic justice for the Muslim Turkish population overflowed into a policy of discrimination against Jews. In the late 1920s, a campaign for the exclusive use of Turkish in the public sphere called "Fellow citizen, speak Turkish!" (Vatandaş Türkçe konuş!) violated Article 39 of the Treaty of Lausanne which provided for freedom of language for all Turkish citizens. Jews were especially hard hit because, in contrast to the Orthodox and Armenians, they often spoke no Turkish, but used only Ladino (Judeo-Spanish) as an everyday language.

During the Second World War, in which Turkey remained neutral until 1945, as the supply situation became increasingly straitened and war profiteers exploited the plight of the people more and more, a "wealth tax" (varlık vergisi) was imposed on 11 November 1942. It was supposed to skim off profiteering gains and simultaneously help reduce the out-of-control state deficit. Its implementation, however, turned into a systematic dispossession of the Christian and Jewish populations. Non-Muslims raised 53% of the special tax, while Muslims contributed 36.5% and resident foreigners 10.5%. In addition, far higher tax rates were placed on them as non-Muslims. The Sabbateans (Dönme) paid double the tax of Muslims, other non-Muslims ten times as much. The leading politicians of the day made no bones about the fact that the wealth tax was also intended to transfer the wealth of non-Muslims to Turkish Muslim businesspeople. In fact, this measure laid the groundwork for businessmen from Anatolia to gain a foothold in İstanbul.[59]

It was not the case, however, that the Jewish community were just collateral damage of a policy that was principally aimed at Christians. In the 1930s, the Turkish state saw the Jewish community in West Thrace, which comprised

---

58 Bayat, "In Pursuit of Homogeneity," 108, 117ff., 121.
59 Hale, *Modern Turkey*, 71. Zürcher, *Turkey*, 200. Lewis, *Emergence of Modern Turkey*, 298. Koçak, *Türkiye'de Milli Şef Dönemi*, 2:506–509, 514ff., 567. A collection of eyewitness reports of the wealth tax can be found in Bali, *Varlık Vergisi*.

more than ten thousand people, as a security risk. It is more than probable that the calls for boycotts and riots against the Thracian Jews in the summer of 1934 were directed by the state.[60] The majority of the Thracian Jewish community subsequently fled to İstanbul or abroad.

It might have actually been an asset for the future of the young Turkey that, in the Treaty of Lausanne, the exclusionary definition as minorities was applied only to non-Muslims. The posture of the Turkish state regarding groups such as the Alevis and Kurds was open in this regard, but it slid very soon into the pattern of an exclusionary cooptation. The existence of the Kurdish population in Turkey revealed the ambivalence of the Turkish national idea: there was no racist conception of the Kurds that would make their acceptance into Turkish society and their recognition as Turks fundamentally impossible. In practice, however, this acceptance proceeded only under conditions, specifically, at a minimum, acknowledging Turkish as a quasi-native language and, second, the adoption of the "grand narrative" of the Turkish nation. As a result, Kurds have been and are found in all major Turkish parties as members of the National Assembly. However, these parliamentarians—with the exception of those belonging to the currently (still) extant Peoples' Democratic Party (Halkların Demokratik Partisi, HDP)—had to set aside their Kurdish identity and could not pursue any specifically Kurdish concerns. In the end, it's still the case that "In Turkey, a Kurd can be anything—except a Kurd."[61]

The Alevis, on the other hand, fall completely outside the models of order which the Ottoman Empire left to the Republic of Turkey. They stand athwart the traditional Ottoman distinction between Muslims and non-Muslims. They also fall through other screens, because they do not comprise a distinct group either ethnically or linguistically. It's precisely this mercuriality that has made the Alevis into a kind of walking provocation.

It was, however, resistance on the part of those who, from the point of view of the government, were to be counted unambiguously among the winners of the Republic, which cast doubts on the future viability of the Kemalist republic. The modernization agenda decreed from above, somewhat heedlessly, led

---

60 On the course of the antisemitic riots in Thrace in 1934 and on the presumptive responsibility of the state, see Pekesen, *Ende der jüdischen Gemeinden*, 38–54, 255–263.
61 Birand and Yıldız, *Son Darbe*, 112, point to the position paper of Doğu Ergil in his *Doğu Sorunu: Teşhisler ve Tespitler: Özel Araştırma Raporu* (Ankara: Türk Odalar ve Borsalar Birliği, 1995). In the 1990s and 2000s, there appeared a whole series of works which argued for a policy of liberalization towards the Kurds. Atmaca, "Kürt Sorununda Çözüm Süreci," 33–36.

to a double internal emigration among large parts of the rural population. They moved into the big cities and retreated into themselves.

Personality Cult and Moderate Autocracy

In the first decades of the Republic, the milestones of the national movement were highly promoted, even sacralized. Consequently, the later grail guardians of Kemalism wanted to make Mustafa Kemal's multi-day speech (Nutuk) of October 1927 into a "Koran of Kemalism," but the dry and detailed review was incapable of inciting any enthusiasm. The extremely attentive transmission of numerous sayings and deeds of Atatürk is reminiscent of the *hadith* literature, that is, the transmission of the sayings and deeds of the Prophet Muhammad and his companions. The cult of Mustafa Kemal's landing in Samsun on 19 May 1919 suggests a comparison to that of the Hijra, the "emigration" of Muhammad from Mecca to Medina in the year 622.[62] The national holidays of the Republic of Turkey all celebrate the heroic age of the national movement: National Sovereignty and Children's Day (Ulusal Egemenlik ve Çocuk Bayramı) commemorates the opening of the Grand National Assembly on 23 April 1920; Commemoration of Atatürk, Youth and Sports Day (Atatürk'ü Anma, Gençlik ve Spor Bayramı) marks Mustafa Kemal's landing in Samsun on 19 May 1919; Victory Day (Zafer Bayramı) recalls the end of the War of Independence on 30 August 1922 and Republic Day (Cumhuriyet Bayramı) the proclamation of the Republic on 29 October 1923.[63]

The personality cult around Atatürk, above all the indoctrination in schools, military service, and in the public sphere, made Kemalism effective in Turkish society. Many superlatives were invented for Atatürk alongside the aforementioned titles of gazi (heroic defender of the hallowed nation) and *halâskâr* (savior) many variants of which are no longer intelligible to the average Turk because of the language reform: "great" (*büyük*), "genius" (*dahi*), "peerless" (*eşsiz*), "liberator" (*münci*), "exalted" (*ulu*), "creator" (*yaratıcı*), "sublime" (*yüce*), or "marvel of humanity" (*beşeriyet harikası*).[64] But if

---

62   Hanioğlu, *Atatürk*, 187. Jenkins, *Political Islam*, 81.
63   Newly added is the Democracy and National Unity Day (Demokrasi ve Milli Birlik Günü) with time off work on July 15, commemorating the failed coup attempt of 2016. On the AKP governments' dealings with the Kemalist national holidays, see Özyürek, "Commemorating the Coup."
64   Hanioğlu, *Atatürk*, 187.

one puts aside the personality cult around Atatürk, which was thoroughly successful for decades, what can be espied as the essence of Kemalism?

In its ruling praxis, Kemalism may be understood as a variant of authoritarianism, but its contents are not easy to grasp.[65] That it nevertheless enjoyed a great degree of effectiveness despite its relative vagueness is not surprising, as this fuzziness is a fundamental characteristic of all nationalism. Kemalism is thus a nationalism based on Turkey's particular circumstances and promoted by the state. Kemalism saw itself as "modern," "Western," and "secular"— defining itself in unclear terms and thus comparable to other loose ideological constructs like that of Gaullism.[66]

Kemalism's political program isn't particularly helpful in trying to understand it better. At a party congress in October 1927, the Republican People's Party (Cumhuriyet Halk Fırkası, CHP) pledged itself to the four principles of "republicanism" (cumhuriyetçilik), "populism" (halkçılık), "nationalism" (milliyetçilik), and "laicism" (laiklik). These four were expanded in 1931 with the principles of "statism" (devletçilik) and "revolutionism" (inkılapçılık) and, on 5 February 1937, incorporated by amendment into the second article of the Constitution of 1924. The six principles, also the "Six Arrows" of the Republican People's Party, only appear to represent a firm agenda for Kemalism, because they remain all too vague in their details and, even within the Republican People's Party, there was never any attempt to place them into a binding ideological framework.[67]

From the beginning, Kemalist ruling circles were distinguished by an elitism which did not want to be dependent on mass mobilization and which came at the cost of isolation from their own people.[68] Nonetheless, Kemalism did not limit itself to admonition from above, but rather saw itself as justified in indoctrination. As an Ottoman officer deployed to Yemen, İsmet İnönü discovered a collection of records with European music, which he came to like upon repeated listening. "I then realized that our people, too, could come to like Western music if they listened to it all the time."[69]

---

65 Quite justifiably, Plaggenborg, *Ordnung und Gewalt*, 56, points to the "analytic helplessness" in accounts of Kemalism thus far.
66 Compare with Hoffmann and Hoffmann, "De Gaulle as Political Artist," 217, which describes Gaullism in its "ideological emptiness" as "an attitude, not a coherent set of dogmas."
67 Koçak, *Türkiye'de Milli Şef Dönemi*, 1:31ff., 2:82–84.
68 Plaggenborg, *Ordnung und Gewalt*, 126, 256ff.
69 Heper, *İnönü*, 45.

Mustafa Kemal was—aside from his comprehensive military education—an autodidact. A further reason for the vagueness of Kemalism is that Mustafa Kemal's own worldview was conflicted, coupling a confident view of the future with profound mistrust. His egalitarian elitism and readiness to expand his circle of collaborators was joined to a tendency to withdraw into himself. His belief in the achievability of a modern world stumbled over his constant nagging doubts whether his own people could really be won over for it.

The population of Anatolia was in fact not prepared for Kemalism—nor was Kemalism for the Anatolians. Anatolia was the territorial hinge of the Ottoman Empire and thereby the most secure anchor point for the homeless late Ottoman elite, but it was not familiar territory. Mustafa Kemal himself had always only been a fighter on the borders of the empire; until 1919, Anatolia was largely unfamiliar to him.[70] His encounter with Anatolia, a part of his homeland much more conservative than his home city of Saloniki, "came as something of a shock."[71]

An early indication of seething discontent in the Turkish population was the rioting in the town of Menemen near İzmir on 23 December 1930. A certain Derviş Mehmed, a member of the Nakşbendi order, had declared himself the *Mahdi* (literally, "the rightly guided one," a holy, eschatalogical figure in the Islamic religion) in mid-December 1929. Now, in Menemen's marketplace, he was proclaiming an "Islamic revolution." As Reserve Lieutenant Mustafa Fehmi Kubilay (1903–1930), who had been passing by chance, attempted to intervene, he was lynched. The "Menemen Revolt" was in no way any threat to the regime, but it was disturbing nonetheless due to the fact that many bystanders had remained impassive and had not intervened.[72]

We know a lot about Atatürk and can describe him well. However, a historical appraisal remains somewhat difficult, even at the remove of many decades—not least because his person and his work are constantly taken up as continually renegotiated objects of Turkish debates about identity. Another reason may also be that in international historiography, despite the

---

70   Kreiser, *Atatürk*, 182.
71   Hanioğlu, *Atatürk*, 205.
72   Plaggenborg, *Ordnung und Gewalt*, 142. Jenkins, *Political Islam*, 102ff. Impressionistically conducted surveys in periodicals and magazines (in the years 1925–1928) on the expectations and hopes of the population showed no indications of a rejection of the new public order. This is in no way surprising, however, because these utterances took place in the public sphere and thereby under state supervision. Cf. Demirel, *Cumhuriyet Kurulurken Hayallar ve Umutlar*.

Figure 5. The logo of the Republican People's Party (CHP) with its "Six Arrows" illustrates the close connection between state and CHP in the early years of the Republic. In 1937, the arrows were incorporated by amendment as principles in the second article of the Constitution of 1924. The lower part with the acronym in front of the sky is a newer addition.
https://en.wikipedia.org/wiki/Republican_People%27s_Party#/media/File:Cumhuriyet_Halk_Partisi_Logo.svg

thoroughness of the relevant works, the depiction of Atatürk as of a very peculiar kind predominates. The authors refrain from calling him *incomparable*, but he appears to be *beyond comparison*.

Kemalism may, however, be pinned down very well within the pattern of interwar European political culture. The similarities of the Kemalist regime to the moderate authoritarian regimes in Europe—"moderate" relative to National Socialist Germany, Fascist Italy, or the Leninist or Stalinist Soviet Union—like those of Ioannis Metaxas (1871–1941) in Greece, Francisco Franco (1885–1975) in Spain, and António de Oliveira Salazar (1889–1970) in Portugal, are obvious. Turkey's parallels to Poland under Józef Klemens Piłsudski (1867–1935) are also striking. Piłsudski's Poland was also able to secure its own state under different, but similarly extreme difficulties. After the First World War, Poland "had no frontiers, no established territory, no government, no constitution, and no international recognition,"[73] but in the three years after his return to Poland in November 1918, Piłsudski created an independent Poland.

As an architect of a nation-state, Atatürk's merits are undisputed. Building off a clear and comprehensive agenda, he showed audacity and assertiveness. At the same time, Turkey under Atatürk emerged as a moderate autocracy

---

73   Davies, *Im Herzen Europas*, 105. Also, MacMillan, *Paris 1919*, 208.

at whose pinnacle stood not a charismatic leader but a sometimes shy "head teacher." In addition, Kemalism did not evince many of the features that characterized other authoritarian states in Europe. Turkey was not militaristic. It showed no impulses towards an imperialist foreign policy. Although the parliament was a façade after 1925, the foundations for a later transition to democracy were laid. Kemalism never declared the liberal democracies of the West to be a bogeyman. But one doesn't have to take a trip to the far side of the moon to recognize the dark side of Kemalism. As the Young Turks had oppressed the minority that seemed most dangerous to them, the Armenians, so did the Kemalists treat the Kurds.[74] Two burdens laid upon the future were the exclusion of minorities (including the *non*-non-Muslims) from the common state project and the strangely ambivalent position of religion, which was both repressed as a possible threat and simultaneously maintained as a fundamental factor in national identity.

When Atatürk died on 10 November 1938, the shadows of the gathering Second World War were already falling upon Turkey. Atatürk's successors, under the leadership of İsmet İnönü, moved carefully, not wishing to endanger their arduously constructed state. Until the end of the 1940s, their policy was bound to Atatürk's legacy but had to find its own, new path forward—without the support and burden of the towering figure that Atatürk had become since the 1920s.

2. Bound to the Legacy (1938–1950)

In contrast to the highly compressed period of the war years of 1912–1922 and the rapid succession of the Kemalist reforms in the 1920s and early 1930s, the political dynamic slowed markedly in the middle of the 1930s. During the Second World War, the Turkish political elite turned all their energies to the task of leading the country through it unscathed. At the same time, the period from the late 1930s to 1950 was decisive for the continuation and consolidation of the Kemalist legacy. Only after Atatürk's death could a new elite stratum develop fully and prove itself at the same time. By the end of the 1940s, the Kemalist bureaucratic-intellectual-judicial-military complex had become firmly entrenched—a close interaction of Kemalist

---

74   Kreiser, *Atatürk*, 300. Zürcher, *Turkey*, 172.

elites in administration, public relations and universities, jurisprudence, and the military that continued over the following decades. The certainty of having anchored themselves deeply in the state and—to a far lesser degree—society, made it easier for the Kemalist elite under İsmet İnönü to finally permit a political opening.

The Second Man: Ismet İnönü

İsmet İnönü (1884–1973) was the decisive personality in the period between Atatürk's death in 1938 and the elections of 1950 when the Republican People's Party (Cumhuriyet Halk Partisi, CHP), which had previously ruled alone, went into opposition after a loss at the polls. İnönü maintained the fundamental orientation of Kemalist policy and brought Turkey intact through the Second World War, aside from economic crises. İnönü can also justifiably be called the "Second Man" (as he is in the title of a biography of him by Şevket Süreyya Aydemir), as a loyal acolyte of Atatürk during his lifetime and his conservator after his death. İsmet İnönü was possessed of far less charisma than Atatürk and a certain dourness which sometimes could be taken as mental inflexibility, but which was very helpful to him in the tenacious implementation of political goals—a characteristic he had already demonstrated at the negotiations in Lausanne in 1922–23. İnönü's clearly inferior standing relative to Atatürk can be seen in the statues dedicated to him. In 1944, a statue of İnönü by Rudolf Belling was installed in the courtyard of the agricultural faculty of the University of Ankara. Another statue, depicting İnönü as the savior at the defensive battles on the İnönü River in the spring of 1921, planned for İstanbul's central Taksim Square was never installed. The statue, in storage for decades, was not placed in front of İnönü's former house near İstanbul's Maçka Park until 1982.[75]

In the years 1925–1937, when İnönü served as prime minister again after his first brief period in office (1923–24), bad blood repeatedly arose between him and Atatürk. Atatürk had largely withdrawn from the day-to-day affairs of government, but in his actions as prime minister İnönü was frequently vexed by short-term resolutions that came out of the evening "Atatürk table" (Atatürk sofrası) composed of Atatürk and his drinking buddies.

---

75 Dogramaci, *Kulturtransfer*, 291–293.

İnönü's deposition as prime minister in October 1937 had a weightier cause, however: Atatürk sided with the then minister of the economy Celal Bayar in a dispute with İnönü and thus turned against İnönü's policy of an etatist-oriented economic policy.

Nevertheless, when Atatürk died on 10 November 1938, there were no serious candidates opposing İnönü. İnönü was elected president by parliament the very next day. At an extraordinary party conference on 26 December 1938, he was named national chief (Millî Şef) and perpetual chairman (Değişmez Genel Başkan) of the Republican People's Party.[76] From 1938 to 1950, İnönü embodied unopposed the pinnacle of power in the state. From 1938 to 1972, he was chairman of the CHP. İnönü was only forced out of party leadership a year before his death on 25 December 1973.

The Overwhelming State: Economy, Schools, Rail Network

At its origin, the Republic was completely occupied with coping with the consequences of the war decade of 1912–1922. The Great Depression and the Second World War were the next great setbacks along its path. In the 1920s, an economically inexperienced political leadership relied on the strategy of a "national economy" (*milli iktisat*) propagated in the pre-war period.[77] Mustafa Kemal and İsmet (İnönü), who were little versed in questions of state finances and political economy,[78] relied on the initiative of Turkish Muslim entrepreneurs and expected that the rapidly acquired wealth of the new national entrepreneurial class would advance political-economic recovery and development on its own. This expectation remained unfulfilled because the alleged bearers of a new national economy set out upon the much more easily attainable venture of enriching themselves. Beginning in the 1930s, under the impact of the global economic crisis and following a global turn of mind, the Turkish government resorted to a policy of statism, which was one of the six principles of the young state and the Republican

---

76 Koçak, *Türkiye'de Milli Şef Dönemi*, 2:22, indicates that the two titles of *Değişmez Genel Başkan* and *Milli Şef* were already in use under Atatürk. They only became normative terms under İnönü, however.
77 For this, see Toprak, *Türkiye'de Milli İktisat*.
78 Armstrong, *Grey Wolf*, 222, faithful to his rather polemical style of argumentation, remarks that İsmet had less idea about economic and financial questions than "the average Levantine clerk in a Constantinople bank."

People's Party anyway. This reorientation changed nothing about the cautious nature of Turkish economic policy, which was still affected by the impact of the excessive indebtedness of the late Ottoman period.[79]

According to the principle of statism (devletçilik) enshrined in 1931, only the state was possessed of the necessary resources and the capital to build up an industrial base capable of survival and productiveness in Turkey (initially especially in the production of raw materials like steel and cement, or in mining). What exactly the concept of statism meant and how far it might extend was nevertheless contested within the Turkish elite. One may think of the aforesaid confrontation between Celal Bayar and İsmet İnönü in 1937 which led to the latter's resignation as prime minister. It is not clear whether statism was aimed in the direction of a unified national society or whether, in the end, it was dominated by the pragmatic idea that the state should initially take primary responsibility for industrial investments, even if this meant excluding private business.[80] A first five-year plan was put together with the help of Soviet advisors and introduced for the years 1934–1938. Its main goal was primarily to build factories in order to curtail the import of consumer goods and the export of indigenous unprocessed raw materials. A second five-year plan was not implemented in 1938 because of the immediately impending Second World War.

Despite Turkey's successful policy of neutrality in the Second World War, the years beginning in 1939 were shaped by the war economy. The Turkish economy contracted due to the drastic absorption of resources by the maintenance of a million-man standing army. The share of the defense budget as a percentage of total state spending climbed from 30% in 1938 to 55% in 1942, falling back to 40% in 1945. Food prices quadrupled between 1938 and 1944. In the period of 1945–1950, the private sector recovered while the vastly increased state sector only declined gradually. In 1945, gross national product was approximately 35% lower than it had been before the war. In 1950, per-capita income was likely lower than that of 1939.[81]

The constraints of the Second World War also strengthened the tendency, already present, to place all instruments of power in the state's hands. Even in the last few years of Atatürk's life, the Republican People's Party (CHP) lost

---

79   Owen and Pamuk, *Middle East Economies*, 18–20.
80   Plaggenborg, *Ordnung und Gewalt*, 154. Hale, *Modern Turkey*, 55.
81   Koçak, *Türkiye'de Milli Şef Dönemi*, 2:370, 435. Owen and Pamuk, *Middle East Economies*, 24. Hale, *Modern Turkey*, 75.

its character as an independent institution and merged into the state. Recep Peker (1899–1950), who had fought for greater autonomy for the CHP as its general secretary since 1931, was dismissed in 1936. The same year, Prime Minister İsmet İnönü officially proclaimed the alignment of the state apparatus and the party organization. Functions of the CHP were melded with those of the state. In the union of offices between party and state, the prime minister was simultaneously co-chairman of the party; the minister of the interior, general secretary; and the provincial governors the respective leaders of the CHP provincial organization.

This merger of party and state was abandoned in 1939, but in principle, there was no fundamental difference visible in the leadership under Atatürk and İnönü. The Constitution of 1924 actually foresaw a strong role for parliament, but the constitutional demand for the government's responsibility to parliament was never enforced. The president, under Atatürk as well as İnönü, possessed a plentitude of power never anticipated by the constitution. What power was left to parliament devolved almost entirely upon the parliamentary caucus of the CHP. Even they, however, were merely informed of foreign policy questions and had no independent voice.

At the same time, the CHP was not particularly well-anchored in the countryside. Even in the second half of the 1930s, it had no organizational structures at all in the southeast of Turkey.[82] Founded beginning in February 1932, People's Houses (Halkevleri) were supposed to provide a remedy for the missing anchorage of the Kemalist state and the CHP in Anatolia. Their goal was to promote national unity, bring village- and city-dwellers closer together, and explain the principles of the CHP to the people. More modest People's Rooms (Halk Odaları) followed in May 1939 in rural areas with low population density. In total, 478 People's Houses and 4,322 People's Rooms were set up. The original goal of spreading Kemalist ideas was never realized because people tended to stick with what was familiar, but through the People's Houses, in the cities of Anatolia nevertheless came into being a middle class indebted to Kemalism.[83]

The Village Institutes (Köy Enstitüleri) founded in 1940 performed one elementary task. These village schools, usually in the charge of a single teacher, were meant to increase literacy in the countryside and slow the emigration from the village to the city which was already underway. In the cities and towns, four-fifths of children attended school, but in the country

---

82 Koçak, *Türkiye'de Mill Şef Dönemi*, 1:157ff.; 2:54, 96ff., 568–580.
83 Ibid., 2:104–106. Zürcher, "Institution-Building," 104–108.

only a quarter did, because, of the approximately forty thousand villages in the country, three quarters had no school. In addition, the majority of village children left school after only three years and not the five foreseen by the elementary-school system. The Village Institutes now accepted students who only had to have completed the five-year elementary school for an additional five-year term of education. The graduates of the Village Institutes had, in return, to work for twenty years as a teacher at a location determined by the Ministry of Education, during which they would receive, in addition to a meager income, fields and a cottage. (Originally the term of mandatory service was planned to be thirty years.) At the end of the 1930s, as the Village Institutes had produced around twenty-five thousand graduates, momentum flagged. Most of the teachers coming from the city did not fit into the village environment, and the rural population perceived the mandatory construction of the Village Institutes, that is, the school and teacher's house, as forced labor.[84]

An area of particular emphasis in state planning and management was railroad construction. In the 1930s, about a half of all public investment flowed into the expansion of the railway network and other transportation routes. Before the First World War the self-interest of European investors had been determinative in railroad construction. Spur lines extending from port cities served to open up economically profitable hinterlands. The famous Baghdad Railway, which wasn't completed before the First World War, was an exception, because it was meant to bridge the enormous distance between İstanbul and Baghdad; on the other hand, it was governed by the strategic interests of Germany. Beginning in the 1920s, the railway system was adjusted to the national strategic and economic requirements of the Republic of Turkey. All the lines and tracks were nationalized and expansion was driven by the state's interests. By the end of the 1940s, they managed to lay over eighteen hundred miles (three thousand kilometers) of new track.[85]

The vigorous expansion of the railway network helped agricultural productivity climb between fifty and seventy percent in the 1930s, despite a drop in exports due to the Great Depression, which affected eighty to ninety percent of agrarian products, the prices of which declined around 60% between 1928–29 and 1932–33. The slowly growing population could work

---

84 Koçak, *Türkiye'de Milli Şef Dönemi*, 2:115–125.
85 Aydemir, *İkinci Adam*, 1:334ff. Hütteroth, *Türkei*, 430ff. On the embedding of the Baghdad Railway in the contemporary international power constellations, see Schöllgen, *Imperialismus und Gleichgewicht*, 86–176, and McMeekin, *Berlin-Baghdad Express*.

fields previously lying fallow, and numerous railroad lines made these newly productive acreages accessible. The railroad remained the most important means of transport into the 1950s. When railroad construction came to a halt in the Fifties, and busses, personal automobiles, and trucks travelled newly constructed roads, the amount of passenger and freight traffic on the rails sunk rapidly. In 1950, the railroad still carried 63% of freight traffic, the road network 32.5%. In 1970, 73.9% of freight traffic travelled by road, and only 25.8% still travelled by rail.[86] The decades-long neglect of the railroad led to its decline in the last quarter of the twentieth century to Turkey's most impoverished and pitiful means of transportation. Individual prestige projects like the new high-speed trains on the İstanbul-Ankara and Ankara-Konya routes remain islands of quality in an otherwise regrettably bad rail network.

Unscathed by the Second World War

Since the War of Independence, a fundamental pillar of Turkish foreign policy was maintaining a good relationship with the Soviet Union, which in no way meant Turkey understood herself as a satellite of or in any way ideologically subordinate to the USSR. From a position of nonalignment, the guiding principle in the early years of the Republic, Turkey nevertheless came to the insight that one does need a network of friendly relationships and even the backing of a strong power. The Balkan Pact (1934) and the Saadabad Pact (1937, named for a palace in Tehran) were part of the agreements of the 1930s intended to secure Turkey's eastern flank.

The Balkan Pact, concluded on 9 February 1934 in Athens between Greece, the Kingdom of Yugoslavia, Romania, and Turkey, was directed against Bulgaria and Italy, two revisionist-minded states who objected to the terms of the Paris Peace Treaties. Curiously, Italy was one of the victors of World War One and could point to numerous territorial gains. It should have, therefore, belonged to the camp of antirevisionists (like, e.g., Greece, Romania, and Czechoslovakia), but it was dissatisfied because of unrealized territorial demands in Dalmatia. Turkey, as successor to the Ottoman Empire destroyed after the First World War, could have counted itself among the revisionist camp (i.e., countries like Bulgaria, Germany, and Hungary), but it was completely satisfied by the provisions of the Treaty of Lausanne.

---

86   Hale, *Modern Turkey*, 90. Tekeli and İlkin, *Cumhuriyet Harcı*, 3:444.

The Saadabad Pact, concluded on 8 July 1937 with Afghanistan, Iraq, and Iran, was supposed to create security in an easterly direction. This pact, valid for five years, secured friendship on all sides and the recognition of current borders. In addition, it provided for mutual military assistance in case one of the four treaty countries were attacked by another power.[87]

Turkey had concluded a nonaggression pact with Italy in 1928, but the expansionist policy of Fascist Italy in the 1930s reminded the Turks ominously of the Italian aggression of the 1910s, when the Ottomans had lost their Libyan possessions as well as the Dodecanese Islands to Italy. In its search for a sea power who could curb Italian expansion in the Eastern Mediterranean, an ever more conspicuous British-Turkish rapprochement came about in the 1930s. At the same time, Turkey harbored sympathies for Germany's revisionist claims, seeing parallels between the treaties of Versailles and Sèvres. An initially cautiously positive assessment of National Socialist Germany changed, however, with its annexation of Czechoslovakia in the spring of 1939, which was seen in Turkey as the first step in a German policy of expansion towards Southeastern Europe.[88]

During the Second World War, Turkey's foreign policy cupboard was almost bare: an old working relationship with the Soviet Union, a tentative rapprochement with Great Britain, and two pacts (Balkan and Saadabad) which couldn't withstand an autumn storm. It is therefore one of the greatest successes of the young Republic of Turkey that it managed to maneuver undamaged through the Second World War. The strategy of "active neutrality" designed by Numan Menemencioğlu (1891–1958, foreign minister 1942–1944) declared that Turkey would not in any case be allowed to enter into the war too early and to its detriment. In fact, this was a policy of actively directed nonactivity.

German hints about Turco-German "brotherhood in arms" in the First World War, meant as publicity, fell on deaf ears. The memory of the disastrous First World War was much too fresh for the Turkish political elite for them to let Turkey be pulled into the war as a dependent ally of Germany.[89] Turkey's strategy during the war of leaning on Great Britain without joining the Allies was ultimately successful. Turkish foreign policy then returned to its tactic, already well-practiced in the nineteenth century, of intentional

---

87   Türkeş, "Balkan Pact." Volk, "Turkey's Historical Involvement," 16.
88   Deringil, *Turkish Foreign Policy*, 71ff. Koçak, *Türkiye'de Milli Şef Dönemi*, 1:239–241.
89   Koçak, *Türkiye'de Milli Şef Dönemi*, 2:576.

misunderstandings. When, in Anglo-Turkish discussions, it was declared "Turkey should be strong," the British side meant, referring to the Anglo-Turkish mutual-aid agreement of 12 May 1939, that Turkey should be armed for entry into the war, while the Turkish side interpreted it to mean that they should obtain sufficient strength to avoid being drawn into the war. In several situations, like Italy's declaration of war on the Allies on 10 June 1940 or Italy's attack on Greece on 28 October 1940, Turkey should have been required to enter the war, given its treaty obligations. The British side again and again acquiesced in Turkey's being dilatory: a neutral Turkey was better than having a country fighting unwillingly on your side.[90]

Turkey was in fact poorly prepared for the event of war. As in the nineteenth century, its artillery and rifles were of varied provenance. Because they'd considered Italy the principal danger in the pre-war years, the Aegean coast was fortified and furnished with gun batteries. Thrace, however, was not defensible in the case of a massive attack from the west. In March 1941, the defensive line in the west was withdrawn from İstanbul to West Anatolia, thereby potentially surrendering the city on the Bosporus to the enemy as indefensible.[91]

Even if in the first years of the war an invasion by the Axis powers of Italy and Germany had been considered possible, beginning in late 1942, developments favoring the Allies increasingly thrust the Soviet Union to the fore as Turkey's main potential adversary. The fear of a future, overpowered Soviet Union overshadowed the still-unresolved war. In the first years of the war, Turkey hoped for the earliest possible cessation of hostilities leaving Germany strong, because only a strong Germany, in their minds, could brake Soviet expansion into Eastern and Southeastern Europe. The dilemma of Turkish policy in the last years of the war was that they saw the Anglo-Soviet alliance as unnatural and speculated upon its foreseeable ending, but at the same time they could not alienate Britain and its allies during the war.[92] In several hesitant steps, Turkey moved towards officially joining the Allied camp. On 21 April 1944, it ceased deliveries of chrome important for the German armaments industry. On 2 August 1944, Turkey broke off diplomatic relations with Germany, but only declared war on Germany on 23 February 1945, in order to fulfill the basic conditions for acceptance in the United Nations.[93]

---

90 Deringil, *Turkish Foreign Policy*, 112, 144.
91 Ibid., 32–40.
92 On Turkish fears relative to Soviet territorial demands on Turkey, see Koçak, *Türkiye'de Milli Şef Dönemi*, 2:144ff., 147, 149, 154ff., 183, 190. Deringil, *Turkish Foreign Policy*, 166.
93 Koçak, *Türkiye'de Milli Şef Dönemi*, 2:178, 240ff., 264, 273.

To have ridden out the Second World War undamaged despite great economic hardships was a notable political success of Turkish foreign policy. Turkey avoided the burdens of participation in the war and above all did not have to endure its territory's becoming a theater of war. At the same time, there was a cost to pay for its lack of engagement in the war, which was finding itself in an isolated position by 1944 at the latest. It was a fortunate coincidence, then, that the West's reservations concerning Turkey no longer played a role in the broader context, that is, the up-coming confrontation between the United States and the Soviet Union. Only a few years after war's end, Turkey was a solid cornerstone of the Western security architecture.

On the Way to an Opening

Kemalist rule, which had now lasted more than two decades, was not particularly popular among the mass of the population, who were exhausted after the many privations of the war years. The government had additionally lost the support of those with whom they were actually allied: the bureaucratic class suffered under the enormous loss of purchasing power, largely because their salaries had remained the same. Even the well-connected profiteers of the war years demanded a retreat from statism and state interventionism. The commercial bourgeoisie were no longer willing to accept political powerlessness. Large property holders were dissatisfied with the artificially low prices of agricultural products. Faced with living conditions that had been bad for years, and which did not rapidly improve after 1945, rural and urban populations alike found little to praise in the established regime. Especially in the country, where the majority of the population still lived, no visible improvements had taken place. In 1953, only 0.025% of villages were connected to the electrical grid. In 1950, 68% of the population was illiterate, and life expectancy was, on average, 38.1 years.[94]

In this situation, a political and economic opening seemed extremely advisable. On 10 May 1946, a party congress of the autocratic Republican People's Party decreed that instead of continuing with the institution of the perpetual chairman, its party chief should be regularly elected, and that the honorific of national chief granted to İnönü should be changed to that of

---

94 Zürcher, *Turkey*, 206ff. Hale, *Modern Turkey*, 67. In the year 2000, the average life expectancy was seventy-one years (sixty-nine for men, 72.9 for women). İçduygu, "Demography," 331.

party chairman. Further steps towards political openness followed. Forced labor for villagers near mines, necessitated by the war, was abolished. Bans on newspapers and periodicals could no longer be imposed by the then responsible administration, but solely by a court. Within a few months, the one-party government lifted many of the restrictions that they had introduced in the past decades, or at least mitigated them.[95]

Open dissent was possible again and even welcome. Four leading dissidents inside the Republican People's Party, Celal Bayar (1883–1986), Fuat Köprülü (1888–1966), Refik Koraltan (1890–1974), and Adnan Menderes (1899–1961) brought their concerns in a petition to the chairman of the CHP caucus, known as the Memorandum of Four (Dörtlü Takrir). They demanded, among other things, the restoration of parliamentary control over the government and the development of a multiparty system. The four dissenters left, or were expelled from, the CHP in the second half of 1945 and were among the founding fathers of the Democrat Party (Demokrat Parti, DP) established on 7 January 1946, the first significant party alongside the CHP in Turkish party-political history. The Democrat Party was certainly not the first opposition party after the Second World War. The National Development Party (Milli Kalkınma Partisi) founded by the İstanbul industrialist Nuri Demirağ and officially registered on 5 September 1945 was, in the end, insignificant, but its founding signaled the end of the One-Party Era (Tek Partili Dönem) of the CHP.[96]

At this point, Turkey could already look back upon a decades-old but very brittle party-political history. The Second Constitutional Era begun in 1908 was accompanied by the founding of around a dozen parties,[97] followed in 1913 by the monopolization of power by the Young Turk Committee. In the first twenty-five years of the Republic of Turkey, the party landscape was monochrome: on 17 November 1924, the former comrades and then opponents of Mustafa Kemal, among them Abdülhak Adnan (Adıvar, 1882–1955), Kâzım (Karabekir), and Rauf (Orbay), founded the Progressive Republican Party (Terakkiperver Cumhuriyet Fırkası), which stood for the existing social order, political decentralization, and economic liberalization—thereby anticipating the agenda of the conservative parties of the second half of the twentieth century. Mustafa Kemal used the Shaykh Said Revolt of February–March 1925 as a pretext to dissolve the undesired opposition. On 3 June

---

95   Koçak, *Türkiye'de Milli Şef Dönemi*, 2:545. Karpat, *Turkey's Politics*, 159.
96   Karpat, *Turkey's Politics*, 144ff. Koçak, *Türkiye'de Milli Şef Dönemi*, 2:558–560.
97   On the history of the parties after 1908, see Tunaya, *Türkiye'de Siyasal Partiler*.

1925, the Progressive Republican Party was banned for the alleged misuse of religion for political purposes, among other things.

The next experiment with an opposition party got off the ground with the explicit encouragement of Mustafa Kemal. He moved his friend Fethi (Okyar) to found the Free Republican Party (Serbest Cumhuriyet Fırkası) in August 1930. Although this party was not an opposition party in the true sense of the term and sought no connection with the people, Fethi (Okyar) received such a triumphant welcome from the population on a visit to İzmir, that Mustafa Kemal, shocked by the popularity of this just-founded party, pulled the emergency brake.[98] Fethi (Okyar) had to dissolve the party on 17 November 1930, just three months after it was founded with approval at the highest levels.

The partisan democracy after the Second World War began rockily, but it would endure. In the parliamentary elections of 21 July 1945, which were called at the last minute and manipulated on election day in order to diminish the chances of the Democrat Party, which had only been founded a few months before, the DP was only able to win a modest 13.1% of the vote. It was crucial, however, that on 12 July 1947, in a statement on the multiparty system, İsmet İnönü took a position against the hawks in his own party under the leadership of prime minister Recep Peker and explicitly defended the legitimacy of the opposition party.[99] This declaration led to a falling out between İnönü and Peker, who ultimately resigned from office on 10 September 1947. The resistance of the uncompromising camp inside the CHP, which could only imagine an extremely slow transition to multiparty democracy, was broken.

In the elections of 14 May 1950, the Democrat Party won 55.2% of the vote and could thereby take over government.[100] The CHP received 39.6% of the votes but couldn't win a single province in the west of the country; only in the east where the electoral process was still under the control of local notables were they able to pile up considerable margins of victory. Parts of the military, unhappy about the DP's large electoral victory, seemingly had designs on a coup. One must give İnönü "eternal credit" for faithfully holding the course towards a multiparty system and bridling the military.[101]

---

98   Aydemir, İkinci Adam, 1:391.
99   Karpat, Turkey's Politics, 191.
100 Reports of the shares of the vote and parliamentary seats frequently differ from each other (though mostly insignificantly). Consequently, all data on electoral results and parliamentary seats for the period up until 2011 are given following Türkiye İstatistik Kurumu, Milletvekili Genel Seçimleri.
101 Zürcher, Turkey, 218.

Chapter Three

Precarious Pluralism, 1950–1980

Until 1960, the history of the Republic ran along clear lines. The 1950s were marked by conflict between the two parties, the ruling Democrat Parti (Demokrat Parti, DP) and the opposition Republican People's Party (Cumhuriyet Halk Partisi, CHP), but at least in the beginning the two did not diverge very far in their understanding of the foundations of the Kemalist state. On the other hand, and this hand is given more weight here, the breaking of new ground is evident across the 1950s. İsmet İnönü and the power elite surrounding him did not surrender all power, but they nevertheless voluntarily relinquished the most visible parts of it—that is, the government, including the presidency—to another party. When the DP formed a government after the elections of 1950, multiparty democracy became a convincing reality.

With its accession to NATO in 1952, linkage to the West finally became a determining characteristic of Turkey's foreign and domestic policy. The massive internal immigration and urbanization that would change the face of the cities and the character of the entire country took on its full force only beginning in the 1960s, but it very clearly began in the 1950s. The coup of 1960 and the new constitution of 1961 comprise a break but do not alter anything about the basic picture of the three decades between 1950 and 1980: an economic upswing striking in relation to the previous decades, a completely new dynamism but also confusion in politics and society, a political polarization that held the country in an increasingly powerful stranglehold, and finally a securely assigned place and rank for Turkey in the power structure of the Cold War.

1. New expectations, dashed hopes (1950–1960)

Why the leadership around İsmet İnönü decided upon a domestic political opening leading to a multiparty system is not obvious. Did İnönü—in the less probable scenario—push back his goal of political liberalization because of the threats the Second World War had brought with it, and could only pursue this agenda at war's end? Or did the government find itself ready for an opening in order to take the pervasive discontent in the land by the horns and to conform itself to the democratic political culture promoted by Western nations?[1] In any case, the government pivoted to a line of domestic liberalization very quickly after war's end. The Kemalist elite must have in any case conceived— proceeding from their own self-understanding—of a full-fledged democracy as a badge of Western modernity. With the securing of the country through foreign policy, there was no more reason, or perhaps pretext, to delay this project. In economic terms, there was also the wish, very much in the foreground more than twenty years after the founding of the Republic, for Turks not just to enjoy the advantages of an independent nation-state, but to be able to lead a palpably better everyday life. Nothing stood in the way any longer.

The economist Jean Fourastié coined the term *les trente glorieuses* for the period of the economic boom from the end of the war into the early 1970s. While gross domestic product had grown an average of two percent a year in Western Europe in the first half of the twentieth century, in 1950–1973, it grew at "a breathtaking 5 per cent."[2] Resting on its integration into institutions of the Western economic order, like the system of fixed currency exchange rates which existed into the 1970s, Turkey took part in this development, albeit beginning from an exceptionally meager basis. The two major economic downturns, one each at the end of the 1950s and 1960s, were due above all to their own errors and were overcome in a short time. By the end of the 1960s, Turkey had lost the character of a land predominantly

---

1   Koçak, *Türkiye'de Millî Şef Dönemi*, 2:21, 27ff., 360, 561ff., 570, 580, comes to the clear verdict that until 1946, İnönü showed no indications of efforts at liberalization.
2   Patel, *Projekt Europa*, 110.

shaped by agriculture, and by 1973, industry had overtaken agriculture in its contribution to the gross national product. From the 1950s on, people in Turkey could lead a constantly, appreciably improving life. Between 1947 and 1990, the country's per-capita income tripled.[3] This upswing was that much easier for Turkey because, since 1952, its membership in NATO had given the country foreign policy security and a reliable economic environment.

Acceptance by NATO

As protection from the new hegemonic Soviet power, Turkey leaned on the other hegemonic power, likewise created by the Second World War, the United States of America. Already during the late war years, Turkey had feared claims on its territory and sovereignty by the Soviet Union as soon as the USSR could overcome the worst demands of the war. These fears were realized in Summer 1944. On 7 July of that year, Vyacheslav Molotov, People's Commissar for Foreign Affairs, confronted the Turkish ambassador to Moscow with the price for extending the friendship Treaty of Moscow (1921). First, Turkey would have to surrender the northeastern provinces of Kars and Ardahan, which allegedly possessed an Armenian-Georgian majority (which wasn't remotely the case). Second, the Turks would have to enable the erection of Soviet bases on the Bosporus and the Straits of Gallipoli. Third, the terms of the 1936 Montreux Convention Regarding the Regime of the Straits would have to be revised and the Soviet Navy receive privileged right of passage.[4]

President İnönü might conceivably have attempted to continue the line of a neutral foreign policy without the Soviet threats and demands. However, economic and domestic political reasons contributed to the security polity-driven rapprochement with the West, among them the wish to be able to pacify the political opposition at home through economic aid provided by the US.[5] It was Turkey's good fortune that its search for a new anchor alliance coincided with the US's decision not to withdraw from Europe as had originally been planned. Then US president Harry Truman (in office

---

3   Ahmad, *Modern Turkey*, 134. Owen and Pamuk, *Middle East Economies*, 122.
4   Deringil, *Turkish Foreign Policy*, 180.
5   Kirişçi, *Turkey and the West*, 31, 33. Following Koçak, *Türkiye'de Millî Şef Dönemi*, 2:546, however, after World War Two there was no possibility of Turkey's continuing its earlier seesaw policy.

1945–1953) had already come to the conclusion in August 1946 to proceed with all available means against any possible Soviet move for control over Greece and Turkey. This determination was the foundation for the Truman Doctrine, announced on 12 March 1947, with its policy of containment of the Soviet Union.

Turkey's applications to join NATO (founded in 1949) were initially declined. The official explanation was that the geographical location of Turkey was incompatible with the notion of an Atlantic pact. The main reason was likely that Great Britain wanted to integrate Turkey into a still-to-be-created Middle Eastern alliance system under British leadership, in order to mitigate the divisive question of the stationing of British troops along the Suez Canal within the framework of collective alliance commitments.[6]

Along with Turkey's demonstrated readiness to ally and the military capability shown by its deploying twenty-three thousand troops in the Korean War,[7] it was a changed assessment of its geopolitical importance which, above all, led to Turkey's acceptance by NATO. Its strategists saw that a broader deployment of the alliance was necessary and now understood the far-forward location of Turkey in the southeast of Europe as a distinct advantage. Together with Greece, Turkey became a member of NATO on 18 February 1952. Over the following decades, the Republic understood itself as an anti-Soviet and anticommunist rampart.[8] Turkey was—with the exception of a strip of the Norwegian border in the extreme north of Europe—the only NATO member which immediately bordered the Soviet Union. From the ruined Armenian city of Ani, one of the most important sights worth visiting in Turkey, one could see Soviet guard posts on the other side of the deeply cut valley of the little Arpaçay (Akhuryan) River.

Although Turkey hasn't felt threatened by Russia since the 1990s, due to the collapse of the Soviet Union, NATO membership remained the fundamental pillar of Turkish security doctrine and foreign policy into the early 2000s. The alliance with Moscow which arose out of the particular difficulties of the war of 1919–1922 was always conceived of in terms of *Realpolitik* and did not lead to any ideological convergence. By contrast, since the late 1940s, Turkey's relationship with the US was not only characterized by very

---

6 Yeşilbursa, "Turkey's Participation in the Middle East Command," 71.
7 On Turkey's participation in the Korean War, see Solomonovich, *Korean War*.
8 Gasimov, "Turkish Wall," indicates that the anti-Soviet rhetoric in Turkish humanities departments was strongly shaped by Turkic immigrants from the Soviet sphere.

close military cooperation, but the Western hegemon became a cultural and political lodestar for Turkey—or at least its Kemalist elites.

Probation in the Multiparty System

A new era began with the farewell to one-party rule and the victory of the Democrat Party in the parliamentary elections of 1950. In ideological terms, the divisions between the DP and the Republican People's Party (CHP) were not all that large. Both were nationalistically oriented, and the DP shared Kemalism's secularist habitus. Thus, the Republic's third president—after Atatürk and İnönü—Celal Bayar, the DP politician who served in office until 1960, was a fervent admirer of Atatürk.[9] Over the course of the 1950s, however, due to the experiences of mutual slights and insults, the differences between the two parties increasingly deepened.[10] The intertwining effects of ideological conflicts and hostile rhetoric which took on a life of its own led to a deepening crisis in the Turkish political system.

The new government installed by the Democrat Party proved resolute in economic policy. Agriculture and the private sector would have more support, according to its plan. The reputation of the DP in the early 1950s rested on the successes of its economic policy, which they were admittedly able to base on previously introduced reforms. The political liberalization of the late 1940s had been accompanied by a reorientation in economic policy. In 1947, the government decided to put aside the Five-Year Plan and base itself more on the initiative of private capital and the development of agriculture. In the years 1947–1953, agricultural productivity doubled, thanks above all to the expansion of agricultural lands by 55%. The Land Distribution Law passed in 1946 provided legal grounds for the government's forced break up of large landholdings and even those of small estates in areas near cities, but in the end, only government-owned land was distributed and fields previously used communally were given to farmers with small landholdings. In addition, the DP utilized the funds of the Marshall Plan, which opened to Turkey in 1947, in order to import tens of thousands of tractors. Because three-fourths of the

---

9 Dawletschin-Linder, *Diener seines Staates*, 85, 138, 150, 156.
10 Alper, *Jakobenlerden Devrimcilere*, 33n43, indicates that the Kemalist camp first developed the terminology of Kemalism (*Kemalizm*) and Atatürkism (*Atatürkçülük*) for use in the confrontation with the DP and its successor parties in the 1960s.

population was still employed in agriculture, the expansion of production achieved meant a visible economic boom for the entire population.[11]

Though conspicuously successful at first, this economic policy bogged down as early as 1953. In addition to cool summers and crop failures, deeper reasons were present: Prime Minister Adnan Menderes, in office 1950–1960, seemed to have a profound disinclination towards any sort of economic planning. The DP government hardly carried out the goal of transferring the state's economic empire, built up in the first decades of the Republic, into private hands. Its interventions in the economy had little stamina. In agricultural policy, the government resorted to issuing credit and artificially propping up prices. State enterprises had to sell their wares far below value. New state-owned factories produced heedless of the market. Thus, for example, 1960's sugar production achieved a surplus of 54% above the market's demand. Poor management and politically motivated interventions were typical of state enterprises. Policy simultaneously too ambitious and too focused on short-term success, disinclination towards sustained planning, as well as politically targeted investment decisions, led to deficits and rising governmental debt. At the same time, state policy proved incapable of countering unjust developments. In 1955, employees who earned 29% of the country's taxable income paid 40% of its taxes, while large landholders who earned 24% of the income only had to contribute 2% of the tax burden.[12] Moreover, what would become considerably more dangerous for the DP-led government was that government officials and professional military officers had to accept an economic comedown.

The Democrat Party increasingly broke with the CHP and its ideological pet projects over the 1950s to gain popularity—but also out of conviction. The DP government passed the Law on Crimes Committed Against Atatürk (Atatürk Aleyhine İşlenen Suçlar Hakkında Kanun), colloquially the Atatürk Protection Law (Atatürk'ü Koruma Kanunu) which criminalized every form of denigration of the founder of the state. Simultaneously, however, the People's Houses and Village Institutes were closed as instruments of promotions of Kemalism, in 1951 and 1954 respectively. The DP government also claimed to abandon the hard line against Islamic symbols and institutions which had been in place since the 1920s. They lifted the 1936 ban on the call to prayer in Arabic as early as June 1950 (with, it should be noted, the votes of the CHP representatives, who did not want to set themselves

---

11   Owen and Pamuk, *Middle East Economies*, 106ff.
12   Hale, *Modern Turkey*, 88–95, 103. Zürcher, *Turkey*, 225–229.

in opposition to the populace). The following month, religious broadcasts and Koran recitation were permitted on the radio. In 1952, the parliament rescinded the 1945 version of the Constitution which had been linguistically sanitized (into *Öz Türkçe*, that is "Pure Turkish") and voted for the return of the original Constitutional text of 1924.[13] In response to the sharp criticism which the opposition CHP repeatedly directed at the government, the DP increasingly countered with religiously tinged arguments and attempted to discredit the CHP as a party of "infidels" and "crusaders" (*ehlisalip*).[14]

What was new about the Democrat Party was its common touch. Its politicians, above all President Celal Bayar and Prime Minister Adnan Menderes, wanted to—and could—carry the people along with them at their appearances. The DP thus proved itself to be "the first example of a populist government in twentieth-century Turkey."[15] It unceasingly emphasized that it represented the "national will" (*milli irade*) and that the opposition, if it wished to be constructive, had to back the transformation of the country propelled by the DP.[16] The DP government saw itself as continually justified in its conception of politics by its repeated election victories in 1954 and 1957. Turkish election legislation had always favored the strongest party of the moment. With a clear share of more than 40% of the vote, a party does not as a rule require a coalition partner. In 1950, the DP received 416 of 487 seats in the National Assembly with 55.2% of the vote. In 1954, the DP got 503 of 541 seats with 58.4% of the vote, the largest share of the vote ever received by a party in the history of the Republic. In 1957, however, it fell to 48.6%, though without endangering its status as the sole governing party (with 414 of 610 seats in the National Assembly). Over the course of the 1950s, these election results and, above all, their majorities in parliament, led to a "majoritarian syndrome" in the DP. Due to their overwhelming superiority in the National Assembly and the decisive popular will allegedly expressed therein, any opposition appeared to the DP as a deliberate obstruction of their policies.

At the same time, the DP government was inclined to interpret the international environment erroneously. In Summer 1958, the government received a 359-million-dollar stabilization package, the greater part of which

---

13 Hale, *Modern Turkey*, 100ff. Ahmad, *Turkish Experiment*, 365. Dawletschin-Linder, *Diener seines Staates*, 170.
14 Çolak, *Karaoğlan*, 99.
15 Owen and Pamuk, *Middle East Economies*, 110.
16 Zürcher, *Turkey*, 222. Özbudun, *Constitutional System of Turkey*, 8, points out that the concept of a "national will," which incorporates the idea of majority rule in definitive fashion, had already shaped the Constitution of 1924.

was contributed by the United States. It was intended to realign Turkish economic policy, but Prime Minister Menderes saw his assumption that the high strategic value of Turkey for the West would guarantee permanent foreign support—falsely—confirmed by it.[17]

The grounds for the ever more visible alienation between the DP government and the Kemalist elite in the upper bureaucracy, justice system, universities, and the military over the course of the 1950s were manifold: the DP's economic policies which in their breathlessness led to an increasing pressure on the state, the majoritarian syndrome increasingly cultivated by the DP, and the DP's increasingly markedly anti-Kemalist rhetoric. The opposition CHP did its part by decrying the government's inadequacies in absolutes. The political climate of the late 1950s was characterized by numerous public demonstrations and a growing tenor of embitterment. In contrast to the situation to come in the 1960s or even the 1970s, the stability of the state and society were not threatened in any way. Nevertheless, in May 1960 a group of officers committed a coup against the existing government.

The Coup of 1960

The coup of 27 May 1960 went according to plan and met no resistance. Within four hours in the early morning, strategic locations in Ankara and around the country were occupied; the president, the prime minister, the entire cabinet, and all the members of the National Assembly were arrested. It was not difficult for the Turkish elite to commit to silent support of the coup, because they had no sympathy for the Democrat Party in any case. For them, the policies—and above all the polemics—of the Democrat Party had become too unsettling and the goals of the military seemed of a thoroughly noble nature. In their communique read on early morning radio, the junta announced that they had taken power "for the purpose of extricating the parties from the irreconcilable situation into which they have fallen." and that the coup was "not directed against any person or class."[18]

Its easy success concealed the fact that the coup had not been well prepared and breached the hierarchies of the military. The circle of those with knowledge of the coup was also so large that it is amazing that the government did not learn of it beforehand. General Cemal Gürsel (1895–1966), commander

---

17   Gunn, "1960 Coup," 126.
18   Weiker, *Turkish Revolution*, 20ff.

of the land forces, whom the putschists had elevated as their secret leader, was unexpectedly moved into retirement only a few weeks before the coup and therefore could not participate actively in it. In addition, Gürsel did not know most of the officers involved. The politically inexperienced officers only succeeded in drawing up a list of thirty-eight officers who would compose the Committee of National Unity (Milli Birlik Komitesi) under the leadership of General Gürsel three weeks after the coup itself. In addition, disagreement about what was supposed to happen after the coup reigned among the putschists. Alparslan Türkeş, who had read the junta's first announcement on the early morning of 27 May 1960, made a case for long-term military rule in the form of a modernizing dictatorship. However, moderates, who advocated an expeditious return of power to the civilian authorities, prevailed—despite disagreements among themselves. On 13 November 1960, fourteen hawks, including Türkeş, were expelled from the committee.[19] In addition, over five thousand officers and almost all admirals and generals were given mandatory retirement in August 1960. This measure ended the top-heaviness in the Turkish military hierarchy and was supported by the other NATO countries as a step towards conforming with the standards of the alliance.[20]

The first signs of a politicization of the army, with the formation of various factions, had become visible under the political liberalization of the late 1940s. We have already seen that the army's first plans for intervention came to be after the electoral victory of the Democrat Party in 1950. The idea of a coup arose within the military as a consequence of the previously discussed domestic political developments and the economic misery of government officials and officers. While attending NATO training abroad, particularly in the United States, Turkish officers saw how behind Turkey was and returned home frustrated. When, in 1957, a conspiracy of nine officers came to light, President Bayar wanted to pursue a thorough inquiry, but Menderes flinched, likely because of his profound uncertainty as to how the Kemalist-dominated organs of state would react. An immediate impetus for the May 1960 coup may have been that only a few weeks before, on 18 April 1960, the DP majority in parliament resolved to investigate the activities of the CHP opposition. The CHP and the military must have feared that such an inquiry might uncover their close connections.[21]

---

19 Alkan, "Önsöz," x.
20 Dawletschin-Linder, *Diener seines Staates*, 238ff. Weiker, *Turkish Revolution*, 53. Hale, *Turkish Politics and the Military*, 104, 121–125.
21 Dawletschin-Linder, *Diener seines Staates*, 198–200. Ahmed, *Turkish Experiment*, 156. Zürcher, *Turkey*, 240.

In the first three years after the coup of 27 May 1960, the hierarchy of the Turkish military teetered dangerously. Two internal putsch attempts by younger officers, on 22 February 1962 and 20–21 May 1963, were averted. The aftermath of the coup of 1960 shows that Turkey was not immune to taking the path of Arab states like Syria or Iraq which were plagued by a rapid sequence of putsches in the 1950s and 1960s. The ambitions of the military in Turkey and in the Arab states were precisely the same: as torchbearers of progress and modernization, they felt they had to, and were thereby permitted to, force their countries forward.[22]

On 14 October 1960, judicial proceedings were opened against five hundred and ninety defendants, among them President Celal Bayar, Prime Minister Adnan Menderes, Speaker of the Grand National Assembly Refik Koraltan, the entire cabinet, and with a single exception, all the parliamentary representatives of the Democrat Party. The gravamen of the political prosecution referred to Article 146 of the Turkish Criminal Code of 1926 which punished forcible attempts to alter the Constitution with the death penalty. In order to be sure, as many additional charges as possible were dragged in. Some of them bordered on the ridiculous due to their pettiness: Bayar and the former agriculture minister were charged of, among other things, coercing a zoo to buy a dog which Bayar had received from the shah of Afghanistan in his capacity as president.

The Supreme Council of Justice (Yüksek Adalet Divanı) specifically convoked for the purpose sat on Yassıada, an island in the Sea of Marmara off İstanbul converted to a prison and trial venue. It issued its verdicts on 15 September 1961. Bayar, Menderes, Foreign Minister Fatin Rüştü Zorlu (1910–1961), and Finance Minister Hasan Polatkan (1915–1961) were unanimously sentenced to death. In the case of eleven further death sentences, the verdicts were arrived at by mere majority decisions. The Committee for National Unity, which had the right to adjudge death sentences according to the provisional constitutional order, had previously decided to enforce only unanimous death sentences. Zorlu and Polatkan were executed on 16 September 1961, and Menderes a day later. Bayar's death sentence was commuted to a life sentence on the grounds of age (he was seventy-seven years old at the time).

---

22 Picard, "Arab Military," 190. An overview of the state of scholarship on the role of the military in the Arab world of the 1950s and 1960s can be found in Owen, "Role of the Army."

In hindsight it is clear that the military regime made a major mistake in approving the death sentences.[23] Not only was it a disastrous decision to make martyrs of three leading politicians of the DP government, but the Turkish military had placed itself on a slippery slope. In a telegram to the State Department one day after the coup, the US ambassador aired his concern that the military "had opened Pandora's box.... I felt in [the] future [the] military would find it exceedingly difficult not to become involved [in] any divisive political controversy that might involve [the] Turk[ish] people."[24] The ambassador would be proved right.

2. The New Complexity

Until 1960, Turkey's evolution appears clear. After the flight of the leading members of the Young Turk committee in November 1918, a group rose to the top which had emerged from the Young Turk movement during the War of Independence but was nevertheless new. This Young Turk–minded elite held power directly until 1950, first under the leadership of Mustafa Kemal Ataürk until 1938 and thereafter under his successor İsmet İnönü. In the 1950s, however, the Kemalist-inclined Republican People's Party went into opposition and the Democrat Party moved into government. The coup of 1960 restored the old order; the power of the Kemalist bureaucratic-intellectual-judicial-military complex was unbroken.

Let us imagine that Turkey had suddenly been swallowed up by the earth on 28 May 1960, the day after the coup. In that case, the above interpretation would have staying power. In the 1960s, however, a more complex and confusing picture gradually emerged. Turkey pluralized and became much more baffling. Internal migration and urbanization unleashed their full force. The parties splintered. Domestic ideological camp-building and an international environment which was becoming more complicated influenced each other and made political leadership and negotiation increasingly vexed. In the 1970s, the situation deteriorated. The state-driven import-substitution policy hit a dead end, the ideological camp-building produced a powerful political polarization which would almost bring about a civil war, and the parliamentary system almost collapsed under these burdens.

---

23 Weiker, *Turkish Revolution*, 31. Ahmad, *Turkish Experiment*, 164. Dawletschin-Linder, *Diener seines Staates*, 247–258. Hale, *Turkish Politics and the Military*, 144.
24 Ambassador Fletcher Warren in a telegram to the Department of State, 28 May 1960, in *Foreign Relations of the United States 1958–1960*, vol. 10, part 2, 845–848. Quoted in Gunn, "1960 Coup," 120.

Gecekondus and Guest Workers: Rural Flight and Labor Migration

Turkey has been lastingly shaped by the migration from the land into the city and the concomitant urbanization which had already begun in the late 1940s. In the 1950s, three quarters of the population still lived on the land; in 2005, it was only a third. In the decades after the Second World War, Turkey became a country in which millions had the experience of remoteness from their rural homelands and the strangeness of a new, urban environment. *Gurbetçilik*, "finding oneself in a strange land," originally just stood for forms of seasonal migration. Now it increasingly connoted permanent resettlement in the big cities of Western Anatolia and ultimately also those of Western Europe.

Living conditions in the Anatolian countryside were hard. Agrarian acreage could not be expanded much further with the agricultural technology available in the villages. Despite Anatolia's low population density, this bottleneck produced overpopulation and—due to the rules governing inheritance—fragmentation of arable land into inordinately small parcels. The mechanization of agriculture made agrarian production more efficient but simultaneously undermined the livelihoods of over a million smaller farmers who could not keep up with the new developments. They were pushed out of their trade by the over thirty thousand tractors which were introduced between 1946 and the end of the 1950s.

The allure of the city stood in contrast to the forbidding conditions in the country. In the early 1970s, the salary of a casual laborer in the city was double the average income of a rural family.[25] Migrants from the country were used to heavy physical labor and, at least initially, were prepared to take on jobs with little prestige and income. Consequently, they were highly welcome workers, especially in smaller and informal businesses which could use unskilled labor (like construction or simple processing trades).

The population newly drawn into the cities mostly found their new homes in so-called *gecekondu*s, literally housing "built overnight." Gecekondus (Turkish *gecekondular*) are residential structures of all sorts erected without regard to property ownership or construction codes. Beginning in the 1950s, gecekondus shaped the appearance of Turkish big cities. At the beginning of the 1960s, 59.22% of the population of Ankara lived in such structures, 45% in İstanbul, 44.95% in Adana, and 33.42% in İzmir.[26]

---

25 Pamuk, "Economic Change," 281. Hütteroth, *Türkei*, 469.
26 Data from İmar ve İskan Bakanlığı (Ministry of Public Works and Housing), *13 Büyük Şehirde Gecekondu* (Ankara: İmar ve İskan Bakanlığı, 1965), 5–6. Quoted in Karpat,

Gecekondus are not slums (which exist in Turkey, mostly in crumbling old neighborhoods) but rather a form of squatting. Settlement proceeded purposefully: gecekondu residents were ambitious and evinced a high rate of employment—they had come to the city looking for work, after all. Gecekondu occupants and those left behind in the villages should therefore not be regarded as victims of the profound social and economic upheavals in Turkey after the Second World War. Migrants often had property in their villages of origin and came into the cities with capital.[27] In addition, they could rely on networks of solidarity, like the duty for mutual aid between those from the same region (*hemşehrilik*). Meanwhile, the population remaining in villages with strong outmigration could invest in agricultural activity and develop new products thanks to the newly freed-up land and remittances streaming back into the village.[28]

The gecekondu residents' land grabs must also be regarded as a kind of investment, because as a rule they could expect the state lands they alienated to be legalized as private property and real-estate prices to rise. The Gecekondu Law of 1966 (Gecekondu Kanunu) established two categories: those that could be improved and those that should be torn down. With assignment to the former class, gecekondus were secured, even if their connection to municipal infrastructure, like water, electricity, and local public transportation could take years. Initially, therefore, gecekondu residents had little use for political agitation, as they were concerned largely with pressing home their immediate interests, specifically legalizing the property they lived on by getting it entered in a land register (*tapu*).[29]

The large majority of gecekondu inhabitants retrospectively judged their decision to move from the village to the city to have been correct. Women most of all recalled the arduous life in the village, because they were responsible for the bulk of the work in the fields and all of the housekeeping, and

---

Gecekondu, 11. In the following years, the numbers did not rise significantly. At the end of the 1970s, about two-thirds of the population of Ankara lived in gecekondus, and in İstanbul and Adana about 45%. Hale, *Modern Turkey*, 223.

27   Karpat, *Gecekondu*, 26, 28, 58, 87, 134. Owen and Pamuk, *Middle East Economies*, 117. The first slums in the Arab world appeared during the Great Depression, called then as now *'ašwā'iyāt*, "contingencies." Schulze, *Geschichte der islamischen Welt*, 148. The inhabitants of the Arab "contingencies" did not experience the same story of upward mobility as did those of the gecekondus.

28   Karpat, *Gecekondu*, 183. Over the years, these solidarity networks increasingly changed into utilitarian forms of clientelism. Erman, *Urban or Rural*, 557.

29   Hale, *Modern Turkey*, 224. Wedel, "Gecekondu-Viertel," 26. For examples of clearly utilitarian voting behavior among gecekondu residents, see Karpat, *Gecekondu*, 211–225.

because life in a gecekondu possessed less social pressure than life in a village. The gecekondu residents were fundamentally optimistically inclined and believed that their children would advance further than had been possible for them themselves under the prevailing circumstances. They could only imagine a return to the village during their active life in the most extreme circumstances.[30]

The middle and upper classes who had been living in the cities for a longer time at that point had a completely different perspective. They originally assumed that the initial problems of internal migration—like the transformation of the cityscape by a rurally shaped population and the growing number of gecekondus—had to be borne, but that the newcomers would acclimate themselves to the existing ways of city life. When they developed their own, new methods of dealing with the big city, this "failure" to assimilate to established customs was ascribed to their cultural underdevelopment. The gulf between those long-established in the city and those who'd recently arrived persistently shaped the political landscape over the coming decades, fed by a stiff lack of sympathy on both sides.

Labor migration to Europe may be regarded as a variant of the internal migration described above. In both cases, it was driven by a desire to improve one's life prospects in the big city. Expectations of the industrial centers of Western Europe were the same as those of the big cities of Western Turkey. In Western Europe, the odds of achieving a high income were certainly even greater relative to the Turkish countryside—and the loss of an accustomed world even more traumatic.

At the end of 1950s, when indigenous labor became scarce given the continuing economic boom, the industrialized nations of Western Europe began to recruit employees from Mediterranean countries like Italy, Portugal, Spain, Turkey, and Yugoslavia. For the Federal Republic of Germany, an additional circumstance—the construction of the Berlin Wall beginning in August 1961—contributed in that the formerly constant flow of workers from the German Democratic Republic dried up. The recruitments were originally intended to cushion a temporarily elevated need. However, because the migrants took on jobs which the natives no longer wanted to do, they quickly appeared indispensable. The often makeshift accommodations and less-than-friendly reception given to the "guest workers" were often rationalized in terms of the foreign workers' ability to gain experience and take their new

---

30   Ibid., 35, 44ff., 106ff., 140ff., 156–158, 161ff., 173ff.

skills back to their homeland. In fact, on their return, if indeed they went back at all, the former guest workers were generally not capable of transmitting new skills, nor did they want to put their hard-won capital into insecure investments in their home country.[31]

In 1961, there were 6,700 Turks in the Federal Republic of Germany, comprising a hundredth of all foreigners. By 1987, 1,453,700 Turkish citizens lived in Germany, over a third (34.3%) of all foreigners.[32] From then on, the Turkish-descended population in Germany grew tenaciously, but at the same time their share of the total foreign population began to sink. In 2018, people from Turkey remained the largest single community of immigrants but their share lagged at 13.3%.[33]

The Turkish labor migration to West Germany reached its zenith in the years 1968–1973, ending abruptly with the ban on recruitment in 1973. The share of women among labor migrants was strikingly high. In 1975, only 11.6% of women in Turkey were employed, except in agriculture, where their share was very much higher. By contrast, in 1974, women comprised 25.9% of the labor migrants.[34]

As early as the mid-1970s, the German government attempted to encourage foreign workers to return to their homelands.[35] Simultaneously, Turkish immigrants began to send for their families to move to Germany, an understandable decision given the then difficult political and economic circumstances in Turkey. In addition, the number of people from Turkey applying for political asylum climbed from 809 (7.3% of all applications) in 1976 to 57,913 (53.7% of all applications) in 1980. On 18 November 1983, the government of Helmut Kohl passed the Law on Encouraging Foreigners' Willingness to Return (Gesetz zur Förderung der Rückkehrbereitschaft von Ausländern), which was directed at labor migrants (not only from Turkey). It offered a one-time cash payment (DM 10,500 for parents and 1,500 Deutsche marks per child) to those willing to return to their homelands.

---

31   Hoerder, *Cultures in Contact*, 520.
32   Abadan-Unat, *Turks in Europe*, 8.
33   Out of a population of 20.8 million with immigrant background in private households by country of birth, or by country of birth of at least one parent, in 2018. Bundesministerium des Inneren (Interior Ministry of the Federal Republic of Germany), *Migrationsbericht 2018*, 204.
34   According to Abadan-Unat, *Turks in Europe*, 89ff., the readiness of Turkish women to become labor migrants in Europe was likely grounded in the expectation that women alone would be granted family reunification more readily.
35   Some of the relevant regulations proved counterproductive. When, in 1975, in order to reduce social costs, the German government introduced lower allowances for children living abroad, it had the unintended effect that parents increasingly brought their children to Germany.

Turkish workers could also have their contributions to statutory pension insurance, akin to US Social Security, paid out. A quarter million people from Turkey were thus moved to leave the Federal Republic of Germany in 1984.[36]

The early '80s exodus did not interrupt the fundamental demographic trend that the number of people of Turkish descent in Germany was continually growing. Even in the 1980s, German policy had to shelve the false assumption of its policy—and its society—that the presence of Turkish labor migrants and their families in Germany was a passing phenomenon. The majority of them no longer aspired to go "back" to their homeland. The discussion turned to questions like primary education, ghettoization, as well as rights of residence and citizenship. Nevertheless, the experience of a more or less conscious exclusion would still shape the second and third generations of Turks living in Germany.[37] The xenophobic mood in Germany found its tragic zenith in the racist riots in August 1992 in Rostock-Lichtenhagen directed at Vietnamese contract workers and the murders of Turkish families by arson in Mölln on 23 November 1992 and in Solingen on 29 May 1993. Even those who are ready to regard migration from the perspective of the self-interest of the receiving state come to a rather uncomplimentary judgment of how German society and politics handled labor migrants.[38]

The Turkish labor migration into Europe of the 1960s has remained an exceptional phenomenon in the history of the Turkish Republic. By the 2000s at the latest, Turkey had become a receiving or transit country for immigration. Its immigration system diverges considerably from that of most European countries. In Europe, the system is hard on the borders but soft in the interior; in Turkey, it's the other way around. Thanks to an extremely liberal visa regime in the last few decades, travel to Turkey is mostly unproblematic. Gaining a legal residence permit, on the other hand, is almost impossible. Turkey only joined the Geneva Convention on Refugees of 1951 years later, in 1961, and, even then, under the caveat that Turkey would only recognize refugees from the territory of the Council of Europe. Immigration policy in Turkey has always remained limited to the reception of Turks and Muslims and particularly in the stricter sense to those who are both Turks and Muslims.[39]

---

36 Abadan-Unat, *Turks in Europe*, 21ff.
37 See, as merely one example, Ateş, *Große Reise ins Feuer*, 249.
38 Collier, *Exodus*, 70, states that in comparison to Europe, already little receptive, Germany showed a particularly low capacity for absorbing migration. Miller, *Strangers in Our Midst*, 96, 99, 129, criticizes Germany and Switzerland explicitly for denying long-resident labor migrants citizenship, a situation that made them economically vulnerable and subjected them to social exclusion.
39 Parla, *Precarious Hope*, 14–17.

Foreign Policy Options: CENTO, the Balkan Pact, and Other Alliances

In its first decade of NATO membership, Turkey saw itself in complete agreement with the political positions of the United States. However, the withdrawal of the (nuclear-capable) Jupiter missiles from Turkey agreed upon with the Soviet Union as part of the resolution of the Cuban Missile Crisis of 1962 led to profound discontent and sowed seeds of mistrust. The relationship was additionally burdened by a letter of US president Lyndon B. Johnson (in office 1963–1969) of 5 June 1964 in which he dictated two terms relative to the situation in Cyprus which was headed towards a crisis. First, in any military intervention, Turkey (which was seriously weighing one at that time) would not be permitted to use military materiel delivered by the US. Second, Turkey could not rely on NATO assistance if the Soviet Union were to somehow move militarily against a Turkish intervention in Cyprus.[40] Turkey's relations with the US and other NATO members—which had already cooled principally due to the Cyprus question—reached their nadir with Turkey's 1974 intervention in Cyprus. Beginning in the 1960s, Turkish public opinion was characterized by a pronounced anti-Americanism, combined with anti-colonialist motifs.[41] In a search for other possible anchorages and affiliations, but also due to the increasing wealth of the crude-oil producing states in the Middle East, in the 1960s Turkey rediscovered its membership in the Islamic world which it had previously been loath to acknowledge.

In the first years after Turkey's acceptance into NATO, Great Britain and the US had the expectation that Turkey would also serve as a cornerstone of a Western-allied Middle Eastern alliance system. On 24 February 1955, Iraq and Turkey concluded a cooperation and mutual-assistance treaty in Baghdad. This Baghdad Pact was joined by Great Britain, Pakistan, and Iran in the same year. The US officially remained an observer. When Iraq lost its pro-Western government in a coup in 1958 and left the alliance, a new name had to be found. The Baghdad Pact became the Central Treaty Organization (CENTO), now with the US as a full member. The end of the pact finally came, however, when a further founding member, Iran, resigned its membership after its revolution of 1978–1979. The organization never even approached its original goal of becoming a NATO of the Middle East.

---

40 Kirişci, *Turkey and the West*, 37. Harris, "Turkey and the United States," 59.
41 Ataöv, *N. A. T. O.*, 154–170, speaks of an American "cultural imperialism" and "neo-colonialism" in Turkey.

The Baghdad or CENTO Pact may have had little substance, but in comparison, the 1954 Balkan Pact between Greece, Turkey, and Yugoslavia was a mayfly. Signed in Bled (in today's Slovenia) on 9 August 1954, it was aimed in general against feared Soviet attempts at expansion and in particular against Bulgaria, which had been generously outfitted with military materiel by Moscow as a devoted ally of the USSR. The Balkan Pact agreed on reciprocal assistance in the case of an attack on one of the three members. It fell apart very quickly, however, as a quarrel between Greece and Turkey came to the fore once again. After the May 1955 trip of Nikita Khrushchëv (chairman of the Central Committee of the CPSU, 1953–1964) to Belgrade and the signing of a Yugoslav-Soviet declaration on cooperation on the basis of complete equality, Belgrade no longer saw the need for seeking support from noncommunist Balkan countries or nearby states like Turkey.[42]

While its membership in CENTO and the Balkan Pact met the expectations of its Western alliance partners, a second level of Turkish alliance construction was connected to Turkey's seeing itself as isolated in its immediate environment. Thus Israel came into the picture. For its part, Israel was seeking alliances with "peripheral" actors in the region, including the Christian minorities in the area (like Armenians or Lebanese Maronites) and non-Arab states bordering the Arab world, like Ethiopia, Iran, and Turkey. Turkey had recognized Israel on 28 March 1949, but under the impact of the Suez Crisis of 1956, in which Israel had concluded an unfortunate alliance with France and Great Britain, Turkey had downgraded its diplomatic relations with the Jewish state. With the foundation of the "United Arab Republic" by Egypt and Syria on 1 February 1958 and the (aforementioned) shift of Iraq into the pro-Soviet camp two weeks later, closer collaboration with Israel suddenly seemed desirable. A secret meeting between Israeli prime minister David Ben-Gurion (in office 1948–1954 and 1955–1963) and Prime Minister Adnan Menderes in Ankara on 29 August 1958 laid the foundation for an unofficial Turco-Israeli alliance. Apparently the framework of this cooperation even envisioned the erection of an organization which would coordinate the activities of the secret services of the three countries, the Iranian SAVAK, the Israeli Mossad, and the Turkish National Security Service (Millî Emniyet Hizmeti, renamed the National Intelligence Organization, Millî İstihbarat Teşkilâtı in 1965, and commonly referred to by its acronym, MİT).[43]

---

42   Stone, "Balkan Pact." Pirjevec, *Tito*, 299.
43   Guzansky, "Israel's Periphery Doctrine." Schonmann, "Back-Door Diplomacy," 92–94. Bengio, *Turkish-Israeli Relationship*, 42–45.

Beginning in the 1960s, Turkey increasingly subordinated its foreign policy to the smoldering Cyprus question, in which Turkey was internationally isolated. Consequently, Turkey sought the company of the Arab states and campaigned for their support for Turkey's position at the United Nations. In exchange, Turkey was prepared to limit its relations with Israel to a minimum. Ankara joined the Organization of the Islamic Congress (later the Organization for Islamic Cooperation, with its seat in Jiddah, Saudi Arabia), founded on 25 September 1969, in that same year. Its initially half-hearted participation in this pan-Islamic institution was followed by a decidedly stronger engagement with it from the middle of the 1970s.

The Cyprus Question

The Cyprus conflict centers around the question of how the relationship between the Greek Cypriot and Turkish Cypriot populations can be regulated conclusively and amicably and how, in this context, the consequences of their effective division into a Turkish Cypriot northern territory and a Greek Cypriot southern territory could be overcome. With its 3,572 square miles and around seven hundred fifty thousand inhabitants, Cyprus may seem territorially and demographically rather unimportant. The island, however, still has geostrategic significance, and the partition of 1974 made Cyprus an international problem that has been waiting in vain for decades for a solution.[44] To a certain degree, the Cyprus conflict is self-contained and thus appears manageable, but it seems to touch on every dispute that arises in the region, like for example the discovery of large deposits of natural gas in the eastern Mediterranean, leading to a confrontation between Turkey and EU member Cyprus.[45] Moreover, this conflict shows in impressive fashion a fundamental Turkish foreign policy disposition, the willingness to see themselves as on their own.[46]

---

44 The standard works on the history of Cyprus are Mallinson, *Cyprus*, and Richter, *Geschichte der Insel Zypern*.
45 On the political and economic significance of the natural gas deposits in the Eastern Mediterranean, see International Crisis Group, *Aphrodite's Gift*, and Roberts, "Hydrocarbon Resources."
46 Under the influence of the Turkish intervention on Cyprus in 1974 and the consequent Western embargo, the Nationalist Movement Party (Milliyetçi Hareket Partisi, MHP) promulgated the slogan, "The Turk has no friend but the Turk" (Türk'ün Türk'ten

Over the centuries after the Ottomans conquered Cyprus in 1571, a Muslim Turkish community of approximately a fifth of the total population came to be, primarily through emigration from Anatolia. In 1878, Great Britain took control of the island which it had been awarded as a protectorate under formal Ottoman sovereignty (suzerainty) as compensation for its assistance against Russian demands and claims. In 1914, at the beginning of the First World War, Great Britain annexed Cyprus. Finally, in 1925, the island achieved the status of British crown colony. When, in the process of decolonization in the 1950s, Great Britain wanted to surrender direct control over Cyprus, the questions of the division of power between Greek and Turkish Cypriots and the island's relationship to the "motherlands" of Greece and Turkey arose.

Since the creation of an independent state of Greece in 1830, its politicians and intellectuals had advocated the goal of an "union" (*enōsis*) of all areas of Greek settlement, including Cyprus. In 1950, the Greek Orthodox Church of Cyprus, which preached the goal of "union and nothing but union" (Enōsis kai mónon enōsis), conducted a referendum in which 96% of Greek Cypriots opted for unification with Greece. The leading figure representing this Greek Cypriot desire was Michael Christodoulou Mouskos (1919–1977) who served as Makarios III, Archbishop of Cyprus, from 1950 until his death. Turkish Cypriots, however had no desire to live as a minority in a Greater Greece and gravitated ever more closely to Ankara. Beginning in the mid-1950s, they countered the Greek rhetoric of enōsis with the Turkish concept of "partition" (*taksim*).

On both sides, the Cyprus question caused foreign and domestic policy to become increasingly intertwined. From the perspective of Greeks living in İstanbul, they were being squeezed in a vice; but because the community had lost its leadership class over the decades, the pressure on them "just cracked the nutshell, but inside it was hollow."[47] On 6 September 1955, Turkish agents allegedly set off a bomb on the grounds of the Turkish consulate general in Saloniki, right next to Atatürk's birthplace.[48] Parts of the Turkish government

---

başka dostu yoktur). Bora and Can, *Devlet, Ocak, Dergâh*, 49. The Turkish impression that the West was solely supporting the Greek position, among other reasons, led to a tentative rapprochement between Turkey and the USSR beginning in 1964. Karpat, "Turkish-Soviet Relations," 101–105. For the Greek impression, by contrast, that the US ultimately stood on the Turks' side with regard to the Cyprus question, see Clogg, *History of Greece*, 5, 170.

47 Asderis, *Tor zur Glückseligkeit*, 290.
48 In 1969, the KGB *rezidentura* in Athens suggested doing the exact same thing to subvert Greek-Turkish relations, setting it up so the bomber would look like a disgruntled ethnic Greek from Turkey. Moscow Center told them to wait. For a brief discussion of Operation

and military then orchestrated riots against the Greek population of İstanbul, using the fury of the Turkish population over the alleged attack.[49]

Conversations between Great Britain, Greece, and Turkey led to the Treaties of London in February 1959, which laid the foundations for an independent state of Cyprus beginning in 1960. The three guarantor powers pledged to defend the bi-ethnic unity of the Republic of Cyprus. They retained the right to military intervention if the order founded by the treaties were to be endangered. In addition, Great Britain secured two large exclaves on the south coast (Akrotiri west of Limassol and Dhekelia east of Larnaka) which still host military bases today.

While the Turkish Cypriot side was largely in favor of the new governmental construct, the Greek Cypriot side, which had signed the treaties only under pressure from Athens, seemed dissatisfied. This discontent led very quickly to disputes over the implementation of the proportionality regulations which clearly favored the Turkish Cypriots with their share of less than a fifth of the population (the regulations were set at 70:30 for most things, but 60:40 for the military).[50] Mutual blockades, conflicts, and expulsions in 1963–1964 led to the young republic's collapse. The Turkish Cypriots abandoned the common institutions of government and administration and built up parallel administrations in Turkish-majority areas. On 4 March 1964, the U.N. Security Council established the "United Nations Force in Cyprus" (UNFICYP) with Resolution 186 and additionally confirmed that an internationally recognized government existed, represented by the Greek Cypriots.

On 15 July 1974, the military junta ruling Greece instigated a coup against Makarios III (president 1960–7/1974, 12/1974–1977), who barely escaped an assassination attempt and had to flee. In reply, beginning on 20 July, the Turkish military pushed forward from a bridgehead built at Kyrenia/Girne to Nikosia/Lefkoşa. Hastily called negotiations in Geneva were broken off by the Turkish side in the middle of August. In a second offensive which followed

---

Egg (Яцо), as it was called, see Andrew and Mitrokhin, *The Sword and the Shield*, 377, 394–396. (The latter three pages reproduce the memo from Athens, suggesting in detail even where the bomb should be placed, what to do with the bag it was carried in, etc.) My thanks to Bill Walsh for providing this detail.

49   On this, see, in great detail, Vryonis, *Mechanism of Catastrophe*.
50   According to Brey, "Bevölkerungsstruktur," 497, in 1960 there were 442,521 Greek Cypriots comprising 79.5% of the population and 104,350 Turkish Cypriots, with 18.8%. The slightly less than 2% of the remaining population was divided among Armenians, Maronites, and all other population groups.

immediately upon the first, the Turkish military advanced to a line extending from Morphou/Güzelyurt in the west to Famagusta/Gazimağusa in the east, occupying 37% of the territory of Cyprus. While the first Turkish military action in July could be considered understandable, the vast expansion of conquered territory in August could not be reconciled with the right of intervention reserved by the guarantor powers. The battles and expulsions of 1974 resulted in an agreement in the autumn of the same year between the Greek Cypriot and Turkish Cypriot leaderships on a population exchange which left a third of the population of Cyprus refugees. Around 160,000 Greek and 45,000 Turkish Cypriots had to leave their home villages and cities. Today, the segregation of the two groups is almost absolute. At the same time, in the following decades, Turkey systematically settled tens of thousands of Anatolians in Northern Cyprus—in the tradition of Ottoman settlement policy.

For the government in Ankara, the price of the intervention was a far-reaching foreign political isolation—which took place as a poor economic situation descended at home. A resolution of the US Congress of 5 February 1975 on a military embargo of Turkey—in response to the intervention on Cyprus—led to Turkey's decision of 26 July 1975 that the US had to cease all activities on Turkish soil. After the lifting of the embargo three and a half years later (on 26 September 1978), Turkey permitted the US to recommission its military bases in Turkey.[51]

On 13 February 1975, Rauf Denktaş (1924–2012), for decades the decisive political figure among Cypriot Turks, proclaimed the Turkish Federal State of Cyprus (Kıbrıs Türk Federe Devleti). On 15 November 1983, he declared its full independence as the Turkish Republic of Northern Cyprus (Kuzey Kıbrıs Türk Cumhuriyeti), which is to this day only recognized by Turkey, and proclaimed himself president of this state (serving in office until 2005). Today, Northern Cyprus is de facto part of the domain of the Turkish state, the clearest sign of which is the presence of thirty- to forty-thousand Turkish troops.

There were repeated international diplomatic attempts to solve the Cyprus problem. The most promising was the Annan Plan, named after the then general secretary of the UN, Kofi Annan (in office 1997–2006), which foresaw a unification of the two parts in the form of a confederation. The plan, which was put to a referendum on 24 April 2004, failed, however. While 65% of Turkish Cypriots favored it, 76% of Greek Cypriots voted against it.

---

51   Kuniholm, "Turkey and NATO," 220.

Nevertheless, a few days later, on 1 May 2004, the Greek Cypriot part of the island was admitted to the European Union. The misgivings of the Greek Cypriots, very clearly expressed in the referendum, concerned the reliability and feasibility of the agreement, which provided for the complete departure of Turkish troops only after a long period of time. Tactical reasons likely contributed as well, like the assumption that, as an EU member, (Greek) Cyprus could negotiate better terms.[52] In addition, the approximately four-fold greater per-capita income in southern Cyprus may have led Greek Cypriots to view a unification as less worthwhile.

The demand of Greek Cypriots for a common state with a right to free settlement across all Cyprus and the insistence of Turkish Cypriots on extensively autonomous structures loosely connected in a confederation confront each other, unreconciled, to this day. The negotiations over Turkish admission to the EU in the 2000s—if they had been conducted in all seriousness—would have run into the Gordian knot of the Cyprus question. The question of Turkey's admission, however, has never presented a lack of difficult-to-solve, knotty questions.

Turkey and the European Economic Community

Regarded in a larger context, the purpose of Turkish membership in the European Union was thought of as an expansion of and complement to its NATO membership. Belonging to NATO was the solid gun carriage, membership in the European political-economic alliance was supposed to be the cannon. For decades, the cannon was brought again and again into position, in the end hitting only the target of the Customs Union of 1996.

Turkey's accession negotiations reach back to the time of the European Economic Community (EEC) which grew out of the European Coal and Steel Community (ECSC) in 1957, before it became the European Community (EC) in 1993 and finally the European Union (EU) in 2009. On 31 July 1959, Turkey submitted its application for acceptance in the EEC, two weeks after Greece had done so. On 12 September 1963, Turkey signed a treaty of association which was supposed to transition to full membership in a three-stage process in conjunction with a long transitional period. In a first preparatory phase from 1964 to 1973, the EEC granted preferential tariffs and import

---

52   Ker-Lindsay, *Cyprus Problem*, 68–71.

quotas, as well as financial support. An additional protocol on the abolition of tariffs and other barriers signed in November 1970 concretized the conditions of the second phase, which was supposed to extend from 1973 to 1980 at the earliest and 1995 at the latest. After this second phase, the accession process was supposed to be set in motion.

The cooperation which emerged was in no way without friction. The Turkish side complained that the EEC granted free access to industrial goods except those, like textiles, in which Turkey was competitive. In February 1980, the Turkish foreign minister announced that Turkey would apply for full membership in the EEC by the end of the year. The step was obviously motivated by the intention to come to an agreement in principle before Greece's accession to the EEC, scheduled for 1 January 1981, or at least was guided by the interest in receiving advantageous treatment in return for Greece's acceptance.[53] The coup of 12 September 1980 pushed the possibility of accession into the distance for many years.

On the Turkish side, the accession negotiations of the 1960s and 1970s suffered from a disparity between aspiration and economic reality and from a fixation on being treated as similarly to Greece as possible.[54] On the EEC member states' side, on the other hand, the initial satisfaction with Turkey's membership application evaporated, and it became the EEC's most pressing concern "to be able to find the most elastic formula possible" to not openly rebuff Turkey while simultaneously not having to accept it.[55]

Demirel, Ecevit, and Erbakan: Cliffs in the Landscape of the Parties

The original meaning of the terms "left" and "right" refers to the seating arrangement in the French parliament after the Revolution of 1789, and the rapidly solidified division of the parliament into two camps, namely, the "left" who were of the opinion that the revolution was to be extended and

---

53   Hale, *Modern Turkey*, 245–247.
54   See Birand, *Türkiye'nin Ortak Pazarı Macerası*, 41, 70, 94, 96, 100ff., 125, for Turkey's constant self-comparison with Greece and 55, 73ff., 111ff., for the poor preparation of the Turkish side, including lacking exact knowledge over fundamental data regarding their own national economy in the earliest phase of the accession negotiations.
55   Birand, *Türkiye'nin Ortak Pazarı Macerası*, 113.

the "right" who advocated a pause or even a return to the old order.[56] This juxtaposition may be conveyed to the Turkey of the 1960s. One could say that the Kemalists advocated the furthering of the Kemalist "revolution," and the conservative, religious-minded "right" opposed it. With equal justification, one could counter that those who saw themselves as the left, the Kemalists, were actually conservatives as they wished to preserve the "achievements" of Kemalism, while those stigmatized as conservative religious were really the driving political force in the second half of the twentieth century.

The formation of a party spectrum contrasting "left" and "right" goes back to the 1960s. In that decade, political figures who would shape Turkish politics until the turn of the century established themselves simultaneously. Just as the generation born in the 1880s shaped the national movement after the First World War into the early Republican era, those who would determine the course of Turkish politics from the 1960s until the turn of the century were born in the 1920s: Süleyman Demirel (1924–2015), Bülent Ecevit (1925–2006), and Necmettin Erbakan (1926–2011). Politics seemed to affect them like a life-extending magic potion, despite their decades of grueling political confrontations. Alparslan Türkeş (1917–1997), the leading figure of Turkish right-wing nationalism and radicalism was born earlier than the others, but drank equally deeply from the elixir of lifelong political battle. Turgut Özal (1927–1993), although he belonged to the same generation, was an exception, as he only took on a leading role in Turkish politics in 1983 and died in 1993 at the age of sixty-five.

The competition between the Republican People's Party (Cumhuriyet Halk Partisi, CHP) and the Democrat Party (Demokrat Parti, DP) in the 1950s foreshadowed the later ideological-political oppositions of the Turkish party system. Beginning in the 1960s, the fundamental axis of Turkish politics was built between the poles of a left-social-democratic camp and its conservative counterpart. In the 1960s and 1970s, the main roles were played by the CHP, understanding itself increasingly as a party of the left, and the new, conservative Justice Party (Adalet Partisi, AP).

The former chief of the general staff Ragıp Gümüşpala (1897–1964) founded the Adalet Partisi in February 1961. "Its name was its program," because as a successor to the Democrat Party which had been banned following the coup of 1960, it wanted to argue for, among other things, the rehabilitation

---

56 On the extraordinarily rapid construction of a left-right polarity in the French parliament of 1789, see Laponce, *Left and Right*, 47–52. Eßbach is comprehensive in *Religionssoziologie*, 561–659 in the chapter "Ewige Rechte, Ewige Linke" (Eternal Right, Eternal Left).

of the politicians of the Demokrat Parti convicted in 1961.[57] In the late 1940s and 1950s, the word *demokrat* was understood by the uneducated phonetically as *demir kır at* (iron-gray horse), so the DP adopted a horse as its emblem. The Justice Party followed in the DP's footsteps here as well, by making the horse its symbol after a brief initial period of using the initials A and P on an open book.[58] The CHP on the other hand employed the Kemalist symbol with the Six Arrows, as shown above. In earlier decades when the number of illiterates was still very high, party emblems served primarily to denote the parties in a clearly recognizable fashion on election ballots. The tradition continues— even today, most parties in Turkey have pictorial insignia.

Hailing from humble circumstances in West Anatolian Isparta, Süleyman Demirel was general director of the state water authority from 1955 to 1960 and then active in the private sector. In 1964, after Gümüşpala's death, he won the chairmanship of the Justice Party and became the leading figure on the conservative spectrum. More than Menderes or Bayar, Demirel was a politician with whom the rural population could identify. He did not come from the upper bureaucracy or the officer corps which had dominated the country since the Tanzimat, the Ottoman reform period of the nineteenth century, but presented himself as a self-made man who maintained a secular lifestyle. The Justice Party therefore felt compelled to emphasize all the more that Demirel had made the pilgrimage to Mecca, that he had been born in a village called İslamköy (literally "Islam Village"), and that in his parents' house the Koran had been read every day. In the parliamentary elections of 1965 and 1969, Demirel led the AP to a clear majority. The government led by him in 1965–1971 was the last stable government until the military coup of 1980. Demirel returned to active political life in the 1980s, took over the office of president after the death of Özal in 1993, and held it until the year 2000. At the end of his political career, Demirel could look back upon twelve years as prime minister, seven years as president, and twenty-one years in parliament.[59]

Like the Democrat Party, the Justice Party stood for a combination of completely contradictory goals but at the same time could speak for a large number of voters. Their attempt to be close to economic elites was joined by a pronounced populism; economic liberalism accompanied social conservatism,

---

57 Dawletschin-Linder, *Diener seines Staates*, 242.
58 Öktem, *Angry Nation*, 41. Ahmad, *Turkish Experiment*, 237, 377, points out that the graphic with the two letters A and P on the pages of an open book was not so innocuous. The book could be taken to be the Koran and the two letters as the initials for *Allah* and *Peygamber* ("the Prophet" Muhammad).
59 Ahmad, *Turkish Experiment*, 235ff. Türk, *Muktedir*, 73.

Figure 6. Emblem of the Justice Party (Adalet Partisi), the leading center-right party of the 1960s and 1970s. The tradition of combining a party's acronym and logo in a visually striking image continues today. https://en.wikipedia.org/wiki/Justice_Party_(Turkey)#/media/File:Flag_of_the_Justice_Party_(Turkey).svg

which again showed plentiful points of contact with Muslim religiosity. Its differentiation from Kemalism, however, did not mean it placed the latter's foundations—nationalism, a strong role for the state, an affiliation with the West—in question.

On the other hand, Bülent Ecevit was the leading figure for the center-left from the 1970s until the turn of the century. The reorientation of the CHP as a party of the left, which had begun in the 1960s and was initially backed by İsmet İnönü, was conclusively implemented by Ecevit. Ecevit did not possess a university diploma but stood out from other politicians in his intellectuality and his public-relations acumen (among other things, he published around twenty books). Ecevit served as general secretary of the CHP beginning in 1966 but resigned this office in 1971. With his resignation, he turned against the support that İsmet İnönü had provided to the technocratic government installed by the military and initially led by Nihat Erim, because one of the foundational ideas of the leftward-moving CHP was to loosen its tight alliance with the military and upper bureaucracy.[60] At an extraordinary party

---

60 Çolak, *Karaoğlan*, 15, 132–134. Ahmad, *Turkish Experiment*, 261.

FIGURE 7. Symbol of the Party of Justice and Development (Adalet ve Kalkınma Partisi, AKP), in power since 2002. The lightbulb stands for the AKP's claim to bring light into the world and its self-image as a "white [unblemished] party" (*ak parti*). The choice of the lightbulb also stands for the party's unbroken belief in progress.
https://en.wikipedia.org/wiki/Justice_and_Development_Party_(Turkey)#/media/File:Justice_and_Development_Party_(Turkey)_logo.svg

congress on 7 May 1972, Ecevit was finally able to establish his line of a clear reorientation of the party. İnönü, who had led the CHP without interruption since the death of Atatürk in 1938, resigned as chairman of the party and even announced his resignation from the CHP in November 1972, a year before his death in December 1973. Ecevit's sympathies for the Movement of Non-Aligned States did not prevent him from simultaneously championing the national cause. He attempted to transform the successful 1974 Turkish intervention on Cyprus as well as the 1999 capture of the leader of the Kurdistan Workers Party (Partiya Karkarén Kurdistanê, PKK), Abdullah Öcalan—for both of which he was responsible as prime minister—into domestic political strength, in vain as it turned out.

The outermost right wing of the Turkish party landscape was represented for decades by Alparslan Türkeş, whom we have already encountered as one of the leading officers of the 1960 coup d'état. Türkeş was born in Nicosia on Cyprus in 1917, but left the island with his family at the age of fifteen. After the coup of 1960, he was expelled from the military as one of the hawks. Türkeş entered politics and, in 1965, took over the leadership of the right-nationalist Republican Villagers Nation Party (Cumhuriyetçi Köylü Millet Partisi, CKMP) which he renamed the Nationalist Movement Party (Milliyetçi Hareket Partisi, MHP) in 1969. Even today, it represents the right-nationalist to radical right spectrum in Turkish politics, with a potential vote of up to 15% of the electorate. The MHP distinguishes itself by an unconditional Turkish nationalism which does not just represent Pan-Turkist ambitions (that is, the idea that all the Turkic peoples of Asia should be united in a joint nation and under a single government) but also has a racist and pro-violence side. The Gray Wolves (Bozkurtlar) are the extraparliamentary arm of the MHP which is willing to use violence to advance its aims. They call themselves "idealists" (ülkücüler). The Gray Wolves were the most important sponsors of political violence in the 1970s and have in the meantime achieved a strong footing among the Turkish diaspora in Europe.

The radical left of the 1960s and 1970s was less stable, because it was churned up much more frequently by ideological disputes. The Communist Party of Turkey (Türkiye Komünist Partisi, TKP) operated for decades in the underground after being banned in the first half of the 1920s. In 1961, the Workers' Party of Turkey (Türkiye İşçi Partisi, TİP) was founded; it was led by the trade union official Mehmet Ali Aybar (1908–1995) from 1962 to 1969. That the TİP's electoral results of 3.0% in 1965 and 2.7% in 1969 are touted as "successes" shows how peripheral the radical left movement was even at its zenith in the 1960s and 1970s. The TİP, which radicalized markedly after 1969, was banned in 1971 and its leaders were sentenced to long prison terms in October 1972.[61] Since the 1970s, there has been no further significant party on the extreme left.

The first signs of a revived Kurdish political movement trace back to the 1960s. While Kurdish nationalists in the 1920s and 1930s dressed their concerns in religious garb, most Kurdish activists in the 1960s and 1970s understood themselves as socialists. The Revolutionary Eastern Culture Hearths (Devrimci Doğu Kültür Ocakları, DDKO), founded in the late 1960s and shattered under the accusation of separatism in October 1970, combined the ideas of Marxism and Kurdish nationalism.[62] The majority of Kurdish activists saw themselves as campaigners for a radical leftist activism and assumed that with a liberation into socialism, the Kurdish question

---

61   Landau, *Radical Politics*, 97–112, 131.
62   Marcus, *Blood and Belief*, 21.

would solve itself. Only after 1980 would an independent Kurdish political movement concerned primarily with Kurdish affairs become increasingly visible in Turkish politics inside and outside of parliament.

In the 1970s, a stable Islamist current established itself in the Turkish party spectrum. In fact, the Justice Party, the leading conservative party, partially drew upon the same electoral clientele as the Islamist parties, but it never relied solely on an Islamist agenda—in contrast to Necmettin Erbakan, for decades the central figure in the Islamist movement in Turkey. Erbakan came from Sinop on the Black Sea coast, studied mechanical engineering at the Technical University of İstanbul and earned a doctorate at the Rheinisch-Westfälische Technische Hochschule in Aachen (Germany) in 1953. While active in the Union of the Chambers and Commodity Exchanges of Turkey (Türkiye Odalar ve Borsalar Birliği) from 1966 on and taking over its chairmanship in 1969, he achieved national visibility by explicitly championing the demands of small businesses in Anatolia. Erbakan recognized that he had to carry his ideas into the realm of politics in order to have a prospect of realizing them. When the Justice Party did not want to run him as a candidate, Erbakan won the parliamentary seat for Konya as an independent. On 26 January 1970, he founded the National Order Party (Millî Nizam Partisi, MNP) which was banned in 1971, having been charged with the politicization of religion. Its successor party, the National Salvation Party (Millî Selamet Partisi, MSP), founded in 1972, was able to win 11.8% of the vote in the parliamentary elections of 1973. From this point on, the MSP was firmly established within the Turkish party spectrum. Like all the other parties, it was banned after the military coup of 1980, but in 1983, it reappeared—its political objectives unchanged—as the Welfare Party (Refah Partisi, RP).

The relative favor enjoyed by these various political currents in the Kemalist elite complex in administration, justice, and the military may be deduced from how often a party had to change its colors after being banned, often repeatedly, in order to be able to serve the portion of the political spectrum it represented. The Kemalist CHP and the nationalist radical right MHP show the greatest survivability (even given the break after the coup of 1980). On the other hand, it is no surprise that parties on the Islamist spectrum were banned repeatedly, as were Kurdish parties after particularly short intervals.

The history of Turkish political parties up until the turn of the century is even more furcated than this overview suggests. As early as the 1950s, there were more parties than just the DP and the CHP. It is striking, however, how strongly electoral results reflect a fundamentally conservative orientation among the Turkish electorate. Conservative, Islamist, and radical nationalist parties have received 60–65% of the vote from the 1950s to the present.[63] Even the periods of a relatively strong leftist movement and the great, if transient, popularity of the CHP under Bülent Ecevit in the 1970s do not alter this fundamental situation.

3. Polarization and Radicalization (1961–1980)

Even today, the historical interpretation of the 1960s and 1970s has not been able to escape a negative teleology. How could it, given the ever-escalating polarization and radicalization of this time period? The parliamentary party landscape was eclipsed by an extraparliamentary animosity which resulted in conditions similar to a civil war in the second half of the 1970s. The political and economic chaos of the latter half of the 1970s may make the military coup of 1980 seem unavoidable. At the same time, the 1960s and 1970s were the time of the greatest intellectual, cultural, and political variety in the history of the Republic of Turkey in the twentieth century.

Some historians say that, regarded in the correct light, the Cold War began long before the end of the Second World War and came to an end in 1990.[64] For Turkey, one can say that the Cold War shaped the 1960s and 1970s above all. In the 1950s, the country basked in the shade of the American security umbrella. From the 1980s on, Turkey energetically set out in search of economic and political paths which hinted at the new possibilities which would emerge in the 1990s.

One can speak, however, of a Cold War in many respects with regard to the Turkey of the 1960s and 1970s. First, the global conflict between socialist and capitalist alternatives was directly reflected in the polarity between the leftist and rightist camps in Turkey.[65] At the same time, relations between

---

63 Bozarslan, "From Kemalism to Armed Struggle," 119.
64 See, for example, Westad, *Cold War*, 5, which argues that "the Cold War was born from the global transformations of the late nineteenth century."
65 In the domestic Turkish perception, Turkey was an important actor in the Cold War. Presumably because it fulfilled its task as a cornerstone of NATO so well, it is only worth scattered mentions in general accounts of the Cold War. So, for example, in Leffler and Westad, *Cambridge History of the Cold War*, a three-volume work with seventy-two articles, there is not one contribution with direct reference to Turkey. Westad, *Cold War*, conveys a very similar impression.

Turkey and its Western allies cooled dramatically due to disagreements about Cyprus, and finally, the embittered political animosities, especially those of the 1970s, can be construed as a Cold War inside the country.

The ideological straitjacket of the Cold War made it inevitable that domestic and foreign policy would become tightly interwoven. Many observers go so far as to allege that the political violence in Turkey in the 1970s was caused and steered from the outside. So, it is argued, NATO Stay Behind units were not only underground military units kept in reserve but they were supposedly deployed in many countries, including Turkey, to fight communists (and all those considered communists) domestically. With backing from the US (and its institutions, above all the CIA) and the acquiescence of the countries in question, unsavory networks of military, secret-service, and criminal circles were said to be established which damaged democratic culture deeply. Much would speak for the argument that the terror of the 1970s in Turkey was a focused strategy of destabilization.[66] The supposition, as exaggerated it may sound, is not absurd. But even if one day the political archives of the period become completely accessible, we will likely find no conclusive answer. It remains a question of interpretation and evaluation whether the interests and activities of actors like the US intelligence services caused or merely exacerbated the construction of fronts inside Turkey. In any case, Turkey took part in the ideological hostility between left and right particularly conspicuously and thereby in the decisive confrontational model of the Cold War.

Liberal Constitution and Economic Boom

Like the 1950s, the 1960s began full of hopes. The confidence in a democratic and open Turkey was expressed in the Constitution of 1961. A Senate was added alongside the National Assembly as an upper chamber. For the first time, a constitutional court (Anayasa Mahkemesi) was created which was intended not only to review the constitutionality of laws but was also to serve as the entity for initiating impeachment proceedings against officeholders from the president down. The term of office for the president was set at seven years without possibility of extension. The majority representation system of the lower house of parliament (but not the senate) was replaced with

---

66   Ganser, *NATO-Geheimarmeen*, 369 and passim. In this sense, also Öktem, *Angry Nation*, 53, 55, 60.

proportional representation. A particular characteristic of this constitution was detailed clauses on the fundamental rights of Turkish citizens; universities and the press received sweeping guarantees. Never again were civil liberties so broadly conceived in the Turkish Republic as in the Constitution of 1961. At the same time, the constitution was fed by the experiences of the Kemalist elite in opposition in the 1950s; it was intended to bring the government and parliament under control through its wide-ranging provisions.[67]

Only 60.4% of the population approved of the draft constitution in the constitutional referendum of 9 July 1961. Because its rejection was particularly high in Western Anatolia and on the Black Sea, traditional strongholds of the banned Democrat Party, the result may be seen not as a repudiation of the contents of the new constitution, but more as a criticism of the military coup of 1960 and, above all, the mass trial of DP politicians that was on-going at the time of the vote.

In the parliamentary elections of 15 October 1961, the first after the coup, the Justice Party (AP), which had just been founded shortly beforehand, received 34.8% of the votes and lagged just barely behind the Republican People's Party (CHP), with its 36.7% share. Because center-right parties, as well as those even further to the right (all of whom the military suspected of possessing an Islamist agenda), received more than 60% of the votes in total, the military was so disappointed that it weighed a further intervention. They only abandoned the idea because İsmet İnönü and Ragıp Gümüşpala, the then chairman of the AP, agreed to form a coalition under İnönü's leadership. This CHP-AP coalition collapsed on 30 May 1963. Two short-lived coalitions under İnönü followed in 1963–1965, both times without participation by the Justice Party. These years of coalition government under İnönü damaged the CHP and undermined its prospects. The party earned the reputation of a hollow reformism by announcing reforms and never implementing them. Also under the impression of this loss of reputation the CHP shifted to "left of center" (*ortanın solu*). Its change of course was deliberately distorted by the Justice Party, its great opponent, as, "Left of center [runs] the road to Moscow" (Ortanın solu, Moskova yolu). The AP trumpeted their

---

67 Rumpf, *Einführung in das türkische Recht*, 28. Özbudun, *Constitutional System of Turkey*, 11, 122. Çolak, *Karaoğlan*, 104. For the Turkish text of the Constitution of 1961, see https://www.anayasa.gov.tr/mevzuat/onceki-anayasalar/1961-anayasa/, accessed 30 August 2020. For an English translation, see Balkan and Uysal, *Constitution of the Turkish Republic*.

own slogan, "We are right of center, and we are on God's path" (Ortanın sağındayız, Allahın yolundayız).[68]

Ecevit tried to attenuate the traditional alienation of the CHP from the Anatolian population by posing no contradiction between the piousness of the people and social and political progress. "Even when the people pray five times a day, they are progressive. Even when they fast, they are progressive."[69] The Justice Party, now led by Süleyman Demirel, was the clear victor in the next parliamentary elections, receiving 52.9% of the vote in 1965 and 46.6% in 1969. The parliamentary system worked. In 1965, the transition from a CHP-dominated government to an AP government went perfectly smoothly. In addition, the AP governed with a sole parliamentary majority.

After the DP government neglected the direction of the economy in the 1950s, the state took up the instruments of governmental economic planning again. In Article 129 of the Constitution of 1961, the State Planning Organization (Devlet Planlama Teşkilatı) set up in September 1960, received constitutional status. The goals of this agency in developing five-year plans were supposed to be: (a) raising the national income, (b) remedying problems with the balance of payments, (c) the creation of additional employment, (d) a higher degree of social justice, and (e) the elimination of development gaps between regions. The State Planning Organization as a central authority was officially adjacent to other ministries but was de facto superior to them and determined the allocation of credit. Nevertheless, this agency could only realize some of the listed goals, because conservative political forces succeeded in leaving it responsible solely for the planning of state investments.[70] After the regularly executed five-year plans of 1963–1967, 1968–1972, and 1973–1977, the five-year plan for 1979–1983 fell victim to the domestic political turbulence of the late 1970s.

The economic policy of the 1960s and 1970s was contingent upon a plan of import-substituting industrialization. Import-substitution policy desires to limit imports as far as possible by protecting the domestic market and by replacing them with products produced by domestic industry. Thereby, the national economy should—in a kind of self-reinforcing upward

---

68 Ahmad, *Turkish Experiment*, 250ff., 377. From 1972 on, the CHP used the more strongly defined concept of a "Democratic Left" (*Demokratik Sol*). Çolak, *Karaoğlan*, 142–144.
69 Çolak, *Karaoğlan*, 139, here draws upon Bülent Ecevit, *Atatürk ve Devrimcilik* (İstanbul: Tekin Yayınevi, 1976), 7ff.
70 Ahmad, *Modern Turkey*, 132. Hale, *Modern Turkey*, 141–144. Keyder, *State and Class*, 148. Ahmad, *Turkish Experiment*, 275.

spiral—increasingly reduce dependency on imports, ramp up domestic production, and finally achieve international competitiveness. This economic policy did, in fact, effect a rapid growth in production and employment in the manufacturing sector. In 1963–1977, gross national product grew on average 4.3% per annum and real wages almost doubled. In individual industrial sectors, a kind of worker aristocracy developed, receiving very high incomes compared to their counterparts in other countries. In 1977, the wages of Turkish workers in this privileged stratum were double that of those in South Korea.[71]

At the same time, the weaknesses of import-substitution policy in a country like Turkey, which continued to export primarily simple goods like agricultural products or textiles, are obvious. The lowered competition in the domestic market can lead to a loss of competitiveness strengthened by simultaneously increasing inflation and exhausted foreign currency reserves. Beginning in the 1970s, the unfavorable sides of import-substitution policy, namely excessively high production costs and stagnating exports were joined by a lack of competence in the direction of the public economy and inflationary financing of government expenditures.

Turkey never had the good fortune, or perhaps remained protected from the fate, of becoming a "rentier state." This appellation was given to those states of the Arab world in which the overwhelming portion of national income derived from a single source, namely petroleum and natural-gas exports.[72] From the late 1940s into the 1970s, Turkey was, however, a "second-order" rentier state, thanks to plentiful aid payments, above all from the US, and later the remittances from Turkish guest-workers abroad.[73] US support payments to Turkey in the framework of the Marshall Plan and other programs into the early 1960s reached a total of four billion US dollars. In 1960–1978, total project- and program-assistance aid to Turkey amounted to around five-and-a-half billion US dollars.[74]

In the 1970s, remittances from Turks working in Europe skyrocketed. In the first half of the Seventies, remittances corresponded to 70–95% of

---

71   Keyder, *State and Class*, 151ff., 161. Owen and Pamuk, *Middle East Economies*, 112, 251.
72   The political nature of a rentier state is explained (albeit with somewhat essentializing undertones) in Beblawi, "Rentier State."
73   On second-order rentier states, which draw high revenues from their geostrategic significance or remittances from guestworkers abroad, see Schlumberger, *Autoritarismus in der arabischen Welt*, 121.
74   Gunn, "1960 Coup," 104. Hale, *Modern Turkey*, 240.

official export income and led to a positive balance of payments in 1973, Turkey's first since 1946. Simultaneously, beginning in 1973, the Turkish economy was left in the lurch by the pressure of the quadrupling of oil prices. While the leading Western economic powers succeeded, after a short period, in channeling the monstrous profits of the oil-exporting states back into their economies, the aforementioned weakness of Turkey became all too clear. The high remittances in the 1970s led to an overvaluation of the currency and weakened the Turkish economy's export capability. The share of all imports and exports was limited by the import-substitution policy to 16% of GNP, in contrast to an average of 48% in "less-developed" countries, to which Turkey belonged at this point. The weakness of the export industry was particularly conspicuous. The share of industrial exports was under 2% of GNP until 1980.[75]

The liberal Constitution of 1961 provided various classes and interest groups new opportunities to bring forward their concerns.[76] Thus, for example, unions received a right to strike. But new actors would have raised their voices even without the constitution, given the pluralization of society and the transformation of Turkey from a largely agrarian country to an industrial state. In 1952, the Confederation of Turkish Trade Unions (Türkiye İşçi Sendikaları Konfederasyonu, abbreviated Türk-İş, Turkish Labor) was founded, an organization under whose roof congregate a great number of individual unions and which still exists today. Türk-İş declared itself politically neutral in February 1964 and thereafter did not wish to support strikes with political undertones, like, for example, the March 1965 strike by around forty-five thousand miners in Zonguldak (a port city on the Black Sea) against poor working conditions. In 1967, as a protest against Türk-İş's lack of bellicosity, union activists founded the more left-wing Confederation of Revolutionary Trade Unions of Turkey (Türkiye Devrimci İşçi Sendikaları Konfederasyonu, DİSK).[77]

In the then leading periodicals of the Left, like the *Direction* (*Yön*, 1961–1967) or the *Oath* (*Ant*, 1967–1971), intellectuals argued for a "neo-étatism" (*yeni devletçilik*) directed against Western political and economic hegemony but also against large landholders and the urban upper-middle class.

---

75 Hale, *Modern Turkey*, 231. Owen and Pamuk, *Middle East Economies*, 112ff.
76 Alper, *Jakobenlerden Devrimcilere*, vividly depicts the radicalization of the student body in the 1960s which initially saw itself as an ally of the CHP and the military but whose most radical left-wing factions chose the path of armed struggle as early as 1970.
77 Mello, "Radicalization and/or Reformism in Working-Class Politics," 101–103.

This "Turkish socialism" (*Türk sosyalizmi*) was actually not especially revolutionary, but showed many similarities to positions of left-leaning social democracies, comparable to the positions of the British Labour Party at the time. Its demands included the nationalization of key industries, a fair division of national wealth, an appropriate representation of workers in the parliamentary-democratic system, and the protection of workers from employers.[78]

The late 1960s provided a foretaste of the violent confrontations of the 1970s. On 16 February 1969, during a demonstration against the visit of the US Navy's Sixth Fleet in İstanbul, protestors called for an "independent Turkey" (*bağımsız Türkiye*). Counter-demonstrators didn't leave it at chanting for a "Muslim Turkey" (*Müslüman Türkiye*) but attacked. On this day, which became known as Bloody Sunday (*Kanlı Pazar*), there were two fatalities and two hundred injured. A year later, the government viewed a general strike in İstanbul and the province of Kocaeli (east of İstanbul) on 15–16 June 1970 as preparation for a revolution. The government imposed martial law and broke the strike with the help of the military while cutting off all connections to the affected regions.

In 1971, the country was in bad shape. The universities were no longer working. Student groups copied the urban guerillas of Latin America, robbed banks, and kidnapped US citizens and officials working in Turkey. President Demirel indicated repeatedly that the country could no longer be governed by the instruments incorporated in the Constitution of 1961. At the same time, he was losing control over his own party. The Justice Party, a reservoir of the most diverse currents, was torn apart by internal tensions. One group saw itself as "those who honor the nation and what is holy" (*milliyetçi-mukaddesatçı*).[79] Osman Turan (1914–1978), a specialist in the history of the Seljuks and leader of this nationalist-sacralist current, was expelled from the AP in 1967. In 1970, on the other hand, Ferruh Bozbeyli (1927–2019) and forty other parliamentary representatives left the AP and founded the Democratic Party (Demokratik Parti). With a name (almost) identical to that of the Democrat Party of the 1950s, it advertised its aspiration to follow in the former's footsteps. In general, however, it was composed of landowners and provincial notables who considered themselves losers under Demirel's modernization policies. With the schism of the Demokratik Parti, Demirel lost his majority in parliament, was largely incapable of action, and just maneuvered his way until the military intervened again in March 1971.

---

78   Landau, *Radical Politics*, 55ff.
79   According to ibid., 189n114, the *mukaddesatçılar* seemed to have coined this term in order not to make their obvious connection to Islamist positions as explicit.

Military-Technocratic Interlude

On 12 March 1971, the military presented then-president Cevdet Sunay (1899–1982, in office 1966–1973) and the speakers of both houses of parliament with a memorandum that would be read at one p.m. on the radio. The basic tenor of the communiqué: the goals set forth in the Constitution of 1961 are unmet. The military threatened a comprehensive intervention if a strong and credible government did not take the wheel, put an end to anarchy and social unrest, and implement the reforms set forth in the Constitution of 1961. In consequence, as the military expected, Demirel resigned.

In the next two-and-a-half years, a series of technocratic governments ensued under Nihat Erim (1912–1980) and Ferit Melen (1906–1988), both of whom belonged to the rightward camp of the Republican People's Party, followed by Naim Talu (1919–1998) previously a high-ranking official of the central bank. When in Spring 1973, the military came to believe it had to either take power directly or withdraw, it decided for the defensive option. By mid-1973 it had at least partially reached its goals. Two constitutional revisions, in 1971 and 1973, intervened massively in the text of the Constitution. Civil rights were limited, as with supervisory rights of the courts over them were diminished. The liberties of universities and unions were truncated. In addition, the executive was strengthened. The novel instrument of "decree with the force of law" (*kanun hükmünde kararname*) was supposed to make governmental activity more independent of parliament and more effective.[80]

The reason for the ultimatum of 1971 was apparently that, within the military, the impression predominated that President Demirel had lost control. The military did not want to take responsibility for the mistakes of the government and damage itself by imposing order. The exposure of a coup plot by a left-wing faction led by the retired general Cemal Madanoğlu (1907–1993) was a further spur to action. The intervention of 12 March 1971 was followed by a comprehensive purge of officers inclined to the left. Foreign policy considerations also dictated against establishing direct military rule. It was feared at that Turkey would be lumped in with military dictatorships like Greece (1967–1974) and Pakistan (1969–1971).[81]

---

80   Jenkins, *Political Islam*, 131. Hale, *Modern Turkey*, 119ff. Rumpf, *Einführung in das türkische Recht*, 29.
81   Lord, *Religious Politics*, 228. Keyder, "Social Change and Political Mobilization," 27. Hale, *Turkish Politics and the Military*, 192.

For the military, the opponent in the 1971 intervention was unambiguously the radical left movement. On the day the memorandum was made public, state prosecutors opened a case against the Turkish Workers' Party (TİP) which was then banned by the Constitutional Court on 20 July 1971. The press was harassed. Authors like Yaşar Kemal (1923–2015) and Fakir Baykurt (1929–1999) or intellectual journalists like Çetin Altan (1927–2015) and İlhan Selçuk (1925–2010) were arrested. Radical right publications, by contrast, remained untouched. Many of those arrested were tortured, apparently with the goal of dissuading them from further engagement in politics.[82]

The balance of the intervention was murky. The military wanted neither an unambiguous seizure of power nor its rapid relinquishment. Turkish society's previous way of thinking, that the military stood on the side of liberal democratic forces, was dispelled by the intervention of 1971. The experience of the military in 1971–1973, on the other hand, taught them that in the future, any intervention composed of half-measures was to be avoided.[83] The intervention of 1971 stands between the two military coups of 1960 and 1980 and is best understood less as a watershed like 1960 and 1980 but as a milestone along the way to the profound political polarization of the 1970s, which would take on undreamt-of dimensions.

The Derailing of the Political System and the Wave of Violence

The political instability of the 1970s was connected to the fragmentation of the party landscape. The suppression of forces on the left margin initiated in 1971 led to a decline of the legal, parliamentary, and extra-parliamentary left. Above all, though, pervasive violence crippled the country. While the 16 February 1969 confrontation between rightist and leftist activists in İstanbul which left two dead was felt to be so exceptionally brutal as to go down in history books as "Bloody Sunday," in the 1970s a "habituation" towards incessant and capricious acts of violence set in. In summer 1980, barely comprehensible attacks and killings, beatings and shootings, claimed at least twenty lives a day. The notion of a nation split into two halves between the radical right and radical left is, however, incorrect. The vast majority of the population had nothing to do with the violence and suffered from it. At the same time, it was the radical right, led by the nationalist radical right Party of the National Movement

---

82 Ahmad, *Modern Turkey*, 151.
83 Hale, *Turkish Politics and the Military*, 211.

(MHP) which was unambiguously the driving force of the violence, above all in the second half of the 1970s.

The elections of October 1973—the first after the retreat of the military—were seen as a test of whether the new left-of-center orientation of the Republican People's Party under Ecevit would be successful. That the CHP received a great portion of their votes not from the "backwards" regions of the country which had previously been its strongholds but in the industrial cities, showed that urban workers and migrants in the gecekondus now supported the CHP. The CHP won the elections of 1973 with 33.3% of the vote and the elections of 1977 with 41.4% (though with only 213 of 450 seats in parliament). Consequently, they failed to achieve their goal of governing alone. In addition, Ecevit failed to form and lead stable governments. The proportional-representation system introduced in the Constitution of 1961 made the requirements for forming a government more difficult. A personal feud between Ecevit and Demirel contributed as well. A grand coalition always remained a possibility, as the two centrist parties, the AP and CHP, together held more than 70% of the vote total.[84] But, out of tactical considerations, Ecevit entered a coalition with the Islamist National Salvation Party (Millî Selamet Partisi, MSP) on 26 January 1974.

Personal arrogance and false calculations contributed as well. Ecevit, who was responsible for the successful Turkish intervention on Cyprus in Summer 1974, resigned in September 1974 for tactical electoral reasons, because he—the Conqueror of Cyprus (Kıbrıs Fatihi) and defender of the Turkish national interest—hoped for a clear victory at the ballot box.[85] New elections didn't happen, however. Instead, after long months of negotiations, Süleyman Demirel took over affairs of state. Between 31 March 1975 and 22 June 1977, Demirel led the first Government of the Nationalist Front (Milliyetçi Cephe Hükûmeti) together with, among others, the MHP and the Islamist MSP. Another short-lived Government of the Nationalist Front followed from 21 July 1977 to 15 January 1978. These two governments damaged the country's political culture. The smaller coalition partners, the MSP and MHP, held a number of ministerial offices far exceeding their share of the vote.[86] Both parties, but particularly the MHP, used the time to transform the ministries they led into bastions for their own political activities outside of government

---

84 Ahmad, *Modern Turkey*, 159ff., 167.
85 For the term "Conqueror of Cyprus," see Çolak, *Karaoğlan*, 171.
86 In the first Government of the Nationalist Front, the MHP was able to gain three ministerial posts with a total of only three representatives in parliament. Bora and Can, *Devlet, Ocak, Dergâh*, 50.

and parliament. From 15 January 1978 to 12 November 1979, Ecevit once again led the government with some representatives who had defected from the Justice Party, but he could not fulfill the hopes placed in him, neither on the economic nor political plane. So Demirel took over the affairs of state as prime minister yet again on 12 November 1979. The business of parliament increasingly faltered. When the term of President Fahri Korutürk (1903–1987, in office 1973–1980) expired in April 1980, the parties could not agree on a successor. More than a hundred ballots failed to produce a result.

The Turkish national economy ran aground in 1979 at the latest. Due to the dramatic fall of the lira in the second half of the 1970s, the government had to respond with two dramatic devaluations: 79% in June 1979 and a further 48% in January 1980. Only after these two drastic cuts did the lira's official exchange rate coincide with the actual exchange rates on the black market, which had been trading liras at half their official value in March 1979.[87] The measures taken by the post-November-1979 government of prime minister Süleyman Demirel did not only include the devaluation of the currency, but also far-reaching plans for lifting price controls, reducing the public-sector deficit, and deregulating interest rates on the domestic market—the first forerunners of a "neoliberal" politics which would shape Turkish economic policy beginning in the 1980s.

An even greater burden for the country's stability was the radicalization of extra-parliamentary conflicts. Around 1970, radical left organizations took shape which saw their mission as achieving political goals through armed struggle. Even as early as 1965, the Federation of Revolutionary Youth Associations of Turkey (Türkiye Devrimci Gençlik Dernekleri Federasyonu, abbreviated Dev-Genç) was founded. Banned in 1971, Dev-Genç's goal was assisting the peasantry in a revolutionary struggle against imperialism.[88] Similarly, there arose the People's Liberation Army of Turkey (Türkiye Halk Kurtuluş Ordusu, THKO) founded in 1971 under the leadership of Deniz Gezmiş (1947–1972); the People's Liberation Party of Turkey—Front (Türkiye Halk Kurtuluş Partisi—Cephe, THKP-C) under Mahir Çayan (1945–1972); and the Communist Party of Turkey—Marxist-Leninist (Türkiye Komünist Partisi—Marxist-Leninist, TKP-ML) of İbrahim Kaypakkaya (1943–1973), a splinter group of the Maoist Revolutionary Workers' and Peasants' Party of Turkey (Türkiye İhtilalci İşçi-Köylü Partisi,

---

87 Hale, *Modern Turkey*, 237ff.
88 Landau, *Radical Politics*, 39ff.

TİİKP) under Doğu Perinçek (b. 1942). The early and similar death years of Gezmiş, Çayan, and Kaypakkaya (all 1972-1973) are a clue that these organizations were very rapidly crushed by the organs of state. They were likely also as short-lived as they were because they only possessed a very small circle of immediate supporters. The left could bring tens of thousands into the streets for demonstrations, but the number of active radical left militants likely never comprised more than a few thousand, maybe even a few hundred.[89]

The radical right, on the other hand, showed greater ideological coherence from the beginning—given the limited nature of their attempts at interpreting the world, this was no great feat—as well as a much broader milieu of activists. In addition, they could count on the support of various sympathizers in the apparatus of state and probably also the military. The Nationalist Movement Party (MHP) used its participation in both Governments of the Nationalist Front in 1975-1978 and its control of the Interior Ministry to place trusted members in the bureaucracy and to cover for radical right acts of violence. Since the 1950s, the ultranationalist right had organized behind a battle cry against communists. The Associations for the Battle Against Communism (Komünizmle Mücadele Dernekleri), which had achieved semi-official status after the Justice Party's entry into government in 1965, spilled over from the big cities into Anatolia. In 1968, there were already one hundred forty-one branches of the movement. The Gray Wolves (Bozkurtlar) emerged from these associations beginning in the mid-Sixties.[90]

The opposition between "right" and "left" also stood for, or fed off of, further oppositions: Turkish versus Kurdish, Sunni versus Alevi, Sunni versus secular-minded, craftsmen and traders against the urban proletariat.[91] Consequently, the radical right denounced its political opponents as the Three Ks: Kürt, Komünist, Kızılbaş (Kurds, Communists, and Kızılbaş, that is, Alevis). The dynamic was not only about ideology and identity, however. A powerful engine of conflict and willingness to employ violence were social and economic circumstances, especially the poor social integration of youths in the gecekondus of the big cities. For gecekondu residents, the economic crisis in the 1970s meant that their aspirations to social mobility would not be realized—or at least not as easily as they had once appeared. In addition, after

---

89 Kürkçü, "Türkiye Sosyalist Hareketine Silahlı Mücadelenin Girişi," 496, speaks of only "between 100 or 150 militants" who were prepared for armed struggle.
90 Landau, *Radical Politics*, 203ff. Bora and Can, *Devlet, Ocak, Dergâh*, 46-48. Bora, "Narrating the Enemy," 149.
91 McDowall, *Modern History of the Kurds*, 414.

the intervention of 12 March 1971, the state was considerably less indulgent of the gecekondus; some of them were, in fact, torn down. The polarization nourished by the living conditions in these quarters blew back in turn as violence in the gecekondus. City districts ordered themselves, even more than had heretofore been the case, according to group membership—not least for protection. So some larger Alevi quarters came to be in the big cities, whose inhabitants stood unambiguously on the left of the political landscape. In such a politicized society, and given their stigmatization, the Alevis had little in the way of alternatives to affiliation with the left.[92]

Violence was commonplace and could flare up anywhere. To cite just once example, on 13 January 1977, the daily newspaper *Cumhuriyet* reported the following items—virtually under the headline, "Miscellaneous Political Violence in Educational Institutions." At Karlıova High School in the city of Bingöl, thirteen students were arrested after an altercation; Atatürk University in Erzurum was closed for an indeterminate amount of time following the death of a student; sticks of dynamite exploded in the entrance hall of the grammar school of Manisa; at the Teachers' College in Aydın, teachers were attacked with clubs; a brawl broke out at the Capital Journalism School in Ankara.

Assassinations became rampant. On 19 July 1980, Nihat Erim, for several months prime minister after the military intervention of 1971, was murdered leaving an İstanbul beach club. Three days later, on the day of Erim's burial, Kemal Türkler (1926–1980), former president of the Confederation of Revolutionary Trade Unions (DİSK), was murdered, apparently in an act of retribution.

Violence did not simply occur as proof of political commitment, however; it was intended as targeted provocation—almost exclusively by the radical right.[93] On May Day 1977, unidentified gunmen opened fire on demonstrators in İstanbul's central Taksim Square. Because police simultaneously used the sirens on their police cars and had blocked off the main streets leading from the square, a mass panic ensued. Two people were killed by bullets, but thirty four were trampled to death.[94] On 17 April 1978, Hamid Fendoğlu, a representative of the Justice Party, a declared anticommunist, was killed by a mail bomb along with his daughter-in-law and two of his grandchildren. Only years later was it discovered that the bomb had been sent from the

---

92　Erman, "'Liberated Neighborhoods,'" 187, 206.
93　According to Bora and Can, *Devlet, Ocak, Dergâh*, 51, 71–77, it was the goal of the MHP and its numerous subordinate organizations from 1978 on to convulse society in a state of terror.
94　Gourisse, *Violence politique en Turquie*, 265. Birand, *Generals' Coup*, 149. Ahmad, *Modern Turkey*, 169.

National Nuclear Research Center near İstanbul—an institution that was then controlled by the MHP.

Fendoğlu's murder led to anti-Alevi riots in Malatya in Eastern Anatolia, which quickly spread to other cities like Erzurum and Kahramanmaraş.[95] In Kahramanmaraş, following a bomb attack on a movie theater considered right-nationalist on 19 December 1978, an anti-Alevi pogrom broke out and lasted from 22 to 24 December. Only military units, deployed from Kayseri over 150 miles away, were able to contain it. At least a hundred and eleven people were killed in the unrest and over a thousand wounded. On the following day, 25 December 1978, parliament passed the imposition of a state of emergency in thirteen eastern provinces.[96]

The state was helpless, because police and secret-service measures were sabotaged, and information about governmental actions was betrayed to those against whom the measures were aimed. In this regard, one may consider the impenetrable thicket around Mehmet Ali Ağca (b. 1958). Ağca became known to the global public for his 1981 attempted assassination of Pope John Paul II. As early as 1 February 1979, Ağca had already committed murder, killing Abdi İpekçi, publisher of the daily newspaper *Milliyet*. Ağca was arrested but was able to escape from a high-security prison near İstanbul with the help of some guards.[97]

There was a fundamental difference between the terrorism of the left and the right in Turkey in the 1970s. Leftist terrorists were attempting to spur workers to revolution. In contrast, the radical right set about causing chaos and demoralization—with greater force, the secret support of state organs, and much better infrastructure. Especially in Central and Eastern Anatolia, riots instigated by radical right forces could only be prevented when military forces from outside the area intervened. The passivity, indeed the willful connivance, of local security forces at these events was all too apparent. In retrospect, given the crisis pulling Turkey ever deeper into a maelstrom of violence and disintegration, what was surprising about the coup of 12 September 1980 was "not that it happened, but rather that it took so long in coming."[98] Thus, it's only thanks to the vagaries of history that the coup of 1980 did not actually take place in the epochal year of 1979.[99]

---

95 Bora and Can, *Devlet, Ocak, Dergâh*, 84n28. Birand, *Generals' Coup*, 37.
96 Gourisse, *Violence politique en Turquie*, 281–297. Bora and Can, *Devlet, Ocak, Dergâh*, 74, point out that the "overdosed" scale of violence in the massacre at Kahramanmaraş blew up in the MHP's face, as it led to the military's estrangement from the party.
97 Birand, *Generals' Coup*, 49, 51, 56. See also the research of Mumcu, *Papa–Mafya–Ağca*.
98 Hale, *Turkish Politics and the Military*, 232.
99 See for example Bösch, *Zeitenwende*, with chapters on, among others, Iran, Afghanistan, and on the "second oil crisis." Lesch, *1979*, concentrates on the revolution in Iran in

The Coup of 1980

The military was already convinced that an intervention had become unavoidable by the end of 1978. At the same time, leading officers wanted to sit tight. The politicians would have to discredit themselves so completely that no one could doubt the justification of a military intervention. In contrast to the previous interventions of 1960 and 1971, the coup of 1980 was carefully planned and had clear goals.[100] Hierarchy would be strictly observed; no gap arose between the coup's leaders and the commanders of the branches of the military. The military's seizure of power was complete, and the return of power to politicians would follow only gradually and in exactly prescribed individual steps.

In the early morning of 12 September, the military occupied all central points and institutions in the capital Ankara and around the country. The military didn't have far to go, as Ankara, like all other large cities in Turkey, is surrounded by garrisons and military institutions. The leading politicians of the country were arrested in the morning hours. In an address on the day of the coup, Kenan Evren (1917–2015), chief of the general staff and leader of the putschists, laid primary responsibility for the condition of the country at the feet of the politicians. They were said to have acted irresponsibly and thus effected the failure of the entire political system.[101]

The measures taken by the military regime in the following months were extremely harsh. Six hundred fifty thousand people were taken into police custody. One million six hundred eighty-three thousand criminal proceedings were initiated, 517 people were sentenced to death, 49 of whose death sentences were carried out. Thirty thousand people were removed from their positions of employment due to their political sympathies. From 1980–1987, fourteen thousand Turks lost their Turkish citizenship and three hundred thousand people had their passports taken away. In police stations and prisons, torture was given free rein; at least 171 people died under torture in the first years following the coup.[102]

The military intervened in 1960, 1971, and 1980, always citing the political system's having run off the rails. The economic realm experienced a similar

---

February 1979, the Egyptian-Israeli peace treaty in March, and the Soviet invasion of Afghanistan in December.
100   Birand, *Generals' Coup*, 39, 96. Jenkins, *Context and Circumstance*, 38.
101   Ibid., 190ff.
102   Eligür, *Mobilization of Political Islam*, 90. Cemal, *Özal Hikayesi*, 317. Jenkins, *Political Islam*, 141.

derailment. There is a striking relationship between economic development and the military's interventions. On the black market in 1958, the Turkish lira was worth a fifth of its official rate against the dollar. In August 1958, the government had to discontinue all international finance transactions. Under pressure from the International Monetary Fund, it implemented a deep devaluation of the lira (going from 2.80 to the dollar to 9.00 to the dollar), along with further measures like easing imports, changes in export policy, lifting of price controls, higher prices for products manufactured by state enterprises, and the restructuring of governmental debt. This tough stabilization policy brought about a recession which lasted until 1961. This relationship is less obvious, but still visible, with regard to the intervention of 1971. While wages in sectors organized by unions rose 5–7% per year between 1960–1971, they sank by a tenth in 1971–1973 after the intervention. Beginning in 1978, Turkey slid into a severe currency crisis. The International Monetary Fund set strict conditions for its support: the implementation of a stabilization program, drastic curtailment of state subsidies, lifting of import and export controls. In consequence, real wages sank by 34% between 1977 and 1987.[103]

What does this suggestive parallel between the interventions of the military and rigorous economic measures accompanied by sharp declines in earned income tell us? Three answers suggest themselves, in increasing order of cynicism. First, the military may have been concerned that the obvious economic weakness could strengthen political instability, so that it felt compelled to intervene as quickly as possible. The two other possible options are starker, that is, the immediate interest of the military in orderly circumstances, in the sense of a capitalist economic order, or third, the military as the executive arm of international capital interests. Overall, there's much that speaks against the first interpretation because of its naïveté, and some against the third, because it assumes that, in the end, political and economic circumstances in Turkey are solely steered from the outside. The scope of power and the self-image of the Turkish military, which wanted to herald a new era after 1980, speak against this interpretation. It really would be a new era. But it would be shaped by people other than the military.

---

103   Hale, *Modern Turkey*, 106ff. Keyder, *State and Class*, 160. Owen and Pamuk, *Middle East Economies*, 120.

Chapter Four

The Promise of Islamic Conservatism, 1980–2013

One may speak of the "promise" of Islamic conservatism in two senses. In one, beginning in the 1980s "Islam," construed as generally as possible, achieved public visibility and was employed to justify political actions across the entire Islamic world, including the Muslim diaspora. In another, actors outside Islam recognized how useful a "moderate Islam" could be. Thus, the Turkish military regarded Islamic conservatism as a means for social and political moderation which promised to trump the radical left movement. The military junta steering Turkey from 1980 to 1983 also received the approval of its mentor, the US, which for its part saw moderate Islamists as an effective countermeasure against communism in the Islamic world (excepting, of course, those who had held power in Iran since 1979).[1] The fall of the shah in February 1979, the erection of the Islamic Republic of Iran and the Soviet invasion in Afghanistan changed the balance of power in the Middle East and made Turkey all the more significant in Western eyes: Turkey would remain allied to the West and, at the same time, play a weightier role as a moderate force in the Islamic world.[2]

---

1 Westad, *Cold War*, 472, 531.
2 Cemal, *Özal Hikayesi*, 178. Bora and Can, *Devlet, Ocak, Dergâh*, 150–153.

Even movements that were not moderate were sometimes welcome allies. In this regard, one may consider the Western support of the Mujahideen in Afghanistan after the Soviet invasion of December 1979, or the Algerian president Chadli Bendjedid (in office 1979–1992), whose scheme for a controlled ascent of Islamism in the form of the Islamic Salvation Front (Front Islamic du Salut, FIS) quickly slipped out of his control.[3] The Turkish military, which also wanted to use the potential of an Islamic conservatism for its own ends, was likewise overrun by the power of the emerging Islamist movement.

In the Turkey of the 1980s, on the one hand, the political model of the Cold War was still operant. On the other, the country was already beginning to reorient itself. In a European context, Turkey was a bit of a forerunner. The dramatic changes which the post-socialist states of Eastern Europe would experience in the 1990s were anticipated in the global south and Turkey.[4] In the 1980s, Turkey pivoted to a politics of neoliberalism, accompanied by expressions of Muslim piety. Contemporaneous with British Thatcherism (after Margaret Thatcher, British prime minister, 1979–1990), Turkish society was subjected to a regime of market efficiency. Together with the rest of the Islamic world, Turkey acknowledged Islam as a primary characteristic of individuals and societies. With the electoral success of the Party of Justice and Development (Adalet ve Kalkınma Partisi, AKP) in 2002, the triad of democracy, economic success, and Islamic conservatism became a new trademark of the Republic of Turkey. By the 2000s at the latest, the country reentered not only Islamic but world history.[5] Seen from the larger vantage point of the general promise of Islamic conservatism, the AKP's taking power in 2002 is significant, but it is only one episode of many across a time frame stretching from 1980 into the early 2010s.

1. Political Engineers in Power (1980–1983)

With the coup of 1980, the Turkish military concentrated all the instruments of power into its hands. Its leaders would have liked to draw lasting lessons from the embittered domestic political conflicts in the late 1970s, but they also

---

3   Willis, *Islamist Challenge in Algeria*, 111–116.
4   Westad, *Cold War*, 554.
5   Thus, in the narrative of Schulze, *Geschichte der islamischen Welt*, after a detailed discussion of the late Ottoman and earliest Republican periods, Turkey loses any significance for the ensuing decades, only to reemerge conspicuously in the 2000s.

acted under the influence of the Soviet Union's 1979 invasion of Afghanistan and the Iranian Revolution of 1978–1979. While it had always appreciated right-nationalist attitudes as fertile soil for constructing a national identity, the military believed it had found an effective means against left radicalism in Islamic conservatism. Moreover, the military believed they could walk the fine line between promoting a useful Islamic conservatism and avoiding the danger of a strengthened Islamism.

The quarrels between the country's leading politicians in the 1970s, indeed the crippling of the entire political system, confirmed leading military men in their assumption that they were called to undertake fundamental changes in the country's political system and were capable of doing so—without allowing themselves to be drawn into the morass of everyday political combat. However, their all-too-mechanistic perspective on politics misled the military, not only while they directly held power in their hands in 1980–1983, but in the following years when they repeatedly tried to work the levers of power to bring the political machinery into synchronization with their ideas. This arrogance, indeed hubris, broke their back a little later.

The Military as a State Above the State

Since the late nineteenth century the military had seen itself as the tip of the spear of modernization and therefore entitled to an elevated role in government. This self-image did not fundamentally change under the Turkish Republic. Due to the experience of the 1910s, when the Young Turk movement and the military became fatally entangled, however, Mustafa Kemal was convinced that an excessive politicization of the military was deleterious. He therefore wanted to limit the armed forces to the role of an imperium in imperio, comparable to the role of the military in Germany from 1871 to 1914. But even he had to secure the support of top officers for decisive steps like the abolition of the caliphate. Into the mid-1940s, there was no need for the military to intervene to take corrective action, because the ideological gap between the government and military was sufficiently narrow. Since 1960 at the latest, however, the military has seen itself as leader and guardian of the state.[6]

The strong inner cohesion of the Turkish army rests on an unconditional emphasis on Kemalism as an ideology and on the importance of discipline

---

6 Hanioğlu, *Atatürk*, 46ff.

and loyalty. The military consequently looked upon politics with displeasure. Moreover, everyday modes of politics like the laborious and confusing horse-trading of interests were completely foreign to the military mind. Consequently, the military generally desired to keep its distance from party politics—but not from political interventions. After the coup of 1960, the military institutionalized its role as guardian of the state. Article 111 of the Constitution of 1961 gave the National Security Council (Milli Güvenlik Kurulu, MGK), an institution established in 1933, constitutional status. The president held the chairmanship, and it was composed of five civilian and five military members.[7]

After 1960, the military created an independent economic infrastructure for itself, above all through the Army Mutual Aid Society (Ordu Yardımlaşma Kurumu, OYAK) into which all officers paid around a tenth of their income in order to later receive various types of support from the fund. OYAK, an institution shrouded in secrecy, developed over the decades into one of the largest industrial conglomerates in Turkey, thanks not least to a tremendous competitive advantage: the contributions of the members of the armed forces and the assets of the concern were largely exempt from taxes.[8]

The military's supremacy over politics was also evident in the fact that from the foundation of the Republic until the end of the 1980s—with the sole exception of Celal Bayar in the years 1950-1960—the office of president was always held by a former general: Mustafa Kemal Atatürk (1923-1938), İsmet İnönü (1938-1950), Cemal Gürsel (1960-1966), Cevdet Sunay (1966-1973), Fahri Korutürk (1973-1980), and Kenan Evren (1982-1989).

By the same token, one cannot underestimate the military's connection to society—despite all the measures intended to create a firewall around it. The free education offered by military schools was surely always one of the main draws to a career in the officer corps. The educational system at the military schools and academies was as a rule superior to that at civilian educational institutions, thanks to better facilities and closer supervision. The civilian and military schools' curricula were not fundamentally different; but, along with an intensive Kemalist indoctrination, they were transmitted more effectively in the latter. One reason for the military's high esteem

---

7   On the military's side, these were the chief of the general staff and the commanders of the four branches of the armed services, the army, navy, air force, and gendarmerie, as well as the general secretary of the MGK (without voting rights); on the civilian side, the president, prime minister, and foreign, interior, and defense ministers were represented.
8   Thumann, "Geldmaschine der Armee."

in society was that the Turkish officer corps was principally recruited from the lower middle class in provincial cities, thereby avoiding the construction of a self-enclosed military caste. Along with internal migration and state education, the military was over decades a third important prop of national assimilation. Since the reintroduction of mandatory military service in 1927, military service was a critical life experience for the masculine population and, along with circumcision, was one of the most important initiatory rites for adolescent males.[9]

The singular status of the military was thus not the result of a successful autosuggestion, but rather a social reality. In September 1999, when the military was the sole governmental institution capable of providing rapid assistance after a devastating earthquake in the east of İstanbul, a survey reported that only 15% of the population trusted politicians, but 65.1% expressed trust in the military.[10] On the foundation of this self-assurance, the military attempted the impossible in 1980. They would attempt to change much concerning the structure of the political system in order to assure that everything which pertained to the military's power and ultimate veto rights would remain the same as it had supposedly always been in the Turkish Republic.

The Turkish-Islamic Synthesis

The Kemalist project always had a teleological approach. The initially heroic battle would have to be followed by a period of great toil until the Turkish nation would finally be able to enjoy the fruits of their labors. The portions of the population who had no national consciousness or who maintained a false one would inevitably be won over to the common project in the face of the nation's strength and Kemalism's being so self-evidently convincing and right.[11] Economic crises or the necessity of the military's continually having

---

9   Birand, *Shirts of Steel*, 7–8, 10–13. Jenkins, *Context and Circumstance*, 13, 23. Given the low levels of literacy in the 1940s and 1950s, military training may have been more important for the shaping of the male population than schooling. Jenkins, *Political Islam*, 123.
10 Jenkins, *Context and Circumstance*, 16.
11 For the argument for the exemplary function of Kemalism, even on an international level, see a contribution to the parliamentary debate of 29 May 1944 by Cemal Bayar, then a CHP representative: "Like every Turk, I am so sure of the rightness and validity of the Kemalist system of government, that my conviction is that sooner or later all nations of the world will find themselves under a governmental system similar to our regime,"

to take power were seen as a mere delays, not fundamental failures of the enterprise. In reality, however, the Kemalist state not only ran up against its limits, but it drove into a cul-de-sac in which the means it employed to defend that what was sacred to it were turned against it.

In September 1980, the National Security Council (Milli Güvenlik Konseyi), composed solely of military officers, bestowed the office of prime minister on the former general Bülent Ulusu (1923–2015) and that of advisor for economic questions on Turgut Özal. The government was supposed to take care of everyday affairs under the direct supervision of the military. The junta itself set to work in staking its claim as clearly and deliberately as possible. While in 1960, the junta had leading jurists fetched from İstanbul to Ankara on the day of the coup, this time it was more than a year after the coup, in October 1981, when they set up the Constituent Assembly (Kurucu Meclis).[12]

As before 1961, the constitution completed in 1982 recognized only a single parliamentary chamber in the Great National Assembly of Turkey (Türkiye Büyük Millet Meclisi), now with a legislative term of five years. The newly introduced ten percent hurdle was of decisive significance for the representation of parties in the National Assembly over the next decades. A certain sacralization of the Turkish state was particularly conspicuous, which found expression in frequent phrasings like, "the indivisibility of the land and the nation" and "the indivisible integrity of the State with its territory and nation."[13] The president received a certain kind of guardianship over the political system.[14] In addition, the National Security Council (Milli Güvenlik Kurulu, MGK) was strengthened. In 1961 the MGK was tasked with "supporting" the government; in the constitutional amendments of 1971, it became "counselling." Now, Article 118 of the constitution prescribed that the council of ministers would have to "consider" the MGK's recommendations "with priority."

TBMM ZC, Devre 7, İçtimâ 1, Cilt 10, 64. İnikat, 29.5.1944, quoted from Koçak, *Türkiye'de Millî Şef Dönemi*, 2:356.

12   Rumpf, *Das türkische Verfassungssystem*, 91.
13   Özbudun, *Constitutional System of Turkey*, 45ff., here points to the preamble and articles 5, 13, 14, 26, 28 (three times), 30, 68, 81, 103, 122, and 133.
14   Ibid., 19ff., 77, 130. Thus the president names the prime minister and accepts his resignation; he can send legislation back to the National Assembly for reworking; he has comprehensive rights to appoint personnel to significant institutions like the highest courts and university rectorates.

Two days after the constitutional referendum of 7 November 1982 passed with 91.37% of the vote, Kenan Evren was named president. The constitution's Transitional Article 9 endowed him with a special privilege. For a period of six years, the president's veto could only be overridden by a three-quarters majority of the entire parliament. Transitional Article 15 granted the leaders of the coup of 1980 complete immunity from prosecution.[15] One can justifiably say that the constitution of 1982 was drawn up to protect the government from the people.[16]

Even during the period of direct military oversight, further laws were added to the constitution. Law 2945[17] of 9 November 1983 widened the powers of the National Security Council to encompass almost every aspect of national security: it was now the MGK's task to recognize security threats and develop appropriate countermeasures. All relevant documents were issued by the general secretariat of the MGK which was staffed by former officers. The Law on Parties 2820 of 22 April 1983 was particularly harsh in that, among other things, it stated in its Article 81 that parties were not allowed to assert that there were minorities in Turkey, whether of an ethnic, national, religious, or linguistic nature. Law 2932, also of 1983, toughened Articles 26 and 28 of the constitution, which forbade the use of a language other than Turkish. The law prescribed that in Turkey no other language was allowed other than the primary official languages in those countries recognized by Turkey. The obvious purpose was banning Kurdish without doing so by name (Kurdish is officially recognized secondarily after Persian in Iran).[18]

What the constitutional amendments of 1971 and 1973 had heralded was now realized in its entirety: the "weaknesses" of the Constitution of 1961 would be removed by plugging all possible loopholes for uncontrollable liberality. In order to safeguard this in the long term, a conservative consensus in society would be created on the basis of both a Turkish-national and Muslim Sunni identity. The military adopted the idea of the Turkish-Islamic Synthesis (Türk-İslam Sentezi) developed years before by Islamist-nationalist intellectuals.

---

15 Ibid., 130. Rumpf, *Das türkische Verfassungssystem*, 374ff. Those responsible for the coup of 1960 had incidentally already received this same privilege. Özbudun, *Constitutional System of Turkey*, 13.

16 Ibid., 19, 44.

17 All laws can be found on the state websites, https://www.resmigazete.gov.tr or https://www.mevzuat.gov.tr, accessed 20 April 2023.

18 Jenkins *Political Islam*, 144. Özbudun, *Constitutional System of Turkey*, 23. Law no. 2932 was repealed in 1991; the phrase "legally forbidden languages" adopted in the constitution was stricken in 2001. Özbudun, *Constitutional System of Turkey*, 33, 51.

According to the military's interpretation, Turkey's common national culture rested on the three pillars of family, mosque, and military. In this sense and spirit, in 1983 the general staff published a three-volume work with the title *Atatürkism (Atatürkçülük)*, in which Atatürk was portrayed as a pious Muslim. His reforms were said to ultimately have been aimed at removing just those elements of religion which kept the people trapped in ignorance and superstition. In 1986, the Ministry of Education revised all schoolbooks to harmonize them with the idea of an indivisible connection between "religion and state" (*din ü devlet*).[19]

The military thus believed they had recognized and employed religion's potential for mobilization. In fact, they achieved their immediate goal of strangling the left to radical left current so relatively strong in the 1960s and 1970s and weakening the unions—but a twofold price would have to be paid for this. First, the Kurdish and Alevi activists who had identified with the political left for the previous two decades went their own way. In the parliamentary system, Kurdish parties even took over from the 1990s onwards the role of the left and of parties critical of the system. Secondly, the Islamist Welfare Party (Refah Partisi, RP) filled the vacuum created by the destruction of the left by offering themselves as convincing advocates for social concerns in the face of an increasingly ruthless economic and social order.

In the realm of party politics, the military's precautions had, in any case, little durability. All members of the parliament active until 12 September were subjected to a five-year ban from political activity. Two hundred politicians, including Süleyman Demirel, Bülent Ecevit, Necmettin Erbakan, and Alparslan Türkeş, received ten-year bans. On 6 September 1987, however, the fourth transitional article of the Constitution of 1982, according to which the ten-year ban on political activity would have run until 1992, was lifted in a referendum by a bare majority of less than a percent.[20] The greats of the 1970s could return to politics, and they first took part in parliamentary elections again on 29 October 1987.

The military only permitted three of more than fifteen newly founded parties to run in the first parliamentary elections of 6 November 1983 to take place after the coup. Two were ginned up by the military, the Nationalist Democracy Party (Milliyetçi Demokrasi Partisi) and the Populist Party (Halkçı Parti). The center-right Motherland Party (Anavatan Partisi, ANAP), founded by Turgut Özal, was the sole other party admitted to the election

---

19 Jenkins, *Political Islam*, 142. Kaplan, "Din-u Devlet," 120.
20 Jenkins, *Political Islam*, 142. Cemal, *Özal Hikayesi*, 240.

under pressure from the West.[21] The military's expectations were deeply disappointed. The Nationalist Democracy Party under former general Turgut Sunalp (1917–1999), which the military favored, was the big loser with only 23.3% of the vote. The Populist Party, which was supposed to represent the former constituencies of the CHP, got 30.5%. Mehmet Keçeciler (b. 1944), an advisor to Özal in the 1980s, prophesied before the vote that a "seed produced by the military will not thrive in the political soil of this country."[22] The clear winner was the Motherland Party (ANAP) with 45.1% of the vote.

The basic party spectrum, which had already evolved in the 1960s, now resurfaced after its forcible suppression at the hands of the military. The party of the Islamist electorate, which, after 1987, could once again be led by Necmettin Erbakan, was yet again called the Welfare Party (Refah Partisi, RP). The newly founded True Path Party (Doğru Yol Partisi, DYP), initially steered by Süleyman Demirel in the background, understood itself explicitly as the successor to the Justice Party (Adalet Partisi, AP) of the 1970s and 1980s.

Nevertheless, four significant changes may be observed in the Turkish party structure after 1983. First, parties left of the social-democratic/Kemalist spectrum were hardly to be seen in the polity, much less represented in parliament. Second, Kurdish political activists no longer saw their interests represented by the existing parties and attempted to pursue them through their own parties. Third, the center-right camp became divided between two parties, the ANAP, led by Özal, and the DYP, steered by Demirel. And finally, the center-left camp spread across two, and even temporarily (1992–1995) three parties: the Democratic Left Party (Demokratik Sol Parti, DSP), which Bülent Ecevit led from its founding, initially behind the scenes and openly after the 1987 lifting of his ban from politics; the Social-Democratic Populist Party (Sosyaldemokrat Halkçı Parti, SHP)[23] led by Erdal İnönü (1926–2007), son of İsmet İnönü and a professor of theoretical physics; and finally the Republican People's Party (Cumhuriyet Halk Partisi, CHP), refounded in 1992 and which absorbed the SHP in 1995.

From 1983 to 1991, the Motherland Party could govern alone, thanks to favorable electoral results. Thereafter a series of progressively weaker coalition

---

21 Ibid., 48–55.
22 Ibid., 41.
23 On the other hand, the SHP was created from the merger of the unviable Populist Party (Halkçı Parti) and the Social Democracy Party (Sosyal Demokrasi Partisi) led by Erdal İnönü.

governments followed in rapid succession. Even the wily Süleyman Demirel, president from 1993 to 2000, failed to unite the center-right camp.

At first glance, the paths which Turkey and Iran took in the transition from the 1970s to the 1980s were completely contradictory. While Turkey anchored itself even more deeply in the Western alliance system after the coup of 1980, Iran not only severed its earlier close alliance with the US, but became an especially militant opponent of the West. While in Turkey, Kemalism, which understood itself as secular, was still the official leading ideology, Iran saw itself as an ideal Islamic polity—or at least as on the way towards becoming one. At the same time, however—and here the always noteworthy parallels between the two countries emerge—the Turkish Constitution of 1982 not only closely followed that of the Fifth Republic of France proclaimed by Charles de Gaulle in 1958 but also the new constitution of the Islamic Republic of Iran—despite all the latter's Islamist rhetoric.[24] A further similarity suggests itself: the Islamic Republic of Iran, which only apparently foreswore nationalism, wanted to export its revolutionary Islam across the Islamic world, but finally failed in exporting and internationalizing its revolution, because it was founded upon certain particularities of Iranian society and intellectual history, above all the role of the Shi'ite clergy.[25] Turkey was similarly constrained: thanks to its historical character and the imprints taken on during the period of the Turkish Republic, a peculiarly Turkish variety of political-minded Islam developed, becoming increasingly apparent in the 1990s.

2. Excursus: Nation and Islam

Up until now, we have spoken in self-evident fashion of the conservative Motherland Party (Anavatan Partisi, ANAP), the Islamist Welfare Party (Refah Partisi, RP), and the right-wing Nationalist Movement Party (Milliyetçi Hareket Partisi, MHP)—all parties which can be assigned to the political right.[26] In this excursus, we will limn the three basic currents of Turkey's political right—conservative, Islamist, and radical nationalist—and their respective

---

24   Ahmad, *Modern Turkey*, 186. Abrahamian, *Khomeinism*, 15.
25   Halliday, "Iranian Foreign Policy," 92. Skocpol, "Rentier State and Shi'a Islam."
26   In the small Anatolian cities of the 1970s, there often emerged a sort of political division of labor—older brothers joined the center-right AP and younger brothers the MHP. Bora and Can, *Devlet Ocak, Dergâh*, 54.

proportions of admixture of the two most important ingredients of Nation and Islam.[27]

Let's begin the at the most fundamental level: the Islamic religion and the Turkish nation can very easily be distinguished from one another. However, when we are dealing with Turkish identity and Turkish identity politics, there is a direct interplay between the two. Along with the question of what relationship Turkey should have with "the West," the relationship between nation and Islam has been decisive for the self-understanding of modern Turkey, because at this intersection, we find an answer to the questions of what the Turkish nation should ultimately be based upon, and how Turkish Muslims—beyond religious practice—can find their way in the public and political realm.

Turkish nationalism in the Kemalist mode gave persuasive answers to the demands of the nineteenth and early twentieth centuries, at least within the parameters of its internal logic. It answered the question how the new state would be tailored. Coexistence within a multiethnic state no longer seemed in keeping with the times, and congregating in a nation-state, by contrast, appeared the natural solution. The national War of Independence became the primordial basis of pride; the natural home of the Turks would be Anatolia.

Nevertheless, Islam was indispensable for Kemalism, not as a religion as such, but as a criterion for membership in the nation. On 5 May 1968, the Egyptian state-adjacent newspaper *al-Ahram* (Pyramids) reported on a Marian apparition at the Coptic Church of the Virgin Mary in Cairo's Zeitoun neighborhood. An article whose subtitle contained the pull quote, "The appearance of the Virgin is a sign God will be with us in our victory, and that Heaven has not abandoned us" explained that the Virgin Mary wished to rebuild the nation after the Six Day War lost to Israel in June 1969, and that she mourned East Jerusalem which had been loss to the Israeli Army.[28] That a (more or less credible) religious apparition in a church could lead to the improvement of the nation was and is unthinkable in the Turkish context. While intellectuals of Christian confession participated materially in the formulation of Arab nationalism,[29] such a collaboration in the context of Turkish nationalism was unimaginable.[30]

---

27 For a comparable categorization, see Bora, *Türk Sağının Üç Hâli*, 8, which describes nationalism as the "solid," Islamism as the "liquid," and conservatism as the "gaseous" form of the Turkish right.
28 *Al-Ahram*, 5 May 1968, p. 3. Cited in Wild, "Gott und Mensch in Libanon," 225.
29 Dawisha, *Arab Nationalism*, 25–32.
30 Alevis are not to be found among the theorists of Turkish nationalism, unlike Kurds such as Ziya Gökalp (likely the most important pioneer of Turkish nationalism) or Jews such as Munis Tekinalp (*né* Moiz Kohen).

In its confessional exclusivity, Turkish nationalism closely resembles Southeastern European nationalism. As in Southeastern Europe (where, for example, the Orthodox confession is extremely closely associated with being Serbian and the Catholic with being Croat), the "right" confessional affiliation is a fundamental requirement for membership in the nation. One may presume that the project of a secular society in the Republic of Turkey was not only a product of the striving for Western modernity, but also— more unconsciously than consciously—served as a counterweight to the confessional core of the Turkish national concept. Kemalism's very instrumental understanding of religion speaks in favor of this interpretation— the Islam "purified" by the Kemalist state, that is, constrained in its reach, should not be "exploited" as a political instrument beyond the criterion of confessional membership.[31]

Let us look back again at the classical animosity between the Kemalist secularist and religious-conservative camps in Turkey. The self-image of the Kemalist elite was that, through the reforms of the 1920s and 1930s, they had pruned religion back to its immediate ritual requirements and had smashed the network of religious institutions and symbols which had grown up over centuries. Following the French as a paragon, they championed the principle of laïcité (laiklik), but Turkish laicism was "much more of a political motto than an analytical concept,"[32] because the Turkish state never intended a separation of religion and state but rather the control of religion by the state.

To describe the religious policy of the Kemalist state as laicism, then, is a mistake not only made abroad but inside Turkey as well. At the same time, one can't use the term "secular" in generally recognized fashion for the portion of the society which regards the Kemalist reforms as the natural and even pride-inspiring foundation of a progressive and modern Turkey. In the self-understanding of the secular camp, "secularity" stands for more than secularization, specifically for a comprehensive and affirmative definition of one's own political self-understanding and one's way own life. In the years of Kemalist dominance, "secular" could mean a lifestyle completely alienated from belief and everyday religious practice, but at least as strong was the

---

31 Lewis, *Emergence of Modern Turkey*, 264. This depiction of religion, tactically deployed in the 1920s and 1930s, has distorted the view of later authors on its complex role. See for example, the many maladroit suggestions in Ahmad, *Turkish Experiment*, 242, 371–373, 375, 377, 382, that religion was not permitted to be "exploited."
32 Schulze, *Geschichte der islamischen Welt*, 109.

affirmation of a modernity (albeit vaguely imagined) to which one felt one belonged and which one denied to "the other."

One can therefore speak of a design flaw or at least an unacknowledged weak point in Kemalism, namely the desire to discard religion as a relic of the lost Ottoman Empire and as a dangerous competitor and, at the same time, the belief that it was unavoidable to rely on common membership in Sunni Islam as a connective element for the nation. This construction of the Turkish citizen as Turk and Muslim is probably the legacy anchored most deeply in the political culture of Turkey, more so than all the other elements of Kemalism.

Before the three currents named above are discussed in detail, some explanations of the terminology used below are indispensable. One is not using straightforward terms, even when one is just speaking about "Islam" or describing a tradition or action as "Islamic." "Islam" is the comprehensive label for everything pertaining to the Islamic religion, but can also be employed in an even broader sense. Thus, an Islamic state is not merely a state with a Muslim majority, but rather a state like, for example, the Islamic Republic of Iran, which grounds its legitimacy and political ethic in the religion of Islam.[33] Analytically seen, the consideration that "all forms of political action in Islamic modernism were basically secular,"[34] speaks against the use of the term "Islamic" for political positions. Even if one wished to follow the premise that political intentionality in Islam is shown more strongly than in other religions, we might be dealing with an exceptional phenomenon that will recede in the coming decades.[35] In any case, the political charging of Islam which began in the nineteenth century and continues today is likely not best regarded as a regression in the face of the excessive demands of Western-dominated modernity,[36] rather as an attempt at coping with it by using its

---

33   According to Hallaq, *Impossible State*, the idea of resurrecting an ideal Islamic state resting on Shari'a in the modern world is not only pointless but downright impossible. At the same time, Hallaq argues against the self-assured Western position that there is no alternative to the modern state as created in the West.
34   Schulze, *Geschichte der islamischen Welt*, 80.
35   For the confident authors Courbage and Todd in *Unaufhaltsame Revolution*, 36, ahead of the Islamic world—after a phase of potentially violent Islamism in which we now find ourselves—"looms, in all probability, a de-Islamized Muslim world which has passed through the same development as the Christian Occident and the Buddhist Far East once did."
36   As a particularly vivid example of such a negative skein of interpretation, see Lewis, *What Went Wrong?*, which argues that Muslims had failed to find an appropriate answer to modernity and therefore took refuge in religious and cultural regression.

own terminology. It's surely not wrong to say that as a missionary religion like Christianity, the language and instruments of power are not alien to Islam.

In this book, the term "Islamism" is used in preference to "political Islam." Islamism in Turkey has shown fluid crossovers with conservative and radical nationalist camps and thereby possesses more ambiguity and vagueness than the action-oriented term "political Islam" conveys. As an adjective corresponding to "Islamism," we use "Islamist." This admittedly militant-sounding adjective should be regarded in the same derivational relationship as "nationalist" has to "nationalism." Of course, the parallels between the two conceptual pairs—Islamism/Islamist, nationalism/nationalist—are limited. While nationalism historically brought about the existence of nations, no one would argue that Islamism created Islam. Islam is a religion that appeared on the Arabian Peninsula in the seventh century of Western calendar. Turkish nationalism appeared around 1900 and the Turkish nation even later. It is valid, however, to maintain that every variation of Islamism is potentially capable of bringing about *its own* Islam.

For reasons of analytical clarity, in the following, the conceptional pair of Islam/Islamic will basically be used only to describe aspects of religion or other cultural or social phenomena immediately derived from the religion. In principle, scholarship would need an additional term like "Islamizing" to connote the broad and confusing realm which lies between the concepts of "Islamic" and "Islamist," and which contains all the attitudes invoked by cultural images and ideas which receive a religious covering without being directly subject to the political goals of Islamism at the same time.

The Right-Conservative Current: Conservative, Nationalist, Proximate to Islam

The reservoir and power source of the right-conservative current,[37] of which the center-right parties are only a part,[38] is the Sunni-Turkish population of Anatolia, which has always been the largest single group in the Republic of Turkey—both as the rural populace and later after their large-scale migration into the cities.

---

37 It is essential to speak here of a "right-conservative" movement and not only a "conservative" one, as there was a "left-conservative" movement represented by the Kemalist main current.
38 For examples of organizations belonging to the conservative current outside the political parties, see Lord, *Religious Politics*, 218.

The Janus-faced nature of the center-right parties, which in the main rest upon this conservatively inclined and religiously minded majority but sometimes appear very close to the secular-Kemalist camp and other times to the Islamists' position, explains the vagueness and indecisiveness which appears again and again in analysis of the Turkish right. For example, were the Democrat Party (Demokratik Parti, DP) of the 1950s, the Justice Party (Adalet Partisi, AP) of the '60s and '70s, or the Motherland Party (Anavatan Partisi, ANAP) of the '80s and '90s, basically conservative and only had overtones reminiscent of Islamism? Or were these parties connected to Islamism in some fundamental fashion? Formulating a clear answer is obviously difficult.[39] The typical meandering around ideological positions in the center-right parties was less a problem than an opportunity for them. While the Kemalist camp was forbidden from admitting any contradictions in its ideology, the much less restrained center-right parties could bounce to and fro between the poles of conservatism, Islamism, and nationalism without being disloyal to themselves.

One could even go so far as to say that, in the second half of the twentieth century, the Kemalist power establishment was confronted by a right-conservative complex which could not, initially at least, take on the former in terms of institutional power, but which was, at the same time, superior in its interpretive power. After some decades of paralysis, the Islamist movement and the right-conservative movement in its wake had recognized Kemalism's above-described mistake in the construction of the Turkish nation-state: it had made membership in Sunni Islam fundamental but simultaneously discarded it as a cultural guidance system.

The right-conservative current thus had several triumphs in hand. Contra the argument which was still persuasive in late Ottoman times that the religion of Islam stood for weakness, it could now credibly point to the anchoring of modern Turkey in the nation *and* Islam. It could unreservedly and authentically represent the triad of conservatism, Islamism, and nationalism. It could effortlessly fill Kemalism's emotional lacunae. They just had to succeed in winning over the conservative and religiously minded electorate.

Central to the self-image of the right-conservative *and* Islamist spectrum in Turkey is the feeling of having been pushed to the margins for the first eighty years of the Republic, indeed of having been a victim. The practice of religion

---

39   Right-conservatism is, however, not so volatile that it can't be studied by political-scientific research. See, for example, the numerous contributions in Belge and Çiğdem, *Muhafazakârlık*.

was never forbidden, as it was in, for example, Enver Hoxha's Albania, but it was supposed to be expressed only in an Islam that was state-adjacent and approved by Diyanet officials. In this sense, one could describe—however exaggeratedly— the rural Muslim Turkish population of Anatolia as *the largest minority* which the Kemalist state created. They experienced the Kemalist reforms as an alienation from their customary cultural and religious environment. Center-right and Islamist politicians consequently repeated like a litany that the silent majority had, over decades, been thrust into the status of a *lesser majority*.

The Islamist Movement: Victim Myth and the Headscarf Question, Dervish Orders and Fethullah Gülen

In contrast to the right-conservative current, Turkish Islamism openly rejected Kemalism, although it backed some of its central characteristics as a matter of course, like emphatic nationalism or unconditional insistence on the territorial integrity of the country. In this sense, the Islamist movement was more honorable and serious, if more withdrawn into itself, than the right-conservative current.

In terms of a "hard no," the Islamist movement could not agree with the Turkish state's so-called laicism, let alone *laïcisme à la française*. Islamism attributes such a central significance to the morality of a society that its being driven out of many areas of public life seems impermissible. At the same time—and likely more importantly—Islamism is a position which intends "to be able to derive immediate and universally definitive rules for the organization of the body politic from religious sources."[40] Following the doctrines of a globally active Islamism, one also sees Turkish Islamism committed to the goal of erecting an ideal, global Islamic community (ümmet), though with the decisive caveat that it would have to be a community which does not level out national and ethnic differences.

Turkish Islamism adopts argumentative models that Islamism uses across the Islamic world, like contrasting Western materialism with its own spirituality,[41] with the inherent premise that the West is therefore hollow and doomed to collapse in the end. On the other hand, the Islamist movement in

---

40   Bielefeldt, *Muslime im säkularen Rechtsstaat*, 41.
41   The deprecatory comparison between a materialist West and a spiritual Orient is a general phenomenon in the contention of Asia's intellectuals with the West. Conrad, *Global History*, 30, refers to the examples of Tenshin Okakura (1862–1913) in Japan and Rabindranath Tagore (1861–1914) in Bengal.

Turkey shows no desire to give up the borders of its country, its language, or its own culture.[42]

The Islamist movement has created its own victim mythology. In contrast to representatives of the right-conservative current, it can point to persecution by the Kemalist state as an additional form of legitimation possessed by it alone. While, according to Kemalist myth, the Turkish nation almost went under due to hostilities with the European great powers and was only able to secure its own state due to its heroic resistance, the Islamist myth proclaims that the identity of the Sunni Muslims of Anatolia would have been all but extinguished had they not stubbornly resisted the assault of the Kemalist state.

One of the crucial achievements of Islamist-nationalist intellectuals after the Second World War (more on whom in the following subchapter) was going on the offensive and, using the argument of a Turkish-Islamic Synthesis, calling for the fusing of nation and religion as an essential prerequisite for national greatness. The Kemalist reforms, according to this thesis, led to Turkey's loss of its patrimony and language and destroyed the spiritual strength of the Turks. Only a new elite, able to break up the templates of Kemalism, could bring the Turkish nation, which had been robbed of its true role, back into balance once again.[43]

Along with the rhetoric of a long history of suffering oppression, a second crucial argument, that of authenticity, came to the fore. That was, only politicians on the Islamist spectrum could give appropriate expression to the voice and will of the people. Both arguments were of great power in mobilizing people. This mobilization was not only a rhetorical appeal in campaign speeches but rested upon a genuine social foundation. Its pronounced distance from the general public was always simultaneously both a strength and a weakness of Kemalism. It lent the elites the capability of sober rationality but at the same time alienated them from their own people.[44]

By contrast, the Welfare Party (Refah Partisi, RP) of the 1980s and 1990s could connect with the cultural institutions and experiences of the migrant population in the big cities, not only with a better common touch but with a very effective grass-roots effort which also recognized the potential of women as intermediaries. This mobilization succeeded through emotional appeals

---

42 But see Vömel, "Turkish Islamism," which notes an international orientation in the Turkish Islamism of the 1970s.
43 Yavuz, *Secularism and Muslim Democracy*, 138.
44 Plaggenborg, *Ordnung und Gewalt*, 80.

to the religious-traditional worldview of individuals. Of particular help were the social networks which, to a great extent, were rooted in the migration era and the concomitant experience of solidarity. The mechanisms of mutual aid (*imece*) and the granting of protection and patronage (*himaye*) which people from rural Anatolia took with them into the gecekondus and outskirts (*varoş*) of the great Turkish metropolises, strengthened the parties' grass-roots activism. The Islamist parties succeeded best when conveying these ideas of cooperation and assistance in slogans like "service" (hizmet) and "order" (*nizam*).[45]

For their "long march through the institutions," the Islamist movement brought the requisite patience as well as the ability to employ different forms and paths for mobilizing opinion. As a result, the wearing of headscarfs in public institutions like universities (this right was never limited in public) was a particularly suitable means not only for emphasizing their own ethical standards and demanding a conspicuous role in the public sphere, but also for reshaping that sphere according to their own ideas. Women who conform to the rules of *tesettür* (the appropriate form of covering overall, thus extending beyond the veil) earn the protection of every pious Muslim and receive "ostentatiously chivalrous treatment" from men.[46] Veiling was and is—not only in Turkey but elsewhere—an expression of personal pious conduct, a means for self-determination in one's own environment, religious self-empowerment, and a political instrument at the same time.

In the 1970s, increasing numbers of women in cities began to cover themselves in "Islamically appropriate" fashion. Consequently, on 8 December 1978, the government led by the Republican People's Party (Cumhuriyet Halk Partisi, CHP) issued a decree forbidding women working in public service from covering their heads in the workplace. From the 1980s to the 2000s, the headscarf was the object of a constant back-and-forth struggle in Turkish society, an incessant series of decisions, revisions, and abrogations of revisions. The headscarf debate took a dramatic turn after the parliamentary election of 18 April 1999. Among the female candidates of the Virtue Party (Fazilet Partisi, FP), the successor party to the Welfare Party (which had been banned shortly before), there were eight veiled women, but only one of them, Merve Kavakçı (b. 1968), was elected to parliament. When Kavakçı wanted to take her oath of office at the opening of parliament on 2 May 1999 wearing a veil, this led to an uproar among the representatives. Kavakçı was not

---

45   White, *Islamist Mobilization*, 71. Türk, *Muktedir*, 223ff.
46   White, *Islamist Mobilization*, 74.

sworn in, and shortly thereafter her parliamentary mandate was withdrawn. On 7 May 1999, the state prosecutor filed a motion with the Constitutional Court to ban the Virtue Party for antisecularist activities. Into the late 2000s, the Constitutional Court and the government led by the Party of Justice and Development (Adalet ve Kalkınma Partisi, AKP) traded fire in a bitter struggle over the question who would be able to conclusively determine the headscarf question and on what legal basis. From today's standpoint, one can say that the Islamist movement won that battle.[47]

Sufism was another resource for Islamist mobilization in Turkey. Sufism is the Islamic variety of the mysticism which is found as a fundamental current in all religions. It is however not the case, that Islamic mysticism poses a uniformly clear contrast with Orthodox varieties of Islam. It serves much more as a different way of approaching God and partially as a different form of religious living. This is particularly true for the *tarikat*, the Sufi brotherhoods which gradually developed beginning in the twelfth century. The *tarika* (literally "way" or "path," a loanword from Arabic) rests, according to Sufi doctrine, on a higher level of consciousness than the Shari'a, but beneath the final goal of the vision and knowledge of the true nature of God (*hakikat*).[48] The members of these Sufi brotherhoods, also known as dervish orders, do not live celibately in cloisters, but pursue a worldly life and gather only on certain occasions in convents (known in the Ottoman-Turkish context as a *dergah*, *tekke*, or *zaviye*). A hierarchical relationship between master ("sheikh," *şeyh*, or *pir*) and his students seeking instruction and guidance is characteristic of Sufi orders.

The Sufi brotherhoods diverged into different currents. The Bektashi order (Bektaşilik), then, so important in Ottoman history incorporated Shi'ite elements, drew upon ecstatic practices. The Bektashis were banned in 1826, because they were closely tied to the Janissary Corps which was destroyed that same year. On the other hand, the Nakşbendis (Nakşibendilik), a Sufi order significant not only in Turkish Islam, reject conspicuous ritual practices and place probity in everyday life in the foreground as the proof of one's belief.[49] In fact, all Sufi brotherhoods were banned in 1925, but many succeeded in maintaining networks which escaped the gaze of the state.

---

47 Jenkins, *Political Islam*, 139, 165. In 2008, the ban on the headscarf at universities was eliminated. In 2014, girls ten and older in schools were permitted to wear them. Rogg, *Türkei*, 202.
48 Schimmel, *Mystische Dimensionen des Islam*, 16, 148.
49 Ibid., 68ff. On the Nakşbendis in the context of global Islam, see Weisman, *Naqshbandiyya*.

Because he Nakşbendis lacked religious expressivity, they were particularly well outfitted for such almost-invisible activity.

Said Nursî (1876–1960) stood in the tradition of the Nakşbendis. He took part in the failed counterrevolution of 1909, thereafter keeping a low profile, politically, and concentrating on his writings, which were later collected in the comprehensive work, the Risale-i Nur (Treatise of Divine Light). A new and final phase in Said Nursî's life began in 1950, when the Democrat Party's taking power opened up new political opportunities for him and made him honored once again as a significant personality. Nursî's fundamental concern was the revitalization of Turkish religious culture. This revival would not take place through political activities or force, but rather through "positive action" (*müspet hareket*), which meant the re-anchoring of Islamic mores in society by everyday example. The Nurcu movement, which is to say the adherents who succeeded Said Nursî, is considered fragmented; the ideological alignments of the various subcurrents extend from Pan-Islamists to Kurdish groups who see in Said Nursî a devout Kurdish nationalist.

The Gülen movement stands in the tradition of Said Nursî. Its founder, Fethullah Gülen, was born in 1938 in the village of Korucuk near Erzurum, received instruction in a local Nakşbendi convent, and occupied himself with the writings of Said Nursî even as a youth.[50] As a qualified imam, Gülen was sent by the Diyanet to İzmir in 1965. There he was the superintendent of a Koran school connected to a mosque, but at the same time was already famed as the leader of the movement named for him. In 1999, he emigrated to the US, where he still lives today.

Just like the Nurcus, the Gülen movement dispensed with important elements of Sufi brotherhoods, like initiation (acceptance into the brotherhood and simultaneously a consecration into a higher level of consciousness), firmly defined religious practice, and a fixed master-disciple relationship, because it no longer believed these organizational forms to be in keeping with the times. In addition, the goal was presumably to be better able to avoid state repression by means of an unclear organizational structure. An orientation towards the master, however, remained dispositive, even if the Gülen movement represents itself as a loose network of volunteers who are merely inspired by Fethullah Gülen. The Gülen movement declines the label of "movement" (*hareket*) and prefers to speak of itself in terms like "[the]

---

50 The Gülen movement attributes so much significance to the study of the writings of Said Nursî that they have even been accused of neglecting the study of the Koran.

service" (hizmet). The instrument of ambiguity, deployed in thoroughly strategic fashion, makes it possible for the movement to maintain that Gülen initiated the transnational efforts of the Gülen movement but simultaneously has absolutely no part in the leadership and guidance of the movement.[51]

The desire to raise up a "golden generation," who would succeed in executing the fundamental turn towards an Islamic order in state and society, was typical of the Islamist movement as a whole in Turkey. The Gülen movement was unusual, however, in how much emphasis it placed on intensive instruction in modern natural sciences in the schools it ran.[52] Gülen schools claimed to be free of any kind of indoctrination; however, the movement's message was transmitted in more subtle fashion. The teachers, who were in general committed to the Gülen movement, proved to be extremely engaged and model instructors.[53] Religious schooling ensued during students' contacts with educators outside school classes, primarily in the attached boarding schools. A further pillar of engagement and the public visibility of the Gülen movement was intercultural and interreligious dialogue. These activities were not aimed at deeper hermeneutic contention, but rather stressed the commonalities of the three monotheistic religions, Judaism, Christianity, and Islam, and served as a platform for personal encounters.[54] All these activities must be spoken of in the past tense, as in 2013 the Gülen movement was accused by the Turkish state of having built a "parallel state" (*paralel devlet yapısı*) and would be persecuted unmercifully as the puppet masters of the failed coup attempt of July 2016 (and more so thereafter).

The state and military reacted to the challenge of Islamism partially with harshness, partially with cooptation. When Said Nursî died in 1960 in the Southeastern Anatolian city of Şanlıurfa, Cemal Gürsel, chief of the then regnant military junta, ordered his exhumation and burial in an unknown location in the Western Anatolian city of Isparta in order to prevent the establishment of a saintly cult of veneration at his grave.[55] However, twenty years later, when the Nakşbendi shaykh Mehmet Zahit Kotku (1897–1980),

---

51 Tee, *Gülen Movement*, 24. Hendrick, *Gülen*, 72.
52 Lord, *Religious Politics*, 194. Mardin, *Religion and Social Change*, 80ff., 87, notes that in the late Ottoman era Said Nursî advocated the foundation of a Kurdish university in Van in Eastern Anatolia in which traditional Islamic sciences would have been taught alongside modern philosophy and natural sciences.
53 According to Balci, *Islam in Central Asia*, 59, the Gülen movement employed a strategy of attraction through active "representation" (*temsil*) in the schools they ran in Central Asia, due to the strongly secular character of the population and the political elite.
54 Tee, *Gülen Movement*, 124–126.
55 Lord, *Religious Politics*, 225.

superintendent of the İskender Paşa convent in İstanbul, with close relationships with politicians like Necmettin Erbakan and Turgut Özal, died, the National Security Council regnant since the coup of 1980 secured permission for Kotku to be buried in the cemetery of the Süleymaniye, the most important Ottoman mosque in İstanbul—making Kotku the first individual buried there since the founding of the Republic.

The Radical Nationalist Movement: Pan-Turkists and Gray Wolves

In this subchapter, our object is not the everyday nationalism omnipresent in the Republic of Turkey, but rather those forms of radical and activist nationalism which are mostly found among groups on the extreme political right. We have already seen that, in the Turkish party spectrum, this position has been represented since the 1960s primarily by the Nationalist Movement Party (Milliyetçi Hareket Partisi, MHP). The MHP is not alone on this section of the spectrum, however; as in all the other camps, other parties may be found, like for example the Great Unity Party (Büyük Birlik Partisi, BBP) founded in 1993 by Muhsin Yazıcıoğlu (1954–2009) and characterized by a stronger Islamist orientation. They are joined by other organizations inclined to radical Turkish nationalism, like the Türk Ocağı (literally, "Turkish Hearth") founded in 1911 and by 1920 in possession of around thirty thousand members,[56] or by the Aydınlar Ocağı (literally, Hearth of the Enlightened), an elitist circle of right-oriented intellectuals founded in 1970. Among its members numbered individuals like İbrahim Kafesoğlu (1914–1984) and Muharrem Ergin (1923–1995) who contributed to the development of the Turkish-Islamic Synthesis (Türk-İslam Sentezi).[57] This ideology, which was so strongly promoted by the military in the 1980s, found much more approval in radical nationalist circles than in the Islamist movement.

One striking characteristic of Turkish nationalism is that it actually stands for two nationalisms: for an unconditional Turkish nationalism, that is for the defense and strengthening of the Republic of Turkey, and at the same time for Pan-Turkism (Türkçülük or Pan-Türkizm), that is, the idea that all the Turkic

---

56 Landau, *Pan-Turkism*, 42.
57 Eligür, *Mobilization of Political Islam*, 96–102. Bora and Can, *Devlet, Ocak, Dergâh*, 128–155 (including a notable comparison of the *Aydınlar Ocağı* with *Opus Dei* on pages 135–137).

peoples of Eurasia should combine into a single realm—under, it goes without saying, Turkish leadership. Pan-Turkism can be differentiated from the Pan-Turanism in this regard. The latter term, which arose in the nineteenth century, derives from the old Iranian word *Tūrān*, which denoted the lands northeast of Iran. Pan-Turanism was conceived of in much milder, broader fashion, including even Mongolian, Finnish, and Hungarian in the "Turanian" languages.[58] Pan-Turkism is more focused, but its goal is practically unattainable and utopian even in the eyes of its adherents. It seeks a pan-Turkic empire that would not only gather in today's Turkic republics of Azerbaijan, Kazakhstan, Kyrgyzstan, Turkmenistan, and Uzbekistan, but also all the other Turkic-speaking populations scattered widely across Eurasia into a common Turkic home. The above-mentioned Gray Wolves, the militant arm of the MHP, are an example of the two faces of radical Turkish nationalism. Their emblem, the gray wolf (*bozkurt*), derives from pan-Turkist mythology, but at the same time, their political efforts are primarily directed at the Republic of Turkey.

The pan-Turkist relationship to Turkish nationalism can be seen in many of its pioneers who were born or grew up in the Russian Empire, but later moved to the Ottoman Empire, in particular Turkey. Among them number Hüseyinzade Ali Turan (1864–1941) and Ahmet Ağaoğlu (1869–1939) from Azerbaijan, Yusuf Akçura (1876–1924) from Simbirsk (now Ulyanovsk) on the Volga, and Sadri Maksudi Arsal (1878–1957) from near Kazan, or the two Bashkir scholars Abdülkadir İnan (1889–1976) and Zeki Velidi Togan (1890–1970).[59]

Beginning in the 1950s, the radical nationalist current in Turkish politics took a decisive turn, becoming increasingly open to Islamist thought. However, openness to Islamic concepts was present in Turkish nationalism quite early. For example, the thought of Ziya Gökalp (1875/6–1924), who may be considered the most important conceptual progenitor of Turkish nationalism in general, does not rest exclusively on European thinkers like Émile Durkheim and Ferdinand Tönnies, but also owes debts to intra-Ottoman and intra-Islamic intellectual traditions.[60] In addition, this Islamically colored nationalism received state cover during the decades of the Cold War because it seemed to be an effective counter-weapon against the communist threat. Today, Turkish radical nationalists are still always

---

58   Lewis, *Emergence of Modern Turkey*, 347.
59   Zürcher, "Children of the Borderlands," 282, is fundamental with regard to this phenomenon.
60   Topal, "Ziya Gökalp in Context and Tradition," 2017.

nationalists in the first instance, but Islamist thought has become the second pillar of their political identity.

Over time, the radical nationalist movement split into various streams. In the 1930s and 1940s, German nationalism served as a model for some radical Turkish nationalists, with its hatred for Slavs, antisemitism, and racism; we can name Alparslan Türkeş, Nihal Atsız (1905–1975), and his brother Nejdet Sançar (1910–1975) in this regard. Atsız went so far as to adopt some of Hitler's mannerisms. However, when Atsız and some others from the extreme right edge of radical Turkish nationalism wanted to take over the Nationalist Movement Party from within in the late 1960s, they were defeated by Alparslan Türkeş, who saw the opportunity for helping the MHP garner more votes provided by the opening to Islamist positions. At the end of the '60s, Türkeş was already proclaiming the slogan, "We are as Turkish as the Tian Shan Mountains and as Muslim as Mount Hira" (Biz Tanrı dağı kadar Türk, Hira dağı kadar Müslümanız). The Central Asian Tian Shan Mountains point to the alleged original home of the Turks in Central Asia, and Mount Hira to an area near Mecca where, according to Islamic tradition, the Archangel Gabriel first revealed the Koran to Muhammad. The MHP's 1969 choice of a party emblem with three crescent moons and not a gray wolf was likely a signal of its openness to the Islamist milieu.[61]

An affinity for the state is striking among all the possible permutations and variations within the radical nationalist movement. The converse is true as well, that is, there has been considerable understanding and sympathy for this current among many representatives of the state. Under the influence of the initial military success of Germany after its attack on the Soviet Union in June 1941, the hopes of Pan-Turkists swelled, thinking they would somehow be able to realize their dreams in an alliance with a Germany dominating Eurasia. The Turkish government, with whose seesaw policy in World War II we have already familiarized ourselves, at first placed no clear limits on these Pan-Turkic ambitions. However, beginning in 1944, the Turkish state kept a close eye on Pan-Turkic activities in order not to provoke the Soviet Union, whose victory over Germany was at that point clearly foreseeable. When anticommunist demonstrations took place outside the restrictions of martial law on 3 May 1944, more than thirty leading Pan-Turkists and their sympathizers were arrested a few days later. Among them were the aforementioned Nihal Atsız, Nejdet Sançar, Alparslan Türkeş, and Zeki Velidi Togan, but

---

61   Bora and Can, *Devlet, Ocak, Dergâh*, 48.

also other radical nationalists like Peyami Safa (1899–1961), Hikmet Tanyu (1918–1992), and Reha Oğuz Türkkan (1920–2010). The ensuing trials lasted until March 1947 and ended with the acquittal of all the defendants. As soon as the state elite recognized that sentences would not improve relations with Moscow, or that such concessions were no longer needed, they were overturned.[62] Nihal Atsız received a fifteen-month prison sentence for radical speech in 1973, but President Fahri Korutürk (in office 1973–1980) pardoned him in January 1974. When İsmet İnönü, chairman of the Republican People's Party (Cumhuriyet Halk Partisi, CHP), spoke to President Cevdet Sunay (in office 1966–1973) about the danger to the state presented by the Gray Wolves, the latter answered, "My friend, they are just kids fighting communism" (Canım, onlar komünizme karşı mücadele eden çocuklar).[63] In fact, in the 1970s, the Gray Wolves understood themselves to be unofficial helpers of the state. Consequently, their disappointment was all the greater when, after the coup of 1980, the military junta distanced itself from the movement, prosecuted them criminally (though of course to a much lesser extent than the radical left), and eschewed their support as an irregular force.[64]

Tanıl Bora and Kemal Can insist in powerful terms that the radical nationalist movement in the 1970s was neither a purely criminal group nor a firmly consolidated fascist organization nor even a homogenous political movement; that it can be neither understood solely as Anatolia's resistance to cosmopolitanism and modernization, nor exclusively as a fraction of the reactionary right, nor as a subculture of a lumpenproletariat—and that it was all of this at once.[65]

Islamism in Turkey shows a more independent development,[66] but Turkish radical nationalism nevertheless possesses also a hard, ideological core. Thus the radical nationalist movement pushed to the extreme the Kemalist demand that non-Turkish Sunnis and non-Sunni Turks must conform to the dominant national model and categorically excluded all non-Turkish non-Sunnis from the outset. The fascist slant to the radical nationalist movement was not a mere episode of the 1930s and 1940s, but belongs to its basic political inventory. The honorary title *başbuğ*, which Alparslan Türkeş bore within the MHP after 1967, drew upon the National Socialist term *Führer*, although its etymology goes back to the mythology of Central Asia. The Gray Wolves

---

62   Landau, *Pan-Turkism* 115–118. Koçak, "Türk Milliyetçiliğinin İslam'la Buluşması," 602.
63   Bora and Can, *Devlet, Ocak, Dergâh*, 48.
64   See ibid., 87–126, for the MHP's shock at their treatment by the military junta after 1980.
65   Ibid., 68.
66   Landau, *Pan-Turkism*, 115–118. Akgün and Çalış, "Tanrı Dağı Kadar Türk," 599.

were influenced by Nazi organizations like the Hitler Youth and SS in their organization and ideology.[67]

At the end of this broad excursus across the right-conservative current and the Islamist and radical nationalist movements, it's worth once again keeping in mind that murky borders between the three have always been a feature of the Turkish right. This is true as well for the many subcurrents of the Kemalist power complex overlapping with the radical nationalist movement. Some readers might feel the need for a similarly in-depth discussion of the currents and movements on the left in Turkey. It is however the case that the world of the left and left radicalism has always been much more influenced by international schools of thought and—with the exception of unusual manifestations as, for example, in Kurdish activism—consequently has been considerably less "original" than that of the political right. Armed with more exact knowledge of the attitudes and ways of thinking of these three fundamental currents of the Turkish political right, we can return to our history of the events of the 1980s.

3. Unrestrained and Restrained Liberalization (1983–1993)

The rhythm of Turkish political history has its own regularities; in the realm of the economy, however, its parallels to global development are obvious. Beginning in the 1980s, a fundamental turn towards a neoliberal economic order proceeded hand-in-hand with the promises of an Islamic conservatism. Since the '80s, then, Turkey has shared in the global phenomenon of a lasting weakening of unions.[68] Neoliberal economic orders, however, in no way always signify unbridled economic development. Turkey's growth rates in the 1980s (4.1%) and 1990s (4%) lagged behind those of the 1960s (6.4%) and 1970s (4.7%).[69]

Nevertheless, in the decade between 1983 and 1993, the foundations of Turkey's later economic success after the turn of the century were laid. Turkey soon deployed the instruments of a liberalized economic policy developed in the 1980s. This policy would later been known under the rubric of "the

---

67 Tapia, "Turkish Extreme Right-Wing Movements," 305.
68 Streeck, *Gekaufte Zeit*, 119. Per Herr and Sonat, "Fragile Growth Regime," the percentage of the labor force represented by unions sank from 35.3% in 1975 to 5.8% in 2008.
69 Herr and Sonat, "Fragile Growth Regime," 37fn18. Harvey, *Neoliberalism*, 88, notes the weak growth in the US and UK in the 1980s, for South America one can even speak of a lost decade.

Washington Consensus," meaning it came out of the agreement between institutions located in Washington, D.C., such as the US Treasury Department, the International Monetary Fund (IMF), and the World Bank, on the need for structural reform programs in many national economies around the world.

Critics of neoliberalism see in it a project of capitalist elites who wish to reinstate the extraordinarily great income and wealth differentials which existed before the Second World War.[70] It is said to be a variety of counter-revolution.[71] This term can be profitably employed in understanding Turkey from the 1980s into the 2010s—but in a different sense. It was not a case of the old elites of the Republic's further enriching themselves, rather it had to do with the ascent of a new political-economic elite class which had played no important economic role, much less a political role, in either the late Ottoman era or the early Republic. Beginning in the 1980s, however, Anatolia and the Anatolians achieved economic and political significance. The "Anatolian Tigers"—rapidly developing industrial centers such as Çorum, Denizli, Gaziantep, Kahramanmaraş, Kayseri, Konya, and Malatya—were not actors able to pull themselves out of the morass of underdevelopment by their own bootstraps or became so competitive merely by virtue of low wages, long workdays, and very flexible employment arrangements.[72] There is a backstory. As early as the end of the 1960s there were "priority development regions" (*kalkınma öncelikli yöreler*) designated, for example, in Denizli and Gaziantep, which would create impressive development on these foundations beginning in the 1980s.[73]

A report of the European Stability Initiative (ESI), located in Berlin, on "Islamic Calvinists" shows the challenge of discerning the real relationship between politics, religion, and economy in the case of the Anatolian Tigers. The ESI report from 2005 comprehensively documents the economic success story of large enterprises in Konya in Central Anatolia, one of the most conservative cities in Anatolia. The political goal of this report was obvious: to allay the fears of the European public of a "deep" Anatolia shaped by Islam, stereotypically incompatible with Europe, and unready for accession to the European Union, in contrast to cosmopolitan İstanbul. The argument's equation of economic success with readiness for accession is not the only

---

70   Harvey, *Neoliberalism*, 16, 19, 83, 119. Streeck, *Gekaufte Zeit*, 87, 93, 96.
71   Ibid., 153.
72   Pamuk, "Economic Change," 291.
73   Lord, *Religious Politics*, 171, 174.

noteworthy thing about the report. At the same time, the report faces the same dilemma that confronted Max Weber in his investigations into the origins of the 'Protestant work ethic,'[74] namely whether religion is the chicken or merely the egg laid by dynamic economic forces, embedded in a corresponding religio-cultural attitude.[75]

In any case, beginning in the mid-1980s, Turkey stepped out of the shadows of the Cold War and its military regime. The years under Prime Minister and, later, President Turgut Özal remain in memory as a decade of a first economic and foreign policy opening—incomplete but nevertheless exemplary for the following decades.

The Özal Decade

The years from 1983 to 1993 were shaped by Turgut Özal. In the years 1983–1989, he was chairman of the Motherland Party (Anavatan Partisi, ANAP) and prime minister. From 1989 until his death in 1993, he was in office as president. He was therefore the second president, along with Celal Bayar (1950–1960), who had no military background. Özal, who first stepped onto the political stage in the 1980s, stood in many respects for the same political spectrum as Süleyman Demirel, albeit with a much stronger dose of economic liberalism and a personal inclination to Islamism. According to Özal, the Motherland Party which he founded and led, was not in the line of any earlier party. The ANAP, he claimed, covered the spectrum of all important party currents of the 1960s and 1970s. It would be conservative like the Justice Party (Adalet Partisi, AP), traditionalist (i.e., Islamist) like the MSP, and nationalist like the MHP. In fact, it could embody the goal of social justice just as credibly as the social democrats.[76]

Born in the Eastern Anatolian city of Malatya in 1927, Turgut Özal grew up in a religiously observant family. His father received an education as an imam before pursuing a career in the state Agricultural Bank (Ziraat Bankası).

---

74 Although Weber tries to demonstrate in his *Protestant Ethic and the Spirit of Capitalism* (1904–1905) how Calvinism unmercifully drives people to unceasing professional work with its doctrine of predestination, he nevertheless sees himself compelled to issue the caveat that he should not be understood as advocating in his work the "stupid, doctrinaire thesis" that "capitalism as an economic system was a creation of the Reformation." Weber, *Protestantische Ethik*, 105ff.
75 European Stability Initiative, *Islamische Calvinisten*, 28.
76 Jenkins, *Political Islam*, 149. Ahmad, *Modern Turkey*, 192.

His mother, an elementary-school teacher, had close connections to the Nakşbendis.[77] In the 1950s, Özal worked in the State Planning Organization (Devlet Planlama Teşkilatı, DPT). After the military intervention in 1960, he worked for the World Bank in Washington for two years, but then returned to Turkey and was active in the private sector. Along with his brother Korkut, he joined the National Salvation Party (Millî Selamet Partisi, MSP) in the 1970s. Korkut Özal was elected into the National Assembly as a representative of the MSP in 1973 and served in office as minister of agriculture and the interior. Turgut Özal himself ran unsuccessfully as an MSP representative from İzmir in 1977—which was ultimately a stroke of luck for him, because if he had been elected he would have been struck with a multi-year ban on political activity after the coup of 1980.[78] When Süleyman Demirel became prime minister in October 1979, he named Özal undersecretary of the State Planning Organization. In January 1980, Turgut Özal was tasked with implementing the stabilization package backed by the International Monetary Fund and a consortium of international banks. In July 1982, having served since the coup as advisor to the prime minister on economic issues, he had to resign because of a bank scandal—not directly attributable to him—and was considered finished, politically. But another fortunate twist of fate ensured that the Motherland Party he had founded was the only party beside the two artificial parties created by the military admitted to the parliamentary elections of 6 November 1983 in which ANAP won a brilliant victory. On 6 December 1983, Özal took over the office of prime minister.

With the 1978–1979 revolution in Iran and the Islamic Republic of Iran's strict anti-Western position, Turkey had clearly gained strategic and security-political weight. International organizations like the IMF were particularly well-disposed towards the country in the 1980s, and saw in it a "shining example of the correctness of orthodox stabilization and restructuring programs."[79] Özal continued this policy of liberalization further after his election as prime minister. While in the 1970s the share of industrial exports had stayed below 2% of GNP, it climbed to 8.5% as early as 1990. As Turkey became an important supplier to both sides in the long (1980–1988) war

---

77 When his mother Hafize died in May 1988, the government led by Özal published a decree permitting the burial of his mother next to the grave of Mehmet Zahit Kotku on the grounds of the Süleymaniye Mosque. Cemal, *Özal Hikayesi*, 158.
78 Türk, *Muktedir*, 158ff.
79 Per Owen and Pamuk, *Middle East Economies*, 119, who in no way share the opinion of the IMF at that time.

between Iraq and Iran, the Middle East took over from the EEC as Turkey's greatest export market.

Özal laid the foundations for an export-oriented, globally competitive Turkish market economy. His goal was for foreign capital to stream into Turkey and domestic capital to be mobilized for productive investment. On this foundation—or so went the expectation—production and exports would climb and ultimately create a stable national economy no longer plagued by inflation.[80] However, growth in the 1980s was restrained and was purchased through a rapidly increasing indebtedness (of ten billion US dollars in 1980 and more than fifty billion ten years later). The weaknesses in Özal's governing style were obvious: he conducted himself like an autocrat and did not understand the importance of a strong legal framework for sustainable development. The pervasive corruption of the 1990s was one legacy of his politics.[81]

Like his predecessors Menderes and Demirel, Özal dissociated himself from the established leadership class in politics and the economy. He declared he had not been born in Dolmabahçe Palace (the nineteenth century sultanic palace built directly on the shore of the Bosporus) but was, like the majority of Turks, "a child of Anatolia."[82] Even more than his predecessors, Özal, who was very proud of his economic competence, employed the rhetoric of a developmental leap under his government: "Look, in five years, forty dams have been built in our country; in the era of one-party rule, over twenty seven years [i.e., 1923–1950] only three were built."[83]

Özal's politics showed similarities to the recipe the Democrat Party had whipped up in the 1950s: economic recovery in conjunction with traditional cultural values, which were in turn connected to the Islamic religion. Since Özal's time, the *iftar* (the communal evening meal with which the end of the daily fast during Ramadan is marked) has been used for political purposes. Özal was furthermore the first politician in the center-right camp who presented himself in public as a believing Muslim. In July 1988, he undertook the

---

80 Cemal, *Özal Hikayesi*, 306.
81 Pamuk, *Economic Change*, 287–289.
82 Turgut Özal on 27 March 1989. In *Başbakan Turgut Özal'ın Yurtiçi-Yurtdışı Konuşmaları: 13.12.1988–31.10.1989* (1989), 115, quoted following Türk, *Muktedir*, 150.
83 Turgut Özal on 16 September 1989. In *Başbakan Turgut Özal'ın Yurtiçi-Yurtdışı Konuşmaları: 13.12.1988–31.10.1989* (1989), 92, quoted following Türk, *Muktedir*, 144.

pilgrimage to Mecca, as the first sitting Turkish prime minister to do so.[84] His taking part in Friday prayers in the Kocatepe Mosque in Ankara in November 1989, shortly after he became president, was a pointed gesture.

After some break-ins during by-elections in 1986, Özal lost his political dominance and had to worry about his position of power following the re-admittance of formerly leading political figures like Demirel and Ecevit to political life in September 1987. In consequence, he no longer oriented his economic policy towards stability, but rather expansion. Consequently, Özal undermined his substantive achievements, as the successes of his economic policy were founded in a considerable extent on auto-suggestion.[85] The same was equally true in foreign policy.

New Foreign Policy Coordinates in the East

Turkey's renewed application for admission into the European Economic Community (EEC) on 14 April 1987 was less borne by the hope that it would quickly succeed than by the calculation that the economy would be spurred by the chance of admission. The admissions application was rejected by the EEC in December 1989, with reference to Turkey's economic problems and difficult human-rights situation. It is however obvious that the EEC applied stricter standards to Turkey than to other countries like Greece (admitted in 1981), Spain, and Portugal (both admitted in 1986), and found fault with conditions that they studiously ignored in the others' cases.[86]

The sustained poor relations with Greece in the 1980s (in 1984, Greece enacted a defense doctrine which declared Turkey, rather than the USSR, its chief threat) were primarily related to the proclamation of the Turkish Republic of Northern Cyprus. A severe Greco-Turkish crisis in March 1987 was ignited by Turkish oil exploration in the Aegean. In 1988, under Özal and the then Greek prime minister Andreas Papandreou (in office 1981–1989 and 1993–1996), relations briefly brightened: Turkey declared Greeks exempt from visa requirements, and Özal made a state visit to Athens, the first Turkish prime minister to do so in sixty-three years. However, by the end

---

84 Turkish politics thus stand in the tradition of the Ottoman Empire. Not a single Ottoman sultan ever undertook the Hajj, even though Mecca was Ottoman territory for four centuries. Rafeq, "Arab States and the Ottoman Heritage," 349.
85 Cemal, *Özal Hikayesi*, 200–203.
86 Patel, *Projekt Europa*, 206ff.

of 1988, relations were already darkening again. Turkey objected to the Greek position that the only contentious issue between Greece and Turkey (other than Cyprus) was the demarcation of the continental shelf in the Aegean. In their mind, further unsolved problems included the disputed demarcation of national airspaces, Greece's militarization of the Aegean islands, and the status of the Turkish minority in West Thrace.[87]

So while Turkey had no real outlets from many domains of conflict, elsewhere new opportunities opened up. The field of "Islamic banking" is a particularly vivid example of a point of intersection between the liberalization of the economy, a new orientation in foreign policy, and an Islamist-tinted domestic policy. The Motherland Party (Anavatan Partisi, ANAP) government enabled the construction of an Islamic banking system which uses other forms of profit-sharing instead of charging interest, which is forbidden by the Koran. Immediately after Özal's entry into government in December 1983, the appropriate legal framework was established with a law on "special financial institutions" (özel finans kurumları). The decree had two obvious goals: to inject into financial circulation the savings of pious Muslims who did not want to deposit their money in regular banks, and to attract capital from the Muslim world, above all the Gulf States.[88] The first institutions of this type founded were the Albaraka Türk Özel Finans Kurumu, that is, a Turkish private bank in cooperation with the Saudi Arabian Al Baraka Bank (from Arabic *al-baraka*, "blessing, prosperity") established in January 1985 and the Faisal Finans Kurumu (presumably named after the Saudi King Faisal, r. 1964–1975) established in April 1985. Both of these were Turco-Saudi joint ventures. The Islamic banking system has never become a really significant arm of the Turkish financial system, however. In January 2014, its share amounted to 6.6% in Turkey—compared to 21% in Malaysia and 51% in Saudi Arabia.[89]

The fall of the Berlin Wall on 9 November 1989, the collapse of the Warsaw Pact, and eventually the dissolution of the Soviet Union itself in December 1991 represented a foreign policy and geostrategic sea change for Turkey. Old threats like the Soviet Union disappeared; new flashpoints became visible. One thinks of the conflict that had already ignited in 1988 between Armenia and Azerbaijan, or of Operation Desert Storm, the military action by the United States and its allies against Iraq in 1991. At the same time,

---

87   Clogg, *History of Greece*, 191ff.
88   Jenkins, *Political Islam*, 151.
89   Lord, *Religious Politics*, 204–206.

new opportunities, like in trade, and new spaces, like in Central Asia, were opening up. With the independence of Azerbaijan in the South Caucasus and Kazakhstan, Kyrgyzstan, Turkmenistan, and Uzbekistan in Central Asia, the Turkish government—all too optimistically—glimpsed a "Turkish century" dawning on the horizon.

Since the Soviet-Turkish treaty of March 1921, Turkey had neglected its relations with the "Turks abroad" (*dış Türkler*) and had only felt responsible for the Turkish population on Cyprus, in Greek West Thrace, and in Bulgaria. The dissolution of the Soviet Union was initially regarded with caution that nevertheless turned to excitement by the end of 1991—in absolutely tumultuous fashion. On 16 December 1991, the leading Uzbek politician and later president Islam Karimov (1938–2016) arrived for a visit in Ankara. The reception committee included the Soviet ambassador, as befit a republic of the Soviet Union. The Soviet, Turkish, and Uzbek flags were hoisted. However, at mid-day immediately after the official recognition of Uzbekistan by Turkey—completed just then—all Soviet symbols were promptly removed.[90]

Western states supported Turkey's ambition to become a patron power for the Turkic states of Central Asia. Turkey, as a model of a secular, democratic country—went the West's thinking—could help avoid the emergence of a vacuum somewhere in the newly founded Central Asian states.[91] The euphoria of the years 1991–1993 and the Turkish attempt to take a leadership position among the new Turkic states were followed by the realization of Turkey's limited opportunities for action, especially with respect to economics, then a return to a policy dictated by circumstances.

At the beginning of the 1990s, institutions and instruments intended to drive the foreign policy agenda of the country came into being in rapid succession under President Özal. These included the Turkish Cooperation and Coordination Agency (Türkiye İşbirliği ve Koordinasyon Ajansı Başkanlığı, TİKA), founded in 1992, and the television program *TRT Eurasia* (*TRT Avrasya*) broadcast by satellite since April 1992. Turkey also engaged in the founding of new international associations, like the Organization of the Black Sea Economic Cooperation (*sic*, BSEC), in 1992.[92]

This dynamic initiated by Özal lasted beyond his death in the realm of foreign policy. Both foreign ministers Hikmet Çetin (in office 1991–1994)

---

90 Aydın, "Relations with the Caucasus and Central Asia," 755.
91 Ibid., 757.
92 See the organization's website: www.bsec-organization.org, accessed 20 April 2023.

and İsmail Cem (in office 1997–2002) continued the policy of openness and stronger integration in the region. Many elements of the foreign policy which would become known as Neo-Ottomanism and Zero Problems with the Neighbors (Komşularla sıfır sorun) were found under İsmail Cem, who stood for rapprochement with Greece above all.[93]

In the 1980s, military and security-policy cooperation with Israel resumed. The cooperation, aimed at common enemies like Syria and Iraq, was undergirded on historical occasions like the 1992 celebrations of the five-hundredth anniversary of the beginning of Ottoman reception of Sephardic Jews expelled from Spain. On 3 November 1994, the Turkish prime minister, Tansu Çiller (in office 1993–1996) travelled to Israel—this was a first.[94] More Turco-Israel agreements followed, on economic cooperation, free trade, promotion of bilateral investments, and prevention of double taxation. The agreement of 23 February 1996 on military cooperation received much attention. The backbone of their relationship remained, as in the late 1950s and early 1960s, military and security cooperation; only this time, their relations were much closer, more openly displayed to the rest of the world, and promised longer-term sustainability.[95]

The Turkey of the 1980s evinced an unusual combination of dynamics. The leaden weight of the military dictatorship still weighed on its shoulders, but, at the same time, the decade was distinguished by a spirit of optimism in economics and foreign policy. In the 1990s, however, the drive forward flagged, and Turkey's unresolved problems returned to the fore.

4. Political and Economic Stagnation (1993–2002)

In some regards, the 1990s recalled the 1970s. There were: repeated political stalemates precipitated by, among other things, personal animosities among leading politicians; political instability with rapid changes of government;

---

93   For examples of a neo-Ottoman agenda under İsmail Cem, see Örmeci, *Portrait of a Turkish Social Democrat*, 20, 62, 97, and passim.
94   Only a few days before, on 26 October 1994, the peace treaty between Israel and Jordan was signed. Israel was no longer a pariah in the Arab world, and consequently close contacts between Turkey and Israel seemed less offensive.
95   Thus Bolukbasi, "Turkish-Israeli Alliance," 29ff., argues that, because of the continuing disagreements between Turkey and Syria and Iraq about the mass of water in the Tigris and Euphrates, there would henceforward exist good preconditions for Turco-Israeli collaboration.

high levels of violence; and economic decline. If one exchanged five thousand Turkish lira (TL) for one US dollar in January 1994, by April of the same year, that dollar was worth TL 38,000. Faced with galloping inflation, the daily papers announced with ironic assurance that, in Turkey, everyone would soon be a millionaire.[96] High rates of inflation averaging well over 50% in the 1990s and economic slumps in 1991, 1994, and 1998 finally climaxed in the dramatic crisis of 2001 in which the gross national product shrunk by almost a tenth and Prime Minister Ecevit felt compelled to approach the International Monetary Fund for help again.

After Özal's death in 1993, there was no political personality who would be able to shape the following decade. A new face in the 1990s was Tansu Çiller (b. 1946), whose trip to Israel was mentioned above. An American-educated professor of economics teaching at Boğaziçi University (Boğaziçi Üniversitesi, "University of the Bosphorus"), Çiller joined the True Path Party (Doğru Yol Partisi, DYP) in November 1990, and in 1993, the DYP leadership elevated the attractive and urbane woman to its chairmanship as the party's hoped-for show piece. The same year, she ascended to the prime ministry when Süleyman Demirel moved to the presidency. She was able to stay in office until 1996 in a coalition with the Social-Democratic Populist Party (Sosyaldemokrat Halkçı Parti, SHP). Çiller advanced the culture of self-enrichment established by Özal to the point that her own party, the DYP, was "all but transformed into a family business."[97]

The second leading figure of the center-right camp in the 1990s was Mesut Yılmaz (b. 1947) who took over as chair of the Motherland Party (Anavatan Partisi, ANAP) in 1991 and served as prime minister three times in the 1990s: June–November 1991, March–June 1996, and—at least this last time for a whole year and a half—June 1997–January 1999. Çiller and Yılmaz could not come to an understanding, so after the election of 24 December 1995, the coalition hammered out between the ANAP and DYP shattered under their personal rivalry. The center-right ANAP and DYP, who ideologically speaking were divided by almost nothing, never managed to find themselves in the same camp.

The center-left camp could also not overcome factionalism; in its case, between the Democratic Left Party (Demokratik Sol Parti, DSP) and

---

96 When on 1 January 2005, the new Turkish lira was introduced (with the symbol ₺) at a rate of one to one million old lira, a million of the old lira were worth less than a Euro.

97 Birand and Yıldız, Son Darbe, 50, interview with İsmet Sezgin (1928–2016; DYP minister of the interior, 1991–1993).

the Republican People's Party (Cumhuriyet Halk Partisi, CHP) under the respective leaderships of Bülent Ecevit and the luckless Deniz Baykal (b. 1938). Bülent Ecevit remained the decisive person on the center-left party spectrum, however. In the years 1999–2002 he was prime minister for a fifth and final time, though already showing signs of age-related infirmities.

Only one current party saw itself in the ascendant in the 1990s. The Islamist Welfare Party (Refah Partisi, RP) achieved a strong position in parliament in the 1990s and advanced into the middle of society.

The Inexorable Rise of Islamism

Since the founding of the National Order Party (Millî Nizam Partisi, MNP) in January 1970, the Islamist movement had been securely represented on the party spectrum and in parliament. The National Salvation Party (Millî Selamet Partisi, MSP), founded as a successor to the MNP in 1972, was included in three governments during the half-decade between 1974 and 1979.[98] The Welfare Party (Refah Partisi, RP), newly founded in 1983, could not immediately capitalize on the previous Islamist parties' successes at the ballot box. On 29 October 1987, the RP took part in parliamentary elections for the first time, but failed to clear the ten percent hurdle with only 7.2% of the vote. The next parliamentary election on 20 October 1991 saw them rise to 16.9% of the vote, but they were only the fourth-strongest party and in fact only reached their result in an electoral alliance with two other parties. In the snap elections on 24 December 1995, the Welfare Party succeeded in becoming the strongest force in parliament with 21.4% of the vote, very slightly ahead of the two center-right parties, the Motherland Party and the True Path Party. This success was adumbrated by local elections in 1994, when the Welfare Party was not particularly strong nationally with 19.1% of the vote but was still able to win the mayoral offices of several large cities, including İstanbul and Ankara.

What were the reasons for the rise of the Welfare Party in the mid-'90s? For one, the stalemate between Tansu Çiller's DYP and Mesut Yılmaz's ANAP played into its hands. Also of significance was the fact that the Sufi brotherhoods (tarikat) and religious associations (cemaat), which had previously always voted center-right, supported Islamist parties for the first time.[99]

---

98   Türk, *Muktedir*, 180–182.
99   Birand and Yıldız, *Son Darbe*, 61.

In addition, the promotion of the Turkish-Islamic Synthesis by the military and state in the 1980s must have seemed arbitrary in its distinction between a state-desired conservative Islam versus a "reactionary" (*irtica*) Islam. İrtica had become a fighting word for the secularist camp in order to denounce an allegedly backwards Islamism. However, the strengthening of Sunni institutions by the state, on-going for decades and forced since the 1980s, inevitably made an impact. An obvious example is the schools in which imams and Friday preachers were educated. These *imam-hatip* schools, which were set up at the outset of the Republic, were closed in 1930 and reopened in 1951. Within the organs of state there was indeed resistance to this type of school, because it recalled the duality of the education system in late Ottoman times, with *medrese*s (educational institutions for religious jurisprudents) on one hand and secular schools on the other. In 1973, the curriculum of the imam-hatip schools was broadened. In opposition to the comprehensive schools a parallel system came into being, in which religious-conservative families wanted to have their children educated. Accordingly, the number of imam-hatip students rose from 48,895 in 1973 to 200,300 in 1980–1981 and 511,502 in 1996–1997.[100]

At the same time, beginning in the late 1980s, the alliance of institutions anchored in the Islamist milieu broadened. The Independent Industrialists and Businessmen's Association (Müstakil Sanayici ve İşadamları Derneği, MÜSİAD) clearly differentiated itself from TÜSİAD, the Turkish Industrialists and Businessmen's Association (Türk Sanayici ve İşadamları Derneği) founded in 1971.[101] The acronym MÜSİAD differed from TÜSİAD only in its first letter, M, which officially stood for *müstakil*, "independent," but it also stood, without explicitly saying so, for *Müslüman*, "Muslim." Three-quarters of the firms associated with MÜSİAD were founded after 1980, whereas only a fifth of TÜSİAD's firms had been. While TÜSİAD had always represented large, established industrial firms and businesses, MÜSİAD championed smaller businesses located outside the traditional economic and industrial hub of İstanbul. By the middle of the 1990s, MÜSİAD had over two thousand member firms and represented about a tenth of Turkey's gross national product.[102]

---

100 Lord, *Religious Politics*, 181–191.
101 Today, the "Turkish Industrialists and Businesspeople's Association" (Türk Sanyici ve İş İnsanları Derneği).
102 Jenkins, *Political Islam*, 154ff.

Beginning in the 1980s, TÜSİAD turned away from the statist model of the 1960s and 1970s and saw itself as a bearer of the Western economic order as well as the further democratization of Turkey. MÜSİAD, by contrast, relied on international Islamic solidarity and the compatibility of Islamic morality with a dynamic free-enterprise system; consequently, it viewed the emerging Muslim national economies of Southeast Asia as models, especially Malaysia's. The first president of MÜSİAD, Erol Yarar (b. 1960) declared that the Western *homo œconomicus* had to be replaced by *homo islamicus*.[103]

The concept of a "just order" (*adil düzen*) formulated by Necmettin Erbakan in the 1970s aimed at establishing a more just economic order and a new society aligned with Islamic principles.[104] The National Vision (Millî Görüş), the nonparliamentary arm of the movement founded by Erbakan, is a multifaceted concept. *Millî* is translated as "national" in contemporary usage, but at the same time it carries with it the older Ottoman conception of a religious community, in this case of Sunni Muslims. (*Millî* is the adjectival form of *millet*, the religio-political organizational units we met in chapter 1.) The demand for a just economic and social order and a "national vision" found its object and its cause in the underdevelopment of Anatolia. The capitalist order was not placed in question, rather the goal became assisting the "lesser majority" of Anatolia to a just share of the country's economic goods.

Erbakan's charisma in his own political milieu was explicable by the absoluteness of his declarations. His anti-Western polemic described a complete contrast between the soulless materialism of the West and Islam, which alone could enable simultaneous material and spiritual development. In Erbakan's worldview, no one could escape this opposition. All political parties but his own were just trying to ape the West and make common cause with it. Outsiders must have found Erbakan's utterances disturbing when he spoke of "Crusaders" and "Freemasons" and when his antisemitism peeped out from beneath the mantle of anti-Zionism. For Erbakan, the European Economic Community was a clique of Freemasons steered by "International Jewry," and so accession would be a disaster for Turkey. American Jews would live on the top floor of the EEC house, European workers on the ground floor, and the Turks would now to move into the basement as the janitor.[105]

---

103 Buğra, "Class, Culture, and State," 531.
104 Jenkins, *Political Islam*, 154ff.
105 Türk, *Muktedir*, 174. Birand and Yıldız, *Son Darbe*, 56. Ahmad, *Turkish Experiment*, 383 (here referring to the *Cumhuriyet* of 28 April 1970). On the (alleged) role of freemasonry in the late Ottoman period and the Republic of Turkey, see Dumont, "Freemasonry in Turkey."

Necmettin Erbakan was radical in his rhetoric, but some things connected him with right-conservatism, like his mechanistic understanding of society and unbroken belief in progress. It is in any case striking that Islamism's leading light and the two most important representatives of the conservative current, Süleyman Demirel and Turgut Özal, were all engineering students at the Technical University of İstanbul at the same time (Erbakan graduated in mechanical engineering in 1948, Demirel in civil engineering in 1949, and Özal in electrical engineering in 1950).[106]

In 1996, a revolutionary moment occurred in the Turkish Republic: the head of an Islamist party became prime minister. After Tansu Çiller (DYP) and Mesut Yılmaz (ANAP) could not agree on a government, Çiller turned to the Welfare Party (RP). On 28 June 1996, the DYP and RP coalition was announced (and nicknamed with a portmanteau of their names, Refahyol), with Necmettin Erbakan as prime minister. In the second half of the legislative session, Erbakan was supposed to turn over the office to Çiller.

The leading forces in the bureaucracy, justice system, media, and military eyed this new political orientation suspiciously. Erbakan made his first trip abroad to Iran, Pakistan, Singapore, Malaysia, and Indonesia. On 22 October 1996, he announced plans to found a group of liminal Muslim states as a counterweight to the association of leading industrial states, the G7 ("Group of Seven"). This new group would be called the D8, for "the Developing Eight," and would be composed of Bangladesh, Egypt, Indonesia, Iran, Malaysia, Nigeria, Pakistan, and Turkey. The D8, which was officially brought into being on 15 June 1997 at a meeting of the heads of state in İstanbul, still exists but has never become an influential actor.[107]

Erbakan's innovations in the country's domestic-political culture were the most provocative to his opponents. On 11 January 1997, Erbakan invited the leaders of Sufi brotherhoods to a fast-breaking meal at which many of them appeared in their orders' regalia. Perhaps Erbakan only wished to reconcile the brotherhoods with the state with this invitation, but the secular camp feared that Turkey could follow a path similar to Iran's. When, on 13 January 1997, the cabinet determined that working hours in government institutions would be harmonized with the month of fasting in Ramadan, the decree

---

106 Erbakan repeatedly pointed with pride to the high degree of education in his party. Among the candidates taking part in the 1973 elections, there were 160 engineers across eight parties. Half of them were members of the National Salvation Party. Türk, *Muktedir*, 198.

107 See the organization's website at https://developing8.org/, accessed 20 April 2023.

was abrogated by the Council of State (Danıştay) due to its violating the principle of secularism. On 31 January 1997, a celebration of Jerusalem Day, so-called, in the district of Sincan in Ankara, to which the Iranian ambassador was invited, was particularly provocative. The occasion was already political, because Quds Day, falling on the last Friday of Ramadan, had been created by the Ayatollah Khomeini in 1979, to show the solidarity of the Islamic world with the Palestinians and Jerusalem. On this particular evening in Sincan, propaganda posters of Lebanon's Hezbollah and Palestinian Hamas were hung and a tent erected in the shape of the al-Aqsa Mosque on Temple Mount.[108]

Even before the incident in Sincan, specifically on 22–24 January 1997, a decision had been made at a meeting of the commanders of the armed forces to remove the Welfare Party from power. The first decisive step was the session of the National Security Council (Milli Güvenlik Kurulu, MGK) on 28 February 1997, at which the military demanded the implementation of a bundle of measures from the government. Among other things, courses in the Koran should be administered by Diyanet officials only and the Sufi brotherhoods (tarikat) should cease their activities. The central demand of the military was to raise the length of elementary education from five to eight years in order to cut the legs out from underneath the imam-hatip middle schools. The military pointed to the fact that this class of school was producing over fifty thousand graduates a year, while the Diyanet couldn't recruit more than about two thousand imams. In Turkey, the consequences are referred to as the 28 February Process (28 Şubat süreci) because it was not comprised of a one-time catalog of measures, but a period over several months in which the military wanted to permanently straighten out the Welfare Party and its supporters. They forced the media to support this agenda through "informational events." In order to escalate the fear of a potential coup, the general staff left the lights on in its building at night.

On 18 June 1997, Erbakan gave up and resigned from the office of prime minister. Representatives of his coalition partner, the DYP, had been steadily resigning; the coalition had lost its majority in parliament. On 21 May 1997, the state's attorney applied for a ban on the Welfare Party at the Supreme Court (Yargıtay). On 16 January 1998, the party was banned with the justification that they had allegedly become a hub for activities against the principle

---

108 Birand and Yıldız, *Son Darbe*, 193–195, 198.

of secularism. Erbakan and some other RP politicians were banned from all political activity for five years.[109]

The military had thus achieved the paramount goals of its policy of attrition, the resignation of Necmettin Erbakan, the banning of the Welfare Party, and the drying up of the imam-hatip middle schools. After the introduction of the eight-year elementary school curriculum on 17 August 1997, the number of imam-hatip students dropped back from more than a half million to only 64,534 in 2002;[110] though, of course, it rose dramatically from then on.

In the early 1990s, given the break in the ten-year pattern of military interventions (1960, 1971, and 1980), academics allowed themselves to be led astray by the hopeful appraisal that the relationship between politics and the military had in the meantime become comparable to that in Western democracies.[111] The "postmodern" intervention of 1997, however, contradicted this all too optimistic assumption. The military damaged itself with its constant interventions, even after Erbakan had been driven from power and his party had been forbidden, because its attempted micromanagement of politics proved unworkable. As with every military intervention, the question of long-term consequences arose. Had the military not intervened and the politicians of the Welfare Party and their supporters not been made martyrs, would there perhaps never have been "neither Tayyip Erdoğan nor the AKP?"[112] In fact, the surmise is justified, in that the "28 February Process" cleared the field for the overwhelming success of a new party—the Party of Justice and Development (Adalet ve Kalkınma Partisi, AKP).[113] The military's hope that the Islamist movement would require at least ten years to recover from the blow of 1997 was in vain.[114] Only five years later, the AKP won the parliamentary elections of 3 November 2002; and, another five years later, the AKP camp struck out at the military.

Islamism was not the only challenge for the Turkish state in the 1990s. The Alevi and Kurdish questions persisted as well. Compared to the Kurdish issue,

---

109 Jenkins, *Political Islam*, 161ff. Birand and Yıldız, *Son Darbe*, 211, 222, 225. Along with Erbakan, these were the former minister of justice Şevket Kazan, four RP representatives, and the mayor of Kayseri, Şükrü Karatepe. Jenkins, *Political Islam*, 164.
110 Lord, *Religious Politics*, 181–191.
111 Thus Hale, *Turkish Politics and the Military*, 290–295.
112 Birand and Yıldız, *Son Darbe*, 245, refer to a statement by Hasan Ekinci (representative of the DYP from the province of Artvin).
113 Ibid., 249, refer here to an interview with Meral Akşener, then a DYP politician and interior minister in Erbakan's cabinet.
114 Jenkins, *Political Islam*, 164. Interview by Jenkins in February 1998 with General Doğan Beyazit, general secretary of the National Security Council (MGK) from 1993 to 1995.

the Alevi question was both simpler and more convoluted at the same time. It remains convoluted because down to the present; because—even though this is absolutely not their goal—the Alevis alone place into question the foundations of the Turkish nation (with Sunni Turks as its "real" constituents) due to the character of their (religious) culture, based on their internal religio-cultural differences and political-organizational fragmentation.[115] The relationship of the Turkish state to the Alevis in the 1990s was, on the other hand, simpler than its to the Kurds, because the Alevis were not demanding the right to secession from Turkey or at least autonomy within it.[116] Such a demand would have been nigh impossible anyway, because the settlement areas with a strong Alevi share of population are located in the middle of Anatolia. In addition, the Alevis were increasingly found in the large cities of Anatolia and Western Europe due to the migration process of the past decades. However, expectations that the Alevi milieu would dissolve in the big cities and that they would disappear into the Sunni majority were not fulfilled.[117] The Kurdish question, by contrast, was much more pressing in terms of security policy, but at the same time was understood in time-tested fashion. The Kurds' demands for national rights broadly corresponded to the late Ottoman experiences with Christian minorities.

The Alevis' Dichotomy

From the beginning of the Republic, the Alevis' relationship with the state was conflicted. The state secularism on offer from Kemalism had an attractive side to the Alevis. The close coupling of Turkish citizenship with a Sunni identity was, however, an impediment. With the political radicalization of the 1970s, an Alevi identity emerged publicly, although in indirect fashion, because the Alevis collectively located themselves on the political left and conflated their self-perception as an outsider religious minority with that of a disadvantaged

---

115 According to Massicard, *Alevis in Turkey and Europe*, 65, the only neutral symbols of Alevidom accepted on all sides are *semah* (ritual dance) and *saz* (the long-necked lute).
116 Ibid., 142, notes, however, that the idea of creating an Alevistan circulated in the 1980s.
117 In 1966, İbrahim Elmalı, then-director of the Diyanet authority, believed he was able to discern a dissolution of the Alevis. Massicard, "Alevis in the 1960s," 55. Hütteroth, *Türkei*, 277, rashly presented the prospect that the Alevis would dissolve into the general population of Turkey "even before one was able to be sufficiently informed of their numbers, much less their heterodox beliefs."

social class.[118] The inordinate share of Alevis in socialist parties and groupings is incidentally not unusual, as the same phenomenon can be observed with many religious and ethnic minorities in the Middle East: Alevis, Armenians, Berbers, Druze, Jews (before 1948), Kurds, and Shiʻites.[119]

Attacks on Alevis did not remain a part of the violent conflicts of the 1970s but persisted in the following decades. An arson started by a mob in the Madımak Hotel in Sivas on 2 July 1993 was directed at those gathered at the hotel participating in the yearly celebrations in honor of Pir Sultan Abdal, a poet and rebel of the sixteenth century revered by Kurdish-speaking Alevis. The author Aziz Nesin (1915–1995), who happened to be present drew particular ire, as he had shortly before published a partial translation of Salman Rushdie's *Satanic Verses* in Turkish. Nesin was able to narrowly save himself; nevertheless, thirty-five people died in the fire started at the hotel, which was not prevented by the security forces and was fought all too belatedly by the fire department.[120]

On 12 March 1995, automatic weapons fire from a moving car shot up a café patronized by Alevis in the İstanbul neighborhood of Gezi. One Alevi cleric (*Dede*) was killed, and twenty-five customers were injured. In the ensuing protests by outraged Alevis in İstanbul, twenty-two more people were killed and over five hundred injured by security forces. The political and legal reckoning which followed was telling: Necmettin Erbakan and Alparslan Türkeş pointed to the alleged influence of foreign forces while at the same time the official investigations were dragged out. Twenty-two relatives of those killed appealed to the European Court for Human Rights, which ordered Turkey to pay compensatory damages. Officially, the perpetrators and those responsible have not been able to be identified to this day.[121]

The pogroms against Alevis display a conspicuously recurrent pattern, in which the role of the authorities extends from tacit approval up to open support. It is therefore unsurprising that the Alevis have sought new answers and paths since the vision of a class-free society in which all ethnicities are equal finally collapsed with the coup of 1980. They backed away, disillusioned, from purely secular explanations and have turned towards religious and cultural explanatory models.

---

118 Bumke, "Kurdish Alevis," 518. Vorhoff, *Alevitische Identität*, 82.
119 Sing, "Tempestuous Affair between Marxism and Islam," 69.
120 Birand and Yıldız, *Son Darbe*, 29–39. On the transformation of the hotel into a memorial in the early 2010s, see Çaylı, "Conspiracy Theory as Spatial Practice."
121 Birand and Yıldız, *Son Darbe*, 97–103, name high officials as the presumed string-pullers.

Because the Alevis, in contrast to the Kurds, showed no signs of demanding rights in a militant fashion, it was and is natural for the Turkish state to bind them to itself, despite the alienation created by their religio-cultural resistance. Turkish Sunnis, for example, can barely place Pir Sultan Abdal (c. 1480–1550), the key figure for Kurdish Alevis. By contrast, Hacı Bektaş Veli, an Islamic mystic in thirteenth-century Anatolia and the leading figure for Turkish-speaking Alevis, offers numerous points of reference with regard to Sunni Islam—clearly visible, for example, in the Bektaşi Sufi order which professes the Sunnah.[122]

The first attempts to bind the Alevis closer to Sunni Islam took place in the 1960s. Among them was the Diyanet authorities' attempt to establish the unitary Directorate for Religious Communities (Mezhepler Müdürlüğü).[123] These all foundered in the face of resistance from the Sunni camp and were only taken up again in the 1990s. Demands from Alevi associations proceeded in the same direction, namely equality with Sunnis. Beginning in the 1990s, however, Alevi leaders gradually seem to have come to the understanding that official approval of the construction of Alevi assembly halls and Alevi representation among Diyanet officials could lead into the trap of cooptation by the state. Consequently, some Alevis began to demand instead that the Diyanet authorities be dissolved and the maintenance of religious institutions be placed directly in the hands of the faithful, or even to be transitioned to a system of funding like Germany's Church Tax (Kirchensteuer). The fundamental desires of Alevi associations have not changed to this day: recognition of their holy places and the lifting of the requirement of mandatory religious education with exclusively Sunni content in the schools.[124]

The Kurdish Question and the PKK's Challenge

Irrespective of all its ideological changes, of course, the Kurdish national movement of the twentieth century was defined by two fundamental goals: to achieve a form of self-determination and, moreover, to modernize their own society. "The first goal is unrealized, the second only

---

122 Whose global center today sits, incidentally, in the Albanian capital of Tirana. See Elsie, "Derwischsekten Albaniens," 3–7.
123 The proposal even went so far as to name a well-known Alevi, Feyzullah Ulusoy, former deputy of the Hacı Bektaş Convent as director of this new department.
124 Lord, *Religious Politics*, 142–150. Vorhoff, *Alevitische Identität*, 180, 188. Bardakci et al, *Religious Minorities*, 102ff.

rudimentarily achieved."[125] One reason why only the Kurds in Northern Iraq have been able to gain a stable, self-administered territory is the sheer, overweening power of the central state in the Middle East, against which the Kurds have either been unsuccessful in defending themselves or with which they could only negotiate a meager profit.

The alliance between Kurdish tribal leaders and the Turkish state which has developed since the early Republic is rooted in a certain sense in the Ottoman era. After the incorporation of Kurdish territories into the Ottoman governmental apparatus, İstanbul and the Kurdish tribal elite worked out a stable relationship from the sixteenth to the nineteenth century. In any case, this second phase of relative peace in the Republican era would not last centuries, as under the Ottomans, but only a few decades. As early as the 1960s, the Kurdish question made its way to the surface again. The coup of 1980 was in this respect a catalyst. It destroyed the—already utopian—project of a socialist state in which the Kurdish question would resolve itself of its own accord, dried up the radical left movement, and contributed thereby to the Kurdish question's being posed directly.

Southeast Anatolia is the region of Turkey in which Kurds compose either the majority or at least an above-average portion of the population. As a crude rule of thumb, one can say, the further southeast, the more Kurdish. Southeast Anatolia can be described as a rectangle reaching from Iğdır on the Turco-Iranian border to Erzincan, just 310 miles to the west. From there, roughly following the course of the Euphrates, one can draw another line south, also about 310 miles long, to the Turco-Syrian border, south of Urfa.[126] The rectangle thus formed (the other two sides consist of the Turkish border with Iran in the east and Iraq and Syria in the south) describes an extended Southeast Anatolia, in which Kurds composed three-quarters of the population before the large-scale internal migrations. This is also the region of the First General Inspectorate (Birinci Umumi Müfettişlik)[127] established on 1 January 1928, and thus the territory which the Turkish state itself defined very early—without openly saying so—as Kurdistan. The same can be said

---

125 Strohmeier and Yalçın-Heckmann, *Die Kurden*, 146.
126 Nestmann, "Ethnische Differenzierung," 546, describes this border simultaneously as the "main-culture divide" between a primarily Turkish-settled area (in the west and north) and a Southeastern Anatolian space populated by minorities which may be "understood as a province which culturally borders and transitions into the Caucasus, Iran, and Syro-Arabia."
127 Aydemir, *İkinci Adam*, 1:309, 311, 343n1.

for the State of Emergency Zone (Olağanüstü Hâl Bölgesi, OHAL) of 1987–2002, composed of the twelve provinces of Batman, Bingöl, Bitlis, Diyarbakır, Elazığ, Hakkâri, Mardin, Muş, Siirt, Şırnak, Tunceli, and Van. This zone was defined much more expansively than the actual area of military confrontations with the Kurdish revolutionary movement. Despite all the changes in recent decades, these areas in Southeast Anatolia fundamentally have a Kurdish-majority population.

The Kurds took part in the migration and urbanization waves beginning in the 1950s. They were drawn into the Big Three—Ankara, İstanbul, and İzmir—but also into cities like Adana and Mersin. The Kurds, however, were not just caught up in the general migration dynamic; beginning in the 1980s, their migratory behavior was shaped by war and expulsion. Kurdish migration and urbanization thus show particular characteristics: during the late 1980s and early 1990s alone, when something approximating a war was occurring there, approximately a million people left their homes in Southeast Anatolia. Around a third of all rural settlement units in the enormous State of Emergency Zone were depopulated; more than three thousand villages in Southeast Anatolia were destroyed. Many Kurds sought a first refuge in the large cities of Southeast Anatolia, like Diyarbakır, whose population consequently tripled in the 1990s.[128] Such cities, which were shaped by the ubiquity of the military and the security services and which had only developed with difficulty into industrial centers, could not cope with the enormous growth in population. The cities of the Southeast therefore served as springboards for a later, westward emigration—or for the path into Kurdish terrorism.

The Kurdish question is tightly connected to the question of the underdevelopment of Southeast Anatolia. In Turkey, as in every other country, there persist inequalities between individual regions. The superior weight of its three metropolises, however, was overwhelming. In 1976, Turkey had 23,400 doctors, of whom 16,600 or 71% practiced in İstanbul, Ankara, or İzmir. The defining gap between West and East presented itself even more sharply in Southeastern Anatolia. In 1975, the Turkish literacy rate was 62% (75% among men, 48% among women). In the same year, the literacy rate in the thirteen southeastern provinces lay at only 32.8%, thus at approximately half the national average.[129]

Despite the strength of the Turkish state, the political elite showed themselves to be helpless, to a certain degree, before the phenomenon of

---

128 International Crisis Group, *Turkey's Kurdish Impasse*, 2.
129 Hale, *Modern Turkey*, 222–225.

Southeastern Anatolia. They could only interpret it as a kind of sickness, "which could never be overcome and healed."[130] They could not make heads or tails of where the deeper causes of this sickness lay, except in internal problems of the region like tribal structures and a lack of education. Southeastern Anatolia is not just a region of especially pronounced underdevelopment, though. Here, terms like "internal colonialism" are not ideas conjured out of thin air.[131] The late Ottoman and Young Turk state destroyed the power structures of the Kurdish feudal lords which had grown up in the region over centuries without deploying effective state rule in their place and really dismantling the remaining feudal structures. The state's answer, for which İsmet İnönü's policy in the 1920s and 1930s stood, was "to understand [Southeastern Anatolia] not as an issue affecting the entire nation and as a question of development, but to be satisfied with administrative and military interventions alone in this region."[132]

When leaders of the Turkmen minority were murdered in the chaos of the 1958 military coup in Iraq, a parliamentary representative of the Republican People's Party (Cumhuriyet Halk Partisi, CHP) called for reprisals against the Kurds in Turkey as revenge. Kurdish demonstrations against this outlandish demand led to the imprisonment of fifty Kurdish students and intellectuals. When one of them died in custody, the Group of Forty-Nine (Kırk Dokuzlar) came into being and was accused of "Kurdism and communism." This group was novel in the sense that they were members of the younger generation who had not lived through the repression of the 1920s and 1930s and, moreover, came from modest social backgrounds, that is, they did not belong to leading families of Kurdish notables.[133]

As early as the 1970s, Kurdish activists became estranged from the Turkish left in a quarrel over the question whether Turkish rule over Kurdistan was to be regarded as a form of colonialism.[134] The PKK, founded in 1978 in the village of Fis near Diyarbakır, emerged from the milieu of radical left student groups in Ankara. Despite its name, it was anything but a Kurdistan Workers' Party (Partiya Karkerên Kurdistanê). By 1975, Abdullah Öcalan and his early collaborators had already made the strategic decision to no longer conduct

---

130 Aydemir, *İkinci Adam*, 1:308.
131 The idea of Turkish colonialism in Kurdistan is associated with İsmail Beşikçi (b. 1939), who nevertheless sees the political status of Kurdistan and the Kurdish people as "very far below that of a colony" in the ordinary sense. Beşikçi, *Kurdistan*, 16. On Beşikçi's intellectual and political personality, see Ünlü, "İsmail Beşikçi."
132 Aydemir, *İkinci Adam*, 1:317.
133 Çelik and Garapon, "Nouvelle génération d'élites kurdes."
134 On this, see Yegen, "Turkish Left and the Kurdish Question," 166ff.

the struggle with the Turkish state in the big cities, as radical left groups in the 1970s had done, but to carry the war into the Kurdish-inhabited areas in Southeastern Anatolia.[135] The main object of their fight was not initially the Turkish state, but large Kurdish landholders and tribal leaders who had entered into alliance with the Turkish state.[136]

The military coup of 1980 hit the PKK hard indeed, but their leader Abdullah Öcalan (b. 1949 in the village of Ömerli in the province of Şanlıurfa) had already fled to Syria in July 1979 and had placed himself under the protection of the Syrian state. From his new domicile in Damascus, Öcalan summoned all PKK activists to Syria. With Syria's indulgence, the PKK fighters attended Palestinian organizations' paramilitary training camps in the Bekaa Valley in eastern Lebanon. The PKK received its first combat experiences as allies of the Palestinians in battle against the Israeli army which invaded Lebanon in Summer 1982 and advanced as far as Beirut.

Hafiz al-Asad, then-ruler of Syria, would never have been prepared to grant the Kurds in Syria the rights that the PKK were demanding for Kurds in Turkey. But the PKK would serve as an opportune thorn in Turkey's side—Syria had demanded the return of Alexandretta, and Turkish control of the headwaters of the Euphrates always vexed Syria—as long as its provocations were not too blatant. As a result, the PKK's military activities were not permitted to proceed from Syrian soil, especially as the flat border area between Turkey and Syria did not lend itself to guerrilla warfare. The mountainous and therefore difficult-to-monitor Turco-Iraqi border region, on the other hand, was an ideal base of operations. In February 1991, a no-fly zone was established over northern Iraq for the protection of Iraqi Kurds as part of Operation Provide Comfort, after the Iraqi state under Saddam Hussein brutally suppressed uprisings of Shiites in the south and Kurds in the north, which had flared up in the wake of Iraqi's defeat in the Gulf War. This laid the foundations for today's autonomous Kurdish entity in northern Iraq. The PKK, whose number of fighters had climbed to probably around ten thousand (a third women!) at the beginning of the 1990s, seized the moment and greatly expanded their activities from 1991 on.

---

135 Urbane and educated people often return to their countries (thus to some degree swimming against the prevailing current of social transformation), but not to cultivate the land. The Kurdish nationalism of the PKK was no different in this respect than other nationalisms. They talk about peasants and the soil but create city folk. On this effect, see Gellner, *Nations and Nationalism*, 107.
136 McDowall, *Modern History of the Kurds*, 399–402, 421, 423.

The PKK differentiated itself from all the other Kurdish organizations by its unconditional profession of armed struggle and the iron allegiance to its leader, Öcalan, who not only tolerated no contradiction, but mercilessly eliminated every possible opposition emerging on the horizon. Öcalan's paranoia went so far that he had several dozen young Kurds from the big cities of Western Turkey who had joined the PKK at the end of the 1980s murdered on the suspicion that there could be Turkish agents among them.[137]

The Turkish political elite initially countered the challenge of the PKK with haughtiness. In 1986, the then prime minister Turgut Özal spoke of the PKK as "two and a half bandits."[138] Due to their military successes, the group was gradually elevated to the rank of "political banditry" and compared with the Armenians or Macedonians in late Ottoman times, who were also supposedly backed by foreign powers. In 1985, the buildup of units of loyal village guards (köy korucuları) began, and by the end of the year, they contained thirteen thousand men. They recalled the Hamidiye units set up by Sultan Abdülhamid II in the 1890s, irregular troops withdrawn from the command of the local provincial administration, who became notorious for their attacks on the civilian population, above all the Armenians, and were principally recruited among the Kurds.[139]

The superiority of the Turkish state was overpowering. Alongside special forces, police, and the village guards, whose strength amounted to a hundred thousand men around the year 2000, around two hundred twenty thousand soldiers were deployed in Southeastern Anatolia.[140] Likely decisive for the Turkish military's success was, however, that with the comprehensive clearance of settlements by the Turkish army, the PKK lost their infrastructure and the support of the village populace. The Turkish army, which had initially been trained for the conduct of wars between states, changed its tactics to conduct irregular warfare. From the middle of the 1990s, it was clear to both sides that the PKK could not win the military conflict. However, the Turkish military was still convinced that they could achieve a conclusive victory over the PKK.

At the end of the 1990s, after Turkey credibly threatened Syria with war if they continued to support the PKK, the Syrian regime jettisoned Öcalan and

---

137 Marcus, *Blood and Belief*, 94, 96, 108–110, 134–140, 145–151, 172ff., 217, 245, 260–266.
138 Turgut Özal, "Kimseden Korkumuz Yok," *Milliyet*, 27 August 1986, 6. Quoted in Aydin and Emrence, *Zones of Rebellion*, 90.
139 Marcus, *Blood and Belief*, 97ff. On the role of the Hamidiye's successor organizations in the First World War, see Klein, *Margins of Empire*, 170–183.
140 Marcus, *Blood and Belief*, 248ff. Aydin and Emrence, *Zones of Rebellion*, 104.

forced him to leave the country in October 1998. Öcalan's odyssey through various countries ended when the Turkish secret service caught up with him in Kenya on 15 February 1999. In June 1999, he was sentenced to death. With the abolition of the death penalty in October 2002, his sentence was commuted to life in prison. Since 1999, Abdullah Öcalan has lived in solitary confinement on the prison island of İmralı in the Sea of Marmara. After his capture, the PKK withdrew its units into Iraq in August 1999 and declared a permanent armistice, which would in actuality last until June 2004.

While repressing the Kurdish population of Southeastern Anatolia, the Turkish state sincerely intended to develop the region economically. The Southeastern Anatolia Project (Güneydoğu Anadolu Projesi, GAP) went back to the 1970s and was extraordinary in both scope and ambition, encompassing at least a tenth of the surface area of Turkey, with today's provinces of Adıyaman, Batman, Diyarbakır, Gaziantep, Kilis, Mardin, Siirt, Şanlıurfa, and Şırnak. GAP had the goal of economically developing the southeast and thereby solving the Kurdish question through economic satisfaction. Indeed, the region will become an economic powerhouse for the Middle East, if the Turkish state gets its wish. The economic boom in Southeastern Anatolia since the late 1990s has actually been conspicuous, though at the price of sharpening the conflict with Syria and Iraq over the waters of the Tigris and Euphrates Rivers. The GAP could not, however, fundamentally remedy many of the weak points of Southeastern Anatolia, like the one-sided structure of landholding which leaves a great portion of the rural population landless, or investments in a few places which already possessed a quite respectable economic infrastructure.[141]

While the Turkish state increasingly recognized the necessity of an economic strengthening of the region, the PKK took a long and thorny route to ideas which were more oriented towards reality. Their positions always reflected the course of the military confrontation, despite the cast-iron ideological positions put out for show. In the 1980s, the PKK saw the Kurds as victims of the Turkish state and Western imperialism, which was guilty of splitting up the region and hadn't permitted a Kurdish state after the First World War. Given their military failures beginning in 1993, the PKK then tried to represent the Kurdish question as a question of human rights affecting the entire international community. The association of the Turkish political class with Marxist concepts of "oriental despotism" and "the Asiatic

---

141 Bilgen, "Southeastern Anatolia Project": 134. Strohmeier and Yalçın-Heckmann, *Die Kurden*, 190.

means of production" were replaced by the representation of a divided ruling class. The PKK finally gave up its ambitions of independence, with the argument that such an independent Kurdistan would be economically unviable. Its demands today are limited to the rights of freedom of expression, education in Kurdish, and self-administration. By the end of the 1990s, then, the positions of the PKK had become much closer to those which had long been brought forward by the moderate Kurdish and parliamentary opposition, arguing a solution must be found within the framework of a territorially sovereign Turkey; in return the Turkish state must guarantee Kurds the right to fair political representation and decentralization and eliminate all forms of discrimination like the policy of systematic imprisonments and long prison sentences for nonviolent political activists.[142]

Since the beginning of the 1990s, Kurdish politicians have expressed their concerns by means of their own political parties. When Kurdish parliamentarians of the Social-Democratic Populist Party (Sosyaldemokrat Halkçı Parti, SHP) led by Erdal İnönü were expelled for taking part in a conference at the Institute Kurde de Paris in October 1989, they founded the People's Labor Party (Halkın Emek Partisi, HEP) in June 1990. In the 1990s and 2000s, the HEP was followed by a sizeable number of Kurdish parties which were constantly subjected to bans and sanctions. Despite the confusing succession of Kurdish parties, which did not peel off from each other seamlessly and did not always occupy identical positions, they were all unambiguously located on the left side of the party spectrum. Initially, the Kurdish parties could only achieve direct political participation in cities and towns with a clear Kurdish majority, however they did so with great success. Thus the People's Democracy Party (Halkın Demokrasi Partisi, HADEP) captured the majority of municipal offices in Kurdish cities in 1999. Finally, in 2012, the Peoples' Democratic Party (Halkların Demokratik Partisi, HDP) was founded; it is still active today. In the parliamentary elections of June and November 2015 and June 2018, the HDP succeeded in clearing the ten percent hurdle, not least because its political program extends beyond purely Kurdish issues, and it is accepted as a party that represents the general issues of the political left.[143]

---

142 Aydin and Emrence, *Zones of Rebellion*, 36ff., 45–48. Strohmeier and Yalçın-Heckmann, *Die Kurden*, 111. International Crisis Group, *Turkey's Kurdish Impasse*, i.

143 Because the ten percent hurdle doesn't apply to "independent" candidates, Kurdish politicians were able to win twenty-four and thirty-six seats for themselves in the 2007 and 2011 elections, respectively. Sayarı, "Political Parties," 187.

Turkey on a Slippery Slope

In the early 1990s, the Turkish state achieved in overpowering militant Kurdish separatism. To that end, it put everything it had in the balance. The state's expenditures on the war were massive. In the period from 1984 to 2005, the state likely spent between 150 and 170 billion dollars on the war against the PKK, that is around 7–8 billion dollars a year.[144] In the struggle with the PKK, all legal and extralegal means of combat were regarded as legitimate. This style of warfighting allowed violence to escalate boundlessly, with executions, torture, bomb attacks, and assassinations whose perpetrators remain in the dark. Was the Kurdish threat really so great as to be worth degrading the rule of law far outside the combat zones in Southeastern Anatolia? Prime Minister Tansu Çiller (in office 1993–1996) at first set signals of reconciliation and proposed a "Basque model," but then had to climb down in the face of advocates of a hard line. Consequently, Çiller advanced the idea of an "all-encompassing fight" (*topyekûn savaş*) to which the Turkish state leadership committed, ominously summarizing, "It will end one way or another" (Ya bitecek, ya bitecek).[145]

The Turkish conduct of the war never even approached the extent of brutality that the Iraqi government under Saddam Hussein showed the Kurdish population in northern Iraq, however. During the so-called Anfal campaign of 1988, well over one hundred thousand Iraqi Kurds were killed and about one-and-a-half million were driven from their homes. On 16 March 1988, a single poison-gas attack on the town of Halabja only a few kilometers from the Iranian border killed fifteen thousand civilians.

Nevertheless, the blank check the politicians cut led to an unprecedented brutalization of the security forces and undermined the foundations of the rule of law in the country. Thus, the 1990s were characterized by a large number of assassinations "perpetrator unknown" (*faili meçhul*), not only in Southeastern Anatolia, but in the big cities of Western Anatolia—far away from the actual war. Prominent assassination victims in the Turkish metropolises included intellectuals of various political orientations, but all of whom held liberal convictions. There was even a suspicious death in the military. The commander of the Gendarmerie, Eşref Bitlis, who had spoken out against

---

144 Mutlu, "Economic Cost," 73.
145 Tansu Çiller, "Ya bitecek, ya bitecek," *Sabah*, August 11, 2009, http://www.sabah.com.tr/Siyaset/2009/08/11/tansu_ciller_ya_bitecek_ya_bitecek.

the activities of the infamous Gendarmerie Intelligence and Counter-Terror organization (Jandarma İstihbarat ve Terörle Mücadele, JİTEM) died in a dubious airplane crash on 17 February 1993.[146] The premature death of former president Turgut Özal on 17 April 1993 also seemed suspect to many. Shortly before his death, Özal had showed himself open to a federal solution to the Kurdish question and had confidentially sent a delegation of the Kurdish Democracy Party (Demokrasi Partisi, DEP) to Damascus for discussions with Öcalan. His successor as president, Süleyman Demirel, willingly yielded the field to the military.[147]

Eşref Bitlis and Turgut Özal may have died natural deaths, but assassination victims certainly did not. Who gave the orders? Who conducted the assassinations? The so-called Susurluk scandal of 1996 laid bare the proliferating connections between the organs of state, criminal elements, and right-wing extremists. On 3 November 1996, three occupants of a car died in a traffic accident in Susurluk (north of Balıkesir in Western Anatolia): Hüseyin Kocadağ, deputy chief of police in İstanbul, Abdullah Çatlı, a militant right-wing extremist wanted by Interpol and a leading member of the Gray Wolves, and the former beauty queen Gonca Us. Sedat Edip Bucak, a parliamentary representative of the True Path Party (Doğru Yol Partisi, DYP), large land holder, tribal chief, and leader of Kurdish village-guard units, survived with serious injuries.

One perceives the long lines of a "deep state" (*derin devlet*) in these networks; that is, a secret state-within-a-state working underground, which stretches back to the time of the Ottoman-Turkish cataclysm of 1912–1922.[148] The Special Organization (Teşkilat-ı Mahsusa), already active in the First Balkan War, took part in the Armenian genocide during the First World War and produced many leaders of the later national movement. All of these past connections and the excesses of the fight against the PKK led to "collateral damage" in society and politics. In reaction to the Susurluk scandal, civil protests occurred, beginning in February 1997. Every evening at nine o'clock, everyone was asked to turn out their lights for one minute to emphasize a demand for transparency in politics. The then minister of justice of the Welfare Party (Refah Partisi, RP) Şevket Kazan (1933–2020) subsequently

---

146 Birand and Yıldız, *Son Darbe*, 16ff. Herzog, "Small and Large Scale Conspiracy Theories," 198.
147 Birand and Yıldız, *Son Darbe*, 18ff. McDowall, *Modern History of the Kurds*, 433, 437ff.
148 Per Gingeras, "Last Rites," 173, the extreme emphasis on the security of the state led to the creation and perpetuation of a "deep state" from the late Ottoman era to the present. Gingeras, *Heroin*, 259, is more careful.

described this scornfully—"They are playing the Candle-Has-Gone-Out game" (Mum söndü oyunu oynuyorlar)—thereby equating the civil protests with a centuries-old Sunni calumny against the Alevis, whose religious ceremonies were alleged to culminate in sex orgies.

With the goal of weakening the PKK, the state promoted competing militant Kurdish organizations like Hizbullah (the Party of God, with no substantive connection to the Lebanese Hezbollah), which wanted to erect an Islamic state in Kurdistan. Around six hundred political murders in 1992 and 1993 alone have been ascribed primarily to this organization. Kurdish Hizbullah was clever in recruitment, developed conspiratorial techniques, and was a serious competitor that drove the PKK out of many cities in Southeastern Anatolia in the first half of the 1990s.

While Turkish organs of state might not have been responsible for the emergence of organizations like Hizbullah, they tolerated and even supported them, because they appeared too valuable as intra-Kurdish competition for the PKK. Some of the militant organizations emerging in the 1990s were promoted by Iran, which has wanted to export its revolutionary Shi'ite ideology around the entire Islamic world since its revolution in 1979. The organization The Jerusalem Warriors (Kudüs Savaşçıları) in Turkey was blatantly under the direct control of the Iranian secret service. This organization, uncovered and destroyed in the year 2000, was likely responsible for the murder of at least these four individuals: Muammer Aksoy, law professor and founder of the Association for Atatürkist Thought (Atatürkçü Düşünce Derneği), on 31 January 1990; Bahriye Üçok, columnist and former dean of the Department of Theology at the University of Ankara, on 6 September 1990; Uğur Mumcu, an investigative journalist for the newspaper *Cumhuriyet*, on 24 January 1993; and Ahmet Taner Kışlalı, political scientist and commentator, on 21 October 1999. The Organization of the Islamic Movement (İslami Hareket Örgütü), founded in Batman in 1987 and smashed in 1996, set itself the goal of provocation through assassinations and causing political escalation. The cooperation of this organization with the Iranian secret services was so extensive that they kidnapped Iranian dissidents living in Turkey and delivered them to Iranian agents.[149]

In the 1990s, a lamentably bad economic situation coincided with the erosion of domestic political conditions. Macroeconomic instability ensued due to a rash liberalization of capital markets in 1989, among other things. This liberalization led to banks' acquiring credit abroad in order to loan the

---

149 Aydin and Emrence, *Zones of Rebellion*, 65ff. Jenkins, *Political Islam*, 185–200.

money at the much higher interest rates prevailing domestically, and thus making the Turkish banking system vulnerable. The inflation rates in the 1990s went from 60.3% in 1990 to 106.3% in 1994.[150] The unstable and depressed 1990s culminated in the severe economic crisis of 2001.

Even outside of politics and economics, fate was not kind to Turkey. On 17 August 1999, at three in the morning, the tension between the Anatolian and Eurasian tectonic plates released in a powerful earthquake whose epicenter was in Gölcük (on the east end of the Gulf of İzmit and situated in the metropolitan area of İstanbul), killing almost eighteen thousand people. The Turkish people learned in the following weeks that their country possessed a vital civil society, and that their country was not surrounded by enemies. Private Turkish and international organizations brought in aid, while governmental organizations—with the exception of the military—appeared paralyzed. At the turn of the century, Turkish society's weariness with the smug complacency of its politicians, the insufficiently controlled violence of the organs of state, and economic misery had become immense.

5. Departure (2002–2013)

The 2000s were distinguished by the extraordinary story of the success of the Party of Justice and Development (Adalet ve Kalkınma Partisi, AKP). In 2001, a group of dissidents left the Virtue Party (Fazilet Partisi, FP), the successor party to the Welfare Party (Refah Partisi, RP) banned in 1998 and whose own existence was already endangered. These dissidents founded the AKP on 13 August 2001, with Recep Tayyip Erdoğan (b. 1954) as its chairman and Abdullah Gül (b. 1950) as his deputy. In contrast to Necmettin Erbakan's movement, the AKP wanted to be open to more milieux within Turkish society and thereby become capable of winning an electoral majority. At the same time, the AKP contrasted itself with all previous parties by, for example, endowing the initials AKP with the additional meaning of Ak Parti, or White Party, in the sense of the party's having an "unspotted" history and stance at odds with the prevailing sense of corruption. When the Welfare Party was ousted from power in 1997, two possible options presented themselves: radicalization, perhaps as in Algeria when the Islamic Salvation Front (Front islamique de salut, FIS) was robbed of their electoral victory in 1991, or moderation.[151] The AKP of the 2000s followed the latter path.

---

150   Herr and Sonat, "Fragile Growth Regime," 38–40.
151   Cagaptay, *New Sultan*, 82.

Fortune smiled upon the young party. Facing the serious economic crisis of 2001, the government invited the Turkish economist Kemal Derviş (b. 1949), then at the World Bank, to take on the position of minister of state for economic affairs. With the help of the IMF, Derviş enforced fiscal discipline, stabilized and reformed the financial system, introduced a free-floating exchange rate, and laid the foundation for later budget surpluses. The consequence was that gross domestic product, after a sharp contraction of around a tenth in 2001, climbed around 35% over the next four years.[152] Thus, the difficult-to-digest medicine of the International Monetary Fund had already been administered and the worst was over by 2002.

The political constellation in 2002 also favored the AKP. The voters held the quarreling center-right and center-left parties responsible for the failings and mistakes of the 1990s. The military had damaged itself in its running battle with the Welfare Party and thereby intensified the victim status of the Islamic movement. In addition, the biases of the Turkish electoral systems worked favorably for the AKP in historically unique fashion. The AKP received 34.3% of the votes in the 3 November 2002 elections, but received two-thirds of the seats in parliament, winning 363 out of 550. The victory of the new party right out of the gates was astonishing, as was the voters' complete overthrow of the party system. Heretofore, several relatively equally weak parties which had fairly reliably overcome the ten percent hurdle faced off. The votes of other, smaller parties which could not clear the hurdle were lost. This time, however, the share of lost votes comprised over 46% of the total vote. None of the parties elected to parliament in 1999 succeeded in reentering, neither the two center-right parties, the Motherland Party (Anavatan Partisi, ANAP) and the True Path Party (Doğru Yol Partisi, DYP) nor the Democratic Left Party (Demokratik Sol Parti, DSP) led by Bülent Ecevit, nor the Nationalist Movement Party (Milliyetçi Hareket Partisi, MHP). Some, like the DYP, barely missed the ten percent hurdle. Others were atomized. The DSP had been the strongest party, with 22.2% in the elections of April 1999, and had placed Bülent Ecevit in the prime ministership. Now, in 2002, it declined to an obliteratingly tiny 1.2%. Only the Republican People's Party (Cumhuriyet Halk Partisi, CHP), which had been under the ten percent hurdle in 1999, was able to enter into parliament again, with 19.4% of the vote.

Attempts to abolish the ten percent hurdle, which was introduced after the coup of 1980, were not pursued in the 1990s. The then majority parties saw it as a way to prevent the entry of a Kurdish party into parliament, since, given

---

152   Pamuk, "Economic Change," 290ff.

the political fragmentation among the Kurds, they could as a rule unite less than a tenth of the electorate. The electoral law passed in 1983 was amended four times between 1983 and 1987, always to the effect that the strongest party would be overly favored.[153] The ten percent hurdle, which the established parties never believed would affect them, now became their undoing. Center-right parties, which significantly shaped Turkish politics since the 1950s, have not been represented in parliament since 2002. Even the still-extant Islamist Felicity Party (Saadet Partisi, SP), which carries on the legacy of Necmettin Erbakan, who died in 2011, has remained well below the ten percent hurdle in every election since 2002. The AKP thereby inherited a two-fold patrimony: It bound the electorate from the Islamist spectrum to itself and could, at the same time, completely take over the bankrupt assets of the center-right party spectrum.

Until the parliamentary elections of 2015, the AKP possessed the absolute majority of the seats in parliament. This model of success planted the idea in the AKP—no later than their third victorious parliamentary election in June 2011—that their crushing majority in parliament was an expression of the popular will and, therefore, that the government's actions needed no further justification. In this conviction of holding a majoritarian mandate, the AKP followed the Democrat Party (Demokrat Partisi), which maintained a similar conviction after it had won consecutive elections in 1950, 1954, and 1957.

Since 2002, then, the parliamentary system has been dominated by the AKP, and the overview of parties represented in parliament is easy—too easy. The AKP fluctuated between 40 and 50 percent in the following five elections in 2007, 2011, June and November 2015, and finally in June 2018; the CHP between 20 and 26 percent; and the MHP between 11 and 16 percent. The Good Party (İyi Parti, İP), which is between the CHP and the MHP in its orientation, just made it into parliament in 2018 with 10.0% of the vote. However, the deck was shuffled anew above all because the Kurd-aligned Peoples' Democratic Party (Halkların Demokratik Partisi, HDP) succeeded in clearing the ten percent hurdle in the last three elections (June and November 2015 and June 2018). In answer to this challenge, and faced with a threat to their absolute majority in parliament, the AKP has buttressed itself with an alliance with the nationalist, radical right MHP since 2015.

But back to 2002. An important reason for the AKP's enormous popularity with the electorate was that the responsibility of the established parties

---

153 Cagaptay, *New Sultan*, 88. Ahmad, *Modern Turkey*, 196.

for the economic crisis of the year before was very fresh in voters' memory. The great acceptance accorded the AKP in subsequent elections, on the other hand, rests to a considerable extent on the success of the Turkish economy in the 2000s. The AKP was not solely responsible for the boom, which was built upon the liberalization of the economy under Turgut Özal in the 1980s and on the restructuring measures in collaboration with the International Monetary Fund at the turn of the century. Under the governance of the AKP, however, economic dynamism escalated and resulted in a multi-year boom.

Erdogan's AKP: Euphoria and Zeal for Reform

The AKP succeeded not only in remaining in government for a very long time, but it changed Turkish society and the political order from the ground up. It persistently ground down the Kemalist bureaucratic-intellectual-judicial-military complex which had ruled Turkey for decades. The AKP was seen and promoted by the Western international community—but also the liberal public in Turkey—as a model for the compatibility of democracy and a moderate Islamism. New leadership in the Turkish economy came to light. The ascent of Anatolian cities like Konya, Kayseri, and Gaziantep as economic and industrial centers was now complete. In the 2000s, a new pluralism came to be, in which the old elites faced newly ascendant elites.

The most visible track record of the AKP was the country's economic up-swing. Between 2002 and 2015, the average annual growth rate of the Turkish economy was 4.8%.[154] The thoroughly pro-business center-right parties had always expressed the ambition to make Turkey a leading economic power. In the election of 1957, then-president Celal Bayar articulated his hope that "in thirty years, this blessed land of fifty million people will be a little America."[155] The electoral program of the Justice Party (Adalet Partisi, AP) of 1977 was headlined by the electoral slogan of "Great Turkey" and declared a goal of achieving an economy as large as that of the Federal Republic of

---

154 Kirişçi, *Turkey and the West*, 137.
155 Dawletschin-Linder, *Diener seines Staates*, 194, refers to a report in the newspaper *Cumhuriyet* of 21 October 1957.

Germany by century's end.[156] The AKP expressed similarly grandiose aspirations—but this time, reality followed the rhetoric more closely.

Turkey recovered very quickly from the sharp contraction in 2001 and achieved an average growth rate of 7.5% over the years 2002–2006. The inflation rate, so high in the 1990s, retreated tremendously after 2002, and by 2004 first reached single-digit territory, at 9.4%.[157] Almost everyone had more money at their disposal,[158] but early on shadows fell upon the AKP governments' "economic miracle." From 2001–2011, the share of consumer credit climbed sevenfold to 21% of gross national product.[159] The unequal income distribution, the quite high and partially hidden unemployment, and poor and unsure working conditions made the Turkey of the 2000s a land with uneven living conditions. The country was not following the model of East Asian states which strove for permanent growth through a more just distribution of incomes. In addition, the privatization of the education and health-care systems led to inadequate provision of public goods and thus stood in contradiction to the principle of society as a whole's participation in economic growth. A comparison with South Korea, which in the mid-1960s showed a similar production structure to Turkey's, lends itself in this case. Turkey implemented no consequential industrial policy, even in the 2000s, and made fewer investments relative to gross domestic product than South Korea. Consequently, Turkey today possesses a smaller share of high-value technological products in its range of production—with the exception of some individual armament products like military drones.[160]

Turkey's boom is also reflected in its urban landscape. The gecekondus which characterized its big cities for decades receded and were replaced by large housing projects of the state housing authority founded in 1984 (literally, the Presidium for the Administration of Mass Housing, Toplu Konut İdaresi Başkanlığı, TOKİ) or private developments. The migrant quarters were replaced, not just materially but mentally. In the 1980s, there appeared the new term "suburb" (varoş). Varoş does not denote any exact form of housing, geographically or architectonically, but is rather a sort of umbrella term for traditional values and modes of behavior, like a Muslim

---

156 Hale, *Modern Turkey*, 124.
157 Herr and Sonat, "Fragile Growth Regime," 40.
158 Acemoglu and Ucer, *Ups and Downs of Turkish Growth*, 6.
159 Berlinski, "How Democracies Die."
160 Herr and Sonat, "Fragile Growth Regime," 40, 57ff. Taymaz and Voyvoda, "Beat of a Late Drummer," 105–110. Pamuk, "Economic Change," 271.

lifestyle, veiling, and patriarchal family structures in a long-established urban environment of former internal migrants from the country.[161]

The AKP took up the impetus for reform that had developed after the nomination of Turkey as a candidate for accession to the European Community on 11 December 1999. It was borne by the unanimity of the political elites and society in Turkey around the turn of the century that accession to the European Community was both worth striving for and possible. In consequence, on 6 February and 26 March 2002, the government led by Bülent Ecevit concluded two harmonization packages which were intended to adapt Turkish legislation to the Acquis Communautaire, the "common asset" of legal regulations of the EC. The resistance of the Nationalist Movement Party, then a coalition partner, to a third harmonization package led to the call for new elections on 3 November 2002. The nine packages of legal changes and the two constitutional reforms in the years 2002–2004 under the AKP government were shaped by the prospect of admission to the EC.[162] Even in its intention to push the military back into its proper area of responsibility, the AKP built upon a reform process introduced before their entry into government.

The AKP did not succeed at everything. In 2004, parliament passed a legislative package on education that, among other things, saw to the abolishment of the discriminatory hurdles for graduates of the imam-hatip schools. When President Ahmet Necdet Sezer (b. 1941, in office 2000–2007) exercised his veto, the government withdrew the bill on 3 July 2004.

Some of what the AKP undertook was not a departure. In September 2004, in the framework of a reform of the criminal code, a clause criminalizing adultery was inserted. When the EU opposed this, Erdoğan irately declared the EU had no right to meddle in the internal affairs of Turkey, but he dropped the new clause. A similar disagreement arose around the question of the headscarf. On 29 June 2004 and again, following an appeal, on 10 November 2005, the European Court for Human Rights (ECHR) rejected the suit of the medical student Leyla Şahin, brought with the backing of the government. Because she had worn a headscarf on campus, the University of İstanbul imposed disciplinary measures on Şahin in 1998 and subsequently refused her entry. The ECHR argued that this measure did not violate the Convention for the Protection of Human Rights and Fundamental Freedoms and that the headscarf was a "powerful external symbol." The Turkish government, with Prime

---

161 White, *Islamist Mobilization*, 59.
162 Jenkins, *Political Islam*, 168. Özbudun, *Constitutional System*, 140.

Minister Erdoğan in the lead, interpreted the verdict as a lack of support for their fight against the narrow-minded Kemalist tradition of laicism. Erdoğan added that no court had the right to decide the headscarf issue, which belonged solely to Islamic jurisprudents, the so-called ulema.[163]

Not everything that the AKP undertook contributed to a liberalization of politics and society. The constitutional referenda of 21 October 2007 and 12 September 2010, which were no longer influenced by the prospect of EU accession but were driven by domestic political considerations, could only charitably be described as corrections to the illiberal Constitution of 1982. In 2007, a 67.51% majority approved direct election of the president and the shortening of the legislative term from five to four years. Here, Turkey took the first steps towards a semi-presidential system. With the politically divisive referendum of 2010, a 58% majority approved the removal of the clause in the Constitution of 1982 guaranteeing immunity from prosecution to those responsible for the military coup of 1980.[164] The number of judges on the Constitutional Court and in the Supreme Council of Judges and Prosecutors (Hâkimler ve Savcılar Yüksek Kurulu) was significantly increased.

The AKP government also wanted to make new approaches to the Alevis and Kurds, but ran into deep-seated mistrust. The Alevi associations only perceived the AKP's policy of openness to Alevis in 2007–2010 as an attempt at Sunni cooptation.[165] In May 2009, in the framework of a "Kurdish opening" (*Kürt Açılımı*), the government guaranteed, among other things, the right to use the Kurdish language, permitted Kurdish television broadcasts, and allowed Kurdish politicians to conduct their electoral campaigns in the Kurdish language. They submitted amnesty offers to PKK members and attempted to restore old Kurdish placenames. Ahmet Türk (b. 1942), chairman of the Kurdish-aligned Democratic Society Party (Demokratik Toplum Partisi, DTP), opined that "The mountain labored and didn't even bear a mouse."[166]

In 2009–2011, MİT, the Turkish secret service, held talks in Oslo with representatives of the PKK in exile in Brussels, followed by a direct exchange with Öcalan. However, even the AKP governments succumbed to the grim logic of the conflict between the Kurdish movement and Turkish state. After the

---

163 Jenkins, *Political Islam*, 173ff., 178.
164 Özbudun, *Constitutional System*, 75, 140. Öktem, *Angry Nation*, 184.
165 Bardaki et al., *Religious Minorities*, 109–121.
166 Atmaca, "Kürt Sorunda Çözüm Süreci," 42.

conversations in 2014 faltered, the relationship returned to open hostilities in Summer 2015. Since then, the Turco-Kurdish fronts have hardened again.

With regard to the problems with the state's relationship to the Kurds, which had seemed unsolvable up to that point, the AKP government extended the frontiers of the sayable and the imaginable further than they ever had been, but their readiness to change their spots was also stretched to its limit. What, then, about the mistake in constructing the Kemalist Republic based on confessional membership and simultaneously excluding religion? Could the AKP heal this breach? The AKP arrogated and arrogates to itself the representation of the entire breadth of the conservative party spectrum and, at the same time, the ability to credibly address a religiously minded electoral milieu by its origins as well as its symbolic language. At the same time, the AKP has always declined to use designations like "Islamic" or even "moderate Islamic" for itself. They maintain that parties fundamentally "are not religious."[167] Moreover, they aver Islam knows no radicality, and the moderation always inherent in the religion does not need to be recognized by an explicit designation.[168]

Were one to go by the AKP's self-portrait, the reasons for its success and crucial elements of its self-understanding would be unintelligible. In any case, large portions of its membership are practicing Muslims. A survey in spring 2002 reported that 90% of AKP voters prayed at least once daily and 99% fasted in Ramadan. Eighty-one percent see themselves first as Muslims, then as Turks. Only 44% of those who voted for the AKP called for women to cover their heads, but 93% expected that the AKP will take steps to rescind the headscarf ban (then still in force).[169] While, at the beginning of the 2000s, around two thirds of women in Turkey covered their heads, the percentage among the AKP's women voters was 94.6%.[170] It would not be accurate to define the AKP principally as a Islamist party, as one could with justification in the case of the various parties led by Necmettin Erbakan. However, the AKP has been a coalition movement from the beginning; in that sense, its connection to Islamist

---

167 In an interview with the daily newspaper *Sabah* on 16 August 2003, Yalçın Akdoğan, AKP ideologue, rejected any AKP connection to political Islam and even refused the label "Muslim democrat." Yavuz, *Secularism and Muslim Democracy*, 2. On the same note, see Erdoğan's statement of 7 December 2009, quoted in Türk, *Muktedir*, 33.
168 Ibid., 330.
169 Jenkins, *Political Islam*, 169, refers here to a survey of Boğazici University recounted in a series in the daily newspaper *Milliyet*, November 15–18, 2002.
170 Tarham Erdem, "Turban Dosyası," *Milliyet*, May 27, 2003. Description following Jenkins, *Political Islam*, 178.

thought has never been severed. The AKP's outstanding leadership figures in the 2000s did not stand in the tradition of Turkish right-centrism, but rather that of Islamism.

In retrospect, we can say that the 2000s were a golden age with a transitory equilibrium between the old Kemalist elites in the justice system, military, administration, economy, and academia, who had not been completely disempowered, and the AKP government, which had not yet achieved total plenitude of power. The political, social, and economic participation of large portions of the population who had previously seen themselves as being excluded, was now possible. The AKP's ascent was greeted by liberal intellectuals inside and outside Turkey as an act of emancipation, even liberation. Everyone was swept up in the excitement.[171] All the more understandable, then, did the AKP government's desire to take up the fight against the old power structures seem.

The Battle Against the Paramount State and the Deep State

Attacks by "perpetrators unknown," so characteristic of the 1990s, were almost unknown in the 2000s. Violence in Turkey declined significantly. Nevertheless, the country continued to be plagued by individual assassinations. On 19 January 2007, Hrant Dink, Armenian intellectual, activist, and publisher of the Armenian- and Turkish-language newspaper *Agos* was shot to death by an assassin then just sixteen years old—in retaliation for Dink's having allegedly insulted the Turkish people. Dink was conciliatory in inclination, but often reminded Turkey in no uncertain terms about its suppressed history of violence. Two years before, that is, in 2005, he had been sentenced to six months' probation under Article 301 of the Turkish criminal code, which in broad terms defines culpability for attacks on Turkishness (*Türklük*). His appeal of the sentence lay before the European Court of Human Rights at the time of his death. The murder of Hrant Dink led to an upheaval in civil society, thousands of people, only a very few among them non-Muslims, engaged in protest marches under the slogan, "We are all Hrant, we are all Armenians" (Hepimiz Hrant'ız, hepimiz Ermeniyiz).

---

171 In a lecture in the mid-2000s, the author of this book himself asserted that, in a best-case scenario, the AKP could evolve into a kind of "Muslim CDU" (Christian Democratic Union—the leading center-right party in Germany). See also the optimistic judgement of Hermann, *Wohin geht die türkische Gesellschaft*, 141, that Recep Tayyip Erdoğan had "taken the long road from Islamist to Muslim democrat."

This murder, committed by a killer of opportunity hired by radical nationalist circles, did not remain an isolated incident. On 5 February 2006, the Italian priest Andrea Santoro was murdered in Trabzon, also by an underage assassin; on 2 July 2006, the Catholic pastor Pierre Bruinessen was stabbed to death in Samsun. Murderers slit the throats of three Christian missionaries, two Turks and a German citizen, on 18 April 2007 in the Eastern Anatolian city of Malatya. The chairman of the Turkish conference of bishops, Luigi Padovese, was stabbed to death and decapitated, presumably by his driver, on 3 June 2010, ostensibly without any political motive. Was there a connection between these murderous attacks? Was it that Christian missionaries' activities had long been met with suspicion in the Turkish Republic? State Diyanet authorities had tasked all imams with announcing in the mosques on 11 March 2005 that Christian missionaries were comparable to medieval Crusaders.[172] Nevertheless, the sudden wave of violence against missionaries and Turkish converts to Christianity beginning in 2006 came as a surprise. It was frequently speculated that the assassins ultimately were in the service of the "deep state" (derin devlet), attempting to undermine the still half-optimistic accession negotiations with the European Union.[173]

The liberalization of society and politics, tied to a greater visibility of Islam in the public sphere, deeply disturbed the old Kemalist elites and their hardest core, the military. The military harbored suspicions of the new AKP government, not least because these politicians did not offer the military the deference that they had always been paid in the previous decades. It is striking, however, how toothless and wan the military's resistance was in the end.

Already on 9 December 2002, thus mere days after the AKP's taking over the government, the military submitted a dossier on Islamist activities to Prime Minister Gül. The government did not act on it and let it be known that they wished to direct their entire attention to the stabilization of the economy and the reform process as a foundation for accession to the EC. When, on 20 November 2002, President Sezer flew to a NATO summit in Prague, he was seen off by the parliamentary speaker, Bülent Arınç (b. 1948), accompanied by his headscarf-wearing wife. At this early point in time, only a few weeks after the AKP's first electoral victory, the public appearance of a

---

172 Jenkins, *Political Islam*, 179.
173 European Stability Initiative, *Mord in Anatolien*, comprehensively and factually reports about the ultranationalist background of the assassinations and on their tacit support from the organs of the state.

"veiled" spouse of a representative of a constitutional body was still an affront. In admonition, the commanders of the branches of the military forces, under the leadership of the chief of the general staff, Hilmi Özkök (b. 1940, in office 2002–2006) visited Arınç in his office, sat in silence for several minutes, and then left the room. On 3 March 2004, Aytaç Yalman (b. 1940), commander of land forces, took part in a conference of the Association for Ataturkist Thought (Atatürkçü Düşünce Derneği) in the company of other high officers—another intended gesture of warning to the government.[174]

Why was the military's resistance to the AKP so feeble? The military had damaged its reputation and its influence in the late 1990s with some all too blatant manipulations. In addition, its top leadership fundamentally supported Turkey's accession to the European Union. Many of the regulations in the 2000s which weakened the power position of the military were part of the EU harmonization packages, and consequently it was difficult for the military to repudiate the AKP lock, stock, and barrel. The military's return to its primary task of the defense of the country appeared sensible from the perspective of increased democratization and a clearer division of responsibilities. Hilmi Özkök, chief of the general staff from 2002–2006, was not only a mild-mannered personality and a practicing Muslim, but he also saw the dilemma that opposition to the reform packages from the military could be characterized as sabotage of the EU accession process. With a few exceptions, civil society also supported the reform policies of the AKP.

At the end of August 2006, Özkök was replaced as chief of the general staff by Yaşar Büyükanıt, also born in 1940 but possessed of a personality markedly rougher around the edges. Büyükanıt issued his first warnings at the change of staff on 28 August 2006,[175] but even under his leadership, the military choked on the AKP. Consequently, they made various forays towards disempowering the party but shied away from the most direct path, another coup. In 2007, the AKP named Abdullah Gül the successor to the outgoing president, Ahmet Necdet Sezer. To the military, Gül was like a red rag to a bull, above all because of his wife Hayrünnisa, who not only wore a headscarf but who had lodged a complaint with the European Court of Human Rights because of her earlier denial of admission to university. Gül was elected president on 27 April 2007 in the third round by a simple majority boycotted by the two opposition parties, in particular the Republican People's Party (CHP). On the

---

174 Jenkins, *Political Islam*, 170, 173.
175 Ibid., 170, 172, 180ff.

same day, at eleven at night, the military published a warning on its website, which became known as the E-Memorandum (E-Muhtıra). The military, it declared, would not hesitate to follow its entrusted duty, namely protecting the principle of secularism. On 1 May 2007, the Constitutional Court ruled, on precarious legal grounds, that two thirds of the members of parliament had to be present at the election of a president.

Consequently, under a boycott by the parliamentary opposition, Gül's election as president would have been fundamentally impossible. The AKP then called for new elections on 22 July 2007, which it won with 46.6% of the vote (and 341 of 500 seats). This was a great victory, but nevertheless not enough for a two-thirds majority in parliament. On 25 July 2007, however, Devlet Bahçeli (b. 1948), then as now chairman of the MHP, declared that his party would appear in parliament for the presidential vote. This assured the presence of two-thirds of the representatives of the Turkish National Assembly. Gül was able to be elected president on 28 August 2007 without a further appeal to the electoral process.

A final attempt to drive the AKP from power was undertaken in the following year. On 14 March 2008, the chief Prosecutor opened a great number of indictments against the AKP which were intended to move the Constitutional Court to ban the party. The Constitutional Court had, at the latest under the Constitution of 1982, set itself up as an iron advocate of the Kemalist legacy with reference to the indivisibility and territorial integrity of the state as well as its secular character. With Abdullah Gül's taking the office of president in 2007, the presidency was no longer a protective institution of the Kemalist state, so that the Constitutional Courts importance as a bulwark of the Kemalist secularist camp rose even higher.[176] On 30 July 2008, the court decided to accept the charge that the AKP had undermined the principle of secularism and, as punishment, halved the state grants to the party for the following year. The necessary three-fifths majority to ban a party, which had been added in the constitutional amendments of 2001, was not reached.[177] If the military's intervention in 1997 had been a "postmodern putsch," then the attempts to push the AKP out of power in 2007 and 2008 weren't much more

---

176 See Özbudun, *Constitutional System*, 133–143, with a clear criticism of the Constitutional Court's usurpation of regulatory authorities, unrooted in the constitution. Özbudun was also chairman of a scholarly board which, in 2007, received the assignment of drawing up a new constitution. The undertaking was not realized.
177 Ibid., 32.

than "postpostmodern" coup attempts. From then on, the military would be on the defensive—it had its back to the wall.

The AKP governments in the 2000s had to fight against a "paramount state" which looked down upon the AKP, full of mistrust, from the heights of the general staff, the Constitutional Court, and the state bureaucracy. The AKP could also point with justice to the fact that they were not only opposed by this visible state but also had to wrestle with the structures of a "deep state," that is kinds of informal and even criminal collaboration for the ostensible good of the state and the nation. We have already seen how, in the 1990s, the state and the military considered themselves justified in deploying every possible means in the fight against the PKK, using every conceivable ally, including criminal networks. The deep state—which, as a legacy of the Young Turks, belongs to the long, unholy bloodlines of Turkey's authoritarian state tradition—found itself on a new updraft.

For decades, informal units inside the military had withdrawn themselves from the control of democratically elected governments. In 1952, the military set up a unit for unconventional warfighting, the Mobilization Study Council (Seferberlik Tetkik Kurulu) which was converted into the Special Warfare Department (Özel Harp Dairesi) in 1965 and renamed again in the 1990s as the Special Forces Command (Özel Kuvvetler Komutanlığı).[178] The goal of the Special Warfare Department, which was structured in groups and networks isolated from each other, was the guidance of the population in resistance in the case of an occupation of the country by a foreign power. These units, ostensibly dissolved only in 2013, would have also been part of the secret Gladio organization within NATO.[179] In order to enforce the military's demands of 28 February 1997, Çevik Bir (b. 1939), then-deputy chief of the general staff, deployed Working Group West (Batı Çalışma Grubu). Several million dossiers were compiled; the intensity of surveillance by this working group "reached Stalinist proportions."[180]

The need to gain control of these secret structures, constructed or at least tolerated by the military over decades—and which acted with a certainty that they would never be brought to account—immediately suggested itself to the AKP. In the so-called Ergenekon trials which ran from 2007 to 2013, the

---

178 According to Öktem, *Angry Nation*, 45, the "September Events," that is, the pogrom against the Greek Orthodox community of İstanbul in 1955 was probably planned and directed by the Seferberlik Tetkik Kurulu.
179 Jenkins, *Between Fact and Fantasy*, 14ff. Lord, *Religious Politics*, 217n8.
180 Öktem, *Angry Nation*, 108.

Ministry of Justice opened a multitude of cases against high-ranking officers, but also against a wide circle of other people.[181] Ergenekon is a legendary valley in the Altai Mountains of Central Asia in which the earliest Turks found refuge after a defeat. A she-wolf named Asena is said to have led them out of the hidden valley again. Ergenekon was also allegedly the name of a secret network that wished to depose the ruling AKP government, but whose existence could never be proven by these trials. Many convicted received life sentences, among them, for example, İlker Başbuğ (b. 1943), chief of the general staff from 2008 to 2010. It was clear very early on that there was something more than a little strange with these trials. Their course was always similar: an anonymous informant would produce extremely detailed information, combined with exact information about weapons caches. State prosecutors produced huge dossiers of evidence of often trivial and deceptive content. The judges' verdicts did not go beyond the arguments in the indictments. The Gülen movement, which had in the meantime brought the Ministry of Justice well in hand in its march through the institutions, was the decisive actor. The positions in the military vacated in the Ergenekon trials were systematically filled by adherents of the Gülen movement. Instead of its ostensible intention of drying up the structures of the deep state, it increasingly appeared that the AKP camp meant to create its own, new deep state.[182]

On 29 July 2011, Chief of the General Staff Işık Koşaner (b. 1945, in office since 2010) as well as the commanders of the army, navy, and air force, resigned in protest against the arrest of around a tenth of active generals in the framework of the Ergenekon trials. Such an action would have been unimaginable a few years before,[183] but even less imaginable was that this protest faded away without effect. In any case, the Ergenekon trials adumbrated much of what would clearly come to light in the 2010s: the perversion of the principle of suspicion (whoever was considered suspicious, was suspicious) and the manipulation of public opinion—in short, the undermining of the rule of law and democracy in the service of "higher goals."

---

181 The Ergenekon trials fell apart into sub-trials, like, for example, the Balyoz ("sledgehammer") trials beginning in 2010.
182 Rodrik, "Ergenekon and Sledgehammer," 106ff. Cagaptay, *New Sultan*, 110. Jenkins, *Between Fact and Fantasy*, 56, 62, and passim, refers to the untenability and conspiracy-theoretical bases of the indictments.
183 See, however, the resignation of the general staff chief Necip Torumay (1926–2011, in office from 1987 to 1990) who was in disagreement with Özal's unilateral policy with regard to supporting US policy in the Gulf War and argued (as the US incidentally did as well) against Turkey's sending troops to the Gulf. Ahmad, *Modern Turkey*, 201.

Foreign and Trade Policy with a New Self-Confidence

In the initial decades after the Second World War, Turkish foreign policy, indeed Turkey's relationship to the rest of the world full stop, was limited to, essentially, its NATO membership and strategic alliance with the United States. So, relations with all of its neighboring countries were tense, or at least not friendly. As in economic policy, the foreign policy of the AKP governments were a continuation of the efforts of the 1980s and 1990s to open up the country. What was new, beginning in the 2000s, was that Turkey's foreign policy had a much stronger economic backing. The budget of the state development assistance organization, the Turkish Cooperation and Coordination Agency (Türk İşbirliği ve Koordinasyon Ajansı Başkanlığı, TİKA) amounted to eight-five million dollars in 2002, but had climbed to about 3.5 billion dollars in 2015.[184] The budget for the Turkish emergency-management organization, the Disaster and Emergency Management Presidium (Afet ve Acil Durum Yönetimi Başkanlığı, AFAD), founded in 1999 after the earthquake in İstanbul, had grown to about three hundred million Euros by 2015. In the meantime, AFAD had undertaken many missions abroad.[185]

The new ambitions of Turkish foreign policy showed themselves in regions of the world far from Turkey's own, like in Subsaharan Africa beyond the Maghrib states with which Turkey had cultivated relations over decades. In 1999, the Turkish government first settled on the intention to undertake a permanent and coordinated Africa policy, but it lacked the means to seriously implement this policy. In 2005, however, the AKP government proclaimed a "Year of Africa" and laid the foundations for a comprehensive Africa policy. They increased their number of embassies on the continent from twelve in the middle of the 2000s to thirty-four by the end of 2012. Trade volume with Africa climbed from 3.7 billion dollars in 2003 to 17 billion in 2011. Turkish Africa policy not only emphasized dealing on an equal footing but was infused with an anticolonial message. President Abdullah Gül emphasized in a 2011 speech that, in contrast to the Europeans, Turkey did not simply wish to export raw materials from Africa.[186]

---

184 Kirişci, *Turkey and the West*, 60.
185 See the projected budget 2015 in *Hürriyet*, October 13, 2014, https://www.hurriyet.com.tr/ekonomi/butcede-aslan-payini-maliye-bakanligi-aldi-27371830.
186 Hazar, "Türkiye Afrika'da": 33, 36. Vahap Munyar, "Biz Avrupalılar gibi hammaddeyi götürmeyiz," *Hürriyet*, March 26, 2011, quoted in Afacan, "Afrika Acılımı," 17. The argument of anticolonialism is carried to historically untenable lengths by overly enthusiastic Turkish observers of Africa policy. According to them, the Ottoman Empire

Along with aspirations to world-spanning diplomacy came the more tangible ambition to establish Turkey as a kind of cultural protective power in the former area of Ottoman rule.[187] A first target, close at hand, were the former Ottoman areas of rule in Southeastern Europe. The Turkish public had shown a much greater emotional reaction to the Yugoslav Wars of Dissolution in the 1990s than, say, the Lebanese Civil War in the 1970s and 1980s.[188] The new Turkish foreign policy in Southeastern Europe was simultaneously marked by caution. In the late 1990s, it was difficult for Turkey to openly place itself on the side of the Kosovo Liberation Army (Ushtria Çlirimtare e Kosovës, UÇK) in its battle against Serbia, because the possible parallels between the objectives of the UÇK in Kosovo and the PKK in Turkey were all too obvious.[189] Nevertheless, over the course of the 2000s, Turkey became an important stakeholder in Southeastern Europe. Fears of too great an influence from fundamentalist Islam, driven by states like Iran or Saudi Arabia, moved Western countries to grant Turkey a free hand in the Southeastern European countries with Muslim majorities.[190]

The AKP government, which had just come to power in 2002, wanted to affirm their reliability of as an ally of the West and therefore agreed that the US could use Turkey as the northern deployment zone for the attack on Iraq in March 2003. In return, Turkey would receive comprehensive aid in the amount of thirty billion US dollars. At the vote in the National Assembly on 1 March 2003, however, around a hundred AKP representatives voted against the deal.[191] Parliament's refusal to agree could be seen on the one hand as a foul-up on the part of the still-young AKP government, but on the other hand, it was a harbinger of the alienation between Turkey and the US which would become more and more visible in the following decade.

---

halted the further Spanish and Portuguese colonial expansion, due to its possessions in Africa. Hazar, "Türkiye Afrika'da," 30ff.
187 Since 1999, a good overview of the activities and expectations of Turkish foreign policy is contained in the semi-official periodical *Insight Turkey* which is published by the government-adjacent think tank SETA (Siyaset, Ekonomi ve Toplum Araştırma Vakfı, the Foundation for Political, Economic, and Social Research). See https://www.insightturkey.com and https://www.setav.org/en/, accessed 20 April 2023.
188 Kentel, "Identité nationale turque," 367. This analysis composed by Kentel around the turn of the century (thus about the Turkish public's lack of interest in violent conflicts in the eastern Arab world) no longer applies in the wake of the Syrian War of the 2010s.
189 Ganglof, "Politique balkanique," 344.
190 Öktem, *New Islamic Actors*, 22–25.
191 Jenkins, *Political Islam*, 171ff.

In the years 2008 and 2009, a very auspicious rapprochement between Armenia and Turkey was to be seen, brought about by the Armenian president, Serzh Sargsyan (in office 2008–2018) and the Turkish president, Abdullah Gül (in office 2007–2014). In September 2008, Gül became the first president to make a short visit to Yerevan to take in a soccer game between the Armenian and Turkish national teams. In October 2009, Armenia and Turkey signed two protocols in Zurich on the establishment of diplomatic relations and the opening of borders. The conflict in Nagorno-Karabakh and the question of the genocide were excluded, but Armenia had to accept the fixing of the Armenian-Turkish border of 1921 in advance. The process then stalled, presumably due to hefty resistance from Azerbaijan. One day after the signing of the Zurich protocols, Erdoğan demanded that Armenia withdraw from areas of Azerbaijan beyond Nagorno-Karabakh, which Armenia had occupied in the war for Nagorno-Karabakh until the armistice in 1994.[192] Turkey's official position declared that they were not demanding that Armenia withdraw from Nagorno-Karabakh itself, but merely from Azerbaijan proper.[193] During the war between Armenia and Azerbaijan in September–November 2020, however, it became apparent that Turkey would in no way cease its support of Azerbaijan when Azerbaijani troops pushed into Nagorno-Karabakh proper.

A break with Israel came about with much ado at the World Economic Forum in Davos on 29 January 2009, when, in a conversation with Shimon Peres, then-president of Israel (in office 2007–2014), Recep Tayyip Erdoğan attacked Israel as a brutal, "child-killing" country. In the following years, the slogan "Israel is a baby-killer" (İsrail bebek katili) could be read on many building walls in İstanbul. The Turco-Israeli relationship was additionally shaken by Israel's storming the Turkish ship *Mavi Marmara* in May 2010. The *Mavi Marmara*'s crew wished to bring aid materiel into the Gaza Strip against the instructions of the Israeli navy and likely looked forward to its becoming an international scandal. Since then, relations have remained frosty, despite an Israel apology for the *Mavi Marmara* incident. Turkey has freed itself from the expectations of its Western allies in this regard as well. From today's perspective, the scandal at Davos is to be seen not only as the announcement of an estrangement from Israel, but also a turn towards a more ideologically motivated foreign policy directed by domestic political considerations.[194]

---

192 Waal, *Caucasus*, 242ff.
193 Aydın, "Relations with the Caucusus and Central Asia," 774, 777.
194 Kirişçi, *Turkey and the West*, 157–158.

Turkey's EU Accession: The History of a Failure

In the 1990s, there were only cautious steps towards convergence between Europe and Turkey. The customs union introduced between the EC and Turkey barely received any attention in the country; the refusal anew of an application for acceptance in the EC in 1997 was received with bitterness. In December 1999, at the EC summit in Helsinki, a breakthrough came about when the European Council categorized Turkey as fundamentally capable of accession. The Council determined at the summit in Copenhagen in December 2002, that in two years it would decide whether Turkey fulfilled the criteria of a functioning democracy, and immediately thereafter accession negotiations would commence. In a meeting in December 2004, the Council of Europe recognized Turkey had fulfilled the Copenhagen criteria; and, in October 2005, accession negotiations were opened.

The horrifying complexity of the accession negotiations require that one brings the processes to a conclusion as quickly as possible, if one is acting in good faith.[195] At the beginning of 2021, however, in the case of the accession negotiations between the EU and Turkey—which are officially still underway—only sixteen of thirty-five chapters had been opened and only that with regard to academia and research had been concluded. Why was and is there a lack of readiness and ability to bring the negotiations to a successful conclusion? On the European side, there has never been a collective determination by all the relevant actors to allow the project of Turkey's accession to become a reality. The simulacrum of accession negotiations was practiced too long, identity-political reservations were too strong, and the challenge too great in being able—and being inclined—to find an appropriate place within the Union for this powerful state, which is kicking so many fundamental, open, domestic-political questions down the road.

A critical point Turkey has levelled with justification over decades at Europe's mindset is that of its ambiguity. After the Second World War, Europe saw Turkey as part of the Middle East—a region where they could practice classical power politics. On the other hand, they wanted to impose requirements on Turkey based on the argument that, as a potential European country (though that would not be entirely decided yet), it had to adhere to European values—values which, by the way, were in no way always observed by Europe

---

195 Cagaptay, *New Sultan* (2017), 97. All member states must assent to all thirty-five individual chapters.

and the European Union themselves. From the Turkish perspective, its history of becoming closer to Europe reaches back into the late eighteenth century. How then could anyone turn away a country that had already been knocking on the gates of Europe for two hundred years?

For Turkey, the experience of being the sole accession candidate put off for decades has been formative. Even if Greece's acceptance in 1981 without considering Turkey was understandable given the coup of September 1980, the acceptance of the Greek Cypriot Republic of Cyprus on 1 May 2004, despite the failure of the referendum on the Annan Plan a few days before, was unfortunate, even provocative. For Turkey, it was a deep mortification that Eastern and Southeastern European countries rolled past Turkey in several waves of accession.[196]

Consequently, the Turkish side's reproach of "the EU's failure to see Turkey and the Turks as a part of its 'self'" is justified.[197] The argument advanced by many European politicians, like the previous EU enlargement commissioner Günter Verheugen (in office 1999–2004), that the reason for Turkey's alarming political development since the late 2000s is its rejected application to the EU displays, however, arrogance couched as humility. Such arguments proceed from the practiced assumption of the previous decades that a country's acceptance into the EU inevitably exercised a democratizing effect. The escalating authoritarianism in several Eastern European member states shows, however, that such a "civilizing" effect of the EU, at least in the sense of Western European liberality, is in no way to be taken for granted. A member-state Turkey taking a negative course similar to the one it actually has would have been a burden hardly bearable by the community.

The reproach often made by the Turkish side, that the EU ultimately did not want to admit Muslim Turkey to its "Christian club," is not made up out of whole cloth. However, it is not the sole reason. In the case of a further large enlargement round—however improbable at that time—including the Southeastern European states which remained outside the EU (i.e., Albania, Bosnia-Hercegovina, Kosovo, North Macedonia, Serbia) one wouldn't want not to accept Albania or Kosovo for the sole reason that they are majority Muslim. It also is not just the Islamic character of Turkey, but also that with its accession, a country would have become a

---

196 On 1 May 2004, alongside Cyprus, the Czech Republic, Estonia, Hungary, Latvia, Lithuania, Malta, Poland, Slovakia, and Slovenia joined the EU. On 1 May 2007, Bulgaria and Romania joined, and on 1 July 2013, Croatia did as well.
197 Kirişçi, *Turkey and the West*, 77.

member of the European Union which, on the basis of its size and self-attributed importance, would demand a leading role in the EU. Turkey's not seeing itself solely as a European state is precisely what would have made it so worthwhile as a member. Its identitarian connections extend in the most varied directions. At the same time, as a member state of the European Union, Turkey would have had difficulties with defining its position within the EU which would have put far into the shade those which Great Britain had as a member state until January 2020. It's obvious that the debates quickly became all about the big picture, namely the question of relations between Turkey and Europe in general.

The genre of political-science dissertations about Turkey's possible accession to the European Union which flourished over the past few decades is now a part of academic history. Because one should not pretend that the question of Turkey's accession to the European Union is open. One could speak of a window of possibility in the early 2000s, because, on the Turkish side, the elites and the large majority of the Turkish population supported accession, as did an important part of the political class on the European side. This window has closed for the foreseeable future. The European Union would have had to take several years of exclusive lead time to prepare for Turkey's accession. However, such an intention was only partially present, and never among all the important actors in the European Union.

The Turkish public understood the decision of the Council of Europe in 2002 on the possible initiation of accession negotiations erroneously, as if imminent membership were a fact. Shortly after the accession negotiations were formally resolved upon in 2004, support for accession shrank significantly.[198] In the meantime, Turkey has turned its back on the accession project. This ambition has fallen to the bottom of the list of priorities in Turkish politics—also demonstrating a new political orientation that no longer desires to be reliant on the EU. At the fourth regular party congress of the AKP in October 2012, on a list of sixty-three priorities for a vision of Turkey in the year 2012, the goal of EU membership landed in sixtieth place.[199]

The possibility of Turkish accession in the early 2000s set off very lively identity-political conflicts in European countries. The vehemence of the

---

198   Jenkins, *Political Islam*, 178, cites 67.5% agreement in 2004, 57.4% in 2005, and 32.2% in 2006. Jenkins bases this on the results of a survey published in *Milliyet*, October 24, 2006, under the headline "The People Do Not Trust the EU" (*Halk AB'ye güvenmiyor*). For different numbers with a comparable trend, see Kirişçi, *Turkey and the West*, 18.
199   Ibid., 139.

arguments was indicative of the hostile stereotypes employed, the most potent of which was surely the contrast between "[Christian] Europe" and "Islam."[200] This rhetoric invoked not only the secular political order and society of Europe but also an alleged "Judeo-Christian" identity which seemingly effortlessly secured a majority with two of the three monotheistic religions.[201] Liberal intellectuals argued to the contrary that precisely because the Turks were not Christian, the "future European Turks would likely be inclined even more than other Europeans to emphasize the secular, tolerant, and liberal dimensions of European identity."[202]

Declared opponents of Turkish accession, like the German historians Hans-Ulrich Wehler and Heinrich August Winkler or the jurist Ernst-Wolfgang Böckenförde, argued on the level of identity, saying that due to Turkey's historical and cultural roots it could and should never be a member of the European Union.[203] The advocates of accession, on the other hand, did not counter this identity-politics-based rejection with a clear assertion of Turkey's belonging to Europe, but rather preferred to fall back on practical arguments like the opening of a large new market for the European economy or the relevant geostrategic advantages.[204] Fundamentally, the early 2000s discussion of Turkey's accession was just one episode in a larger argument of how European society and policy—faced with a bevy of Mediterranean countries with Muslim-majority populations and constantly growing Muslim populations in Western European counties—should deal with "Islam."

---

200 Sing, "Against All Odds," 139, justifiably points out that this dichotomous perception is prejudiced in advance in that Europe appears as a self-evidently important entity in contrast to "Islam," a clearly problematic entity.
201 For a more recent example, see "Kurz will, dass die EU die 'christlich-jüdische Identität schützt,'" *Der Kurier*, November 21, 2019, https://kurier.at/politik/inland/kurz-will-dass-die-eu-die-christlich-juedische-identitaet-schuetzt/400681271.
202 Judt, *History of Europe*, 767. It's striking that Tony Judt, who here so unambigiously affirms the Europeanness of Turkey, only mentions the country in passing in his comprehensive narrative of Europe after the Second World War (with a scope encompassing all of Eastern Europe).
203 Wehler, "Türkische Frage;" Winkler, "Ehehindernisse;" Böckenförde, "Nein zum Beitritt der Türkei," 35.
204 For this, see the pro-accession contributions in Leggewie, *Die Türkei und Europa*.

Chapter Five

The Road to Another Republic, 2013 to the Present

Opinions about developments in Turkey in the 2010s—and almost everyone has one—diverge wildly. On the one hand, there are those who defend the "new Turkey," its structure as a presidential regime and its path to a modern conservatism and a dynamic authoritarianism. One only has to regard how many obstacles this new course has had to overcome and of what achievements the contemporary Republic is capable and will be capable in the future. Given its decades-long experience of being continually rebuffed by the West and by Europe in particular, Turkey seems to have sorted itself out again.

Conversely, others see the significant decline in Turkey's democratic culture as undoing the achievements of the liberal period in the 2000s, and even as potentially endangering modern Turkey's history of success in toto. Recall the euphoria of the 2000s for Turkey, inside and outside the country. The judgment at the time was that the policy of "apartheid" cultivated by the Kemalist elite with regard to the rural or rural-heritage population was now coming to an end. A new pluralism had been created with the coming of a new elite, supported by the Justice and Development Party (Adalet ve Kalkınma Partisi, AKP) which came to power in 2002. In short, Turkish politics and society had managed to free itself from the straitjacket of state Kemalism. If the 2000s were a decade of liberation, and if the AKP and its milieu displayed so many positive characteristics, how could one not want or be able to continue travelling down this promising path? How, in the last few years, did Turkey take a turn into authoritarianism?

Without doubt, memory of being on the receiving end of decades of paternalism has not faded among the religious-conservative population of Turkey, and they remain unreconciled to their being pushed to the margins of the Turkish Republic for the first decades of its existence. It remains beyond question that the stalled negotiations over Turkey's accession to the European Union and the disappointment engendered by its rejection for membership yet again after applying for decades led to a hardening of political positions in Turkey. The experience of the coup attempt in July 2016 surely recalled the traumatic memories of the earlier, successful putsches by the military.

But how far do such justifications for the authoritarian turn go? Can one really say that these experiences and circumstances created a path dependency that was so clear-cut that the AKP, the government constituted by it, and the political elites recruited from it inevitably had to submit themselves to the "dark side of power?" It would follow from such an argument that, given its more or less heavy burdens, the evolution of Turkey in recent years was inescapable. One would have to deny the free will of Turkey's political elites and its people.

In any case, the beginning of the 2010s was once again characterized by euphoria. The Arab Spring, or the "Arabellion," the wave of peaceful revolts against authoritarian rulers in the Arab world, created excitement. For decades, Arab potentates had locked down their positions of power, to mention only Muammar al-Qaddafi in Libya since 1969, Ali Abdullah Saleh in Yemen since 1978, Hosni Mubarak in Egypt since 1981, and Zine el-Abidine Ben Ali in Tunisia since 1987. When the Arab Spring petered out, the disappointment was that much greater—in Turkey as well, where the hopes of a new, favorable political order in the region had climbed to exuberant heights.

At the same time, the AKP government displayed an increasing impatience with those who did not share its opinions. At the latest, the government's answering the Gezi Park protests of May 2013 with nothing but repression disillusioned the liberal camp, which may have perceived the AKP as increasingly unsympathetic but still wanted to see in it a decisive force for the transformation of the country. The evolution into a state culture of authoritarianism peaked in the government's exceptionally harsh reaction following the failed coup attempt on the night of the fifteenth and sixteenth of July 2016.

The Republic of Turkey is looking into the future and seeing several milestones ahead of it. Preparations for the hundredth anniversary of the founding of the Republic on 29 October 2023 are imminent, but Turkish historians also already looking at the six-hundredth anniversary of the conquest of Constantinople on 29 May 2053, and—in the far distance, but a particularly round-numbered jubilee, the thousandth anniversary of the Battle of Manzikert/Malazgirt on 26 August 2071. These commemorations will serve, as is always the case in national cultures of memory, as self-assurance of the rightness of the path taken. The road that Turkish politics has taken since the early 2010s has, at any rate, led into a new Republic.

1. Old and New Guiding Lights

The first conjectures that a First Turkish Republic had come to an end appeared after the military coup of 1960.[1] In later years, a Second and even Third Turkish Republic were continually invoked as well. In contrast to France, however, which has without a doubt been living under its Fifth Republic since 1958, there is no consensus in Turkey over which Republic, if it's no longer the First, they now find themselves in. Despite deep disjunctions—like for example the coups of 1960 and 1980 and the ensuing constitutions of 1961 and 1982—a periodization of different Republics has never gained acceptance, neither inside Turkey nor in international historiography. The reason for this is likely the Kemalist power complex's abiding staying power until the beginning of the twenty-first century. Nevertheless, with the final collapse of the Kemalist paradigm in the 2010s and the meanwhile wholesome exchange of elites in administration, military, judiciary, and even the university (including the complete alienation of the formerly allied Gülen movement), Turkey is en route to another Republic. When exactly the break took place is an open and likely moot question. The beginning of the Ergenekon trials in 2007, the collective resignation of the general staff in July 2011,[2] the collapse of the accord between moderate Islamism and intellectual liberalism occasioned by the Gezi Park protests in Summer 2013, the alienation and finally open hostility between the Gülen movement and the AKP in 2013–2016, or the failed

---

1   See Robinson, *First Turkish Republic*. Celal Bayar, president from 1950 to 1960, spoke in his later publications of a "Second Republic" founded by the coup and thereby illegitimate. Dawletschin-Linder, *Diener seines Staates*, 266. According to Türk, *Muktedir*, 183, Erbakan was arguing as early as c. 1975 that a new republic had begun with the end of one-party rule in the late 1940s.
2   Thus the journalist Aslı Aydıntaşbaş offered the opinion that with the collective resignation of the Turkish general staff in July 2011 a new republic had arrived. In Tuysuz and Tavernise, "Top Generals Quit."

coup attempt in the night of 15–16 July 2016? The constitutional referendum of 16 April 2017 on a presidential system of government and the parliamentary and presidential elections of 24 June 2018 are, in any case, conclusions and not the beginning of the evolution. Much speaks for viewing 2013 as the decisive turning point. The Gezi Park protests and their suppression poisoned the social climate; the falling out between the Gülen movement and the AKP boiled over into an open slugfest; and the hopes of the Arab Spring had dispersed two years after their beginning.

Arab Spring, Neo-Ottomanism, and the War in Syria

The 2010s began with great confidence in the entire Middle East. In December 2010, a popular rebellion broke out in Tunisia, which drove President Zine al-Abidine Ben Ali, who had ruled since 1987, out of power and, in addition, demanded political participation, social dignity, and economic improvement. When it became clear in January 2011 that the Arab Spring had not remained contained in Tunisia, but had spread to many further Arab countries, the excitement was great—in the Arab lands themselves but also among Western publics. Early analyses of the Arab Spring compared it with the French Revolution, or at least with the uprisings in Eastern Europe in the 1980s.[3]

The rebels' demands were of a pragmatic nature and not guided by ideology. That the populace revolted rather than charismatic leaders' determining the action could be seen as progress, given the disappointing experiences with the "heroes" of Arab nationalism. On the other hand, the Arab Spring lacked the intellectual and organizational resources to expand into a revolution.[4] The deeper reasons for the unrest lay in the long-broken relationship between elite and people. In the framework of the authoritarian "Arab social contract," the state had secured the people an economic livelihood in exchange for which they had to relinquish political participation.[5]

---

3   Gerges, "Introduction," 2. A report by the International Crisis Group suggested very early that interpretations of the Arab Spring were so divergent that they represented a sort of Rorschach test. Anyone could read in the protests whatever she or he wanted find there. International Crisis Group, *Popular Protest*, 10.

4   According to Paul, "Arabellion," 36–38, the insurgents did not go far enough, in that they simply demanded a change of the top level of leadership rather than striving for a fundamentally new governing principle.

5   Zorob, "Zusammenbruch des autoritären Gesellschaftsvertrags," 229. The Arab world is not alone in this. Compare the collapse of the socialist social contract in Eastern Europe as depicted in Ther, *Neue Ordnung auf dem alten Kontinent*, 42, and in Sakwa,

This social contract had already fallen apart over the course of the economic liberalization which began in the 1980s. The legitimacy of the Arab regime was thus insecure; it only excelled when it came to maintaining its authority.

In European media, excitement was quickly tempered by the concern the Arab Spring could follow a course similar to that of the Iranian Revolution in 1978 and 1979. At that time, the uprising against the shah's regime by highly diverse portions of the population ended up with a theocracy led by Ayatollah Ruhollah Khomeini called the Islamic Republic of Iran. This concern proved way off the mark. No one could have anticipated in the first months the actual, catastrophic path that the Arab Spring took—the slide of three countries, Libya, Syria, and Yemen, into war and ruin. The brutal reestablishment of authoritarian rule by the military in Egypt in Summer 2013 paled in comparison.

The Arab Spring has a gloomy background, namely the destabilization of the eastern Arab world triggered by the American invasion of Iraq in 2003.[6] Today it's beyond question that the occupation of Iraq, ostensibly part of a battle against the "Axis of Evil," was a disastrous step. Despite all its errors, for example in the run-up to the Iranian Revolution in 1978–79, American policy in the Middle East was rather restrained over the previous decades. It was not based on regime change, but the (from the internal perspective of the policy, necessarily) cynical preservation of preexisting political structures and the extant regimes. The American invasion of Iraq in 2003 contradicted this policy of a careful and coolly calculating hegemon. The consequences of this mistake—visible in the Iraqi state's almost collapsing, the strengthening of Iran as a regional power, and the rise of extremely violent organizations like the Islamic State—deterred the US government under President Barack Obama (in office 2009–2017) from allowing itself to be drawn further into the region's conflicts. The escalation of the wars in Libya, Syria, and Yemen in the 2010s is not comprehensible without the retreat of the US from the Middle East. The vacuum left by the inhibited superpower allowed the rise of Russia in the Syrian War since the mid-2010s as a sort of ersatz hegemon. Iran, Saudi Arabia, and Turkey, in turn, have become would-be hegemons in the region.

Putin Paradox, 10, for the Soviet Union. On the revocation of the social contract in the capitalist West, see Streeck, *Gekaufte Zeit*, 127–139, 206.

6   Westad, *Cold War*, 621, describes the US intervention in Iraq after its victory in the Cold War as a "useless war" and the act of a "superpower in decline."

For the Turkish elite, a new and unimagined lesson from the derailment of the Arab Spring was the fact, theretofore unfamiliar to them, that an offensive foreign policy can have repercussions on domestic circumstances.[7] One might just think of Turkey's generous acceptance of around four million Syrian refugees. As well as being a highly creditable deed in itself, it was likely originally conceived of in terms of shaping Turkey's public image as a humanitarian superpower, and proceeded wrongly from the premise that the refugees could soon be repatriated into a new Syria under a Turkish security umbrella after the imminent fall of Bashar al-Asad.[8]

The Arab Spring seemed to offer Turkey the opportunity to export its (admittedly intrinsically fragile) "success story" of democracy, moderate Islamism, and market economy to the Arab world.[9] After the fall of Hosni Mubarak in February 2011, the Egyptian Muslim Brotherhood, who had been in the extraparliamentary opposition for decades, founded the Freedom and Justice Party (Hizb al-hurriyya wa'l-'adalah). The Turkish government had the same view of conditions in Egypt, demographically the most important country in the Arab world, as the Egyptian Muslim Brotherhood. The Ikhwan al-Muslimin spoke of deep structures in the military, security, juridical, and economic fields which reached back even before Hosni Mubarak's era as president (1981–2011). They would never before have let the Muslim Brotherhood come to power; now that the Brotherhood was in government (since 2011), they were placing as many obstacles in their path as possible.[10]

In fact, the Middle Eastern authoritarian regimes displayed a steep learning curve with regard to their resilience a few months after the Arab Spring had challenged them.[11] As rentier states, the Gulf monarchies, above all Saudi Arabia, so long described as ossified political systems one step away from the abyss, showered their respective populations with a cornucopia of financial benefits. In Egypt, the Muslim Brotherhood had nothing with which to counter the propaganda and apparatus of repression of the military, which swept away them—in coup-like fashion—in Summer 2013.

---

7   On comparable mistakes by Saudi Arabia and Turkey in the Syrian War, see Phillips, "Eyes Bigger than Stomachs."
8   Turkish authorities are proceeding from the assumption that there will be around five million Syrians in Turkey in 2028. International Crisis Group, *Syrian Refugee Youth*, 1. Balbay, "Suriye Politikasında," estimates that there are already five million Syrians living in Turkey today.
9   Öktem, "Türkisches Zwischenspiel im Nahen Osten."
10 International Crisis Group, *Marching in Circles*, 9.
11 Heydeman and Leenders, "Authoritarian Learning."

Along with the military's overwhelming position of strength, the ideological weaknesses of the Muslim Brotherhood (including its utopian conception of an ideal Islamic state) and its lack of experience in government and administration led to the Brotherhood's failure.[12]

The political leadership of Turkey was not alone in its original euphoria over the Arab Spring. However, it was perhaps the state which drew the widest-ranging conclusions for the reorientation of its foreign policy, and it clung too long to its initial assessment. Consequently, Turkey indulged in the hope that Bashar al-Asad (b. 1965), who had stepped up as his father Hafiz al-Asad's successor in Syria in 2000, would fall as swiftly as the leaders of Egypt, Libya, Tunisia, and Yemen had, and that Turkey would become the decisive patron power for the new governments in Egypt and Syria. Turkish foreign policy under then-foreign minister Ahmet Davutoğlu interpreted the Arab Spring within the framework of a larger historical narrative, based on the belief that the region was returning to its natural, fundamental geopolitical relations which had been overridden by the European great powers in criminally false fashion after the First World War. To Turkey, then, fell the decisive task, specifically to display an intracivilizational Islamic solidarity with the countries of the Arab Spring and to take on the position of their spokesman.[13] The reason that the Turkish government insisted so strongly on this interpretation was that the Arab Spring seemed to unambiguously confirm their reading of history. The Turkish foreign policy agenda of the 2000s and early 2010s was based on a positive assessment of the Ottoman culture of rule and a confidence that a peaceful coexistence in the former territories of the Ottoman empire could be effected by recourse to the centuries-old patterns of experience in Ottoman policy.[14]

International literature has largely labelled these efforts "neo-Ottomanism" (*Yeni Osmanlıcılık*), generally intended pejoratively.[15] Turkish neo-Ottomanism may be the mark of an all too emotional connection to lost greatness, coupled with a sometimes mistaken understanding of its actual power bases. But was it not actually an intuitive answer to the shifting balance of power in the region? The individual most closely connected to the term

---

12   Sherif, *Egyptian Muslim Brotherhood's Failures*.
13   Kirişci, *Turkey and the West*, 160–162.
14   Bora, "Turkish National Identity," 120, impressively describes neo-Ottoman lines of thought long preceding the AKP's taking office.
15   According to Torbakov, "Neo-Ottomanism versus Neo-Eurasianism," 135, the term "neo-Ottomanism" was coined by the journalist Cengiz Çandar, who was an advisor to Turgut Özal in the early 1990s.

"neo-Ottomanism" is Ahmet Davutoğlu (b. 1959), a professor of political science. He was foreign policy advisor to the AKP government before he became foreign minister in 2009, and subsequently held the office of prime minister in the years 2014–2016. Davutoğlu rejects the concept of neo-Ottomanism—but has simultaneously affirmed it in substance. "I am not a neo-Ottoman. Actually there is no such policy. We have a common history and cultural depth with the Balkan countries, which nobody can deny. We cannot act as if the Ottomans never existed in this region."[16]

Without his political activities, Davutoğlu's book *Strategic Depth*, published in 2001 and difficult to read, is unlikely to have become as well-known as it is.[17] Davutoğlu wishes to move beyond the image of Turkey as a "bridge" between East and West so often deployed in Western narratives, because it allegedly degrades Turkey as an object and moreover misjudges its potential and capability. He sees the land as a "pivot country" (*mihver ülke*) which lies at the intersection of several major regions of the world.[18] From the beginning, the overtly constructive sides of this policy, like having "zero problems" with the neighbors and its inherent self-image as a moderator and arbitrator, ran the risk of hubris, entitlement to a dominant role, and the over-interpretation of deep structures allegedly rooted in history. Comparable approaches could be found under Bülent Ecevit in the late 1970s (in the form of a new national security concept) and under Turgut Özal. What was new this time was the comprehensiveness of the concept and its direct influence on the conduct of security policy.[19]

Recep Tayyip Erdoğan, the prime minister, delivered a memorable example of neo-Ottoman rhetoric at the beginning of the 2010s. In a speech at the fourth regular party congress of the AKP on 30 September 2012, he spoke of a seed of the "civilization of love" which was supposedly planted by Sultan Alparslan, victor of the Battle of Manzikert in 1071. In the hands of Osman Gazi, it became a sprout, then a young plant, and finally a huge plane tree which branched out into the sky, covered the sea, and reached from the Tigris to the Danube. "There is no blood in the shadow of this great plane tree, the Seljuk, Ottoman, and Republican Turkish plane tree. In the shadow of this plane tree, there is no difference and no discrimination, no unjust

---

16   Davutoğlu, "I Am Not a Neo-Ottoman."
17   Davutoğlu, *Stratejik Derinlik*. Davutoğlu, "Principles of Turkish Foreign Policy," is informative because it is arranged in the form of propositions.
18   Ramm, "Politik der 'strategischen Tiefe,'" 52.
19   Hale and Özbudun, *The Case of the AKP*, 120.

treatment, no oppression, no marginalizing of 'the Other.' In the shadow of this beautiful plane tree stand the Süleymaniye and the Selimiye [two particularly important sultanic mosques in İstanbul and Edirne, respectively], the bridge of Mostar and the bridge over the Drina [in Višegrad, Eastern Bosnia]. In the shadow of this plane tree are caravanserais, fountains, medreses, and pious foundations."[20] Ottoman infrastructural achievements in the form of mosques and other charitable institutions do indeed shape the historic cityscapes of many cities of Southeastern Europe. The images and ideas invoked by Erdoğan here go far beyond them and manifest the claim that the Ottoman Empire should be seen as an almost ideal social order.

Under the influence of the Syrian War, the Turkish government began to fundamentally question arrangements in the Middle East. At the same time, they avoided examining the obvious: Just as they wished to see absolutely no connection between the Arab Spring and the Gezi Park protests, they did not consider the Treaty of Lausanne part of the reordering of the Middle East after the First World War and aimed for a revision of the "Sykes-Picot Regime" under the false assumption that such changes would remain without consequence for Turkey itself.[21] In recent years, Turkish foreign policy has sharpened its conduct in such a fashion that now even a change in the territorial terms of the Treaty of Lausanne have become imaginable—but of course only in the sense of an enlargement of Turkey. "As a consequence of lies and diplomatic intrigue," claimed Recep Tayyip Erdoğan in February 2018, "our five-million-square-kilometer fatherland (3.1 million square-miles) was reduced to Turkey's current territory.[22]

Despite all this rhetoric, in the tortuous course of the war for control of Syria, Turkey increasingly became just one player among many. It would be

---

20   Erdoğan, [Untitled]. See Türk, *Muktedir*, 312, for a speech of Erdoğan of 23 August 2013 with similar content. Türk, *Muktedir*, 170, and Birand and Yıldız, *Son Darbe*, 55, describe Erbakan's previous use of the plane tree as a symbol of an organically spreading Ottoman Turkish civilization. The images conjured by Erbakan and Erdoğan likely come from an alleged dream of Sultan Osman I, founder of the Ottoman dynasty c. 1300, of a tree growing from his navel, whose leaves cast shadows upon the whole world. Finkel, *Osman's Dream*, 2.

21   Thus, for example, Foreign Minister Davutoğlu announced in a speech in 2013 in Diyarbakır that Turkey would "break out of these templates prescribed to us by Sykes-Picot." Davutoğlu, "Büyük Restorasyon."

22   Speech by Recep Tayyip Erdoğan on 6 February 2018 before the parliamentary caucus of the AKP, reprinted in *Hürriyet*, February 6, 2018, https://www.hurriyet.com.tr/gundem/son-dakika-cumhurbaskani-erdogan-flas-karari-acikladi-40732853. On this, see also Danforth, "Turkey's New Maps."

going too far to say that Turkey lost its soul in the war in Syria; however, it nevertheless did lasting damage to its reputation in the region. In surveys of public opinion in the Middle East in 2010, Turkey achieved approval ratings of 85%, higher than any other country. In 2013, they had already retreated to 59%, lower than the United Arab Emirates (67%), China (64%), or Saudi Arabia (60%).[23]

A precondition to a solution to the knotty conflict in Syria is that all parties must hit a pain threshold; in addition, there can be no prospect for any of those involved to profitably break through the stalemate.[24] Faced with the multitude of actors in the Syrian War, one has to reach quite far back for historical comparisons, like the Thirty Years' War (1618–1648).[25] Comparable are the confessional front lines overlaid by the obscurity of interests, the great number of external actors using an area (Germany or Syria) as a venue for their conflicts, and a war's feeding on itself.[26] One would hope the Syrian War could end in a new Westphalian peace, as in 1648, wrapping up several lines of conflict in a comprehensive resolution, but it is improbable at the moment.[27] The Syrian War remains an open wound and a threat for Turkey. It was, however, domestic political developments of the early 2010s which were decisive for Turkey's turning into an authoritarian state.

Protests, Attacks, and the Break with the Gülen Movement

On the night of 27–28 May 2013, around twenty environmental activists occupied Gezi Park, a public green space of about nine and one-half acres immediately north of Taksim Square, in order to prevent some upcoming construction. There had originally been a military base in the southern portion of the park, which was torn down in the 1920s in order to make room for a planned parking structure. İstanbul's city administration now wished to use this southern section of Gezi Park for a redevelopment, which would have the

---

23 Akgün et al., *Perception of Turkey* (2011), 10. Akgün et al., *Perception of Turkey* (2014), 8. These surveys, carried out on behalf of TESEV, the Foundation for Economic and Social Studies of Turkey (Türkiye Ekonomik ve Sosyal Etüdler Vakfı) were no longer carried out beginning in 2015.
24 On this, Zartman, "Conflict and Resolution," 16a–b, is fundamental.
25 As two early examples of this argument, see Haass, "New Thirty Years' War," and Lawson "A Thirty Years' War."
26 For such a comparison, see Münkler, *Der Dreißigjährige Krieg*, 817–843.
27 Steinmeier, "Der Westfälische Frieden." Milton et al., *Westphalia for the Middle East*.

façade of the former military base but contain a mosque and a shopping mall. When the police answered the activists' passive resistance with excessive force, a protest movement emerged spontaneously, spreading from İstanbul throughout the whole country. The final clearing of the park in the middle of June could not break the protest movement. There were protests in sixty-nine of the eighty-one provinces of Turkey, in which likely three and a half million people took part, in total. In the first year after the protests, more than five hundred thousand were indicted for taking part in the protests, while incidents of brutality by the security forces went as good as unpunished—and were even praised by the government.[28] The protests, nourished by discontent with the profit orientation of private and state construction firms, broke down the walls of fear which had grown up in the years prior. By September 2013, the end of the protests, which subsided partially of their own accord, partially due an inability to withstand the continually increasing violence of the security forces, eleven protestors had been blinded, five killed, and thousands injured.[29] Even today, security forces are stationed day and night at the entrance to Gezi Park from Taksim Square, ready to smother any attempt at renewed protest in the cradle.[30]

In September 2013, the Gezi Park protests were connected to an almost worldwide spirit of optimism. They seemed join the ranks of a global insurrection against the neo-liberal social order, reaching from Brasilia to Turkey and from Tunisia via Greece and Greenland to New York.[31] What remained of it in Turkey? After summer 2013, the country ultimately divided itself into two camps, those whom the government was able to win over even further with its hard line against the protests, and those who now counted the government as an enemy.

In the parliamentary elections of 7 June 2015, the AKP failed to obtain an absolute majority in parliament, with 40.1% of the vote. It now seemed possible to break the AKP's ability to govern alone, by obliging it to form a coalition with the Republican People's Party (Cumhuriyet Halk Partisi, CHP) or with the Peoples' Democratic Party (Halkların Demokratik Partisi, HDP).

---

28 Amnesty International, *Adding Injustice to Injury*, 5–7 and passim.
29 Özel, "Moment of Elation," 9, 21.
30 The story of Gezi Park has certainly not yet come to an end. In March 2021, the ownership of the property was taken from the city administration and transferred to the General Directorate of Pious Endowments (Vakıflar Genel Müdürlüğü). See, "Gezi Park'ının mülkiyeti İBB'den alındı," *Gazete Duvar*, March 19, 2021, https://www.gazeteduvar.com.tr/gezi-parkinin-mulkiyeti-ibbden-alindi-haber-1516611.
31 See as an example of this explanatory approach, Tuğal, "Resistance Everywhere."

However, the governing AKP, under the informal leadership of President Recep Tayyip Erdoğan (until the constitutional amendment which came in force in 2018, politicians taking the office of president had to surrender their party membership), did not care to accept the electoral results. Summer 2015 was shaped by a new hardening relative to the Kurdish movement, by terrorist attacks with unknown perpetrators, and by an abrupt cooling of the political climate. On 10 October 2015, one hundred and two people died in Ankara, in the worst terrorist attack in the history of Turkey. In the rescheduled parliamentary elections on 1 November 2015, the AKP was able to obtain the very high vote total of 49.5% of the electorate—"the wages of fear."[32]

On the other hand, the breach with the Gülen movement was of tremendous import for power relations within the governing camp. There had long been political differences of opinion between the AKP government and the Gülen movement, without their leading to a permanent rupture. For example, the Gülen movement wanted to avoid a break with Israel like the one initiated by the Turkish government in the wake of the capture of the *Mavi Marmara* by the Israel navy in May 2010; but, on the other hand, the Gülenists were implacable with regard to the Kurdish question. In February 2012, some of the state prosecutors close to the Gülen movement threatened Hakan Fidan (b. 1968), leader of the intelligence service MİT, with prosecution because he had conducted negotiations at the government's behest with the Kurdistan Communities Union (Koma Civakên Kurdistan, KCK), the umbrella organization which arose out of the PKK. But in the end, neither their political nor even ideological positions were crucial, just the fact that it had come to an open power struggle between the two former allies. When, in the beginning of the 2010s, it was clear that all other opponents had been neutralized, the question arose as to which of the two main currents of Islamist mobilization would prevail—that of party-political wrestling for power, as in the AKP's case, or that of infiltrating state institutions with one's own personnel, as in the Gülen movement's. At the end of 2013, plans for closing the private schools (*dershane*) with supplementary instruction run by the Gülen movement leaked to the public. This was obviously a targeted maneuver to provoke the Gülen movement to open fisticuffs—among other things, the Gülen movement recruited its younger generation there. Subsequently, the Gülen movement responded when, in December 2013, state prosecutors arrested ninety persons, among them sons of ministers, on corruption charges.

---

32   Seufert, "Erdogans Lohn der Angst."

The AKP government quickly got the upper hand, in that they sidelined the prosecutors in question and shrugged off the corruption charges in public as a conspiracy directed from abroad. In December 2014, an arrest warrant was issued for Fethullah Gülen on the grounds of "constructing a parallel state" (*paralel devlet yapısı*). Beginning in December 2015, the Gülen movement was dubbed the Fethullahist Terror Organization (Fethullahçı Terör Örgütü, FETÖ) in investigations.[33] By the middle of the 2010s, the AKP faced no serious enemies any more—but nevertheless a final great challenge loomed, the coup attempt of July 2016.

The Failed Coup Attempt of July 2016

In the late evening of 15 July 2016, the military began to occupy important positions in the cities. Most people initially thought they were security measures taken because of a threatened terrorist attack. The jarring din of fighter planes in the darkness and exchanges of shots around government buildings in Ankara soon proved it was a coup attempt. At 11:00 p.m., prime minister Binali Yıldırım confirmed the facts to the media. Shortly after midnight, President Recep Tayyip Erdoğan appeared on CNN Türk. The coup had already failed by this point. A well-planned coup would not have been conducted in the late evening hours of a Friday, when traffic was still clogging the streets of the big cities, and would never have been allowed to frontally take on the multifarious resistors inside the military and security forces.[34] One of the immediate conditions for the success of the coup would have been detaining President Recep Tayyip Erdoğan and other leading politicians of the governing party. In addition, there was on the one hand the communiqué of the putschists, calling themselves the Council of Peace at Home (Yurtta Sulh Konseyi), alluding to Atatürk's famous motto, "Peace at home, peace in the world" (Yurtta sulh, cihanda sulh). Their message was read out by a news anchor and transmitted only on the state radio and television broadcaster TRT. On the other hand, there was the president's summons and the call from the minarets of almost all ninety thousand mosques to take to the streets and oppose the putschists. By the end of the night with the putschists'

---

33   Cagaptay, *New Sultan*, 137. Türk, *Muktedir*, 262–290. Lord, *Religious Politics*, 272–275.
34   According to Gürsoy, "15 July 2016 Failed Coup," 287ff., the loyalty of the uppermost echelons of the military, the intelligence service (MİT), and large parts of the police thwarted the success of the coup.

capitulation, thirty-six partisans of the coup and 240 of its opponents had been killed, as well as 49 partisans and 2,195 opponents injured.[35]

Because the Turkish government contributed little to a convincing explanation of the coup attempt in the months following, its true causes likely lie between two—equally unlikely—poles of interpretation. The government's explanation is that the coup attempt by the Gülen movement came as a complete surprise and it was only averted thanks to the heroism of the state leadership and of the people.[36] This contrasts with the supposition that the coup attempt was staged by the state leadership in order to ensure the destruction of its opponents once and for all.[37] Much speaks for the case that the Gülen movement was involved in the coup attempt or was responsible for it. There are also some indications, however, that the government learned of the coup plans well in advance and had sufficient time to prepare for it.

The failed coup attempt is historically extraordinary in the sense that, previously, resistance by the government and the people to the overwhelmingly powerful Turkish military had always failed. But the military had already foundered through its weakening as an independent political actor in previous years. The military's limbs had been amputated, but its old reflexes allowed it to believe it could strike once more. After the failed coup attempt of July 2016, the military finally, permanently lost its role as political guardian of the nation.

The AKP's decision *not* to use the enormous gain in legitimacy it had earned in thwarting the coup attempt as an opportunity for national reconciliation (by only punishing a narrow circle of masterminds) also represented a crossroads. The AKP chose instead the path of hunting down everyone who fundamentally did not share the political goals of the AKP, and thereby hardened the assumption that the coup suited their political calculus. Some measures served indeed the legitimate goal of finally securing civilian control over the military. The established military academies were shut down, and a National Defense University was established. Around a third of all military personnel were dismissed in October 2016. The number of active soldiers sank from 518,166 to 355,212. The share of civilians in the Supreme Military Council (Yüksek Askeri Şura), which decides all important promotions and

---

35 Altınordu, "A Midsummer Night's Coup."
36 Yavuz, "How Credible Are Alternative Coup Scenarios?" supports the interpretation of the Turkish government's seeing a sole leading role for the Gülen movement in the coup attempt and all other explanatory approaches as mistaken.
37 The chairman of the Republican People's Party (CHP) advanced the scenario of a controlled coup attempt. Kılıçdaroğlu, "Hükümet darbeyi biliyordu."

retirements in the military, was raised to ten while the number of military members dropped to four.³⁸

If one believes the Gülen movement was behind the coup, then the destruction of its entire network in Turkey is understandable.³⁹ The excessively harsh reprisals, however, that the state undertook in the weeks and months after the failed putsch, suggest a "counter-coup" by the state. For example, liberal intellectuals demonstrably had no interest or participation in the coup attempt. Retroactively attributing sympathies for or even complicity in the coup to them, then, was nothing but an arbitrary exploitation of the enlarged room for maneuver that the failed coup attempt had put at the government's disposal. In the framework of the state of emergency imposed on 20 July 2016 and repeatedly extended until 18 July 2018, thousands of dismissals from state service took place without proper investigation, as did confiscations of property without due process, thousands of imprisonments without the possibility of contact, and police custodies of up to thirty days without judicial hearings. In the two years of the state of emergency, the government issued thirty-two decrees with the force of law (*kanun hükmünde kararname*, akin to the US president's executive orders) and thereby circumvented parliament as the legitimate legislative branch. A broad circle of individuals were subjected to bans on leaving the country and on employment. Of the approximately four million officials in Turkey before the coup attempt, about one in twenty-five were dismissed by summer 2018 for alleged involvement in the coup attempt.⁴⁰ These measures may not have been harder and more comprehensive than those after the coup of 1980; however, they certainly lasted longer and were less predictable.

The AKP government expended great effort to anchor the coup attempt of 2016 as a new national myth. The southernmost and oldest of the three Bosporus bridges in İstanbul was renamed the Bridge of the Martyrs of 15 July (15 Temmuz Şehitler Köprüsü), as was the central Red Crescent Square (Kızılay Meydanı) in Ankara, which became the National Will of 15 July Red Crescent Square (15 Temmuz Kızılay Milli İrade Meydanı). In July 2017, on the occasion of the first anniversary of the failed coup, heroic paintings were displayed which were composed in exactly the same sepia tones familiar from depictions of the Turkish War of Independence. Giant billboards declared

---

38   Lord, *Religious Politics*, 269, 277.
39   In fact, the Gülen movement is now just a shadow of its former self, but under the circumstances, it will survive as a diaspora movement.
40   Lord, *Religious Politics*, 276. Tartanoğlu, "Türkiye Ağır Yaralı."

solemnly, "We have not forgotten — we will not forget — we will ensure it is not forgotten" (Unutmadık — ununmayacağız — unutturmayacağız).

The Presidential Republic Since 2018

The constitutional referendum of 16 April 2017, which was passed with a majority of 51.41% of the vote, laid the foundations for a new political system which was implemented through the parliamentary and presidential elections of 24 June 2018. The rationale for the transition to a presidential regime was that the Constitution of 1982 was said to be in need of reform and had to be fundamentally overhauled.[41] The changes placed before the people for approval, however, were largely limited to allocating as much power to the president and as little to parliament as possible.

Since 2018, the cabinet has been named directly by the president without parliamentary approval. The office of prime minister, previously so central, does not exist anymore; its rights now belong to the office of the president. The president can dissolve parliament at any time. However, the president must run for reelection himself in new elections. Parliament requires a three-fifths majority of the members' votes to dissolve itself on its own. Parliament's rights of oversight over the ministers are limited. Only an absolute majority can *request* an investigation, and only a two-thirds majority can *order* an investigation.[42]

Just as people have always referred to the disastrous sides of Kemalism, in the future there will be discussions of the costs consequent to Tayyipism (Tayyipçilik, an ironic analogy to Kemalism, derived from Atatürk's second personal name), the presidential republic installed by Recep Tayyip Erdoğan with its authoritarian outlines. The parallels of Tayyipism in the 2010s to the Khomeinism in Iran in the 1980s are eye-catching, even given the differences in the details: the emphasis on nationalism and borders; the marked Islamic modernism; the focus on socio-political questions but without ever questioning the principle of private property (above all for their own clientele); the rhetoric of mutually exclusive opposites; the warning of the threat of imperialists and Zionists; the similarities to the tradition of Latin American populism.[43]

---

41 See for example the suggestion of Özbudun, *Constitutional System of Turkey*, 21, that the sixteen constitutional amendments in the years 1982–2010 did not suffice to undo the illiberal character of the Constitution of 1982.
42 Lord, *Religious Politics*, 278–282.
43 For the case of Iran, see Abrahamian, *Khomeinism*.

The authoritarian turn has torn Turkish society even more drastically into two hostile camps, and in addition has led to much financial and intellectual capital's leaving Turkey since 2015, as well as the Turkish economy's losing its previous competitiveness. The paramount role of Recep Tayyip Erdoğan has been a bottleneck in the Turkish political system for years—but with the constitutional amendments passed in 2018, it became official. Everything must run through the presidential palace, every decision of a certain import must be placed before the president and approved by him.

Political competition was neutralized along with the rule of law, which Turkey in fact no longer possesses. The rise of the Peoples' Democratic Party (Halkların Demokratik Partisi, HDP) and its success in the parliamentary elections of 2015 dynamited the party system which had been frozen since 2002, with the AKP as governing party and the Republican People's Party (CHP) and the Nationalist Movement Party (MHP) as eternal opposition parties. The HDP succeeded in winning new constituencies outside national-minded Kurds by opening and positioning itself as a left-liberal party. In the parliamentary elections of 7 June 2015, the HDP cleared the ten percent hurdle for the first time with 13.1% of the vote. They succeeded again in the parliamentary vote on 1 November 2015 and the most recent parliamentary election of 24 June 2018 (with 10.8% and 11.7%, respectively). Charged with "terrorist propaganda," the HDP's leading politicians, Figen Yüksekdağ (b. 1971) and Selahattin Demirtaş (b. 1973), lost their parliamentary mandates after the lifting of their parliamentary immunity in 2016 and have been in prison since. The pressure of the state on the HDP and its representatives, including mayors belonging to the HDP in Southeastern Anatolia, continues unabated.[44]

Alongside ever more nakedly displayed authoritarianism, an Islamization of education and everyday life has proceeded apace. Islamic holidays are increasingly celebrated in the schools and Republican holidays marginalized. In Fall 2016, Turkey synchronized its time zone with that of the Gulf States, so that the time difference from the Central European Time Zone is two hours during winter. It is surely no coincidence that this changeover took place on 29 October, the anniversary of the founding of the Republic.[45]

---

44 According to Pabst, "Die Mafia mischt im Kurdenkonflikt mit," of the sixty-five HDP mayors elected in the municipal elections of 2019, there were only two left in office in February 2021, and of the fifty-six HDP representatives elected to the National Assembly in the parliamentary elections of 2018, there was not a single HDP representative who hadn't been charged with a crime by then.

45 Cagaptay, *New Sultan*, 197ff.

2. The Old Turkey and the New Turkey

The AKP government often speaks of a New Turkey (Yeni Türkiye) which is said to have been created in the recent years. And in fact, a new Republic has come about with the destruction of the last remnants of the Kemalist complex, the victory over the former allied Gülen movement, and the transition to a presidential system. But it's not just a farewell to the Old; there is a lot familiar to us from the history of the Republic mixed in with the allegedly New.

The Defeat of Kemalism

For a century and a half, many tremendously gifted thinkers spent all their power and energy on the formulation and development of communist ideology. Nevertheless, the communist regimes of Eastern Europe fell surprisingly quickly from 1989 on. Communism may be dead as a desired form of societal organization, but the instruments of Marxist analysis of the capitalist economic order are not. For Kemalism, however, with its much less specific ideological weight, there will be no reawakening. What remains of it are its effects in the deep structures of Turkish society. No one in Turkey could escape its relentless and often intrusive dissemination in the schools, military, and among the public into the twenty-first century. If one understands the core of an otherwise quite diffuse Kemalism to be the idea of a strong state, indissoluble state unity, and an aggressively propounded modernism, as well as an emphatic demand for assimilation into the majority culture (supplemented by a clearly smaller component of civic voluntarism), then virtually everyone in Turkey is a Kemalist, whether right-Kemalists, left-Kemalists, Islamist Kemalists[46]—or Kemalokemalists, to coin a name for the dogged species of unbroken, convinced Kemalists, however many fewer they have become in the interim.

The party which has stood for the legacy of Kemalism for decades is the party Atatürk founded himself, the Republican People's Party (CHP). Its greatest success in recent years was winning back the office of the mayor of İstanbul in the municipal elections of 31 March 2019, which had fallen in 1994 to the Welfare Party (Refah Partisi, RP) and its candidate, Recep Tayyip

---

46   See the further suggestions in Lord, *Religious Politics*, 14, on the use of the term "Islamist Kemalists" in Turkish journalism. Cizre, "Fear and Loathing," uses the image of Kemalist DNA borne by the AKP under Recep Tayyip Erdoğan.

Erdoğan. While Erdoğan's presidential government accepted the loss of Ankara and has dismissed İzmir, pro-CHP for decades, as a hopeless case, they did not want to accept the loss of İstanbul and forced a renewed election on 23 June 2019 by means of the Supreme Electoral Council (Yüksek Seçim Kurulu). Their calculations did not pan out. Even though the CHP's candidate, Ekrem İmamoğlu (b. 1970), had won by a hair's-breadth margin of less than fifteen thousand votes on 31 March, on 23 June 2019, he expanded his margin of victory to over eight hundred thousand votes, winning 54.12% of the vote. Ekrem İmamoğlu, who belongs to the conservative wing of the CHP, succeeded in his campaign under a slogan completely devoid of content: "Everything will be very beautiful" (Her şey çok güzel olacak). The CHP can only invoke the Kemalist legacy to which they still feel bound very indirectly if they want to be successful in elections. Winning by dint of their own efforts is no longer possible. In İstanbul they likely only succeeded because İmamoğlu had the support of all parties outside the alliance the AKP had with the MHP, from the Kurdish-adjacent HDP to the nationalist and right-leaning Good Party (İyi Parti) under Meral Akşener (b. 1956).

Kemalism's strengths were simultaneously its weaknesses. Thus from the beginning, the crucial element of Kemalism was nationalism. Nationalism, however, is an extremely undemanding and flexible growth, which can thrive in virtually any ideological soil. Because really all parties in Turkey which appeal to the Turkish Sunni majority population were and are nationalistic, not much remains for Kemalism now that its sole right to administer the nation and the state have been taken out of its hands. The Turkish foundational myth, so important for national self-consciousness, isn't at all original. One notices the similarities to the foundation myth of socialist Yugoslavia, specifically "the explanation of the nation's origin (there, the Second World War), the figure of the founding father (Tito), and the motif of martyrdom (war of liberation) as well as the highest object of fascination, its miraculous rescue from extreme danger (e.g., the Battle on the Neretva)."[47] In the Turkish case, these are—in astonishing parallel—the First World War and the War of Independence (1919–1922); the founder of the Republic, Mustafa Kemal Atatürk; and the narrow defensive victories against the Greek advances in the year 1921.

With the defeat of Kemalism, "post-Kemalism," the classic left-liberal criticism of Kemalism, also doesn't have much life left in it. Since the beginning of

---

47   Calic, *Geschichte Jugoslawiens*, 204. See also Calic, *Tito*, 280.

the 1980s in Turkey, "almost all social scientists and scholars in the humanities working and publishing according to international standards" have been subject to "the paradigm of post-Kemalism,"[48] which saw its chief task the fundamental criticism of the project of Kemalist modernity, coupled with the wish to display this critique's compatibility with global post-modernity and post-colonialism. Consequently, there was a kind of partnership of convenience and coalition of interpretation between the Islamist and left-liberal camps. An argument on which the conservative Islamist milieu and the left-liberal critics of Kemalists converged was the distinction between White Turks (Beyaz Türkler) and Black Turks (Kara Türkler). According to this schema, the "White Turks" are the urban gentry, in part with long roots back into the elites of the late Ottoman era. The "Black Turks" on the other hand are the simple Anatolian rural population who came to the cities later as migrants. For the entire history of the Republic, the Black Turks are said to have been pushed to the margins by the Whites and treated contemptibly. The post-Kemalists were quite varied among themselves, but they were united by the conviction that amends had to be made for the marginalization of the Kurds and conservative Anatolians. In the case of the former, they didn't get very far. In the latter case, the debt is likely overpaid.

In their disappointment over the false promise of Islamic conservatism, Turkish intellectuals may be inclined to compulsively repeat their assessments of earlier years. In their new political homelessness (Turkey has become a difficult place for many, intellectually as well as physically), they may attempt to evoke a sense of belonging by reflexively attributing responsibility for the undesirable developments to the main prop of the Kemalist complex, the military. In this sense, the military coup of 1980 becomes a kind of second original sin of the Turkish Republic—along with the corruption of the original, noble goals of the young Republic with the turn to authoritarianism in 1925 and, above all, during the one-man rule of İsmet İnönü after the death of Atatürk in 1938.

While a paternalistic perspective on Turkey is out of the question, in the future an explanatory model of inverse paternalism, as is often found among foreign and domestic observers, should be avoided. Inverse paternalism doesn't look presumptuously upon Turkey, but the exaggerated claim to see the people of Turkey as victims of foreign mistakes or even machinations can result in interpretive dead ends. To provide just one example: Turkish

---

48   Aytürk, *Post-Post-Kemalism*. Aytürk, "Post-Kemalizm Nedir," 5.

left-liberals often succumbed to the temptation—with legitimately emancipatory intentions—to ascribe excessively great influence to foreign forces. In this mode, Turkish policy would be a supine object of superior interests and powers, and the opinions and positions of the people in the country would mean little. It is the case, however, despite all its dependencies and all its influences, the Turkish Republic determined the course of its policy in its first hundred years largely on its own—for good and ill. Even in authoritarian systems, like that which Turkey has become since the 2010s, the people do not just endure their rulers but also create them.[49]

The fact that Kemalism's weapons grew ever duller over time contributed to its defeat. The Kemalist elite manipulated the people for decades with the accusation of the misuse of religion. Even the very first opposition party, the Progressive Republican Party (Terakkiperver Cumhuriyet Fırkası) was banned in 1925 under the charge of misusing religion. This accusation seemed to be a reliable instrument in the battle against the right-conservative and Islamist camps right up until no one wanted to hear about that alleged danger any more.

If we look for an example to the Presidium for Religious Affairs (Diyanet İşleri Başkanlığı), an authority with around a hundred and twenty thousand employees, a new organizational law, Law No. 6002 from the year 2010, expanded the remit of the authority and elevated it to the rank of an undersecretariat of state in the institutional hierarchy. In 2012, the president of the Diyanet was promoted in the state protocol from the fifty-first rank to rank ten. Since 2014, the Diyanet no longer reported to the deputy prime minister but directly to the prime minister (and, since 2018, it reports directly to the president). Between 2002 and 2016, the personnel of the Diyanet grew 52%, while the number of mosques only grew 15% (to 87,381) in the same time period, and the population grew 21%. Since 2017, imams reporting to the Diyanet can solemnize religious and civil marriages simultaneously; the mandatory civil marriage ceremony has been dropped.

It might seem as if the Diyanet was treated shabbily by the state until the AKP's taking power in 2002 and only flourished thereafter. The Diyanet's share of the state budged in the middle of the 1940s was 0.2%, its nadir. It climbed until reaching 1.2% in the middle of the 2010s. In addition, the Diyanet had advised against the introduction of the Turkish-language call to prayer in the

---

49 Greene and Robertson, *Putin v. the People*, 205, uses the term "co-construction" for the Russian people's contribution to the stabilization of the system of rule under Putin.

1930s and, beginning in the 1980s, favored the idea that the headscarf could be worn in state institutions like universities—that is, it sometimes opposed the will of the state elite.

However, that first impression of a neglected agency is not borne out by history. Since the 1950s, the Diyanet has experienced a continuous institutional expansion. Law No. 633 of 11 June 1965, which comprehensively regulated the legal mandate of the Diyanet, emphasized its monopolistic position as an employer of the Islamic clergy; degrees could only be obtained from educational institutions which stood under the Diyanet's control, like the imam-hatip schools and departments of theology. At the same time, it enjoyed ever larger budget increases, not just the 172% in 1951 shortly after the Democrat Party (Demokrat Parti, DP) took power, but even a 107% increase as far back as 1946.[50]

The AKP and Erdoğan see themselves as anti-Kemalists, but by that they only mean enemies of the establishment which dominated Turkey into the 2000s. The AKP can live just fine with the Six Arrows, Kemalism's squishy principles. Kemalists always understood laicism to mean that religion had to be controlled by the state. The enormous state Diyanet authority names imams, determines the content of textbooks for religious instruction, and composes the sermons for the Friday preachers. The AKP gladly inherited this legacy of Kemalist "laicism." Revolutionism, another of the six principles, is to be understood as the profound restructuring of society, as determined by the state leadership—even against the will of parts of the population. What is worth improving in this principle? In the eyes of the AKP, Kemalism is not to be abolished, it just has to be turned on its head.

The AKP under Recep Tayyip Erdoğan can credibly portray itself as the legitimate representative of all currents of conservatism and Islamism. In addition, it can seriously contend, at least to its partisans, that it can offer everything positive that Kemalism had to offer without being burdened by its disadvantages. That the AKP's attacks on others have had an impact and the others' attacks on the AKP have remained ineffectual show its unfailingly favorable strategic position in Turkish policy since the turn of the century. At the same time, the AKP elite infer a mandate to lead the land according to a higher truth from the elections they've consistently won and their self-imposed task of rectifying the partially erroneous Kemalist reforms. According to this theory, an authoritarian form of government appears, in

---

50   Lord, *Religious Politics*, 93–95, 97, 100, 113, 115–117, 127. Jenkins, *Political Islam*, 127.

historic perspective, appropriate, indeed unavoidable. Has the AKP, now in power since 2002, succeeded in finding the ideal compound of authoritarianism and populism in the form of its leading figure, Recep Tayyip Erdoğan?

The New Atatürk: Recep Tayyip Erdoğan

In today's Turkey, everything revolves around the person of Recep Tayyip Erdoğan. Before its profound enhancement, the Turkish office of president was already more powerful than, for example, that of the German Federal president but far from that in a presidential system à la française. But with a bare majority's passing the constitutional referendum of 16 April 2017, the office of the Turkish president became disproportionately powerful. The entire political system of Turkey thereby consolidated around the person of Erdoğan.

The basis of Recep Tayyip Erdoğan's success can be found in his defeats. On 12 December 1997, in the Southeastern Anatolian city of Siirt, Erdoğan, who had been mayor of İstanbul since 1994, read the following lines from a poem: "Minarets are bayonets, cupolas helmets; mosques are our barracks, the believers soldiers. God is great, God is great."[51] This poem was in fact contained in a list of recommended reading for elementary schools put together by the Ministry of Education, but Erdoğan was nevertheless sentenced to ten months in prison by the State Security Court (Devlet Güvenlik Mahkemesi) on 21 April 1998, citing Article 312 of the penal code regarding "open incitement to hate and enmity." He appealed the sentence in vain, and reported to prison on 26 March 1999, only to be released again on 24 July 1999. During these four months in jail, Erdoğan received seven thousand five hundred letters, all of which he allegedly answered.[52] Along with the 1998 sentence, he received a five-year ban from active participation in politics. The ban had barely expired on 9 March 2003, when Erdoğan was elected to parliament in by-elections as a representative for Siirt, the very city where he had read the poem. Only five days later, on 14 March 2003, the National Assembly named him the fifty-ninth prime minister of Turkey. He remained in this

---

51 "Minareler süngü, kubbleler miğfer; camiler kışlamız, müminler asker. Allahû ekber, Allahû ekber." The "Soldier's Prayer" ("Asker Duâsı") by Ziya Gökalp which is sometimes cited as its source does not contain these lines. See Tansel, *Gökalp Külliyatı*, 58. On Cevat Örnek, the apparent author of the poem, properly named "İlahi Ordu" (the Divine Army), see this article in the *Hürriyet* of September 23, 2002, https://www.hurriyet.com.tr/gundem/o-siiri-kimin-yazdigi-yillardir-biliniyordu-99423.
52 Birand and Yıldız, *Son Darbe*, 265ff.

office until 2014. Since 28 August 2014, Recep Tayyip Erdoğan has been the twelfth president of the Republic. With the introduction of the presidential system in 2018, his term-limit clock has been reset.

Alongside Erdoğan, the political personnel of the 2000s and 2010s remain negligible and in the end are basically staffage. Abdullah Gül became foreign minister when he surrendered the office of prime minister to Erdoğan in March 2003. When President Ahmet Necdet Sezer reached the end of his term of office, Abdullah Gül was elected president (in office 2007–2014), only to disappear into the woodwork when he fell out of favor with Erdoğan. Erdoğan's successors as prime minister were Ahmet Davutoğlu in 2014–2016, succeeded by Binali Yıldırım (b. 1955) who held the office until its abolishment in 2018.

Erdoğan's aura comes from his story of migration, his difficult economic situation, and his marginalization in his childhood and youth. He was born in 1954 in Kasımpaşa quarter of İstanbul, the son of a migrant from the Black Sea region. Kasımpaşa lies on the western shore of the Golden Horn, which was shaped by shipyards and industrialization in the late Ottoman period. With the explosive growth of İstanbul in the second half of the twentieth century, the quarter lost its function as an industrial area and became a point of arrival for poor migrants from Anatolia. Erdoğan deploys his background aggressively. He has always cited his origins in Kasımpaşa for his decisiveness and absoluteness today. He explains his unyieldingness with his experience of exclusion, "We only bow to pray."[53] That he never smiles or laughs in public is prized by his adherents as a sign of his manliness and resolve, but he occasionally cries openly and is therefore cherished by his followers as "authentic."[54]

After primary school, Erdoğan attended an imam-hatip school. Subsequently, he studied at a trade school, from which he graduated in 1981. In 1978, Erdoğan married Emine Bülbaran whose family—in quite the portent of fate—hailed from the aforementioned Siirt, and is of Arab descent. He was active in Islamist parties and organizations even in his youth. In 1984, he was deputy chairman of the Welfare Party (Refah Partisi, RP). At the same time, Erdoğan pursued an economic career. When he was elected mayor of İstanbul in 1994 at the age of forty, he was already an established businessman

---

53   Türk, *Muktedir*, 367, refers here to a statement of Erdoğan's of 5 February 2014.
54   Yavuz, *Secularism and Muslim Democracy*, 118–143, assigns Erdoğan to the archetype of the "tough guy" (*kabadayı*) rising from his parochial social environment and sees in Abdullah Gül the archetype of the "victim" (*mağdur*). In fact, the role of victim is also important in Erdoğan's self-presentation. Temelkuran, *Euphorie und Wehmut*, 125, 196.

in Ülker, a huge Turkish grocery concern. Earning money "was one of the main goals in his life."[55]

Erdoğan's ascent to the apex of the state was anything but predictable—but is nevertheless easy to comprehend. His success is thanks to the rise of Islamism in Turkey since the 1990s, but also his political skill and unscrupulousness—even within his own party.

Erdoğan's former comrade Abdullah Gül was considerably more experienced on the international level. Gül, born in 1950 in Kayseri in Central Anatolia, studied economics at the University of İstanbul and, like Erdoğan, was active in the student organization of the Milli Görüş movement, the National Turkish Students Union (Millî Türk Talebe Birliği). After graduation, he did two years of post-graduate study in Great Britain and held a position with the Islamic Development Bank in the Saudi port city of Jeddah in 1983–1991. Gül was minister of state and the government's spokesman during the period of the Refahyol coalition between the Welfare Party (Refah Partisi, RP) and the True Path Party (Doğru Yol Partisi, DYP) in 1996–1997.[56] Nevertheless, in 2003, Gül took a back seat to Erdoğan, where he remained until he was finally pushed to the margins in the 2010s.

Erdoğan has long left his former comrades by the side of the road, allowing him to become the most significant politician in modern Turkey after Atatürk. Indeed, there have been others, like Süleyman Demirel or Bülent Ecevit, who managed to shape Turkish politics over decades, but they could never achieve a sole, dominant position. On the basis of a new constitution envisioned in 2021 (apparently shelved for the time being), Erdoğan, like Vladimir Putin, would have been able to extend his right to the office of president into the 2030s.[57] Mustafa Kemal only lived to the age of fifty-seven; Erdoğan reached that age in 2011. Atatürk dominated Turkey for more than fifteen years, from the end of the War of Independence in 1922 until his death in 1938. In the meantime, Recep Tayyip Erdoğan has governed the country for almost twenty years, passing Atatürk not only in lifespan but time in office.

What unites these two men, and what separates them? Erdoğan is a Kemalist in the sense that the unconditional defense of national sovereignty and a strong state are important to him. He believes he himself knows what's good for the people in the country. In the eyes of Erdoğan and his loyalists,

---

55 Yavuz, *Secularism and Muslim Democracy*, 126.
56 Jenkins, *Political Islam*, 166ff.
57 Sayın, "Yeni anayasa."

they need to remedy the narrow-minded biases of Kemalist modernization policy. The Kemalists' policy of authoritarian modernization, which marginalized broad swaths of the population, must be replaced by a compensatory and genuine modernization in such a fashion that modern Turkey can regain contact with its cultural and religious roots. A religious way of life must become a recognized part of the nation again. In order to achieve these goals, Erdoğan, an "anti-Atatürkist Atatürk," uses exactly the same instruments with which Kemalists worked: state institutions and the techniques of top-down social engineering.[58]

Atatürk and Erdoğan are also connected by a manner in which people try to discredit them. Like Atatürk, Erdoğan is sometimes alleged to not be of real Turkish descent. One can hear that Erdoğan is a Laz (which might be halfway acceptable, since the Laz are considered culturally assimilated) or even of Armenian descent.[59] These allegations obviously recall the earlier suppositions that Atatürk was a Sabbatean (Dönme).[60]

One difference between the two men particularly catches the eye. Atatürk had a clearly defined, substantive goal which he believed he had achieved around 1930. Perhaps he did not use the years that were left to him particularly meaningfully, or perhaps he willfully reduced their number with his alcoholism, but he was ready to be satisfied with that which he had achieved. Erdoğan, by contrast, is distinguished by an insatiable striving for power and glory, the driving force in his political dealings, which leads him and his government into ever more spirals of polarization and suppression of its opponents.[61]

From the beginning, Erdoğan has possessed the character traits of an "authoritarian loner" and "unbridled ambition stemming from the belief God has anointed him to lead Turkey," according to a report from the US embassy in Ankara written only a few months after Erdoğan had become

---

58 Cagaptay, *New Sultan*, 8.
59 Kirişçi, *Turkey and the West*, 92.
60 Mango, *Atatürk*, 452; Baer, "An Enemy Old and New." Bozarslan, "Alevism and the Myths of Research," 7, points to speculations that Atatürk was a Bektaşi. For the background of comparable conjectures that Tito was not a South Slav, see Pirjevic, *Tito*, 39, and Calic, *Tito*, 19, 127.
61 The occasional excesses of today's Turkish foreign policy are not solely due to the character of an individual, that is, Recep Tayyip Erdoğan, but are connected to new methods of recruitment. Until 2002, Turkey's diplomatic corps was largely drawn from graduates of the Department of Political Science at the University of Ankara (the former *Mülkiye*). Today, they largely come directly out of the cadres of the AKP. Hansen, "The Era of People Like You Is Over."

prime minister.⁶² In his own party, Erdoğan is revered as the "chief" (*reis*). An AKP mayor of the city of Of (located on the Black Sea coast east of Trabzon) stated in 2010, that one had to show one's gratitude for Erdoğan every day with two *rekât* (a unit of ritual movements in Islamic prayer).⁶³

A Tradition of Populism and Authoritarianism

What is Erdoğan's secret ingredient? What makes his great success possible? Erdoğan constantly allies with new partners, only to drop them after a while or to push them aside. He was supported by the liberal media and public when he fought the superior power of the Kemalist complex. He then allied with the Gülen movement to conquer the bureaucracy, military, and judicial bodies from within. Since 2015, by contrast, he has entered into a pact with the Nationalist Movement Party (Milliyetçi Hareket Partisi, MHP).⁶⁴

Is Erdoğan a populist? Certainly. His rhetoric is not primarily Islamist, but populist. Despite their differences, Menderes, Demirel, Özal, and Erdoğan, the main proponents of conservative populism in the history of the Republic of Turkey, share certain fundamental characteristics. They all speak of an absolute division between a decrepit old elite and "real" people.⁶⁵ They elevate the "national will" (milli irade) to a fetish and justify electoral autocracy with reference to it. They cultivate a nationalist conservative Islamist populism and exercise a marked pragmatism in power.⁶⁶

Demirel was the first to master the complete register of conservative populism. The Justice Party (Adalet Partisi, AP) was said to have sprung from the breast of the people. His time in government, as part and representative of the people, was said to be an "era of great works" (*büyük eserler dönemi*). The benefits of civilization could only be preserved through "development" (kalkınma). Demirel distinguished himself sharply from the Republican

---

62   Öktem, *Angry Nation*, 131, refers to Wikileaks' publication of the internal correspondence of the US Embassy in Ankara with Main State in Washington, DC, in 2004.
63   However, when an AKP representative from Aydın in Western Anatolia called Erdoğan a "second Prophet" in the same year, i.e., 2010, Erdoğan rebuked the statement as unacceptable, and the representative had to resign. Türk, *Muktedir*, 425.
64   Cagaptay, *New Sultan*, 139.
65   Mudde and Kaltwasser, *Populism*, 5ff., describe how populism posits two antagonistic camps: the "pure," who represent the will of the people, confront the "corrupt [former] elite."
66   For a comprehensive discussion of these characteristics, see Türk, *Muktedir*, 433–438.

People's Party (Cumhuriyet Halk Partisi, CHP). They were not only representatives of an old, privileged minority, but nothing less than an enemy of the people. Only the Justice Party, in his telling, had succeeded in bringing "stability" (*istikrar*) to Turkey.⁶⁷ Characteristic was his denial and dismissal of all class differences. "For us, the nation (*millet*) is everything. When we say nation, then we make no distinction between class and group, between old and young, rather we think of these things as a unity, as a connected whole."⁶⁸

Demirel may have been the first to perfect the fashion in which such arguments are presented, but he was not the first to employ them. Adnan Menderes, prime minister from 1950–1960, ceaselessly returned to the comparison between past and present, which stood for the contrast between scarcity and prosperity. Menderes proudly pointed to the enormous construction activity and the explosion in street construction in the 1950s, which far surpassed the achievements of past decades (and were, incidentally, responsible for the destruction of historic districts of İstanbul).⁶⁹

The populist mode of confronting one's political opponents also applied to Menderes. The Republican People's Party (CHP) was not paying attention to the national will; those who criticized his government belonged to a privileged minority. The contrast between an overweening and "tyrannical state" (*ceberrut devlet*) and the "oppressed nation" (*mazlum millet*) was decried, although Menderes and the Democrat Party comprised the government for ten years. Menderes even spoke of himself as "oppressed" (*mazlum*) and a "victim" (*mağdur*), although he came from a large landholding family in Western Anatolia and had himself been a parliamentary representative of the CHP from 1931 to 1945.

Erdoğan and his predecessors have always spoken critically to derogatorily of the CHP, which has existed since the foundation of the Republic (with a short interruption after the coup of 1980). This criticism attacks the CHP's authoritarian record and simultaneously attributes complete responsibility for

---

67 Türk, *Muktedir*, 80ff., 89–97, 102.
68 Süleyman Demirel, 27 November 1996. In Süleyman Demirel, *Kongre Konuşmaları ve Bazı Konular Hakkındaki Konuşmalardan Özetler*, quoted in Türk, *Muktedir*, 78.
69 In a speech in Balıkesir in 1953, Menderes said he was sorry to always be speaking of numbers, only then to immediately report that the number of radios in the country had grown from two hundred thousand to over six hundred thousand inside of three years. Turkey, he said, would soon make a great leap and reach the level of Europe and the US. See Türk, *Muktedir*, 43. For a comparison, see Landau, *Radical Politics*, 83, 230, 234, 241, for visions of a strong Turkey circulating in the 1960s, both on the left to radical left camps (personified in the form of the intellectual Doğan Avcıoğlu, 1926–1983) and on the radical right (led by Alparslan Türkeş).

the violent disorders in Turkish history to the CHP. A notable example of this is Erdoğan's speech of 23 November 2011, when he apologized in the name of the Turkish state for the violence in Dersim in 1937–1938. At the same time, he demanded that the chair of the CHP, Kemal Kılıçdaroğlu (b. 1948), apologize in the name of the party which was in power at the time.[70] The attack on Kılıçdaroğlu combined with Erdoğan's simultaneous apology was both wily and reprehensible at the same time. He completely absolved his political camp from any responsibility for early Republican history, publicly shamed his political opponents (Kılıçdaroğlu is, incidentally, a descendent of Dersim Alevis) and, in addition, painted Alevis as allies of the Kemalists.

Of all the parties in the history of the Republic, the Motherland Party (Anavatan Partisi, ANAP) of the 1980s was closest to the AKP. In both cases, liberal-minded members were pushed out of leadership positions over time or left the party of their own free will. Such as the AKP in 2002, Turgut Özal, founder and leader of the ANAP, had good luck—after the coup, the ban on political activity for politicians active before 1980 left a big hole, which he filled with men of rural backgrounds who otherwise would never have had a chance to achieve high office. Özal arrogated to himself the role of speaking for the "central pillar," that is, the middle of society.[71] When, however, he increasingly came under pressure in the late '80s, he turned without hesitation to nationalist/radical right actors—just as Erdoğan did after the election of June 2015, when he lost his absolute majority.

The similarities between Özal and Erdoğan are, in fact, astonishing. Like Erdoğan, Özal had an instrumental understanding of democracy, sought a presidential regime, already had the vision and the claim—in the 1980s— to lead a party uniting the entire rightward spectrum with an antagonistic center-left party as a permanent opposition. Özal based his legitimacy on economic successes, combined an Islamist-tinted populism with economic liberalism, harbored neo-Ottoman ambitions, and had a broken relationship with Europe, particularly the European Union.[72] Both Özal and Erdoğan shared a rhetorical approach of selling the desire for an Islamist-ordered society as liberalization. One statement of Özal on the headscarf battle, from July 1989 when he was still in office as prime minister, displays this attitude vividly. "We want to achieve a society in which no one is judged for their religious

---

70   Ayata and Hakyemez, "Turkey's Past Crimes."
71   Ahmad, *Modern Turkey*, 192–194.
72   Cemal, *Özal Hikayesi*, 74, 79, 155, 179–183, 187, 195, 198ff., 223, 243, 253–255, 307ff., 313, 319, 350.

convictions; at the same time, we are striving so that those who want to wear this or that based on their religious convictions are not prevented from doing so."[73]

Erdoğan could and can build on these well-grounded pillars of Turkish right-populism. He too characterizes the CHP as standing for economic failure and stagnation and, simultaneously, the arrogance of the old elite. The quantifying ideology of progress remains unbroken: Erdoğan continually cites the—incidentally really remarkable—amount of road construction under the AKP government. While "the others" built 6,100 kilometers (3,790 miles) of highway in sixty-nine years, "we" have built 17,100 kilometers (10,625 miles) in ten years,[74] a great service to the nation, "because streets mean civilization, development, progress."[75]

Among the amazing performance characteristics of Turkish populism is the fact that its waving the bloody shirt of a putative victim status, though endlessly repeated and in reality long outdated, still has not yet fundamentally worn out its effectiveness with voters.[76] Erdoğan could present himself until the early 2020s with undiminished success as an "avenger of the disenfranchised" and as an opponent of the system. His rhetorical style swings between folksiness and Ottoman-sounding words, without the latter being considered antiquated—instead they conjure up lost worlds and traditional connections.[77]

Erdoğan's famous-infamous statement of 1993 that democracy is a vehicle to be used as needed and then gotten off[78] can be interpreted in the obvious sense of cynical opportunism. In Erdoğan's political universe, however,

---

73 Ibid., 161.
74 Türk, *Muktedir*, 374.
75 See ibid., 218; see also 314 for the basis of the AKP's building mania in their idea of civilization.
76 Another example of the long-term effects of such charges and resentments is Israel. The predominance of the Labor Party which had existed since the founding of the country was already broken in 1977 with the coming to power of Menachem Begin as prime minister. Nevertheless, to this day, right-populist politicians like Benjamin Netanyahu are able to refer with effect to the experience of marginalization and poor treatment under the former secular Zionist-minded Ashkenazi elite among audiences of Sephardic Jews, and even among Russian Jews who emigrated to Israel in the 1990s.
77 Depending on the occasion, the register of Erdoğan's speeches switches between aggression, Islamism, nationalism, and insincere cosmopolitanism. The aggressive Islamist rhetoric in a speech marking the 562nd anniversary of the conquest of Constantinople stands in contrast to his apparently conciliatory rhetoric on the one hundredth anniversary of the battles on Gallipoli (albeit still mixed with attacks on alleged European Islamophobia and unjustified Armenian demands). Erdoğan, "İstanbul'un Fethi." Erdoğan, "Çanakkale 100. Yıl Barış."
78 Jenkins, *Political Islam*, 166, refers here (without a page reference) to Metin Sever and Cem Dizdar (eds.), *2. Cumhuriyet Tartışmaları* (Ankara: Başak Yayınları), 1993.

democracy has likely always had an ancillary role relative to overarching higher truths. Thus, in the same year, Erdoğan attacked a saying of Demirel's, that democracy should be the goal—democracy could never be a goal, he argued, only a means.[79]

Today's Turkey shows parallels to many other countries whose governments exhibit authoritarian features and which enthusiastically point to each other as models.[80] However, outside the global wave of authoritarianism, is there not perhaps a particular persistence of authoritarianism in Turkey or perhaps a pendulum swing in its political culture between democracy and dictatorship visible into the present?[81] Certainly the cataclysms of the 1910s and 1920s, the stress of the migration into the cities in the 1950s and 1960s, the being ripped from the familiar world of village society, the coexistence of patriarchal family structures and open societal systems, and finally a strict upbringing in the schools and the military, have made Turks susceptible to authoritarian explanatory and behavioral models. But it is also true that the argument that Turkey today is supposedly "a democracy without democrats"[82] can be countered with the fact that substantial portions of the Turkish population are more "democrats without a democracy." According to Freedom House, Turkey today is "not free" with comparable ratings of unfreedom as Iraq, Burma, Nicaragua, Thailand, and Uganda. On Reporters Without Borders list of press freedoms, Turkey has dropped from 99th in 2002 to 154th (of 180 countries) in 2020. In the 2020 *World Justice Report*, Turkey ranked 117th out of 128 countries.[83]

The persecution of Turkish intellectuals, journalists, and politicians who dare to act in a fashion uncongenial to the government continues unabated as

---

79 Türk, *Muktedir*, 176.
80 Thus, the prime minister of Hungary, Viktor Orbán, referred to China, Russia, and Turkey as models. Kirchick, "Order from Chaos."
81 According to Bischoff, *Ankara*, 212–216, the Turkey of the day could be interpreted as either a democracy or a dictatorship, depending on one's perspective.
82 Kirişçi, *Turkey and the West*, 183. On "democracy without democrats" in the Arab world, see Salamé, "Small is Pluralistic," 86, 97.
83 https://freedomhouse.org/countries/freedom-world/scores; https://www.reporter-ohne-grenzen.de/tuerkei; https://www.reporter-ohne-grenzen.de/fileadmin/Redaktion/Downloads/Ranglisten/Rangliste_2002/Reporter_ohne_Grenzen__Rangliste_2002.pdf; https://worldjusticeproject.org/sites/default/files/documents/WJP-ROLI-2020-Online_0.pdf. All sites accessed 20 April 2023. On Turkey's descent in the 2010s from a "democracy" (two steps below "full democracy") to a "closed anocracy" (four steps above the lowest level of autocracy), see in addition Marshall et al., *Global Report* (2009), 12, and Marshall et al., *Global Report* (2017), 32.

it has for years. In order to name a few exceptionally well-known cases from the year 2020: In February, the court acquitted the philanthropist Osman Kavala (b. 1957), who, among other things, founded the Anadolu Kültür Foundation and the İletişim publishing house (with intellectually ambitious publications on societal themes), of the absurd charge of having been the mastermind of the Gezi Park protests of 2013. Kavala, who had been in pre-trial detention since October 2017, was freed only to be imprisoned again a few days later, this time on the basis of the no less nonsensical allegation of having supported the coup attempt of July 2016 in cahoots with, among others, George Soros. In June 2020, parliament (with the votes of the AKP and its ally the MHP) withdrew immunity from three representatives in order to allow them to be imprisoned: Enis Berberoğlu of the CHP, as well as Leyla Güven and Musa Farisoğulları of the Peoples' Democratic Party (Halkların Demokratik Partisi, HDP). In July, a court sentenced Deniz Yücel (b. 1973), a former German correspondent in İstanbul, in absentia to a prison sentence of over two years for "terrorist propaganda." His previous incarceration of almost a year seriously damaged Turco-German relations until he was released from custody in February 2018 and immediately left the country.

Erik Jan Zürcher has made the telling observation that Turkey experienced liberal, pluralistic phases in 1908–1913 and 1919–1925 which were followed by authoritarian phases in 1913–1918 and 1925–1950.[84] The second half of the twentieth century likely lends itself to description—with certain gray areas—by means of such a wave-form model of the cycle of liberal opening and authoritarian hardening. This model has repeated itself particularly clearly under the AKP's governance since 2002. The liberal and pluralistic phase of the AKP in the 2000s was followed by the turn to authoritarianism. Has Turkey entered into a new authoritarian phase which will one day make way for a liberal and pluralistic phase, then? Nothing speaks against such an optimistic assessment. Nevertheless, it is worth considering that authoritarian regimes which are established in good economic times can root themselves deeply in state institutions in order to be able to stay in power during later phases of increasing unpopularity and economic decline.[85] Moreover, historical experience shows that authoritarian phases last longer in Turkey than liberal awakenings.

In the meantime, an electoral autocracy has come into being. There will be elections in Turkey in the future, because they lend legitimacy and encourage mobilization, but when the elections—already strongly circumscribed in

---

84 Zürcher, *Turkey*, 4.
85 Kisilowski, "Poland."

their fairness—are over, then the power of those in government is meant to be unlimited. Much like the legal system in Turkey, elections are thus robbed of their proper function in a democratic system and conceal the reality of a system far distant from one which could properly be called a democracy. The "national will" (milli irade) can be expressed at the ballot box. If, however, the electoral returns do not correspond to the expectations of the government, the "national will" can retreat to a higher level of meaning which is only accessible to the initiates in power. The appeal to higher truths in domestic politics may work its effect as ever, but some realities are capable of defying rhetoric. Here, undiminished, sits the Kurdish problem.

The Kurdish Achilles Heel

What many Turks feel—that they can't really trust anyone—is actually true for the Kurds. Nourished by British interests, in the Treaty of Sèvres (1920) there was still a Kurdish entity foreseen in the areas of today's southeastern Turkey and northern Iraq. By the Treaty of Lausanne (1923) there was no more talk of a Kurdistan. After the collectively fought Anatolian war of independence, the Kurds were pushed aside by their former Turkish allies. In an agreement in Algiers on 6 March 1973, Iraq made concessions to Iran on the question of the course of their common border in the Shatt al-Arab (the confluence of the Tigris and Euphrates before its mouth at the Persian Gulf). In exchange, Iran dropped its years-long support of the Democratic Party of Kurdistan (Partiya Demokrata Kurdistanê, PDK) led by Mustafa Barzani in northern Iraq. In Autumn 2019, the American government announced to withdraw its support for the Kurdish military units in Syria and Iraq which had provided reliable service in the fight against the Islamic State, accompanied by the remark of the US president Donald Trump (in office 2017–2021) that the Kurds were "no angels" themselves.[86] For states in the region, the Kurds were and are an annoyance or even a threat. For external actors like Great Britain or later the USSR and the United States, the Kurdish question was always just a "dependent variable."[87] With friends like these, who needs enemies?

---

86   "Trump claims Kurds 'no angels' as he boasts of his own 'brilliant' strategy," *Guardian*, October 16, 2019, https://www.theguardian.com/us-news/2019/oct/16/trump-claims-kurds-are-much-safer-as-us-troops-leave-syria.
87   Shareef, *The United States, Iraq, and the Kurds*, 173.

A fundamental problem of Kurdish politics in the twentieth century was that different Kurdish movements had no chance against the much better-armed forces of national states, divided as they were because of a lack of coordination and fragmentation (whether political, religious, linguistic, or economic).[88] In the 2000s, the relationship between the Turkish state and Kurds in Turkey was still a purely national question, in the sense that, the Kurdistan Workers' Party (Partiya Karkerên Kurdistanê, PKK) was alone in fighting for the demands of Turkish Kurds while Iraqi Kurds were pursuing their own interests within the framework of the Iraqi state. The situation beginning in the 2010s differs from all periods after the First World War in that the political movements of the Iraqi, Syrian, and Turkish Kurds (though much less so of the Iranian Kurds) have in the meantime become interwoven and thereby a common, supranational Kurdish space has come to be. The way back to containing the Kurdish question as a domestic problem of any given state is hardly imaginable. The impossibility of a purely military solution to the Kurdish problem has long been obvious; now, however, the pointlessness of limiting the Kurdish question to an individual national question in a given state has become manifest.

Since Öcalan's capture in 1999, the political orientation and the rhetoric of the PKK have changed. Under the influence of the libertarian-anarchist American philosopher Murray Bookchin (1921–2006), the PKK has subscribed to the concept of a "democratic confederalism," composed of elements like "direct democracy, conciliar government, the equality of the sexes, the recognition of cultural plurality, and collective ownership of natural resources." Non-Kurdish and non-Muslim minorities, it is claimed, would be able to find a home among the "Peoples of Kurdistan."[89] The project of democratic confederalism was supposed to find its first application in West Kurdistan (Rojava),[90] proclaimed on 30 January 2014 and consisting of the three cantons (from east to west) Cizire, Kobane, and Efrin. The Syrian-Kurdish Democratic Union Party (Partiya Yekitiya Democrat, PYD), which emerged out of the PKK, rose to become the crucial power among the Kurds of Syria during the Syrian War, along with its military arm, the

---

88 McDowall, *Modern History of the Kurds*, 184, 192, 197, 207.
89 Seufert, "Von der Lösung der Kurdenfrage," 56ff. Seufert, "Kurden als zentraler Faktor," 70.
90 According to Lack, "In den kurdischen Gebieten Syriens," 66, the term *Rojava* was dropped in December 2016 in favor of "the Democratic Federal System of Northern Syria" in order to back off from a claim to solely Kurdish representation in the region which shone through the term *Rojava*.

People's Defense Units (Yekîneyên Parastina Gel, YPG).[91] Democratic federalism, as it has been managed by the PYD, has proved to be more of a guided democracy, similar to those set up in Eastern Europe after the Second World War. Real power lies with the military leadership of the PKK in the Qandil Mountains in Iraq.[92] Faced with the exigencies of the war and the unavoidable necessity of making compromises—for example, working sub rosa with the Asad regime in Damascus, which has maintained a continuous presence throughout the 2010s in northern Syrian cities like Qamishlo/al-Qamishli and Haseke/al-Hasaka[93]—makes a conclusive verdict about the seriousness and future prospects of the project of Kurdish democratic confederalism impossible at this point.

Since the 2000s, Turkey has been able to live with a Kurdish entity in northern Iraq, because the opportunity for cooperation presented itself immediately. Along with economic advantages (Iraqi Kurdistan as an important location for investments and a sales market for Turkish products), close collaboration in energy policy (a pipeline between Iraqi Kurdistan and the Turkish Mediterranean port of Ceyhan opened in 2014), and a common enemy in the PKK, made Turkish patronage of Iraq's Kurds, who are dependent on Turkey for access to the sea, alluring. In addition, Turkey saw the advantages of having a Kurdish entity in Iraq as a conservative Sunni palisade against a Shi'ite-dominated Iraq.[94] The Turkish state's reaction to the rise of a Kurdish entity in northern Syria was entirely different. Turkey saw in it the beginnings of the PKK's lengthening arm and a direct danger.

Turkey's goals today are to have a say in the future (or, alternately, the nonfuture) of Syria, to weaken Kurdish military units as much as possible, and to prevent the consolidation of a territorial corridor ruled by the Syrian Kurds along the Turkish border.[95] As a result, a strange ambiguity has emerged in Turkish policy. The government looks on the Kurdish question, as ever, as a domestic political issue, but at the same time, it feels justified in carrying the conflict with the Kurds beyond its own borders. Since the

---

91 On the very close relations between the PKK and PYD, see Kaya and Lowe, "PYD-PKK Relationship."
92 Savelsberg, "Kurdish PYD and the Syrian Civil War," 359.
93 Lack, "In den kurdischen Gebieten Syriens," 72–74.
94 Harris, *Quicksilver War*, 108.
95 International Crisis Group, *Russia and Turkey*, 3. The idea of a buffer zone was already contemplated on the Turkish side in 2011-2012. Harris, *Quicksilver War*, 32.

1990s, Turkey has repeatedly pushed into Iraqi territory to destroy PKK havens. Turkey's intervention in Syria since 2016, however, serves a more comprehensive agenda and is conjoined with the ongoing presence of Turkish troops in northern Syria.[96]

Just as Turkey has been unable to solve the problem of the PKK inside the country for decades, it will not succeed in silencing the PKK and its offshoots on the international level. The PKK possesses units with military firepower, it is deeply anchored in the Kurdish diaspora of Europe, and in addition, it boasts organizational structures in Syria, Iraq, and Iran—and of course also in Turkey![97] In order to solve the conflict with the Kurds, the Turkish state must be ready to make more far-reaching concessions, specifically the right to education in one's native language, decentralization, the lowering of the ten percent hurdle in parliamentary elections, and an ethnically neutral constitution.[98] For now, there is little prospect of such concessions. With Turkey's deep entanglement in the Syrian conflict, the Kurdish question is, in any case, no longer dependent solely on a settlement within Turkey itself. It can only be part of a comprehensive solution of the conflict in Syria—which, however, is in no way visible on the horizon.

Between East and West

Examples of Turkey's quarreling with European countries are legion. Just to take a few examples from 2020: At the end of February 2020, the Turkish president declared the Greco-Turkish land border as "open," followed by an—ultimately unsuccessful—stampede of refugees and migrants from a very wide variety of countries upon Greek border posts. On 10 June 2020, there was almost a Franco-Turkish clash in the Mediterranean. Two Turkish frigates on escort duty for a freighter underway from İstanbul to the Libyan port of Misrata forced aside a French frigate which wished to check the freighter under the framework of the EU Operation Irini policing the weapons embargo on Libya. In July, a survey mission of the Turkish research ship

---

96   The most important operations (*harekât*) were Euphrates Shield (Fırat Kalkanı Harekâtı, August 2016–March 2017), Olive Branch (Zaytin Dalı Harekâtı, January–March 2018), Peace Fountain (Barış Pınarı Harekâtı, October 2019), and Spring Shield (Bahar Kalkanı Harekâtı, February and March 2020). In the meantime, Turkey possesses more than ten bases in Iraq with several hundred troops stationed there. Rogg, "Die Türkei verlegt den Kampf."
97   Seufert, "Ernüchternde Bilanz kurdischer Politik," 83.
98   International Crisis Group, *Human Cost of the PKK Conflict in Turkey*, 2.

Oruç Reis south of the Greek island of Kastellorizo (over sixty miles east of Rhodes) brought Greece and Turkey closer to the brink of war than they had been since 1969. Turkey does not accept Greece's claim to an exclusive economic zone of two hundred nautical miles around each of its islands in the Mediterranean. Kastellorizo lies less than two miles from the south coast of Turkey, the Turkish foreign minister, Mevlut Çavuşoğlu (b. 1968) explained in July 2020, but 310 miles from the Greek mainland.[99]

The signs of a general disassociation from the West were also clear in 2020. On the occasion of the Friday prayers on 24 July, the Hagia Sophia (Ayasofya) was reopened as a mosque with the attendance of the president. In terms of form, everything went well. The Supreme Administrative Court (Danıştay) repealed the cabinet decision of 24 November 1934 which had ordered its conversion into a museum. The reconversion of the Hagia Sophia, which served as a mosque from the Ottoman conquest of İstanbul in 1453 until 1931, was surely aimed at distracting from the country's economic problems, but at the same time it fulfilled a decades-long dream harbored by Islamists inside and outside Turkey alike.[100]

Recently, however, since the beginning of 2021, Turkey has made advances towards European countries again and is even discussing accession to the European Union anew. One should not read anything more in this than a maneuver by Turkey (which has not backed off hard repression at home) owing to its economic difficulties and growing foreign policy isolation.

On 2 March 2021, the president announced the comprehensive Human Rights Action Plan (İnsan Hakları Eylem Planı) whose "ultimate goal" would be "a new, civilian constitution." However, on 17 March 2021, the state prosecutor of the Court of Cassation (Yargıtay) requested a ban on the Kurdish-aligned HDP and a multi-year ban on political activity for around six hundred HDP politicians. It is quite possible that the elections for parliament and the presidency in 2023 might see the defeat of an opposition that has been dismantled in advance with every trick in the book. Only a few days later, on 19 March 2021, the Turkish government withdrew from the İstanbul Convention on Preventing and Combatting Violence Against Women and Domestic Violence. The treaty, according to the government, was being misused to destroy the unity of the family and to conduct propaganda for sexual minorities. At the time of its signing in İstanbul by the members of

---

99   Hermann, "Säbelrasseln im Mittelmeer."
100 On the circumstances attendant to the conversion of the Hagia Sophia to a museum in 1934, see Kreiser, "Das Werk einer verrückten Periode."

the Council of Europe in 2011, it was supposed to be a sign to the world of Turkey's open-mindedness. In 2012, the Turkish government had been the first to ratify the treaty; now it was the first to withdraw from it.[101]

No longer unambiguously anchoring in the Western alliance system, new and apparently enticing perspectives are opening up for Turkey, like, for example, a future in "Eurasia." Adherents of the Eurasia concept in Russia and Turkey derive emotional satisfaction from regarding Europe (and the European Union) as an insignificant appendix of Asia without a future of its own.[102] The idea of a significant role for Turkey in Eurasia, even if it possesses little intellectual or historical depth, can assimilate older concepts like Pan-Turanism, Pan-Turkism, and Neo-Ottomanism, stresses economic aspects like Turkey's position as a transit country for oil and natural gas, can make allowance for the Russo-Turkish rapprochement since the 2000s, and simultaneously expresses the ambition of achieving a position halfway on par with Russia and China.[103]

In several respects, Turkey could in fact be considered a "little China." Although neither was formally a colony, China and Turkey were both shaped by the experience of European imperialism. Both understand themselves as powers that ultimately persevered against European imperialism, and simultaneously can point to the history of their own successful imperialism which they regard—not without justification—as historically outstanding.[104] Like China, Turkey demands to play a role, though of course to a lesser degree, on the basis of its economic capability and political power, but also thanks to its firm belief in its global political uniqueness.[105]

---

101 For the "Human Rights" action plan, see "Cumhurbaşkanı Erdoğan İnsan Hakları Eylem Plan'ını açıkladı," *Haber Türk*, March 2, 2021, https://www.haberturk.com/son-dakika-cumhurbaskani-erdogan-insan-haklari-eylem-plani-ni-acikladi-haber-2990856. For the application to ban the HDP, see "Yargıtay Cumhuriyet Başsavcılığı, 600'den fazla HDP'li hakkında siyasi yasak istedi," Haberler.com, March 17, 2021, https://www.haberler.com/guncel/yargitay-cumhuriyet-bassavciligi-600-den-fazla-hdp-14001400-haberi/. Pabst, "Erdoğan kündigt Istanbul-Konvention."
102 See Lewis, "Geopolitical Imaginaries," 1616ff. and 1626ff. for Russian Eurasianists' perspectives on Europe. A similar downgrading of Europe is present in Kaplan, *Return of Marco Polo's World*, 5–8.
103 Turkish accounts of the concept of Eurasianism are mostly very superficial. An exception is İmanbeyli, "Failed Exodus."
104 According to Burbank and Cooper, *Empires in World History*, 18, the Chinese Empire, along with the Roman, have developed into the two dominant basic patterns of imperial rule in world history, while the Ottoman Empire represents a significant achievement in the synthesis in its combining various (Arab-Islamic, Byzantine, Mongolian, Persian, and Turkish) imperial traditions.
105 For China, see Brown, *The World According to Xi*, 84, 89, 91.

Turkey's connections to and relations with Russia are, however, much closer than those with China, due to closer physical proximity alone. The Tsarist empire and the Soviet Union which followed it represented a direct threat to Turkey for centuries. Even today, Russia cannot really have an interest in a strong Turkey, because Turkey understands itself as a leading Sunni power and thereby could exercise potential influence on the Muslim population in Russia or in the Caucasus and Central Asia, which Russia perceives as its sphere of influence. For its part, Turkey has looked on with concern as Russia has increasingly made the Black Sea its Mare nostrum, above all with the Russian occupation of Crimea in 2014.[106] On 24 November 2015, a Turkish fighter jet shot down a Russian Su-24M attack aircraft operating in Syria which had slightly violated Turkish airspace. Because the Russian sanctions imposed as a result damaged the Turkish economy and Turkey was dependent on Russian support for its own Syria policy, Erdoğan apologized to Russian president Vladimir Putin and likely pledged to no longer attempt to force regime change in Syria.

The apology and the appreciation for Putin's showing support for the Turkish government after the coup attempt of July 2016 entirely renormalized bilateral relations. In December 2017, the Turkish Defense Industry Agency (lit. Presidium for the Defense Industry, Savunma Sanayii Başkanlığı, SSB) announced that Turkey—a member of NATO!—had signed a contract with Russia for the delivery of two batteries of S-400 surface-to-air missiles. In July 2019, the first parts of the system were actually delivered. TurkStream, a gas pipeline leading from Russia to the European part of Turkey, was opened on 8 January 2020 by Putin and Erdoğan together. And the first nuclear power plant in Turkey, in Akkuyu (on the southern Mediterranean coast near Silifke) is being built by the Russian firm Rosatom.

Even military cooperation between Russia and Turkey is thriving. In the war for Nagorno-Karabakh from September to November 2020, which Armenia lost to Azerbaijan, Russia and Turkey found themself in a successful division of roles: Turkey could help Azerbaijan to large territorial gains through comprehensive military assistance, especially its highly advanced drone technology, while Russia played moderator during the cease-fire negotiations and secured further oversight rights along the new Armenian-Azerbaijani borders in Nagorno-Karabakh.

---

106 Before reconciling with Russia in June–July 2016, Erdoğan claims to have told the NATO secretary-general that the Black Sea had almost become "a Russian lake." International Crisis Group, *Russia and Turkey*, 14.

Turkey is also coupled with Russia in their experience of being situated at the European periphery and having damaged relations with Europe.[107] A vivid example of Turkey's new relationship to Europe was the migration crisis of 2015, which must have afforded the Turkish government much satisfaction. One may assume that the Turkish president believed that a larger number of Muslims in the societies of Europe was an investment with long-term profitability. The refugee movement onto Greek islands in the eastern Aegean only separated by a few kilometers from the Turkish mainland, which has significantly lessened since 2015 but continues today, shows Greece, moreover, how exposed these islands are to Turkey. For Western Europeans, the situation of the migrants on the eastern Aegean islands is untenable. The message, however, which Turkey is sending Greece is that these islands immediately off the Turkish mainland are indefensible. In the 2015 migration pact negotiated between the EU and Turkey, Turkey negotiated direct benefits for those Syrian refugees living in Turkey. While Turkey had seen for decades its membership in the West as a fundamental win, it is currently in the process of having Europe and the Western alliance system directly pay for services. The insults to the European public before the parliamentary and presidential elections of 2018 or that of the French president Emmanuel Macron in 2020 may be read as acts of retaliation against a West whose self-righteous claim to be a model worthy of imitation has become tiresome.[108]

Turkey's fundamentally changed self-understanding also can be seen in its relationship with the United States and the NATO alliance. Turkey backed NATO's military operations against the Islamic state in pro forma fashion. Simultaneously, they supported the activities of Islamist militias in Syria which were welcome opponents of the Asad regime and later of the Kurds.[109] With its early entry to NATO in 1952, Turkey wanted to secure itself against the territorial claims of the then extant USSR on Eastern Anatolia and the straits. Given the current, ever more clearly formulated great-power aspirations

---

107 On this, see the many contributions to the special issue "Vergleichende Toxikologie: Herrschaft in Russland und in der Türkey" ("Comparative Toxicology: Governance in Russia and Turkey"), *Osteuropa* 68 (2018). A short, but rich comparison between Erdoğan's and Putin's regimes may be found in Heinemann-Grüder, "Ende der Illusionen."

108 See chapter two of Krastev and Holmes, *The Light that Failed*, 77–137, on the policy of "imitation as retaliation," pursued by Putin since the early 2010, by which he intends to expose the moral haughtiness of the West and to debunk geostrategic interests of the West camouflaged as supposedly universal principles of human rights.

109 On the uncovering of illegal weapons deliveries by the Turkish intelligence service MİT at the beginning of 2014 and its consequences, see Dündar, "I Revealed the Truth."

of Russia, Turkey's surrendering its NATO membership would be a self-inflicted wound, but nothing seems impossible any more.[110] Membership in NATO has always meant a close relationship with the United States, aside from the identity-political complications and confusions which continually arise in relations with Europe and the European Union in particular. But even for Washington, future relations with Turkey threaten "to assume a similar degree of complexity and occasional absurdity as those with Pakistan."[111]

Turkish ruling circles would like to see relations with countries like China and Russia as having become more important than those with Europe. This is not the case, however. Turkey and Europe are closely bound together, not only economically but through the large Turkish-descended migrant population in Western European countries. One will have to get used to new hierarchies, however, or at least get used to the fact that those that were formative in the twentieth century no longer hold sway. The old European self-assurance, indeed condescension, relative to a lower degree of development in Turkey, joined with an admiration for the exotic richness of the country, has little to do with today's realities. In the future, the Turkish-descended migrant population in Europe will take on a greater significance than in the past with regard to relations between Europe and Turkey. The constitutional referendum of 16 April 2017, impressively showed once again the political alignment of the diaspora in Europe. In Turkey itself, 51.41% of the population approved of the referendum; in most European countries, the approval ratings among voting-eligible Turkish citizen were much higher, from Germany and France with significantly more than 60% to the Netherlands, Austria, and Belgium with over 70%. The significantly lower approval ratings in Switzerland, with barely 40%, and the United Kingdom with barely more than 20%, were exceptions reflecting a different history of migration.[112]

The migrant populations from Turkey represent the oldest and most compact groups of Muslims in many countries of Western Europe. At the same time, Turkish governmental organizations have been anchored for many years in the

---

110 See the counterfactual scenario in Hähnlein et al., "Türkei verlässt die Nato."
111 Ammann, "Zweckbeziehung," 5. Cf. Kirişçi, *Turkey and the West*, 164. The danger of the negative effects of the Syria War on Turkey has been described by a former member of parliament as the risk of "a creeping Pakistanization of Turkey."
112 On Germany, see Adar, *Neubetrachtung der politischen Einstellungen türkischer Migranten*. Even if the flight of the Alevis, Kurds, or political activists into Switzerland is conspicuous, it is, however, not resounding. In any case, at around 30–40% of the Turkish-descended migrants, Alevis are disproportionately represented among the migrants. Suter Reich, *Differenz, Solidarität, und Ausgrenzung*, 79, 82.

European diaspora, like the Turkish Islamic Union for Religious Affairs (Diyanet İşleri Türk İslam Birliği, DİTİB) in Germany.[113] The Turkish-descended diaspora stands out among the Muslim population of Europe because Turkey has built an effective influence machine there over recent decades and additionally has at its disposal a very compact migration milieu among the Sunni Turks. The current Turkish government, unlike, say, Saudi Arabia, does not champion a global Islamist agenda, rather a more narrowly composed Islamist-nationalist program, which will presumably not discourage them, however, from aspiring to a "religious protectorate" over Muslims in Europe.[114]

The "Islamization" of the Muslim diaspora in Europe has to do with the errors of European immigration policy, but cannot be attributed exclusively to it.[115] In the Europe of the 1980s, migrant populations from Muslim countries were still seen in the first instance in the light of their individual communities of origin. At that time, in descriptions of Turkish migrant communities Islam was represented only as a subsystem of a comprehensive (as a rule, rurally influenced) social regime that was being brought to Europe with them. Islam as an ordering principle and point of reference was limited to immediate ritual obligations like fasting or praying.[116] In this sense, the German Islam Conference (Deutsche Islam Konferenz, DIK) founded in 2006 by then-interior minister Wolfgang Schäuble with the goal of achieving better religious and sociopolitical integration of Germany's Muslim population, represents a conflicted achievement: The positive and emancipatory claim that Muslims should obtain equality or at least recognition in the society receiving them is opposed by the fact that the DIK assigns all people who come from Muslim countries to the primary category of "Islam."

In debates over the Muslim diaspora in Europe, to which the Turkish-descended community is now to be added,[117] the point of view chosen leads

---

113 The corresponding organization of Diyanet officials in Austria is called the Turkish-Islamic Union for Cultural and Social Assistance of Austria (Avusturya Türk İslam Kültür ve Sosyal Yardımlaşma Birliği) and in Switzerland, the Turkish Religious Affairs Foundation of Switzerland (İsviçre Türk Diyanet Vakfı).
114 For a historical example of attempts at such a protectorate, see Deusch, *K.(u.)k. Kultusprotektorat*, on Habsburg efforts to protect Christian worship and charitable works in Albania.
115 Thus in Kabis, "Interview with Immanuel Todd," Todd speaks of "the Turks' Islamization" by German society.
116 Schiffauer, *Gewalt der Ehre*, is to be read in exactly this sense.
117 In this sense, representations like Herbert, *Geschichte Deutschlands*, which portray the migration of Muslims to Germany exclusively from the perspectives of labor migration of the 1960s and early 1970s are no longer timely.

to completely divergent evaluations, as we have already seen in the question of a possible Turkish accession to the EU. So one can come to the verdict that the Turkish Islamist organization Islamische Gemeinschaft Milli Görüş (IGMG) has entered a post-Islamist phase and is thereby ready to establish itself in a liberal democracy. This is opposed by the argument that an adherence to Islam as an organizational system, from whatever motive, is incompatible with democracy and human rights.[118] Are headscarfs self-conscious signs of religion which harmonize belief and modernity with each other? Or do they, in the final analysis, serve the repression by which women are defined solely by their sex?[119] A quick and amicable resolution of these discussions is of course nowhere in sight.

Janus's Gaze

The experience of the late Ottoman era, of being subjected more or less helplessly to the actions and intentions of the European great powers, shapes the politics of memory of the Republic of Turkey even today. Three examples may make this clear. When the Soviet Union demanded the broadening of their rights in the Bosporus and the Dardanelles, and thereby a revision of the definitions of the Straits Convention of Montreaux of 1936, the then prime minister Şükrü Saraçoğlu (1887–1953, in office 1942–1946) vehemently repudiated this request, combined with the admonishment that Turkey would not tolerate a second Treaty of Hünkâr İskelesi.[120] The Treaty of Hünkâr İskelesi (a boat landing and small district on the European side of the Bosporus) was concluded in 1833 between the Ottoman Empire and Russia under an existential threat to the Ottoman Empire in the form of the advance of Egyptian troops in the direction of İstanbul. The treaty undermined, in exemplary fashion, the status of the Ottoman Empire as a sovereign state. Among other things, under this treaty Russia was able to secure privileged transit rights through the straits. Second, in the 1950s, the Turkish government of the day signed up to a hundred mostly secret treaties for the stationing rights of American military units, an eventuality that

---

118 Here, see the contrary positions of Schiffauer, *Nach dem Islamismus*, 22, 25, and Koopmans, *Das verfallene Haus des Islam*, 250.
119 See the contrary positions of Nökel, *Töchter der Gastarbeiter*, 13, and Kelek, *Die fremde Braut*, 242.
120 Deringil, *Turkish Foreign Policy*, 86, refers here to Feridun Cemal Erik, *Les relations turco-soviétiques et la question des détroits* (Ankara: Başnur Matbaası, 1968), 164.

struck Turkish observers as "a form of modern 'capitulations,'"[121] that is, the escalating extraterritorial rights of European states in the Ottoman Empire in the nineteenth century. Third, in 1993, when the threat of the PKK was at its height, President Süleyman Demirel equated possible autonomy for the Kurds with 1920's Treaty of Sèvres.[122]

Victim and enemy complexes were already employed as a means of political mobilization in the late Ottoman era. Late Ottoman dignitaries argued, for example, that the cause of the decline of the Ottoman Empire since the eighteenth century was "to be sought in the inordinate humanitarianism of the earlier sultans"[123] and did not care to admit that the Ottoman Empire at the height of its power likely played the same instrument of power as the European great powers of the nineteenth century, just in a different key.

The Ottomans, according to the Kemalist state's self-understanding, were to be categorically rejected as the ancien régime. With the political pluralization in Turkey since the 1950s, and the concomitantly greater bandwidth of opinions in Turkish historiography and interpretation, the Ottoman Empire came increasingly to the fore as a legitimate and indispensable component of the complete history of the Turks. Thus it came to be that the conservative and, above all, Islamist movement had a quite distinctive perspective on the Kemalist project: The Ottoman Empire had not been the aberration, but rather Kemalism, because the close connection of Turkish and Islamic identity were the default of an authentic Turkish political culture.[124] Revisionist tendencies in recent decades in international history writing on the Ottoman Empire strengthen—likely rather unknowingly—such perceptions. Thus, for example, it is contended that an independently developing capitalist economy was strangled by European imperialism or that signs of an Islamic Enlightenment in the nineteenth century have been obscured.[125]

---

121 Gonlubol, "NATO, USA, and Turkey," 37.
122 Demirel, "Federasyon, Sevrdir," *Milliyet*, 15 August 1993, quoted following Aydin and Emrence, *Zones of Rebellion*, 96.
123 Pomiankowski, *Zusammenbruch des Osmanischen Reiches*, 162. For an example of this argument's continued life in the apologetically oriented historiography of the Republican era, see Eryılmaz, *Gayrımüslim Teb'anın Yönetimi*, 217.
124 See, for example, Çetinsaya, "Rethinking Nationalism and Islam," 217.
125 According to Gran, *Islamic Roots of Capitalism*, an independent capitalist economy had been constructed in Egypt on the foundation of long-standing trade relations in the Mediterranean sphere, which was displaced by a one-sided relationship of dependence on Europe in the early nineteenth century. On the concept of an "Islamic Enlightenment," see the two articles by Schulze, "Das islamische achtzehnte Jahrhundert," and "Islamische

For the Ottoman Empire in particular, it is argued that the janissaries, the former elite soldiers of the empire in the fifteenth and sixteenth century, had increasingly evolved into a kind of bourgeoisie. In this sense, the destruction of the Janissaries in 1826 was a kind of coup in which a new technocratic-administrative-military elite took power,[126] whose power, one must add, could only be broken in the 2000s.

Today a simple transfer of power after a defeat in parliamentary elections looks more and more unlikely, due to the historical self-image of the elite of the ruling Justice and Development Party. After many decades of rule by a Western-oriented technocratic elite, it is now allegedly a sign of compensatory historical justice that the real majority of the nation leads the government. The current position of the ruling party founds their severity and authoritarianism precisely upon a history of affronts and grievances. History becomes an apparently inexhaustible fount of rationalizations for recycling and cancelling out earlier discrimination.

Are the Turks a happy people? It's a question of perspective. The family of a functionary of the governing AKP, who perhaps was only able to gain admission to a university in the 1990s with tremendous effort, but for whom undreamed of opportunities for advancement have opened up in the last twenty years, will see Turkey with different eyes than the wife of an officer who was sentenced to prison based on (alleged or actual) collaboration with the putschists of July 2016 and who now has to raise her children alone.

Is Turkey a fortunate country? Yes and no, depending on the comparison. A happy providence for Turkey has been that, since the foundation of the Republic, it has remained untouched by major wars. One might note somewhat mischievously that the operations of the Turkish military, aside from its deployment in the Korean War in 1950–1953 and in the 1974 Cyprus intervention, have been expended controlling areas of the Kurdish population.[127] Turkey has, with respect to economic success and standard of living, left countries like Egypt and Pakistan, with which Turkey was happy to be compared in the 1950s and 1960s, far behind. On the other hand, Turkey cannot bear comparison to East Asian countries like South Korea since the 1950s. Its periods of military rule did not inflict effects as catastrophic as those in, for

---

Aufklärung," with an impressive knowledge of European history-of-philosophy debates, but fragmentary when demonstrating an alleged Enlightenment in the Islamic context.
126 Tezcan, "Second Empire."
127 McDowall, *Modern History of the Kurds*, 198, 426.

example, Latin American military dictatorships, however. On the other hand, Turkey hasn't yet succeeded in freeing itself from the up-and-down pattern of liberal and authoritarian phases. In consequence, the younger generation in Turkey really has little to look forward to.[128]

Into the 2010s, everyone, including the governing AKP, saw the growing welfare of the country as a sign of success; a sharp economic decline would have led to the AKP government's being voted out. In consequence of the turn to authoritarianism, the incessant manipulation of the media, and the polarization in Turkish politics, the future of a democratic, free-market order in Turkey is uncertain. Thus, various forms of internal and external migration are occurring. According to the data of the Turkish Statistical Institute (Türkiye İstatistik Kurumu, TÜİK) for the year 2016, 178,000 citizens left the country. In the following year, it was more than a quarter million people. According to information provided by AfrAsia Bank in 2019, at least twelve thousand of the about one hundred thousand Turkish millionaires have transferred their wealth abroad.[129]

The AKP and their chairman Erdoğan's feel for the population is not as sure as in years past. In addition, much remains unclear. Did the AKP accept their loss in the municipal elections in İstanbul with gritted teeth, but still following their democratic convictions? Or was it merely a tactical concession, in order to prevent anyone from saying that Turkey is no longer a democratic country?

Few other events divide the history of the Republic of Turkey into periods as clearly as the military coups. Important events are referred to in Turkey by day and month, like "9/11" for the attacks of 11 September 2001 in the US. Thus, 12 Eylül, that is, 12 September, just goes without saying to the younger generation as shorthand for the coup of 1980. One could even claim that the striking ten-year rhythm of the coups of 1960, 1971, and 1980 has continued in a decade-long rhythm until the failed coup attempt of July 2016. With the referendum of September 1987 and the return of the old political warhorses, Demirel, Ecevit, and Erbakan, to active politics, the coup clock began running again.[130] Ten years later, in 1997, the military forced the resignation of the government under Necmettin Erbakan, then-chairman of the Welfare

---

128 On the extent of unhappiness among Turkish youth, see Mumay, "Schuldlos verschuldet und unglücklich."
129 Gall, "Spurning Erdoğan's Vision."
130 Cemal, *Özal Hikayesi*, 135, even sees Özal's years as prime minister (1983–1989) as a "civilian prolongation of the 12 September regime."

Party (Refah Partisi). Another decade passed and in 2008, the already weakened military took to the Constitutional Court. They only fell slightly short of a majority willing to dissolve the AKP and impose a ban on political activity on its leading politicians. The failed coup attempt of 2016 ensued, the military's last step thus far.

With regard to domestic politics, Turkey has always been characterized by an ebb and flow of authoritarianism and pluralism, but its historical experience does not predetermine its future. Many paths are barred to Turkey, for good and ill. Due to the fall from power of the military, the previous guardian of politics and society, a further military intervention appears extremely unlikely for the foreseeable future. The military can and will not directly intervene in politics and—depending on your point of view—set things to right or derange them.

Much in the current state of affairs, specifically the existence of an electoral autocracy, will not change very quickly. The prospects for success of the Future Party (Gelecek Partisi) founded by former prime minister Ahmet Davutoğlu in December 2019 or the Democracy and Progress Party (Demokrasi ve Atılım Partisi, DEVA) founded by Ali Babacan (who largely determined the economic course of the government until 2015), are deeply unclear. The AKP government has at any rate done everything conceivable to dig itself deep into the hubs of power.

In the long run, Turkey will have to find its way to a new political culture, in which oscillations between self-images as victim and hero and between the emotional states of confidence and wrath, between grandeur and will become less strong. One day—not too far off—the promises of Islamist conservatism will finally ring hollow for all Turks except the grievance AKP's close clientele; at the same time, the return to a Kemalist-dominated, military-guardian state is no longer possible. Turkish society and politics must therefore figure out in the medium term how they wish to understand themselves. As we have seen, the confessional thread woven into the idea of the Turkish nation is a strength and a weakness at once. Along with the moderation of an excessive nationalism, the disentanglement of Turkish national identity from its confessional components could make possible a departure to new shores. In such a—from today's perspective abundantly utopian—polity the participation in politics and society of all the people of Turkey would no longer appear to be a catastrophe, but a prize.

Update on Turkey in the Years 2021–2023

The book in your hands is based on a translation from the German. The original version was published in summer 2021, and the account ended with the Turkish government's withdrawal from the "İstanbul Convention on Preventing and Combatting Violence against Women and Domestic Violence" on March 19, 2021. This short chapter is meant to help the reader understand the most recent developments up to the legislative and presidential elections of May 14, 2023 and to relate them to Turkey's prior trajectory.

Some developments in the past two years since spring 2021, such as the continued growth of Turkey's population, were easy to predict. By the end of the year 2022, Turkey's population counted over eight-five million and has thus surpassed that of Germany, the most populous of all EU member states.[1] Astute observers (the author of this book was not among them) might have anticipated others developments, such as Russia's invasion of Ukraine on

---

1 Türkiye İstastitik Kurumu, *Adrese Dayalı Nüfus Kayıt Sistemi Sonuçları, 2022*, https://data.tuik.gov.tr/Bulten/Index?p=Adrese-Dayali-Nufus-Kayit-Sistemi-Sonuclari-2022-49685. All web pages in this chapter were accessed on May 1-15, 2023.

24 February 2022 and Turkey's efforts to act as a moderator in the conflict while, at the same time, profiting from it.[2]

It was not difficult to also predict that the Turkish government under President Recep Tayyip Erdoğan would continue on its path towards ever-increasing authoritarianism and monopolization of power. According to a 2023 Freedom House report, Turkey is "not free" and has shown a dramatic 29% decline in freedom over the past ten years—only Libya, Nicaragua, South Sudan, and Tanzania have seen a greater decline.[3] Already one of the lowest-ranked countries for political rights and democratic freedoms in 2020, in a 2022 World Justice Report Turkey improved slightly from 117th (out of 128 countries) to 116th (out of 140 countries);[4] yet in a 2023 Reporters without Borders report, Turkey was 165th (out of 180 countries) for media freedom, a significant drop from its position at 154th in 2020.[5]

Observers have noted that the AKP and Erdoğan have lost considerable appeal in the last past few years. But this it is not because of a loss of confidence in Turkey's strongman. The fact is that Turkey's economy has returned to the dire condition it was in when the AKP took power in 2002. It is necessary to recall that inflation averaged well over 50% in the 1990s; and that by 2001—in the wake of the economic slumps of 1991, 1994, and 1998—the gross national product had shrunk by almost a tenth and Turkey had been forced to approach the IMF for help.

Today, Turkey's economy is once again dismal. In the last two years, the Turkish lira has lost 60% of its value against the dollar. Official figures (which are likely manipulated) put inflation at 86% in fall 2022, and it remains above 40%. Turkey is bankrupt: its central bank is thought to owe domestic banks and foreign central banks up to seventy billion dollars. Erdoğan's belief in a form of "voodoo economics"—namely, that minimal interest rates, even during times of high inflation, strengthen the economy—has led not only to an enormous loss in people's purchasing power, but has also fostered cronyism, as credits (up to 35% below the rate of inflation) had to been rationed

---

2 "Who are the Winners in the Black Sea Grain Deal?," *International Crisis Group*, August 3, 2022, https://www.crisisgroup.org/europe-central-asia/eastern-europe/ukraine/who-are-winners-black-sea-grain-deal.
3 Freedom House, *Freedom in the World 2023. Making 50 Years of Struggle for Democracy*, 2023, p. 12, https://freedomhouse.org/sites/default/files/2023-03/FIW_World_2023_DigtalPDF.pdf.
4 World Justice Project, *WJP Rule of Law Index*, https://worldjusticeproject.org/rule-of-law-index/global/2022/Turkey/.
5 Reporters without Borders, https://rsf.org/en/index.

and are presumably dealt out with preference to the government's close supporters.[6] Accordingly, in a March 2022 Optimar survey, 75.4% of the population identified the economy as the country's most serious problem.[7]

Nevertheless, the authoritarian Turkish leadership has shown remarkable resilience in the last few years.[8] Due to the "increasing cost of toleration and decreasing cost of suppression triggered by fear of redistribution,"[9] the government has been able to cultivate the support of parts of the populace outside its base. The AKP has provided many benefits to various large groups, such as the 45% wage increase given to people working in public services that was introduced only a couple of days before the May 14 elections.

While Erdoğan's and the AKP's shine has dulled, their grand rhetoric and gestures continue to speak to important segments of the country's population: Turkey's first aircraft carrier—its planes have to be lifted onto the deck by crane at the moment—recently visited İstanbul and anchored for all to see below the former Sultans' palace, the Topkapı; in Ankara, a new express train line has been built, although it is not fully functional yet; and the Akkuyu nuclear power plant in Mersin province, under construction by the Russian Rosatom company since 2018, and far from being completed, was officially put into service on 27 April when it received delivery of its first nuclear rods.[10]

A particularly telling demonstration of the AKP's still powerful identity politics occurred after the earthquake that hit much of Southern Anatolia and areas in Northern Syria on 6 February 2023— in modern times, the region's most destructive. The two tremors (7.8 and 7.5, respectively, on the Richter scale), the first in the early morning, the second twelve hours later, were catastrophic. In Turkey alone, fifty thousand people died, according to official figures, and there was about thirty-four billion dollars in damage. The state's response to the destruction only made things worse. After the country's last

---

6   "Crossroads at a Crossroads, " *The Economist*, May 6-12, 2023, 16-17.
7   Abdülkadir Selvi, "Ekonomi ve Ukrayna savaşı anketlere nasıl yansıdı," *Hürriyet*, March 24, 2022, https://www.hurriyet.com.tr/yazarlar/abdulkadir-selvi/ekonomi-ve-ukrayna-savasi-anketlere-nasil-yansidi-42028581.
8   On the heuristic strengths and weaknesses of the most commonly used designation for the present Turkish political system—competitive authoritarianism—whereby elections are still real, yet the opposition is confronted with a multiple set of intentional obstructions, see Düzgün Arslantaş and André Kaiser, "The 'Competitive Authoritarian' Turn in Turkey: Bandwagoning Versus Reality," *Third World Quarterly* 44, no. 3 (2023): 496-512.
9   Esen Berk and Sebnem Gumuscu, "Why Did Turkish Democracy Collapse? A Political Economy Account of AKP's Authoritarianism," *Party Politics* 27, no. 6 (2023): 1075-1091.
10 Bülent Mumay, "Erdoğan drückt auf alle Tasten," *Frankfurter Allgemeine Zeitung*, May 10, 2023, 9. https://www.faz.net/aktuell/feuilleton/brief-aus-istanbul/wenn-erdogan-die-wahl-verliert-buelent-mumays-brief-aus-istanbul-18881306.html.

major earthquake, in the Western province of Kocaeli in 1999, the government imposed a new tax specifically allocated to building up a disaster fund. However, when called upon—and because of Turkey's location on various tectonic fault lines it is relatively easy to predict when the next massive earthquake will hit—the thirty-eight billion dollars raised was nowhere to be found and the domestic rescue and relief system was in a very poor condition. Turkey's disaster and management agency, AFAD, which has strengthened Turkey's soft power diplomacy through its multiple deployments abroad, failed in its original task—that is, to support and help people in Turkey during a crisis. The Red Moon (Kızılay), Turkey's equivalent to the Red Cross, was even accused of selling tents meant for humanitarian action for more than forty-six million Turkish Liras (more than two million dollars) to a local NGO.[11] In the 2000s, strict laws were introduced to ensure that all new buildings were quakeproof; but in order to fuel a construction boom in the past twenty years and tie the success of contractors to the size of their political contributions, the AKP undermined building regulations.[12] Furthermore, the Turkish military, in 1999 the only state actor with the ability to come provide aid in Kocaeli, was almost completely absent in 2023.

One might have expected that the apparent indifference and obvious failure of the state after the earthquake in 2023—due to misappropriated taxes, hollowed-out state institutions, corruption, and recklessness—would ultimately turn the electorate against the government. However, the state-controlled media put the blame on contractors, the West was accused of withholding help and resources, and promises were made about reconstructing the affected areas. Enough people in Turkey believed the propaganda and the autocrat survived another day.

Since the resignation of Ahmet Davutoğlu as prime minister in 2016 and the abandonment of his attempt to turn Turkey into the region's wise moderator, the country has developed a policy of assertiveness and strategic

---

11 Sevinç Ünal, "Où est l'Etat? Le contrat social en Turquie à l'épreuve du séisme," *SGMOIK* (blog), May 7, 2023, https://www.sagw.ch/fr/sgmoik/sgmoik/archiv/blog/details/news/ou-est-letat-le-contrat-social-en-turquie-a-lepreuve-du-seisme. Kızılay's president, Kerem Kınık, was to resign finally only two days before the May elections. "Çadır satışı istifa getirdi! Kızılay Başkanı görevini bıraktı," *Hürriyet*, May 13, 2023, https://www.hurriyet.com.tr/gundem/cadir-satisi-istifa-getirdi-kizilay-baskani-gorevini-birakti-42266871.

12 On the "construction rentier system," see Hürcan Aslı Aksoy and Salim Çevik, "Political and Economic Implications of the Turkish Earthquakes. Centralisation of Power Has Eroded State Capacity," *SWP Comment*, March 19, 2023, https://www.swp-berlin.org/publications/products/comments/2023C19_TurkishEarthquakes.pdf.

autonomy.[13] It now acts from "a purely realist perspective."[14] One could argue that Turkey's foreign policy is, nonetheless, driven by values. They are not Western, however. The country is now closer to China, Iran, and Russia, whose agenda is to establish a non-Western world order. Indeed, can we even use the word "Turkey"? The Turkish government wants the world to call the country "Türkiye."[15] Turkey continues to take an ambiguous stance towards the West: it agrees to Finland's application to join NATO, but rejects Sweden's. There may be a principle behind this, but it is much more about the county flexing veto power. As Dimitar Bechev writes, Turkey has become an "entrepreneurial vendor in an increasingly crowded geopolitical bazaar."[16] It has also persevered along its path towards *nationalizing* the issue of the Kurds in Iraq and Syria, and, in this way—unintentionally—*internationalizing* its own Kurdish question.[17] As a result, there are pockets of "Gazafication" inside Syria, and this may have a long-term impact on the interior stability of Turkey.[18]

The legislative and presidential elections on 14 May 2023 were met with both anxiety and enthusiasm by the over sixty million voters in Turkey and the international community. Before voting day, the international media insisted that this year's elections were Turkey's "most consequential . . . in decades"[19] and that they were "the most important anywhere in the world this year."[20]

---

13 See a couple of podcasts on Turkey's assertive foreign policy produced by the International Crisis Group. and released as episodes in its "Hold Your Fire" and "War & Peace" seasons: https://www.crisisgroup.org.

14 Suat Kınıklıoğlu. "Eurasianism in Turkey," *SWP Research Paper*, March 7, 2022, 6, https://www.swp-berlin.org/publications/products/research_papers/2022RP07_EurasianismInTurkey.pdf.

15 Tellingly, the presidential decree in Turkey's *Resmî Gazete* on 3 December 2021 speaks of the word Türkiye "as a brand": https://www.resmigazete.gov.tr/eskiler/2021/12/20211204-5.pdf. The Crisis Group and al-Jazeera English, for example, have adopted this new nomenclature in writing and speech. It must be odd for a French-speaker, in particular, to use "Türkiye," as the Turkish word is almost certainly borrowed from the French "Turquie."

16 Dimitar Bechev, *Turkey Under Erdoğan. How a Country Turned from Democracy and the West* (New Haven: Yale University Press, 2022), 10.

17 See also Mesut Yegen, "Ethnopolitics to Geopolitics: The Turkish State and the Kurdish Question since 2015," *British Journal of Middle Eastern Studies* (2022): 1-18.

18 See also Aslı Aydıntaşbaş, "A New Gaza: Turkey's Border Policy in Northern Syria," *European Council on Foreign Relations*, May 28, 2020, https://ecfr.eu/publication/a_new_gaza_turkeys_border_policy_in_northern_syria/.

19 Nate Schenkkahn and Aykut Garipoglu, "Turkey's Elections Won't Be Free or Fair," *Foreign Policy*, May 3, 2023, https://foreignpolicy.com/2023/05/03/turkey-elections-erdogan-kilicdaroglu-vote-manipulation-suppression-media/.

20 "The Most Important Election This Year," *The Economist*, May 6-12, 2023, 9.

The elections were generally characterized as relatively free, but not fair: in the Turkish media, President Erdoğan received more coverage than his opponents; members of his government stirred up their supporter's anger against opposition candidates; and the government prepared the ground for undermining the integrity of the election results should it lose.[21] Nevertheless, gross manipulation of the elections was considered highly unlikely, as Erdoğan has made success at the ballots the core of his political legitimacy.[22]

The alliance supporting the incumbent president, the People's Alliance (Cumhur İttifakı), is solidly right-wing and nationalist. The major parties are the AKP (dominant since 2002) and the MHP (since 2015), its extreme nationalist junior ally; the alliance also includes Islamist Kurdish party Hüda Par (since March 2023), which has links with the Hizbullah of the 1990s (which is not related to the more well-known Lebanese Hizbullah).

In contrast, the opposition Nation Alliance (Millet İttifakı), brought together in 2018, consists of ideologically very disparate parties. It consists of the ex-Kemalist CHP, under the leadership of Kemal Kılıçdaroğlu, and the İYİ Parti, which split from the MHP and is led by staunch nationalist Meral Aksener; added to these two heavyweights are minor parties such as the Islamist Saadet Partisi, the Europe-friendly Demokrasi ve Atılım Partisi (DEVA), led by Ali Babacan, and the Gelecek Partisi, under the leadership of Ahmet Davutoğlu. Babacan and Davutoğlu are apostates from the AKP. The Nation Alliance is, therefore, prone to internal rife.[23]

At the beginning of 2023, the Nation Alliance outlined what it would do if it won a majority: restore the parliamentary system, fight inflation in order to improve the economy, and respect human rights and democratic norms.[24] As the strictly nationalist İyi Party would not allow a positive word

---

21 on 29 April, Süleyman Soylu, minister of the interior, described the upcoming elections as a potential "political coup" plot machinated by the West. See the Murat Yetkin, *Yetkin Report*, May 1, 2023, https://yetkinreport.com/en/2023/05/01/ruling-akps-final-resort-is-to-intimidate-voters-election-coup/.
22 Aslı Aydıntaşbaş expects that it will be impossible to contest the outcome of the elections if the opposition is leads by more than 2%. See "Letter from Istanbul: Turkey Has Difficult Years Ahead," *Brookings*, April 4, 2023, https://www.brookings.edu/blog/order-from-chaos/2023/04/04/letter-from-istanbul-turkey-has-difficult-years-ahead/.
23 Aurélien Denizeau, "Les coalitions politiques en Turquie à la veille des élections de 2023," *Études de l'IFRI*, April 2023, 29-30, https://www.ifri.org/sites/default/files/atoms/files/denizeau_coalitionsturquie_2023.pdf.
24 Seren Selvin Korkmaz, "Turkey's Visionary Opposition: A Proposal for New Government and Policymaking Structures," *German Marshall Fund*, March 29, 2023, https://www.gmfus.org/news/turkeys-visionary-opposition-proposal-new-government-and-policymaking-structures.

on the Kurdish issue, Kılıçdaroğlu (himself of Alevi descent and thus somewhat suspect in the eyes of the large number of conservative and Islamist-minded voters) made it clear, through conciliatory rhetoric, that he would like to come to an understanding with the Kurdish political movement. The Kurdish Peoples' Democratic Party (HDP)—which, in imminent danger of being barred from participation in the elections, slipped under the umbrella of the Party of Greens and the Left Future (YSP)—again indicated its support for the Nation Alliance by not nominating a candidate of its own for the presidency.

The morning of May 15, the day after the elections (which saw a staggering voter turnout of almost 89%), was sobering for all those who expected or hoped for change. Although most polls had suggested that the Nation Alliance was slightly ahead, the People's Alliance won with 49.34% to the challenger's 35.59%.[25] The oppositional media declared that Erdoğan lost[26] the presidential elections because he was forced into a runoff on 28 May. But as Erdoğan won 49.25% of the vote in the first round and his main contender Kemal Kılıçdaroğlu got only 45.05%, it looks like the incumbent president will be victorious. At the moment, there is no indication any large-scale election fraud took place. Even if one believes that there was a certain amount of interference in the process, one fact cannot be denied: an important part of the Turkish electorate still supports Recep Tayyip Erdoğan and wants his presidency to continue for another five years.

In the next few year, it will become clear—and I think I am right in this prediction—that the Turkish government's ambitious foreign policy is incompatible with its incompetent handling of the economy. Erdoğan can postpone the difficult task of reintroducing economic austerity and stabilizing the country; but when it finally becomes impossible to avoid changing direction, probably in the second half of the 2020s, it will be more painful than it would have been in 2023.

Maurus Reinkowski
15 May 2023

---

25 Results given by T24—https://t24.com.tr—in the morning on May 15, 2023.
26 "Erdoğan kaybetti," *Cumhuriyet*, May 15, 2023, https://www.cumhuriyet.com.tr/yazarlar/olaylarin-ardindaki-gercek/erdogan-kaybetti-2081492?utm_source=Cumhuriyet+Anasayfa&utm_medium=Yazarlar.

Acknowledgements

Alexander Balistreri, Joachim Berg, Tim Epkenhans, Hakan Karateke, Ali Sonay, and Martin Strohmeier read various versions of the manuscript of this book and provided me with many suggestions. I thank Alexander Balistreri and Tim Epkenhans for particularly valuable advice on content and structure.

My thanks to my dear colleague Hakan Karateke for accepting the book for his series "Ottoman and Turkish Studies" at Academic Studies Press. Bill Walsh is assured of my gratitude for his superb translation of the original German version into English.

I have had stimulating and formative conversations about Turkey in recent years with Mehmet Alkan, Metin Atmaca, Hüseyin Bağcı, Fatmagül Demirel, Murat Kaya, Hilmar von Lojewski, Akşin Somel, Anna Vakalis, Richard Wittmann, and Alp Yenen (to whom I owe the inspiration to this book's subtitle). The arguments in this book diverge, in part, very significantly from the opinions of the aforementioned people; they bear no responsibility at all for the content of this book, but I would particularly like to thank you all!

For scholarly hospitality and support, I thank the German Archaeological Institute in Istanbul, the Orient-Institut Istanbul, the Oriental and Eastern European Department of the Bavarian State Library in Munich, and the university libraries of Basel and Freiburg im Breisgau. I would like to dedicate this book to my wonderful wife Ljiljana, who has never lost faith in me despite my countless hours at my desk in recent decades and who constantly encouraged me during the writing of this book.

Maurus Reinkowski, March 2023

Timeline

1071 Aug 26	The Great Seljuks, alongside nomadic Turkic units, win the Battle of Manzikert (Malazgirt) and thus open Anatolia to an influx of Turkic peoples.
1326	Osman I, eponym of the Ottoman dynasty and founder of the Ottoman Empire, dies.
1453 May 29	Ottoman conquest of Constantinople.
1514 Aug 23	The triumphant Battle of Çaldıran, which allows the Ottomans to enforce their claim to Eastern Anatolia against the Safavids.
1793 Feb 24	Establishing the New Order (nizâm-ı cedid) by Sultan Selim III.
1826 June 15	Sultan Mahmud II violently disbands the janissaries (yeniçeri), the former elite infantry of the Ottoman military.
1839 Nov 3	Sultan Abdülmecid I issues the Noble Rescript (hatt-ı şerîf) of Gülhane, initiating the reform policies of the Tanzimat.

1856 Feb 18	Abdülmecid I secures equality before the law for non-Muslims in an imperial rescript (hatt-ı hümâyûn).
1856 Mar 30	In the peace Treaty of Paris, the Ottoman Empire receives the commitment to its participation in the "advantages of the European concert."
1875 Oct 6	The Ottoman Empire declares bankruptcy.
1878 Feb 13	Sultan Abdülhamid II suspends parliament.
1878 July 13	Under the provisions of the Congress of Berlin, the Ottoman Empire loses about a third of its territory and over a fifth of its population.
1908 July 23	The Young Turk Revolution revives parliament and the Constitution of 1876. Beginning of the Second Constitution (İkinci Meşrutiyet).
1912 Oct 8	Outbreak of the First Balkan War (which ends 30 May 1913).
1913 June 16	Outbreak of the Second Balkan War (which ends 10 August 1913).
1914 Aug 2	Secret German-Ottoman agreement on the Ottoman Empire's prospective entry into the war on Germany's side.
1914 Oct 29	The Ottoman Empire enters the First World War, firing on Russian Black Sea ports without prior declaration of war.
1915 Apr 25	Beginning of the Entente powers' landings on the Gallipoli (Gelibolu) Peninsula. The previous night, the Armenian genocide begins (with the first arrests of Armenians in İstanbul).
1918 Oct 30	Armistice of Mudros between the victorious Entente powers and the Ottoman Empire.
1919 May 19	Mustafa Kemal lands in Samsun, which, according to Turkish national historiography, marks the beginning of the war of the Anatolian national movement.
1919 July 23	Opening of the First Congress of the Anatolian national movement in Erzurum (closes 7 August 1919).

1919 Sept 4	Opening of the Second Congress of the Anatolian national movement in Sivas (closes 11 September 1919).
1920 Aug 10	The Ottoman Empire signs the Treaty of Sèvres whose implementation is subsequently hindered by the Anatolian national movement.
1921 Jan 10	Under the leadership of İsmet Pasha, the first of two successful defensive battles on the İnönü River stopping the further advance of Greek troops into Central Anatolia.
1921 Apr 1	Second successful battle on the İnönü.
1921 Sept 13	After a multi-week battle on the Sakarya River, the troops of the national movement succeed in breaking Greek forward momentum for good.
1922 Sept 8	Turkish troops enter Smyrna (İzmir). End of the war of the Anatolian national movement.
1922 Oct 11	Armistice of Mudanya between Great Britain and the national movement.
1922 Nov 1	The Turkish National Assembly abolishes the sultanate.
1923 July 24	Signing of the Treaty of Lausanne.
1923 Oct 29	Proclamation of the Republic of Turkey (Türkiye Cumhuriyeti).
1924 Mar 3	The Turkish National Assembly abolishes the caliphate. On the same day, the Presidium for Religious Affairs (Diyanet İşleri Başkanlığı) is founded.
1924 Apr 20	Parliament ratifies a constitution (Teşkilat-ı Esasiye Kanunu) which replaces the Constitution of 1876.
1925 June 29	Shaykh Said is hanged along with forty-six of his followers in Diyarbakır.
1925 Nov 25	Passage of the Hat Law making it mandatory for men to wear a Western hat in public.
1925 Nov 30	Law forbidding and closing dervish orders, convents, and mausolea.
1926 Feb 17	Resolution of parliament on the introduction of a new civil law code.

1927 Oct 15	Mustafa Kemal begins his marathon speech (Nutuk) to the Second Congress of the Republican People's Party. It concludes on 20 Oct 1927.
1929 Jan 1	Script reform: replacement of the Arabic alphabet by the Latin alphabet.
1935 Jan 1	Mandatory adoption of family names.
1938 Nov 10	Death of Mustafa Kemal Atatürk.
1945 Feb 23	Turkey declares war on Germany in order to fulfill the basic condition for acceptance into the United Nations.
1950 May 14	The Democrat Party (Demokrat Parti, DP) wins the parliamentary elections and takes over governing.
1952 Feb 18	Turkey is accepted into NATO, along with Greece.
1960 May 27	Coup under the formal direction of General Cemal Gürsel.
1961 July 9	On the basis of a constitutional referendum, a newly composed constitution replaces the Constitution of 1924.
1971 Mar 12	The military presents President Cevdet Sunay and the speakers of both houses of parliament with a memorandum and threatens to intervene.
1978 Nov	Founding of the PKK in the village of Fis near Diyarbakır.
1978 Dec 22	Anti-Alevi pogrom begins in Kahramanmaraş, lasting until 24 December 1978, with more than one hundred dead. On the following day (25 December), parliament imposes a state of emergency in thirteen provinces of Eastern Anatolia.
1980 Sep 12	Military coup.
1982 Nov 7	A new constitution is accepted by referendum and Kenan Evren is appointed president.
1983 Dec 6	The National Security Council (Milli Güvelik Konseyi), which has been ruling since 12 September 1980 under the framework of a state of emergency, surrenders the affairs of government to Turgut Özal (ANAP).

1987 Sep 6	In a referendum won by an extremely small majority, the ten-year ban on political activity for two hundred politicians, including Süleyman Demirel, Bülent Ecevit, Necmettin Erbakan, and Alparslan Türkeş, is lifted.
1993 Apr 17	With the surprisingly premature death of President Turgut Özal, an all-encompassing battle against the PKK begins.
1993 July 2	A mob sets a fire in the Madımak Hotel in Sivas, in which the participants in the celebrations in honor of Pir Sultan Abdal have gathered. Thirty-five people die in the fire.
1996 Jan 1	Customs union between Turkey and the EC.
1996 Nov 3	A traffic accident in Susurluk (Western Anatolia) exposes rampant connections between the organs of state, criminal milieux, and right-wing extremists.
1997 Feb 28	A meeting of the National Security Council initiates the February 28th Process, which leads a few months later to the resignation of Prime Minister Necmettin Erbakan and the banning of the Welfare Party.
1999 Aug 17	Gölcük earthquake in the eastern portion of the greater İstanbul metropolitan area with almost eighteen thousand dead.
1999 Dec 11	The Council of Europe recognizes Turkey as wishing to join the EU at its summit in Helsinki.
2002 Nov 3	The AKP wins parliamentary elections and takes over government the same month.
2003 Mar 14	The National Assembly elects Recep Tayyip Erdoğan prime minister.
2005 Oct 3	Beginning of accession negotiations between Turkey and the EC.
2007 Jan 19	Murder of the Armenian activist Hrant Dink.
2007 Apr 27	E-Memorandum (E-Muhtıra) of the military.
2007 Aug 28	Parliament elects Abdullah Gül president.
2007 Oct 21	A constitutional referendum passes, that is, the direct election of the president and the legislature's term is reduced from five to four years.

2008 July 30	The Constitutional Court fails to reach the three-fifths quorum to ban the AKP.
2010 May 31	The Israeli navy captures the ship Mavi Marmara in international waters on its way to the Gaza Strip.
2010 Sep 12	A constitutional referendum abolishes, that is, the clause in the Constitution of 1982 that guarantees the putschists of 1980 amnesty from prosecution. The number of judges in the highest institutions of the judiciary is increased.
2011 Feb 11	High point of the Arab Spring with the resignation of Egyptian president Hosni Mubarak forced by demonstrations.
2011 Mar 17	In Syria, the Arab Spring tips into a war.
2013 May 28	Outbreak of the Gezi Park protests in İstanbul, which spread through all Turkey and last into the fall.
2014 Jan 30	The Syrian Kurdish PYD proclaims the autonomy of "West Kurdistan" (Rojava).
2014 Aug 28	The National Assembly elects Recep Tayyip Erdoğan president.
2015 June 7	In the parliamentary elections, the Kurdish-aligned HDP clears the ten percent hurdle. The AKP loses its absolute majority in parliament for the first time.
2017 Apr 16	Successful constitutional referendum on the transition to a presidential system of government.
2018 June 24	Over the course of the parliamentary and presidential elections, the presidential system of government adopted the year before is introduced.
2019 June 23	The CHP candidate, Ekrem İmamoğlu, wins the mayoralty in the repetition of the municipal elections in İstanbul.
2020 June 10	Near confrontation between ships of the French and Turkish navies in the Mediterranean.
2020 July 24	The Hagia Sophia (Aya Sofya) is reconverted into a mosque as it had been in the years 1453–1931.

2020 Sep 27	Beginning of the war (lasting until November) for control of Nagorno-Karabakh between Armenia and Azerbaijan. Turkish support is decisive for the Azerbaijani victory.
2021 Mar 17	The state prosecutor of the Cassation Court (Yargıtay) applies for a ban on the HDP and a multi-year ban on political activity for about six hundred politicians of the party.
2021 Mar 19	The Turkish government withdraws from the İstanbul Convention for the Protection and Combating of Violence Against Women and Domestic Violence.

Abbreviations

AFAD	Afet ve Acil Durum Yönetimi Başkanlığı—Disaster and Emergency Management Presidium
AKP	Adalet ve Kalkınma Partisi—Justice and Development Party
ANAP	Anavatan Partisi—Motherland Party
AP	Adalet Partisi—Justice Party
BBP	Büyük Birlik Partisi—Great Unity Party
BSEC	Organization of the Black Sea Cooperation [sic]
CENTO	Central Treaty Organization (formerly Baghdad Pact)
CHP	Cumhuriyet Halk Partisi—Republican People's Party
CKMP	Cumhuriyetçi Köylü Millet Partisi—Republican Villagers Nation Party
DDKO	Devrimci Doğu Kültür Ocakları—Revolutionary Eastern Culture Hearths
DEP	Demokrasi Partisi—Democracy Party

DEVA	Demokrasi ve Atılım Partisi—Party for Democracy and Progress
Dev-Genç	Türkiye Devrimci Gençlik Dernekleri Federasyonu—Federation of Revolutionary Youth Associations of Turkey
DİSK	Türkiye Devrimci İşçi Sendikaları Konfederayonu—Confederation of Revolutionary Labor Unions of Turkey
DİTİB	Diyanet İşleri Türk İslam Birliği—Turkish Islamic Union for Religious Affairs (in Germany)
DP	Demokrat Parti—Democrat Party (in the 1950s)
DP	Demokratik Parti—Democratic Party (in the 1970s)
DPT	Devlet Planlama Teşkilatı—State Planning Organization
DSP	Demokratik Sol Partisi—Democratic Left Party
DTP	Demokratik Toplum Partisi—Democratic Society Party
DYP	Doğru Yol Partisi—True Path Party
ECHR	European Court for Human Rights
ESI	European Stability Initiative
FETÖ	Fethullahçı Terör Örgütü—Fethullahist Terror Organization (Gülen movement)
FP	Fazilet Partisi—Virtue Party
HADEP	Halkın Demokrasi Partisi—People's Democracy Party
HDP	Halkların Demokratik Partisi—Peoples' Democratic Party
HEP	Halkın Emek Partisi—People's Labor Party
IGMG	Islamische Gemeinschaft Milli Görüş—National Perspective Islamic Society (Germany)
IMF	International Monetary Fund
JİTEM	Jandarma İstihbarat ve Terörle Mücadele—Gendarmerie Intelligence and Counterterrorism
KCK	Koma Civakên Kurdistan—Union of Communities of Kurdistan

MGK	Milli Güvenlik Kurulu—National Security Council
MİT	Millî İstihbarat Teşkilatı—National Intelligence Organization
MNP	Millî Nizam Partisi—National Order Party
MSP	Millî Selamet Partisi—National Salvation Party
MÜSİAD	Müstakil Sanayici ve İşadamları Derneği—Association of Independent Industrialists and Businessmen
NATO	North Atlantic Treaty Organization
OHAL	Olağanüstü Hal Bölgesi—State of Emergency Zone (in the Kurdish areas of Southeastern Anatolia)
PDK	Partiya Demokrata Kurdistanê—Democratic Party of Kurdistan (in Iraq)
PKK	Partiya Karkarên Kurdistanê—Kurdistan Workers' Party
PYD	Partiya Yekitiya Demokrat—Democratic Union Party (in Syria)
RP	Refah Partisi—Welfare Party
SHP	Sosyaldemokrat Halkçı Partisi—Social-Democratic Populist Party
SP	Saadet Partisi—Felicity Party
THKO	Türkiye Halk Kurtuluş Ordusu—People's Liberation Army of Turkey
THKP-C	Türkiye Halk Kurtuluş Partisi–Cephe—People's Liberation Party of Turkey–Front
TİİKP	Türkiye İhtilalci İşçi-Köylü Partisi—Revolutionary Workers' and Peasants' Party of Turkey
TİKA	Türkiye İşbirliği ve Koordinasyon Ajansı Başkanlığı—Presidium of the Cooperation and Coordination Agency of Turkey
TİP	Türkiye İşçi Partisi—Turkish Workers' Party

TKP–ML	Türkiye Komünist Partisi–Marksist-Leninist—Communist Party of Turkey–Marxist-Leninist
TOBB	Türkiye Odalar ve Borsalar Birliği—Union of Chambers and Commodity Exchanges of Turkey
TOKİ	Toplu Konut İdaresi Başkanlığı—Presidium for the Administration of Mass Housing
TÜİK	Türkiye İstatistik Kurumu Başkanlığı—Presidium of the Statistical Institute of Turkey
Türk-İş	Türkiye İşçi Sendikaları Konfederasyonu—Confederation of Turkish Trade Unions
TÜSİAD	Türk Sanayicileri ve İş İnsanları Derneği—Association of Turkish Industrialists and Businesspeople
UÇK	Ushtria Çlirimtare e Kosovës—Kosovo Liberation Army
UNFICYP	United Nations Forces in Cyprus
YPG	Yekîneyên Parastina Gel—People's Protection Units (military arm of the Syrian PYD)

Bibliography

Abadan-Unat, Nermin. *Turks in Europe. From Guest Worker to Transnational Citizen.* New York, NY: Berghahn Books, 2011.

Abdo, Geneive. *The New Sectarianism. The Arab Uprisings and the Rebirth of the Shiʿa-Sunni Divide.* New York, NY: Oxford University Press, 2017.

Abou-el-Haj, Rifaat Ali. "The Social Uses of the Past: Recent Arab Historiography of Ottoman Rule." *International Journal of Middle East Studies* 14, no. 2 (1982): 185–201.

Abrahamian, Ervand. *Khomeinism: Essays on the Islamic Republic.* Berkeley, CA: University of California Press, 1993.

Acemoglu, Daron, and Murat Ucer. *The Ups and Downs of Turkish Growth, 2002–2015. Political Dynamics, the European Union and the Institutional Slide.* Cambridge, MA: National Bureau of Economic Research, 2015. Accessed March 1, 2023. https://www.nber.org/papers/w21608.

Adar, Sinem. *Eine Neubetrachtung der politischen Einstellungen türkischer Migranten in Deutschland. Analyse des Wahlverhaltens jenseits von "Loyalität gegenüber der Türkei" und "Mangel an demokratischer Kultur."* Berlin: Stiftung Wissenschaft und Politik, 2020. Accessed March 1, 2023. https://www.swp-berlin.org/fileadmin/contents/products/studien/2020S06_Adar_Migranten.pdf.

Afacan, İsa. "Türk Dış Politikası'nda Afrika Açılımı." *Ortadoğu Analiz* 4, no. 46 (2012): 10–18.

Ahmad, Feroz. *The Turkish Experiment in Democracy 1950–1975*. London: Hurst, 1977.

———. *The Making of Modern Turkey*. London: Routledge, 1993.

———. "Ottoman Perceptions of the Capitulations 1800–1914." *Journal of Islamic Studies* 11, no. 1 (2000): 1–20.

Akçam, Taner. *Armenien und der Völkermord. Die Istanbuler Prozesse und die türkische Nationalbewegung*. Hamburg: Hamburger Edition, 1996.

Akgün, Birol, and Şaban Çalış. "Tanrı Dağı Kadar Türk, Hira Dağı Kadar Müslüman: Türk Milliyetçiliğinin Terkibinde İslâmcı Doz." In *Milliyetçilik*, edited by Murat Belge and Tanıl Bora, 584–600. Vol. 3 of *Modern Türkiye'de Siyasi Düşünce*. 4th ed. İstanbul: İletişim, 2009.

Akgün, Mensur, and Sabiha Senyücel Gündoğar, Jonathan Levack, and Gökçe Perçinoğlu. *The Perception of Turkey in the Middle East 2010. Key Findings*. İstanbul: TESEV, 2011. Accessed March 1, 2023. http://tesev.org.tr/en/yayin/the-perception-of-turkey-in-the-middle-east-2010.

Akgün, Mensur, and Sabiha Senyücel Gündoğar,. *The Perception of Turkey in the Middle East 2013. Key Findings*. İstanbul: TESEV, 2014. Accessed March 1, 2023. https://www.tesev.org.tr/wp-content/uploads/report_The_Perception_Of_Turkey_In_The_Middle_East_2013.pdf.

Aksakal, Mustafa, *The Ottoman Road to War in 1914. The Ottoman Empire and the First World War*. Cambridge: Cambridge University Press, 2008.

Alkan, Mehmet Ö. "Önsöz. Darpsız Darbesiz Demokrasi." In *Osmanlı'dan Günümüze Darbeler*, edited by Mehmet Ö. Alkan, vii–xvi. İstanbul: Tarih Vakfı Yurt Yayınları, 2016.

Alper, Emin. *Jakobenlerden Devrimcilere: Türkiye'de Öğrenci Hareketlerinin Dinamikleri (1960–1971)*. İstanbul: Tarih Vakfı Yurt Yayınları, 2018.

Altınay, Ayşe Gül. *The Myth of the Military Nation. Militarism, Gender, and Education in Turkey*. New York, NY: Palgrave Macmillan, 2004.

Altınay, Ayşe Gül, and Fethiye Çetin. *The Grandchildren: The Hidden Legacy of "Lost" Armenians in Turkey*. New Brunswick, London: Transaction Publishers, 2014.

Altınordu, Ateş. "A Midsummer Night's Coup: Performance and Power in Turkey's 15 July Coup Attempt." In *The Dubious Case of a Failed Coup: Militarism, Masculinities, and 15 July in Turkey*, edited by Feride Çiçekoglu and Ömer Turan, 7–39. Singapore: Palgrave Macmillan, 2019.

Ammann, Beat. "Eine immer schwierigere Zweckbeziehung. Der Putschversuch in der Türkei illustriert die zunehmenden Differenzen mit den USA." *Neue Zürcher Zeitung*, July 21, 2016. https://www.nzz.ch/international/putschversuch-in-der-tuerkei/spannungen-im-verhaeltnis-usa-tuerkei-eine-immer-schwierigere-zweckbeziehung-ld.106628.

Amnesty International. *Adding Injustice to Injury: One Year on from the Gezi Park Protests*. London: Amnesty International, 2014. Accessed March 1, 2023. https://www.amnesty.org.uk/files/adding_injustice_to_injury.pdf?CDLPuDOBgZqPGsOR834rmK1hTRvJ5Qih=.

Anastassiadou, Méropi. *Les Grecs d'Istanbul au XIXe siècle. Histoire socioculturelle de la communauté de Péra*. Leiden: Brill, 2012.

Anderson, Matthew Smith. *The Eastern Question, 1774–1923: A Study in International Relations*. London: Macmillan, 1966.

Andrew, Christopher M., and Vasili Mitrokhin. *The Sword and the Shield: The Mitrokhin Archive and the Secret History of the KGB*. New York, NY: Basic Books, 1999.

Andrews, Peter Alford, ed. *Ethnic Groups in the Republic of Turkey*. Wiesbaden: Ludwig Reichert, 2002.

———. "Introduction." In *Ethnic Groups in the Republic of Turkey*, edited by Peter Alford Andrews, 17–52. Wiesbaden: Ludwig Reichert, 2002.

Armstrong, Harold Courtenay. *Grey Wolf: Mustafa Kemal. An Intimate Study of a Dictator*. London: Penguin, 1937.

Asderis, Michael. *Das Tor zur Glückseligkeit. Migration, Heimat, Vertreibung – die Geschichte einer Istanbuler Familie*. Berlin: binooki, 2018.

Ataöv, Türkkaya. *N. A. T. O. and Turkey*. Ankara: Sevinç, 1970.

Atay, Falih Rıfkı. *Zeytindağı*. 4th ed. İstanbul: Dünya Yayınları, 1957.

Ateş, Seyran. *Große Reise ins Feuer. Die Geschichte einer deutschen Türkin*. Berlin: Rowohlt, 2003.

Atmaca, Metin. "Özal'dan Erdoğan'a Kürt Sorununda Çözüm Süreci." In *Türkiye'nin Demokratikleşme. Etnik-Dini Kesimler Üzerinden Değişmenin Analizi*, edited by Halkan Samur and Zelal Kısılkan Kısacık, 19–52. Konya: Çizgi Kitapevi, 2014.

Axworthy, Michael. *Iran. What Everyone Needs to Know*. Oxford: Oxford University Press, 2017.

Ayata, Bilgin, and Serra Hakyemez. "The AKP's Engagement with Turkey's Past Crimes: An Analysis of PM Erdoğan's 'Dersim Apology.'" *Dialectical Anthropology* 37, no. 1. (2013): 131–143.

Aydemir, Şevket Süreyya. *İkinci Adam*. 3 vols. 13th ed. İstanbul: Remzi Kitabevi, 2010.

Aydin, Aysegul, and Cem Emrence. *Zones of Rebellion. Kurdish Insurgents and the Turkish State*. Ithaca, NY: Cornell University Press, 2015.

Aydın, Mustafa. "Relations with the Caucasus and Central Asia." In *Turkish Foreign Policy, 1919–2006. Facts and Analyses with Documents*, edited by Baskın Oran, 750–789. Salt Lake City, UT: The University of Utah Press, 2010.

Aytürk, İlker. "Bir Defa Daha Post-Post-Kemalizm: Eleştiriler, Cevaplar, Düşünceler." *Birikim* 374/375 (2020): 101–119.

———. "Post-Kemalizm Nedir? Post-Kemalist Kimdir? Bir Tanım Denemesi." *Varlık* (2019): 4–7.

———. *Post-Post-Kemalism? Why Is Studying the Turkish Far Right More Relevant Now Than Ever?* Lecture at the Institut d'études de l'Islam et des sociétés du monde musulman und Ecole des hautes études en sciences sociales, May 16, 2018. SoundCloud audio, 56:44, 2019. https://soundcloud.com/iismm/post-post-kemalism-why-is-studying-the-turkish-far-right-more-relevant-now-than-ever-i-ayturk.

Baer, David Marc. *The Dönme: Jewish Converts, Muslim Revolutionaries, and Secular Turks*. Stanford, CA: Stanford University Press, 2010.

———. "An Enemy Old and New: The Dönme, Anti-Semitism, and Conspiracy Theories in the Ottoman Empire and the Turkish Republic." *Jewish Quarterly Review* 103, no. 4 (2013): 523–555.

Balbay, Mustafa. "Olmayan Suriye Politikasında şuursuzluk." *Cumhuriyet*, July 25, 2019. http://www.cumhuriyet.com.tr/koseyazisi/1504006/Olmayan_Suriye_politikasinda_suursuzluk_.html.

Balci, Bayram. *Islam in Central Asia and the Caucasus since the Fall of the Soviet Union*. London: Hurst, 2018.

Bali, Rıfat N. *Model Citizens of the State: The Jews of Turkey During the Multi-Party Period*. Lanham, MD: Lexington Books, 2012.

———. ed. *Varlık Vergisi: Hatıralar – Tanıklıklar*. İstanbul: Libra, 2012.

Balistreri, Alexander E. "Turkey's Forgotten Political Opposition: The Demise of Kadirbeyoğlu Zeki Bey, 1919–1927." *Die Welt des Islams* 55, no. 2 (2015): 141–185.

———. "Writer, Rebel, Soldier, Shaykh: Border Crossers in the Historiography of the Modern Caucasus." *Kritika: Explorations in Russian and Eurasian History* 20, no. 2 (2019): 345–364.

Balkan, Sadık, and Ahmet E. Uysal. *Constitution of the Turkish Republic. Translated for the Committee of National Union*. Translated by Kemal H. Karpat. Ankara, 1961. Accessed February 28, 2023. https://www.anayasa.gen.tr/1961constitution-text.pdf.

Baltacıoğlu-Brammer, Ayşe. "One Word, Many Implications: The Term 'Kızılbaş' in the Early Modern Ottoman Context." In *Ottoman Sunnism*, edited by Vefa Erginbaş, 47–70. Edinburgh: Edinburgh University Press, 2019.

Barbir, Karl. "Memory, Heritage, and History: The Ottoman Legacy in the Arab World." In *Imperial Legacy: The Ottoman Imprint on the Balkans and the Middle East*, edited by L. Carl Brown, 100–114. New York, NY: Columbia University Press, 1996.

Bardakci, Mehmet, Annette Freyberg-Inan, Christoph Giesel, and Olaf Leisse. *Religious Minorities in Turkey: Alevi, Armenians, and Syriacs and the Struggle to Desecuritize Religious Freedom*. London: Palgrave Macmillan, 2017.

Barr, James. *A Line in the Sand. Britain, France and the Struggle for the Mastery of the Middle East*. London: Simon and Schuster, 2011.

Bayar, Yeşim. "In Pursuit of Homogeneity: The Lausanne Conference, Minorities and the Turkish Nation." *Nationalities Papers* 42, no. 1 (2014): 108–125.

Bayraktar, Seyhan. *Politik und Erinnerung: der Diskurs über den Armeniermord in der Türkei zwischen Nationalismus und Europäisierung*. Bielefeld: transcript, 2010.

Beblawi, Hazem. "The Rentier State in the Arab World." In *The Rentier State*, edited by Hazem Beblawi and Giacomo Luciani, 49–62. London: Croom Helm, 1987.

Behrendt, Günter. *Nationalismus in Kurdistan. Vorgeschichte, Entstehungsbedingungen und erste Manifestationen bis 1925*. Hamburg: Deutsches Orient-Institut, 1993.

Belge, Murat, and Ahmet Çiğdem, eds. *Modern Türkiye'de Siyasi Düşünce*. Vol. 5, *Mufazakârlık*. 4th ed. İstanbul: İletişim, 2009.

Bengio, Ofra. *The Turkish-Israeli Relationship: Changing Ties of Middle Eastern Outsiders*. New York, NY: Palgrave Macmillan, 2004.

Benninghaus, Rüdiger. "The Laz: An Example of Multiple Identification." In *Ethnic Groups in the Republic of Turkey*, edited by Peter Alford Andrews, 497–502. Wiesbaden: Ludwig Reichert, 2002.

Berberakis, Stelyo. "Büyükada Rum Yetimhanesi: 1964'te Kapısına Kilit Vurulan ve Restorasyon Çalışmaları Başlayan Binanın Hazin Öyküsü." BBC News Türkçe, October 3, 2020. https://www.bbc.com/turkce/haberler-turkiye-54401378.

Berkes, Niyazi. *The Development of Secularism in Turkey*. New York, NY: Routledge, 1998.

Berlinski, Claire. "How Democracies Die: Guilty Men." *The American Interest*, April 24, 2017. https://www.the-american-interest.com/2017/04/24/guilty-men/.

Beşikçi, İsmail. *Kurdistan: Internationale Kolonie*. Frankfurt a. M.: isp-Verlag, 1991.

Bielefeldt, Heiner. *Muslime im säkularen Rechtsstaat: Integrationschancen durch Religionsfreiheit*. Bielefeld: transcript, 2003.

Bilgen, Arda. "The Southeastern Anatolia Project (GAP) Revisited: The Evolution of GAP over Forty Years." *New Perspectives on Turkey* 58 (2018): 125–154.

Birand, Mehmet Ali, *The Generals' Coup in Turkey. An Inside Story of 12 September 1980*. London: Brassey's Defence Publishers, 1987.

———. *Shirts of Steel. An Anatomy of the Turkish Armed Forces*. London: I. B. Tauris, 1991.

———. *Türkiye'nin Ortak Pazarı Macerası, 1959–1985*. İstanbul: Milliyet, 1985.

Birand, Mehmet Ali, and Reyhan Yıldız. *Son Darbe: 28 Şubat*. İstanbul: Doğan Kitap, 2012.

Bischoff, Norbert von. *Ankara. Eine Deutung des neuen Werdens in der Türkei*. Wien: Holzhausens NFG, 1935.

Bloxham, Donald. *The Great Game of Genocide. Imperialism, Nationalism, and the Destruction of the Ottoman Armenians*. Oxford: Oxford University Press, 2005.

Böckenförde, Ernst-Wolfgang. "Nein zum Beitritt der Türkei." *Frankfurter Allgemeine Zeitung*, December 10, 2004. https://www.faz.net/aktuell/feuilleton/europaeische-union-nein-zum-beitritt-der-tuerkei-1193219.html.

Bolukbasi, Suha. "Behind the Turkish-Israeli Alliance: A Turkish View." *Journal of Palestine Studies* 29, no. 1 (1999): 21–35.

Bora, Tanıl, "Narrating the Enemy: Image and Perception of the 'Communists' among the Radical Right." In *Turkey in Turmoil: Social Change and Political Radicalization During the 1960s*, edited by Berna Pekesen, 137–151. Berlin: De Gruyter Oldenbourg, 2020.

———. "Turkish National Identity, Turkish Nationalism and the Balkan Problem." In *Balkans: A Mirror of the New International Order*, edited by Günay Göksü Özdoğan and Kemâli Saybaşılı, 101–120. İstanbul: Eren, 1995.

———. *Türk Sağının Üç Hâli: Milliyetçilik, Muhafazakârlık, İslamcılık*. 6th ed. İstanbul: Birikim Yayınları, 2009.

Bora, Tanıl, and Kemal Can. *Devlet, Ocak, Dergâh: 12 Eylül'den 1990'lara Ülkücü Hareket*. İstanbul: İletişim, 1991.

Bormuth, Matthias. *Erich Auerbach. Kulturphilosoph im Exil*. Göttingen: Wallstein, 2020.

Bösch, Frank. *Zeitenwende 1979: Als die Welt von heute begann*. Munich: C. H. Beck, 2019.

Bozarslan, Hamit. "Alevism and the Myths of Research: The Need for a New Research Agenda." In *Turkey's Alevi Enigma: A Comprehensive Overview*, edited by Paul J. White and Joost Jongerden, 3–15. Leiden: Brill, 2003.

———. "From Kemalism to Armed Struggle: Radicalization of the Left in the 1960s." In *Turkey in Turmoil: Social Change and Political Radicalization During the 1960s*, edited by Berna Pekesen, 115–136. Berlin: De Gruyter Oldenbourg, 2020.

Braude, Benjamin. "Foundation Myths of the Millet System." In *The Functioning of a Plural Society*, edited by Benjamin Braude and Bernard Lewis, 69–88. Vol. 1 of *Christians and Jews in the Ottoman Empire*. New York, NY: Holmes and Meier, 1982.

Brey, Hansjörg. "Bevölkerungsstruktur." In *Zypern*, edited by Klaus-Detlev Grothusen, Winfried Steffani, and Peter Zervakis, 488–515. Vol. 8 of *Südosteuropa-Handbuch*. Göttingen: Vandenhoeck and Ruprecht, 1998

Brink-Danan, Marcy. *Jewish Life in 21st-Century Turkey: The Other Side of Tolerance*. Bloomington, IN: Indiana University Press, 2012.

Brown, Kerry. *The World According to Xi: Everything You Need to Know about the New China*. London: I. B. Tauris, 2019.

Bruinessen, Martin van. *Agha, Shaikh and State. The Social and Political Structures of Kurdistan*. Rijswijk: Europrint-Secondprint, 1978.

Buğra, Ayşe. "Class, Culture, and State: An Analysis of Interest Representation by Two Turkish Business Associations." *International Journal of Middle East Studies* 30, no. 4. (1998): 521–539.

Bumke, Peter J. "The Kurdish Alevis—Boundaries and Perceptions." In *Ethnic Groups in the Republic of Turkey*, edited by Peter Alford Andrews, 510–518. Wiesbaden: Ludwig Reichert, 2002.

Bundesministerium des Innern [Ministry of the Interior, Federal Republic of Germany]. *Migrationsbericht der Bundesregierung. Migrationsbericht 2018*. Berlin, 2020. Accessed March 18, 2023. https://www.bamf.de/SharedDocs/Anlagen/DE/Forschung/Migrationsberichte/migrationsbericht-2018.pdf?__blob=publicationFileandv=15.

Burbank, Jane, and Frederick Cooper. *Empires in World History. Power and the Politics of Difference*. Princeton, NJ: Princeton University Press, 2010.

Cagaptay, Soner. *The New Sultan: Erdogan and the Crisis of Modern Turkey.* London: I. B. Tauris, 2017.

Çakır, Ruşen. *Ayet ve Slogan. Türkiye'de İslami Oluşumlar.* 3rd ed. İstanbul: Metis, 1991.

Calic, Marie-Janine. *Geschichte Jugoslawiens im 20. Jahrhundert.* Munich: C. H. Beck, 2012.

———. *Tito. Der ewige Partisan. Eine Biographie.* Munich: C. H. Beck, 2020.

Çarkoğlu, Ali, and Mine Eder. "Domestic Concerns and the Water Conflict over the Euphrates-Tigris River Basin." *Middle Eastern Studies* 37, no. 1 (2001): 41–71.

Çaylı, Eray. "Conspiracy Theory as Spatial Practice: The Case of the Sivas Arson Attack, Turkey." *Environment and Planning D: Society and Space* 36, no. 2 (2018): 255–272.

Çelik, Adnan, and Béatrice Garapon. "De l'exil à la représentation parlementaire: une nouvelle génération d'élites kurdes en politique (1946–1955)." *Anatoli—De l'Adriatique à la Caspienne. Territoires, Politique, Sociétés* 8 (2017): 205–232.

Cemal, Hasan. *Özal Hikayesi.* Ankara: Bilgi Yayınevi, 1989.

Çetin, Fethiye. *Anneannem: Anı.* İstanbul: Metis, 2004.

Çetinsaya, Gökhan. "Rethinking Nationalism and Islam: Some Preliminary Notes on the Roots of 'Turkish-Islamic Synthesis' in Modern Turkish Political Thought." *Muslim World* 89, nos. 3–4 (1999): 350–376.

Cizre, Ümit. "Fear and Loathing in Turkey. The Backstory to Erdoğan's Referendum." *Middle East Research and Information Project*, April 26, 2017. https://merip.org/2017/04/fear-and-loathing-in-turkey.

Clark, Christopher. *The Sleepwalkers: How Europe Went to War in 1914.* London: Penguin, 2012.

Clogg, Richard. *A Concise History of Greece.* Cambridge: Cambridge University Press, 1992.

Çolak, Mustafa. *Karaoğlan. Bülent Ecevit.* İstanbul: İletişim, 2016.

Collier, Paul. *Exodus: Immigration and Multiculturalism in the 21st Century.* London: Allen Lane, 2013.

Conker, Orhan, and Émile Witmeur. *Redressement économique et industrialisation de la nouvelle Turquie.* Paris: Sirey, 1937.

Conrad, Sebastian. *What Is Global History?* Princeton, NJ: Princeton University Press, 2016.

Cook, Steven A. *False Dawn: Protest, Democracy, and Violence in the New Middle East.* New York, NY: Oxford University Press, 2017.

Côrte-Real Pinto, Gabriela Anouck, and Isabel David. "Choosing Second Citizenship in Troubled Times: The Jewish Minority in Turkey." *British Journal of Middle Eastern Studies* 46, no. 5 (2019): 781–796.

Courbage, Youssef, and Emmanuel Todd. *Die unaufhaltsame Revolution. Wie die Werte der Moderne die islamische Welt verändern*. Munich: Piper, 2008.

Cremer, Jan, and Horst Przytulla. *Exil Türkei: Deutschsprachige Emigranten in der Türkei*. 2nd ed. Munich: Lipp, 1991.

Criss, Nur Bilge. *Istanbul under Allied Occupation 1918–1923*. Leiden: Brill, 1999.

Danforth, Nick. "Turkey's New Maps Are Reclaiming the Ottoman Empire." *Foreign Policy*, October 23, 2016. https://foreignpolicy.com/2016/10/23/turkeys-religious-nationalists-want-ottoman-borders-iraq-erdogan/.

Davies, Norman. *Im Herzen Europas. Geschichte Polens*. Munich: C. H. Beck, 1999.

Davutoğlu, Ahmet. "Büyük Restorasyon: Kadim'den Küreselleşmeye Yeni Siyaset Anlayışımız." Speech at Dicle University, Diyarbakır, 15 March 2013. https://www.mfa.gov.tr/disisleri-bakani-ahmet-davutoglu_nun-diyarbakir-dicle-universitesinde-verdigi-_buyuk-restorasyon_-kadim_den-kuresellesmeye-yeni.tr.mfa.

———. "I'm Not a Neo-Ottoman." *Balkan Insight*, April 26, 2011. http://www.balkaninsight.com/en/article/davutoglu-i-m-not-a-neo-ottoman.

———. "Principles of Turkish Foreign Policy and Regional Political Structuring." *Turkey Policy Brief Series* 3 (2012): 1–9.

———. *Stratejik Derinlik: Türkiye'nin Uluslararası Konumu*. İstanbul: Küre Yayınları, 2001.

Dawisha, Adeed. *Arab Nationalism in the Twentieth Century: From Triumph to Despair*. Princeton, NJ: Princeton University Press, 2003.

Dawletschin-Linder, Camilla. *Diener seines Staates: Celal Bayar (1883–1986) und die Entwicklung der modernen Türkei*. Wiesbaden: Harrassowitz, 2003.

Deleon, Jak. *The White Russians in Istanbul*. İstanbul: Remzi Kitapevi, 1995.

Demirel, Fatmagül. *Cumhuriyet Kurulurken Hayaller ve Umutlar*. İstanbul: Bağlam, 2019.

Deringil, Selim. *Turkish Foreign Policy during the Second World War: An "Active" Neutrality*. Cambridge: Cambridge University Press, 1989.

———. *The Well-Protected Domains: Ideology and Legitimation of Power in the Ottoman Empire, 1876–1909*. London: I. B. Tauris, 1999.

Deusch, Engelbert. *Das k.(u.)k. Kultusprotektorat im albanischen Siedlungsgebiet in seinem kulturellen, politischen und wirtschaftlichen Umfeld*. Wien: Böhlau, 2009.

Djemal Pascha, Ahmed. *Erinnerungen eines türkischen Staatsmannes.* Munich: Drei Masken Verlag, 1922.
Dmythryshyn, Basil, and Frederick Cox. *The Soviet Union and the Middle East. A Documentary Record of Afghanistan, Iran and Turkey, 1917–1985.* Princeton, NJ: Kingston Press, 1987.
Dogramaci, Burcu. *Kulturtransfer und nationale Identität: deutschsprachige Architekten, Stadtplaner und Bildhauer in der Türkei nach 1927.* Berlin: Gebr. Mann Verlag, 2008.
Dressler, Markus. "How to Conceptualize Inner-Islamic Plurality and Difference: 'Heterodoxy' and 'Syncretism' in the Writings of Mehmet F. Köprülü (1890–1966)." *British Journal of Middle Eastern Studies* 37, no. 3 (2010): 241–260.
Dumont, Paul. "Freemasonry in Turkey: A By-Product of Western Penetration." *European Review* 13, no. 3 (2005): 481–493.
Dündar, Can. "I Revealed the Truth About President Erdogan and Syria. For That, He Had Me Jailed." *The Guardian*, December 28, 2015. https://www.theguardian.com/commentisfree/2015/dec/28/truth-president-erdogan-jailed-turkey-regime-state-security-crime.
Duru, Bülent. "Mustafa Kemal Döneminde Ankara'nın İmarı." In *İcad Edilmiş Şehir: Ankara*, edited by Funda Şenol Cantek, 107–123. İstanbul: İletişim, 2017.
Ecevit, Bülent. *Atatürk ve Devrimcilik.* İstanbul: Tekin Yayınevi, 1976.
Eldem, Edhem. "Capitulations and Western Trade." In *The Later Ottoman Empire, 1603–1839*, edited by Suraiya N. Faroqhi, 283–335. Vol. 3 of *The Cambridge History of Turkey*. Cambridge: Cambridge University Press, 2006.
Eligür, Banu. *The Mobilization of Political Islam in Turkey.* Cambridge: Cambridge University Press, 2010.
Elsie, Robert. "Der Islam und die Derwischsekten Albaniens. Anmerkungen zu ihrer Geschichte, Verbreitung und zur derzeitigen Lage." *Kakanien Revisited*, May 27, 2004. Accessed March 2, 2023. http://www.kakanien-revisited.at/beitr/fallstudie/RElsie2.pdf.
Epkenhans, Tim. "Geld darf keine Rolle spielen, Teil 1: Einleitung." *Archivum Ottomanicum* 18 (2000): 247–250, and "Geld darf keine Rolle spielen, Teil 2: Das Dokument." *Archivum Ottomanicum* 19 (2001): 121–163.
Erdoğan, Recep Tayyip. *Çanakkale 100. Yıl Barış Zirvesi'nde Yaptıkları Konuşma*, April 23, 2015. Accessed March 2, 2023. https://www.tccb.gov.tr/konusmalar/353/32664/canakkale-100-yil-baris-zirvesinde-yaptiklari-konusma.

———. *İstanbul'un Fethi'nin 562. Yıl Dönümü Kutlamalarında Yaptıkları Konuşma*, May 30, 2015. Accessed March 2, 2023. https://www.tccb.gov.tr/konusmalar/353/32584/istanbulun-fethinin-562-yil-donumu-kutlamalarinda-yaptiklari-konusma.

———. Speech to the 4th Justice and Development Party Ordinary Congress, September 30, 2012. Accessed April 10, 2015. http://www.akparti.org.tr/site/haberler/basbakan-erdoganin-ak-part-4.olagan-buyuk-kongresi-konusmasinin-tam-metni/31771#1.

Ergil, Doğu. *Doğu Sorunu: Teşhisler ve Tespitler: Özel Araştırma Raporu*. Ankara: Türk Odalar ve Borsalar Birliği, 1995.

Erickson, Edward J. *Ordered to Die. A History of the Ottoman Army in the First World War*. Westport, CT: Greenwood, 2001.

———. *Palestine: The Ottoman Campaigns of 1914–1918*. Barnsley: Pen and Sword Military, 2016.

Erman, Tahire. "Becoming 'Urban' or Remaining 'Rural': The Views of Turkish Rural-to-Urban Migrants on the 'Integration' Question." *International Journal of Middle Eastern Studies* 30 (1998): 541–561.

———. "'Liberated Neighborhoods': Reconstructing Leftist Activism in the Urban Periphery." In *Turkey in Turmoil: Social Change and Political Radicalization During the 1960s*, edited by Berna Pekesen, 181–210. Berlin: De Gruyter Oldenbourg, 2020.

Eryılmaz, Bilal. *Osmanlı Devletinde Gayrımüslim Teb'anın Yönetimi*. İstanbul: Risale Yayınları, 1990.

Ess, Josef van. *Im Halbschatten: Der Orientalist Hellmut Ritter (1892–1971)*. Wiesbaden: Harrassowitz, 2013.

———. "Ein Jubiläum zum Jahre 2011: Colmar Freiherr von der Goltz." In *Kleine Schriften*, vol. 3, edited by Hinrich Biesterfeldt, 2262–2287. Leiden: Brill, 2018.

Eßbach, Wolfgang. *Religionssoziologie I: Glaubenskrieg und Revolution als Wiege neuer Religionen*. Paderborn: Wilhelm Fink, 2014.

European Stability Initiative, *Islamische Calvinisten. Umbruch und Konservatismus in Zentralanatolien*. Berlin, İstanbul: European Stability Initiative, 2005. Accessed March 2, 2023. https://www.esiweb.org/pdf/esi_document_id_71.pdf.

———. *Mord in Anatolien. Christliche Missionare und türkischer Ultranationalismus*. Berlin: European Stability Initiative, 2011. Accessed March 2, 2023. https://esiweb.org/publications/mord-anatolien-christliche-missionare-und-turkischer-ultranationalismus.

Fahmy, Khaled. *Mehmed Ali: From Ottoman Governor to Ruler of Egypt*. Oxford: Oneworld, 2009.

Feldman, Noah. *The Fall and Rise of the Islamic State*. Princeton, NJ: Princeton University Press, 2008.

Findley, Carter Vaughn. "The Tanzimat." In *Turkey in the Modern World*, edited by Reşat Kasaba, 11–37. Vol. 4 of *The Cambridge History of Turkey*. Cambridge: Cambridge University Press, 2008.

———. *The Turks in World History*. Oxford: Oxford University Press, 2005.

Finkel, Caroline. *Osman's Dream. The Story of the Ottoman Empire, 1300–1923*. London: John Murray, 2005.

Foster, Zachary. "The 1915 Locust Attack in Syria and Palestine and Its Role in the Famine during the First World War." *Middle Eastern Studies* 51, no. 3 (2015): 370–394.

Fromkin, David. *A Peace to End All Peace. The Fall of the Ottoman Empire and the Creation of the Modern Middle East*. New York, NY: Holt, 1989.

Gall, Carlotta. "Spurning Erdogan's Vision, Turks Leave in Droves, Draining Money and Talent." *New York Times*, January 2, 2019. https://www.nytimes.com/2019/01/02/world/europe/turkey-emigration-erdogan.html?action=clickandmodule=Top%20Storiesandpgtype=Homepage.

Gangloff, Sylvie. "La politique balkanique de la Turquie et le poids du passé ottoman." In *Le nouvel islam balkanique. Les musulmans, acteurs du post-communisme 1990–2000*, edited by Xavier Bougarel and Nathalie Clayer, 317–356. Paris: Maisonneuve and Larose, 2001.

Ganser, Daniele. *NATO-Geheimarmeen in Europa. Inszenierter Terror und verdeckte Kriegsführung*. Zurich: Orell Füssli, 2008.

Gasimov, Zaur. "'The Turkish Wall': Turkey as an Anti-Communist and Anti-Russian Bulwark in the Twentieth Century." In *Rampart Nations. Bulwark Myths of East European Multiconfessional Societies in the Age of Nationalism*, edited by Liliya Berezhnaya and Heidi Hein-Kircher, 186–206. New York, NY: Berghahn Books, 2019.

Gellner, Ernest. *Nations and Nationalism*. 3rd ed. Ithaca, NY: Cornell University Press, 1991.

Gelvin, James. *The New Middle East: What Everyone Needs to Know*. New York, NY: Oxford University Press, 2018.

Gençer, Mustafa. "Die Armenische Frage im Kontext der deutsch-osmanischen Beziehungen (1878–1915)." In *Osmanismus, Nationalismus und der Kaukasus. Muslime und Christen, Türken und Armenier im 19. und 20. Jahrhundert*, edited by Fikret Adanir and Bernd Bonwetsch, 183–202. Wiesbaden: Ludwig Reichert, 2005.

Georgeon, François. "Religion, Politics and Society in the Wake of the Young Turk Revolution: The 'Ramadan of Freedom.'" In *The Young Turk Revolution and the Ottoman Empire. The Aftermath of 1908*, edited by Noémi Lévy-Aksu and François Georgeon, 175–195. London: I. B. Tauris, 2017.

Gerges, Fawaz A. "Introduction. A Rupture." In *The New Middle East: Protest and Revolution in the Arab World*, edited by Fawaz A. Gerges, 1–38. Cambridge: Cambridge University Press, 2014.

———. *ISIS: A History*. Princeton, NJ: Princeton University Press, 2017.

Gerlach, Christian. *Extremely Violent Societies. Mass Violence in the Twentieth-Century World*. Cambridge: Cambridge University Press, 2010.

Ghaplanyan, Irina. *Post-Soviet Armenia: The New National Elite and the New National Narrative*. London: Routledge, 2018.

Gingeras, Ryan. *Heroin, Organized Crime, and the Making of Modern Turkey*. New York, NY: Oxford University Press, 2014.

———. "Last Rites for a 'Pure Bandit': Clandestine Service, Historiography and the Origins of the Turkish 'Deep State.'" *Past and Present* 206 (2010): 151–174.

Ginio, Eyal. *The Ottoman Culture of Defeat and the Shifting of Ottoman Identities: The Balkan Wars and Their Aftermath (1912–1914)*. Oxford: Oxford University Press, 2015.

Gokalp, Altan. "Alevisme nomade: des communautés de statut à l'identité communautaire." In *Ethnic Groups in the Republic of Turkey*, edited by Peter Alford Andrews, 524–537. Wiesbaden: Ludwig Reichert, 2002.

Gökalp, Ziya. *Türkleşmek, İslamlaşmak, Muasırlaşmak*. Edited by Osman Karatay. Ankara: Akçağ, 2010.

Gölbaşı, Edip. "Turning the 'Heretics' into Loyal Muslim Subjects: Imperial Anxieties, the Politics of Religious Conversion and the Yezidis in the Hamidian Era." *The Muslim World* 103, no. 1 (2013): 3–23.

Golden, Peter Benjamin. *An Introduction to the History of the Turkic Peoples. Ethnogenesis and State-Formation in Medieval and Early Modern Eurasia and the Middle East*. Wiesbaden: Harrassowitz, 1992.

Goltz, Generalfeldmarschall Colmar von der. *Denkwürdigkeiten*. Revised and edited by Friedrich Freiherr von der Goltz. Berlin: Mittler, 1929.

Gonlubol, Mehmet. "NATO, USA and Turkey." In *Turkey's Foreign Policy in Transition, 1950–1974*, edited by Kemal Karpat, 13–50. Leiden: Brill, 1975.

Gourisse, Benjamin. *La violence politique en Turquie: L'État en jeu, 1975–1980*. Paris: Éditions Karthala, 2014.

Gran, Peter. *Islamic Roots of Capitalism: Egypt 1760–1840*. Austin, TX: University of Texas Press, 1979.

Greene, Samuel A., and Graeme B. Robertson. *Putin v. the People. The Perilous Politics of a Divided Russia*. New Haven, CT: Yale University Press, 2019.
Gunn, Christopher. "The 1960 Coup in Turkey: A U.S. Intelligence Failure or a Successful 'Intervention'?" *Journal of Cold War Studies* 17, no. 2 (2015): 103–139.
Gürsoy, Yaprak. "The 15 July 2016 Failed Coup and the Security Sector." In *The Routledge Handbook of Turkish Politics*, edited by Alpaslan Özerdem and Matthew Whiting, 284–295. London: Routledge, 2019.
Guzansky, Yoel. "Israel's Periphery Doctrine 2.0: The Mediterranean Plus." *Mediterranean Politics* 19, no. 1 (2014): 99–116.
Haass, Richard N. "The New Thirty Years' War." *Project Syndicate*, July 21, 2014. https://www.project-syndicate.org/commentary/richard-n-haass-argues-that-the-middle-east-is-less-a-problem-to-be-solved-than-a-condition-to-be-managed.
Hagen, Gottfried. "German Heralds of Holy War. Orientalists and Applied Oriental Studies." *Comparative Studies of South Asia, Africa and the Middle East* 24 (2004): 145–162.
Hähnlein, Rayk, Markus Kaim, and Günter Seufert. "Die Türkei verlässt die Nato." In *Während wir planten. Unerwartete Entwicklungen in der internationalen Politik. Foresight-Beiträge*, edited by Lars Brozus, 10–15. Berlin: Stiftung Wissenschaft und Politik, 2018.
Halaçoğlu, Yusuf. *Die Armenierfrage*. Klagenfurt: Wieser Verlag, 2006.
Hale, William. *The Political and Economic Development of Modern Turkey*. London: Croom Helm, 1981.
———. *Turkish Politics and the Military*. London: Routledge, 1994.
Hale, William M., and Ergun Özbudun. *Islamism, Democracy, and Liberalism in Turkey: The Case of the AKP*. London: Routledge, 2010.
Hall, Richard C. *The Balkan Wars 1912–1913: Prelude to the First World War*. London: Routledge, 2000.
Hallaq, Wael. *The Impossible State: Islam, Politics and Modernity's Moral Predicament*. New York, NY: Columbia University Press, 2013.
Halliday, Fred. "Iranian Foreign Policy since 1979: Internationalism and Nationalism in the Islamic Revolution." In *Shi'ism and Social Protest*, edited by Juan Cole and Nikki Keddie, 88–107. New Haven, CT: Yale University Press, 2002.
Hamed-Troyansky, Vladimir. "Circassian Refugees and the Making of Amman, 1878–1914." *International Journal of Middle East Studies* 49 (2017): 605–623.

Hanioğlu, Şükrü. *Atatürk: An Intellectual Biography*. Princeton, NJ: Princeton University Press, 2011.

———. *Preparation for a Revolution: The Young Turks, 1902–1908*. Oxford: Oxford University Press, 2001.

———. "The Second Constitutional Period, 1908–1918." In *Turkey in the Modern World*, edited by Reşat Kasaba, 62–111. Vol. 4 of *The Cambridge History of Turkey*. Cambridge: Cambridge University Press, 2008.

———. *The Young Turks in Opposition*. New York, NY: Oxford University Press, 1995.

Hansen, Suzy. "'The Era of People Like You Is Over': How Turkey Purged Its Intellectuals." *New York Times*, July 24, 2019. https://www.nytimes.com/2019/07/24/magazine/the-era-of-people-like-you-is-over-how-turkey-purged-its-intellectuals.html.

Harris, George S. "Turkey and the United States." In *Turkey's Foreign Policy in Transition, 1950–1974*, edited by Kemal Karpat, 51–72. Leiden: Brill, 1975.

Harris, William. *Quicksilver War: Syria, Iraq and the Spiral of Conflict*. London: Hurst, 2018.

Harvey, David. *A Brief History of Neoliberalism*. New York, NY: Oxford University Press, 2005.

Haselsteiner, Horst. "Zur Haltung der Donaumonarchie in der Orientalischen Frage." In *Der Berliner Kongreß von 1878. Die Politik der Großmächte und die Probleme der Modernisierung in Südosteuropa in der zweiten Hälfte des 19. Jahrhunderts*, edited by Ralph Melville and Hans-Jürgen Schröder, 227–243. Wiesbaden: Steiner, 1982.

Hazar, Numan. "Türkiye Afrika'da: Eylem Planının Uygulanması ve Değerlendirme On Beş Yıl Sonra" *Ortadoğu Analiz* 4, no. 46 (2012): 29–38.

Heinemann-Grüder, Andreas. "Das Ende der Illusionen. Wie weiter mit Russland und der Türkei?" *Osteuropa* 68, nos. 10–12 (2018): 261–270.

Hendrich, Béatrice. "Von Pfeilen, Strahlen und Glühbirnen: Das Emblem der 'Partei für Gerechtigkeit und Entwicklung' (AKP)." In *Festschrift in Honor of Ioannis P. Theocharides*, vol. 2, edited by Evangelia Balta, Georgios Salakidis, and Theoharis Stavrides, 105–121. Istanbul: ISIS, 2014.

Hendrick, Joshua D. *Gülen: The Ambiguous Politics of Market Islam in Turkey and the World*. New York, NY: New York University Press, 2013.

Heper, Metin. *İsmet İnönü. The Making of a Turkish Statesman*. Leiden: Brill, 1998.

Herbert, Ulrich. "Europe in High Modernity. Reflections on a Theory of the 20th Century." *Journal of Modern European History* 5 (2007): 5–21.

———. *Geschichte Deutschlands im 20. Jahrhundert*. Munich: C. H. Beck, 2014.

Hering, Gunnar. "Die Osmanenzeit im Selbstverständnis der Völker Südosteuropas." In *Die Staaten Südosteuropas und die Osmanen*, edited by Hans Georg Majer, 355–380. Munich: Südosteuropa-Gesellschaft, 1989.

Hermann, Rainer. "Säbelrasseln im Mittelmeer." *Frankfurter Allgemeine Zeitung*, July 23, 2020. https://www.faz.net/aktuell/politik/ausland/griechisch-tuerkischer-konflikt-saebelrasseln-im-mittelmeer-16872333.html.

———. *Wohin geht die türkische Gesellschaft? Kulturkampf in der Türkei*. Munich: dtv, 2008.

Herr, Hansjörg, and Zeynep M. Sonat. "The Fragile Growth Regime of Turkey in the Post-2001 Period." *New Perspectives on Turkey* 51 (2014): 35–68.

Herzog, Christoph. "Small and Large Scale Conspiracy Theories and Their Problems: An Example from Turkey." In *Conspiracy Theories in the United States and the Middle East. A Comparative Approach*, edited by Michael Butter and Maurus Reinkowski, 194–211. Berlin: De Gruyter, 2014.

Heydemann, Steven, and Reinoud Leenders. "Authoritarian Learning and Counterrevolution." In *The Arab Uprisings Explained. New Contentious Politics in the Middle East*, edited by Marc Lynch, 75–92. New York, NY: Columbia University Press, 2014.

Hillebrecht, Sabine. *Haymatloz. Exil in der Türkei 1933–1945*. Berlin: Verein Aktives Museum, 2000.

Hillman, Jonathan E. *The Emperor's New Road. China and the Project of the Century*. New Haven, CT: Yale University Press, 2020.

Hirsch, Ernst E. *Aus des Kaisers Zeiten durch die Weimarer Republik in das Land Atatürks. Eine unzeitgemäße Autobiographie*. Munich: Schweitzer Verlag, 1982.

———. *Die Verfassung der Türkischen Republik*. Frankfurt a. M., Berlin: Alfred Metzner, 1966.

Hirschler, Konrad. "Defining the Nation: Kurdish Historiography in Turkey in the 1990s." *Middle Eastern Studies* 37, no. 3 (2001): 145–166.

Hobsbawm, Eric J. *Das imperiale Zeitalter 1875–1914*. Frankfurt a. M.: Campus, 1989.

Hoerder, Dirk. *Cultures in Contact: World Migrations in the Second Millenium*. Durham, NC: Duke University Press, 2002.

Hoffmann, Stanley, and Inge Hoffmann. "The Will to Grandeur: De Gaulle as Political Artist." In *Decline or Renewal? France since the 1930s*, edited by Stanley Hoffmann, 202–253. New York, NY: Viking, 1974.

Höpken, Wolfgang. "Türkische Minderheiten in Südosteuropa. Aspekte ihrer politischen und sozialen Entwicklung in Bulgarien und Jugoslawien." In *Die Staaten Südosteuropas und die Osmanen*, edited by Hans Georg Majer, 223–254. Munich: Südosteuropa-Gesellschaft, 1989.

———. "Zwischen Kulturkonflikt und Repression. Die türkische Minderheit in Bulgarien 1944–1991." In *Nationen, Nationalitäten, Minderheiten: Probleme des Nationalismus in Jugoslawien, Ungarn, Rumänien, der Tschechoslowakei, Bulgarien, Polen, der Ukraine, Italien und Österreich 1945–1990*, edited by Valeria Heuberger, Othmar Kolar, and Arnold Suppan, 179–202. Munich: Oldenbourg, 1994.

Hosfeld, Rolf. *Operation Nemesis: Die Türkei, Deutschland und der Völkermord an den Armeniern*. Cologne: Kiepenheuer and Witsch, 2005.

Hurewitz, Jacob C. *Diplomacy in the Near and Middle East. A Documentary Record, 1535–1956*. 2 vols. New York, NY: Van Nostrand, 1956.

Hütteroth, Wolf-Dieter. *Türkei*. Darmstadt: Wissenschaftliche Buchgesellschaft, 1982.

İçduygu, Ahmet. "Demography and Immigration and Emigration." In *The Routledge Handbook of Modern Turkey*, edited by Metin Heper and Sabri Sayarı, 328–337. New York, NY: Routledge, 2012.

Ihrig, Stefan. *Justifying Genocide: Germany and the Armenians from Bismarck to Hitler*. Cambridge, MA: Harvard University Press, 2016.

İmanbeyli, Vügar. "'Failed Exodus': Dugin's Network in Turkey." In *Eurasianism and the European Far Right: Reshaping the Europe-Russia Relationship*, edited by Marlene Laruelle, 145–174. Lanham, MD et al.: Lexington Books, 2015.

International Crisis Group. *Aphrodite's Gift: Can Cypriot Gas Power a New Dialogue?* Europe Report 216, April 2, 2012. Accessed March 2, 2023. https://www.crisisgroup.org/europe-central-asia/western-europemediterranean/cyprus/aphrodite-s-gift-can-cypriot-gas-power-new-dialogue.

———. *The Human Cost of the PKK Conflict in Turkey: The Case of Sur*, Crisis Group Europe Briefing 80, 17 March 2016. Accessed March 2, 2023. https://www.crisisgroup.org/europe-central-asia/western-europemediterranean/turkey/human-cost-pkk-conflict-turkey-case-sur.

———. *Marching in Circles: Egypt's Dangerous Second Transition*, Policy Briefing Middle East and North Africa Briefing 35, August 7, 2013. Accessed March 2,

2023. https://www.crisisgroup.org/middle-east-north-africa/north-africa/ egypt/marching-circles-egypt-s-dangerous-second-transition.

———. *Mitigating Risks for Syrian Refugee Youth in Turkey's Şanlıurfa*, Europe Report 253, February 11, 2019. Accessed March 2, 2023. https://www. crisisgroup.org/europe-central-asia/western-europemediterranean/ turkey/253-mitigating-risks-syrian-refugee-youth-turkeys-sanliurfa.

———. *The Next Iraqi War? Sectarianism and Civil Conflict*, Middle East Report 52, February 27, 2006. Accessed April 12, 2023. https://www.crisisgroup.org/middle-east-north-africa/gulf-and-arabian-peninsula/iraq/ next-iraqi-war-sectarianism-and-civil-conflict.

———. *Popular Protest in North Africa and the Middle East (I): Egypt Victorious?* Middle East and North Africa Report 101, February 24, 2011. Accessed March 2, 2023. https://www.crisisgroup.org/middle-east-north-africa/north-africa/egypt/ popular-protest-north-africa-and-middle-east-i-egypt-victorious.

———. *Russia and Turkey in the Black Sea and the South Caucasus*, Europe Report 250, June 28, 2018. Accessed March 2, 2023. https://www. crisisgroup.org/europe-central-asia/western-europemediterranean/ turkey/250-russia-and-turkey-black-sea-and-south-caucasus.

———. *Turkey and Iran: Bitter Friends, Bosom Rivals*, Crisis Group Middle East Briefing 51, December 13, 2016. Accessed March 2, 2023. https://www. crisisgroup.org/middle-east-north-africa/gulf-and-arabian-peninsula/ iran/b051-turkey-and-iran-bitter-friends-bosom-rivals.

———. *Turkey's Kurdish Impasse: The View from Diyarbakir*, Europe Report 222, November 30, 2012. Accessed March 2, 2023. https://www.crisisgroup.org/europe-central-asia/western-europemediterranean/turkey/ turkey-s-kurdish-impasse-view-diyarbakir.

Jäschke, Gotthard. "Ismet Inönü." *Zeitschrift für Politik* 32, no. 1 (1942): 1–5.

———. "Die Türkei seit dem Weltkriege II. Türkischer Geschichtskalender für 1929 mit neuem Nachtrag zu 1918–1928." *Die Welt des Islams* 12, no. 1/2 (1930): 1–50.

———. "Die Türkei seit dem Weltkriege III. Türkischer Geschichtskalender für 1930." *Die Welt des Islams* 12, no. 4 (1931): 137–166.

———. "Die Türkei seit dem Weltkriege IV. Türkischer Geschichtskalender für 1931–1932." *Die Welt des Islams* 15, no. 1/2 (1933): 1–33.

———. "Die Türkei in den Jahren 1933 und 1934 – Geschichtskalender." *Mitteilungen des Seminars für Orientalische Sprachen zu Berlin* 38 (1935): 105–142.

Jäschke, Gotthard, and Erich Pritsch. "Die Türkei seit dem Weltkriege. Geschichtskalender 1918–1928." *Die Welt des Islams* 10 (1927–1929): 1–154. (Also appeared in book form as *Die Türkei seit dem Weltkriege. Geschichtskalender 1918–1928*. Berlin: Deutsche Gesellschaft für Islamkunde, 1929.)

Jenkins, Gareth. *Between Fact and Fantasy: Turkey's Ergenekon Investigation*. Washington, DC: Central Asia—Caucasus Institute and Silk Road Studies Program, 2009. Accessed March 2, 2023. http://www.silkroad-studies.org/resources/pdf/SilkRoadPapers/2009_08_SRP_Jenkins_Turkey-Ergenekon.pdf.

———. *Context and Circumstance. The Turkish Military and Politics*. Oxford: Oxford University Press, 2001.

———. *Political Islam in Turkey: Running West, Heading East?* New York, NY: Palgrave Macmillan, 2008.

Johanson, Lars, and Éva Ágnes Csató, eds. *The Turkic Languages*. London: Routledge, 1998.

Judt, Tony. *Postwar. A History of Europe since 1945*. London: Vintage Books, 2010.

Kabis, Veronika. "Interview mit Emmanuel Todd." *Die Tageszeitung*, August 19, 2002.

Kafadar, Cemal. *Between Two Worlds: The Construction of the Ottoman State*. Berkeley: University of California Press, 1995.

Kaiser, Hilmar. "Die deutsche Diplomatie und der armenische Völkermord." In *Osmanismus, Nationalismus und der Kaukasus. Muslime und Christen, Türken und Armenier im 19. und 20. Jahrhundert*, edited by Fikret Adanir and Bernd Bonwetsch, 203–235. Wiesbaden: Ludwig Reichert, 2005.

Kaplan, Robert D. *The Return of Marco Polo's World: War, Strategy, and American Interests*. New York, NY: Random House, 2018.

Kaplan, Sam. "Din-u Devlet All over Again? The Politics of Military Secularism and Religious Militarism in Turkey Following the 1980 Coup." *International Journal of Middle East Studies* 34, no. 1 (2002): 113–127.

Karpat, Kemal H. "Introduction: Turks Remember Their Ottoman Ancestors." In *Ottoman Past and Today's Turkey*, edited by Kemal Karpat, vii–xxii. Leiden: Brill, 2000.

———. *The Gecekondu: Rural Migration and Urbanization*. Cambridge: Cambridge University Press, 1976.

———. *Ottoman Population 1830–1914. Demographic and Social Characteristics*. Madison, WI: University of Wisconsin Press, 1984.

———. *Turkey's Politics: The Transition to a Multi-Party System*. Princeton, NJ: Princeton University Press, 1959.

———. "Turkish Soviet Relations." In *Turkey's Foreign Policy in Transition, 1950–1974*, edited by Kemal H. Karpat, 73–107. Leiden: Brill, 1975.

———. "The Transformation of the Ottoman State, 1789–1908." *International Journal of Middle East Studies* 3 (1972): 243–281.

Kaya, Murat. "Western Interventions and Formation of the Young Turks' Siege Mentality." *Middle East Critique* 23, no. 2 (2014): 127–145.

Kaya, Zeynep, and Robert Lowe. "The Curious Question of the PYD-PKK Relationship." In *The Kurdish Question Revisited*, edited by Gareth Stansfield and Mohammed Shareef, 275–287. New York, NY: Oxford University Press, 2017.

Keddie, Nikki R. *Modern Iran: Roots and Results of Revolution*. New Haven, CT: Yale University Press, 2006.

Kehl-Bodrogi, Krisztina. "Das Alevitentum in der Türkei: Zur Genese und gegenwärtigen Lage einer Glaubensgemeinschaft." In *Ethnic Groups in the Republic of Turkey*, edited by Peter Alford Andrews, 503–510. Wiesbaden: Ludwig Reichert, 2002.

Kelek, Necla. *Die fremde Braut. Ein Bericht aus dem Inneren des türkischen Lebens in Deutschland*. 4th ed. Cologne: Kiepenheuer und Witsch, 2005.

Kentel, Ferhat. "Les Balkans et la crise de l'identité nationale turque." In *Le nouvel islam balkanique. Les musulmans, acteurs du post-communisme 1990–2000*, edited by Xavier Bougarel and Nathalie Clayer, 357–395. Paris: Maisonneuve and Larose, 2001.

Ker-Lindsay, James. *The Cyprus Problem. What Everyone Needs to Know*. New York, NY: Oxford University Press, 2011.

Kévorkian, Raymond. *Le génocide des Arméniens*. Paris: Jacob, 2006.

Keyder, Çağlar. "The Consequences of the Exchange of Populations for Turkey." In *Crossing the Aegean. An Appraisal of the 1923 Compulsory Population Exchange Between Greece and Turkey*, edited by Renée Hirschon, 39–52. New York, NY: Berghahn Books, 2003.

———. "Social Change and Political Mobilization in the 1960s." In *Turkey in Turmoil. Social Change and Political Radicalization During the 1960s*, edited by Berna Pekesen, 12–28. Berlin: De Gruyter Oldenbourg, 2020.

———. *State and Class in Turkey: A Study in Capitalist Development*. London: Verso, 1987.

Khalidi, Rashid Ismail. "The Economic Partition of the Arab Provinces of the Ottoman Empire before the First World War." *Review. A Journal of the*

Fernand Braudel Center for the Study of Economies, Historical Systems and Civilizations 11, no. 2 (1988): 251–264.

Kieser, Hans-Lukas. *Talaat Pasha: Father of Modern Turkey, Architect of Genocide*. Princeton, NJ: Princeton University Press, 2018.

Kieser, Hans-Lukas, Kerem Öktem, and Maurus Reinkowski. "Introduction. World War I and the End of the Ottoman World. From the Balkan Wars to the Armenian Genocide." In *World War I and the End of the Ottomans: From the Balkan Wars to the Armenian Genocide*, edited by Hans-Lukas Kieser, Kerem Öktem, and Maurus Reinkowski, 1–26. London: I. B. Tauris, 2015.

Kılıçdaroğlu, Kemal. "Hükümet darbeyi biliyordu, çocuk kandırmasınlar." *Birgün*, January 14, 2017. https://birgun.net/haber-detay/kilicdarolgu-hukumet-darbeyi-biliyordu-cocuk-kandirmasinlar-143086.html.

Kimminich, Otto. *Einführung in das Völkerrecht*. 5th ed. Tübingen: Francke, 1993.

Kirchick, James. "Order from Chaos: Is Hungary Becoming a Rogue State in the Center of Europe?" Brookings Institution, January 7, 2019. Accessed March 2, 2023. https://www.brookings.edu/blog/order-from-chaos/2019/01/07/is-hungary-becoming-a-rogue-state-in-the-center-of-europe/.

Kirişçi, Kemal. *Turkey and the West: Faultlines in a Troubled Alliance*. Washington: Brookings Institution Press, 2017.

Kisilowski, Maciej. "Poland. Authoritarian, Not Patriotic: Jarosław Kaczyński Is Building a State Apparatus that Will Do Whatever It Takes to Protect the Regime." *Politico*, November 28, 2017. https://www.politico.eu/article/poland-far-right-fascist-not-patriotic/.

Klein, Janet. *The Margins of Empire. Kurdish Militias in the Ottoman Tribal Zone*. Stanford, CA: Stanford University Press, 2011.

Koçak, Cemil. "Türk Milliyetçiliğinin İslam'la Buluşması Büyük Doğu." In *Milliyetçilik*, edited by Murat Belge and Tanıl Bora, 601–613. Vol. 4 of *Modern Türkiye'de Siyasi Düşünce*. 4th ed. İstanbul: İletişim, 2009.

———. *Türkiye'de Millî Şef Dönemi (1938–1945): Dönemin İç ve Dış Politikası Üzerine Bir Araştırma*. 5th ed. İstanbul: İletişim, 2010.

Köker, İrem. "Eyalet sistemi: Evren, Özal, İnönü ve Erdoğan ne Demişti?" BBC News Türkçe, April 14, 2017. https://www.bbc.com/turkce/haberler-turkiye-39599042.

Konuk, Kader. *East West Mimesis: Auerbach in Turkey*. Stanford, CA: Stanford University Press, 2010.

Koopmans, Ruud. *Das verfallene Haus des Islam. Die religiösen Ursachen von Unfreiheit, Stagnation und Gewalt.* Munich: C. H. Beck, 2020.
Kramer, Heinz, and Maurus Reinkowski. *Die Türkei und Europa. Eine wechselhafte Beziehungsgeschichte.* Stuttgart: Kohlhammer, 2008.
Krastev, Ivan, and Stephen Holmes. *The Light That Failed. A Reckoning.* London: Allen Lane, 2019.
Kreiser, Klaus. *Atatürk. Eine Biographie.* Munich: C. H. Beck, 2008.
———. "Gotthard Jäschke (1894–1983): Von der Islamkunde zur Auslandswissenschaft." *Die Welt des Islams* 38, no. 3 (1998): 406–423.
———. "Über den 'Kernraum' des Osmanischen Reiches." In *Die Türkei in Europa*, edited by Klaus-Detlev Grothusen, 53–63. Göttingen: Vandenhoeck and Ruprecht, 1979.
———. "Das Werk einer verrückten Periode." *Süddeutsche Zeitung*, July 24, 2020.
Kreiser, Klaus and Christoph K. Neumann. *Kleine Geschichte der Türkei.* 2nd ed. Stuttgart: Philipp Reclam, 2009.
Kriss, Rudolf, and Hubert Kriss-Heinrich. *Volksglaube im Bereich des Islams.* 2 vols. Wiesbaden: Harrassowitz, 1960, 1962.
Kuneralp, Sinan, and Gül Tokay, eds. *Ottoman Diplomatic Documents on the Origins of World War One.* Vol. 7, *The Balkan Wars: 1912–1913.* İstanbul: İsis Press, 2012.
Kuniholm, Bruce R. "Turkey and NATO." In *NATO and the Mediterranean*, edited by Lawrence S. Kaplan, Robert W. Clawson, and Raimondo Luraghi, 215–237. Wilmington, DE: Scholarly Resources, 1985.
Kürkçü, Ertuğrul. "Türkiye Sosyalist Hareketine Silahlı Mücadelenin Girişi." In *Modern Türkiye'de Siyasi Düşünce*, edited by Murat Gültekingil, 494–516. İstanbul: İletişim, 2007.
Kürkçüoğlu, Ömer. *Osmanlı Devleti'ne Karşı Arap Bağımsızlık Hareketi, 1908–1916.* Ankara: Ankara Üniversitesi Siyasal Bilgiler Fakültesi, 1982.
Lack, Katharina. "Die Lage in den kurdischen Gebieten Syriens: Politische Akteure und ihre Entwicklung seit 2011." In *Die Kurden im Irak und in Syrien nach dem Ende der Territorialherrschaft des 'Islamischen Staates': Die Grenzen kurdischer Politik*, edited by Günter Seufert, 58–78. Berlin: Stiftung Wissenschaft und Politik, 2018.
Landau, Jacob. *Pan-Turkism. From Irredentism to Cooperation.* Bloomington, IN: Indiana University Press, 1995.
———. *Radical Politics in Modern Turkey.* Leiden: Brill, 1974.
Laponce, Jean A. *Left and Right. The Topography of Political Perceptions.* Toronto: University of Toronto Press, 1981.

Laut, Jens Peter. *Das Türkische als Ursprache? Sprachwissenschaftliche Theorien in der Zeit des erwachenden türkischen Nationalismus*. Wiesbaden: Harrassowitz, 2000.

Lawson, Greg R. "A Thirty Years' War in the Middle East." *The National Interest*, April 16, 2014. http://nationalinterest.org/feature/thirty-years-war-the-middle-east-10266.

Leffler, Melvyn P., and Odd Arne Westad, eds. *The Cambridge History of the Cold War*. 3 vols. Cambridge: Cambridge University Press, 2010.

Leggewie, Claus, ed. *Die Türkei und Europa. Die Positionen*. Frankfurt a. M.: Suhrkamp, 2004.

Leonhard, Jörn. *Der überforderte Frieden: Versailles und die Welt 1918–1923*. Munich: C. H. Beck, 2018.

Lesch, David W. *1979: The Year That Shaped the Modern Middle East*. Boulder, CO: Westview Press, 2001.

Lewis, Bernard. *The Emergence of Modern Turkey*. 2nd ed. New York, NY: Oxford University Press, 1968.

———. *The Muslim Discovery of Europe*. London: Phoenix, 2000.

———. *What Went Wrong? The Clash between Islam and Modernity in the Middle East*. New York, NY: Perennial, 2002.

Lewis, David G. "Geopolitical Imaginaries in Russian Foreign Policy: The Evolution of 'Greater Eurasia.'" *Europe-Asia Studies* 70, no. 10 (2018): 1612–1637.

Lewis, Geoffrey. *The Turkish Language Reform: A Catastrophic Success*. New York, NY: Oxford University Press, 1999.

Lier, Thomas. "Hellmut Ritter in Istanbul 1926–1949." *Die Welt des Islams* 38, no. 3 (1998): 334–385.

Lijphart, Arend. *Democracy in Plural Societies. A Comparative Exploration*. New Haven, CT: Yale University Press, 1977.

Lord, Ceren. *Religious Politics in Turkey: From the Birth of the Republic to the AKP*. Cambridge: Cambridge University Press, 2019.

Lüdke, Tilman. *Jihad Made in Germany. Ottoman and German Propaganda and Intelligence Operations in the First World War*. Münster: Lit, 2005.

MacMillan, Margaret. *Paris 1919. Six Months That Changed the World*. New York, NY: Random House, 2001.

Makdisi, Ussama. *The Culture of Sectarianism. Community, History, and Violence in Nineteenth-Century Ottoman Lebanon*. Berkeley, CA: University of California Press, 2000.

Mallinson, William. *Cyprus: A Modern History*. London: I. B. Tauris, 2005.

Mango, Andrew. *Atatürk*. London: John Murray, 1999.
Marashi, Afshin. "Performing the Nation: The Shah's Official State Visit to Kemalist Turkey, June to July 1934." In *The Making of Modern Iran. State and Society under Riza Shah 1921–1941*, edited by Stephanie Cronin, 99–119. New York, NY: Routledge, 2003.
Marcus, Aliza. *Blood and Belief. The PKK and the Kurdish Fight for Independence*. New York, NY: New York University Press, 2007.
Mardin, Şerif. *The Genesis of Young Ottoman Thought: A Study in the Modernization of Turkish Political Ideas*. Princeton, NJ: Princeton University Press, 1962.
———. *Religion and Social Change in Modern Turkey: The Cause of Bediüzzaman Said Nursi*. New York, NY: State University of New York Press, 1989.
———. "Turkish Islamic Exceptionalism Yesterday and Today: Continuity, Rupture and Reconstruction in Operational Codes." *Turkish Studies* 6, no. 2 (2005): 145–165.
———. "Youth and Violence in Turkey." *European Journal of Sociology* 19, no. 2 (1978): 229–254.
Massicard, Elise. "Alevis in the 1960s. From Mobility to Mobilization." In *Turkey in Turmoil: Social Change and Political Radicalization During the 1960s*, edited by Berna Pekesen, 49–62. Berlin: De Gruyter Oldenbourg, 2020.
———. *The Alevis in Turkey and Europe. Identity and the Managing of Territorial Diversity*. London, New York, NY: Routledge, 2013.
Marshall, Monty G., and Benjamin R. Cole. *Global Report 2009: Conflict, Governance, and State Fragility*. George Mason University: Center for Systemic Peace, 2009. Accessed March 2, 2023. http://www.systemicpeace.org/vlibrary/GlobalReport2009.pdf.
Marshall, Monty G., and Gabrielle Elzinga-Marshall. *Global Report 2017: Conflict, Governance, and State Fragility*. Vienna, Va.: Center for Systemic Peace, 2017. Accessed March 2, 2023. http://www.systemicpeace.org/vlibrary/GlobalReport2017.pdf.
Mazower, Mark. *Salonica. City of Ghosts: Christians, Muslims and Jews 1430–1950*. London: Harper Perennial, 2005.
McCarthy, Justin. *Death and Exile: The Ethnic Cleansing of Ottoman Muslims, 1821–1922*. Princeton, NJ: The Darwin Press, 1995.
———. *Muslims and Minorities. The Population of Ottoman Anatolia and the End of the Empire*. New York, NY: New York University Press, 1983.

McDowall, David. *A Modern History of the Kurds*. 3rd ed. London, New York, NY: I. B. Tauris, 2004.

McMeekin, Sean. *The Berlin-Baghdad Express: The Ottoman Empire and Germany's Bid for World Power, 1898–1918*. London: Allen Lane, 2010.

Mello, Brian. "Radicalization and/or Reformism in Working-Class Politics." In *Turkey in Turmoil. Social Change and Political Radicalization During the 1960s*, edited by Berna Pekesen, 93–111. Berlin: De Gruyter Oldenbourg, 2020.

Miller, David. *Strangers in Our Midst: The Political Philosophy of Migration*. Cambridge, MA: Harvard University Press, 2016.

Milton, Patrick, Michael Axworthy, and Brendan Simms. *Towards a Westphalia for the Middle East*. London: Hurst, 2018.

Moltke, Helmuth von. *Unter dem Halbmond. Erlebnisse in der alten Türkei 1835–1839*. Tübingen, Basel: Erdmann, 1979.

Mommsen, Wolfgang. *Imperialismus in Ägypten. Der Aufstieg der ägyptischen nationalen Bewegung 1805–1956*. Munich: Oldenbourg, 1961.

Morris, Benny, and Dror Ze'evi. *The Thirty-Year Genocide. Turkey's Destruction of Its Christian Minorities, 1894–1924*. Cambridge, MA: Harvard University Press, 2019.

Mudde, Cas, and Cristóbal Rovira Kaltwasser. *Populism: A Very Short Introduction*. New York, NY: Oxford University Press, 2017.

Mumay, Bülent. "Schuldlos verschuldet und unglücklich. Mehr als die Hälfte der jungen Türken will ihr Heimatland für immer verlassen." *Frankfurter Allgemeine Zeitung*, September 11, 2020. https://www.faz.net/aktuell/feuilleton/brief-aus-istanbul/brief-aus-istanbul-viele-junge-tuerken-wollen-das-land-verlassen-16947226-p2.html.

Mumcu, Uğur. *Papa – Mafya – Ağca*. 3rd ed. İstanbul: Tekin, 1984.

Münkler, Herfried. *Der Dreißigjährige Krieg. Europäische Katastrophe, deutsches Trauma 1618–1648*. Berlin: Rowohlt, 2017.

Mutlu, Servet. "The Economic Cost of Civil Conflict in Turkey." *Middle Eastern Studies* 47, no. 1 (2011): 63–80.

Nafi, Basheer M. "The Abolition of the Caliphate in Historical Context." In *Demystifying the Caliphate. Historical Memory and Contemporary Contexts*, edited by Madawi Al-Rasheed, Carool Kersten, and Marat Shterin, 31–56. London: Hurst, 2013.

Nestmann, L. "Die ethnische Differenzierung der Bevölkerung der Osttürkei in ihren sozialen Bezügen." In *Ethnic Groups in the Republic of Turkey*, edited by Peter Alford Andrews, 543–581. Wiesbaden: Ludwig Reichert, 2002.

Nicolai, Bernd. *Moderne und Exil: Deutschsprachige Architekten in der Türkei 1925–1955*. Berlin: Verlag für Bauwesen, 1998.
Nökel, Sigrid. *Die Töchter der Gastarbeiter und der Islam. Zur Soziologie alltagsweltlicher Anerkennungspolitiken: Eine Fallstudie*. Bielefeld: transcript, 2002.
Nur, Rıza. *Hayat ve Hatıratım*. 4 vols. İstanbul: Altındağ Yayınevi, 1967, 1968.
Öke, Mim Kemal. *Ermeni Meselesi 1914–1923*. İstanbul: Aydınlar Ocağı Yayınları, 1986.
Öktem, Kerem. *New Islamic Actors after the Wahhabi Intermezzo. Turkey's Return to the Muslim Balkans*. Oxford: European Studies Centre, 2010. Accessed March 2, 2023. https://www.academia.edu/1220435/New_Islamic_actors_after_the_Wahhabi_intermezzo_Turkeys_return_to_the_Muslim_Balkans.
———. *Turkey since 1989. Angry Nation*. London: Zed Books, 2011.
———. "Türkisches Zwischenspiel im Nahen Osten. Neo-imperialer Islamismus und die AKP zwischen Farce und Tragödie." *Leviathan. Berliner Zeitschrift für Sozialwissenschaft* 31 (2017): 134–152.
Önder, Zehra. *Die türkische Außenpolitik im Zweiten Weltkrieg*. Munich: Oldenbourg, 1977.
Oran, Baskın. "The Peace Treaty of Lausanne." In *Turkish Foreign Policy, 1919–2006. Facts and Analyses with Documents*, edited by Baskın Oran, 126–140. Salt Lake City, UT: University of Utah Press, 2010,
———. "The Peace Treaty of Sèvres." In *Turkish Foreign Policy, 1919–2006. Facts and Analyses with Documents*, edited by Baskın Oran, 63–77. Salt Lake City, UT: University of Utah Press, 2010.
Örmeci, Ozan. *Portrait of a Turkish Social Democrat: İsmail Cem*. 2nd ed. İstanbul: Libra Yayınları, 2020.
Ortaylı, İlber. *İmparatorluğunun En Uzun Yüzyılı*. İstanbul: Hil Yayını, 1983.
Osterhammel, Jürgen. *Die Flughöhe der Adler. Historische Essays zur globalen Gegenwart*. Munich: C. H. Beck, 2017.
Owen, Roger. "The Role of the Army in Middle Eastern Politics—A Critique of Existing Analysis." *Review of Middle East Studies* 3 (1978): 63–81.
Owen, Roger, and Şevket Pamuk. *A History of Middle East Economies in the Twentieth Century*. London: I. B. Tauris, 1998.
Özbek, Batıray. "Tscherkessen in der Türkei." In *Ethnic Groups in the Republic of Turkey*, edited by Peter Alford Andrews, 581–590. Wiesbaden: Ludwig Reichert, 2002.
Özbudun, Ergun. *The Constitutional System of Turkey: 1876 to the Present*. Basingstoke: Palgrave Macmillan, 2011.

Özel, Soli. "A Moment of Elation: The Gezi Protests/Resistance and the Fading of the AKP Project." In *The Making of a Protest Movement in Turkey: #occupygezi*, edited by Umut Özkırımlı, 7–24. Basingstoke: Palgrave Macmillan, 2014.

Özersay, Kudret. "The Montreux Straits Convention." In *Turkish Foreign Policy, 1919–2006. Facts and Analyses with Documents*, edited by Baskın Oran, 224–232. Salt Lake City, UT: University of Utah Press, 2010

Öztan, Ramazan Hakkı. "Point of No Return? Prospects of Empire after the Ottoman Defeat in the Balkan Wars (1912–1913)." *International Journal of Middle East Studies* 50, no. 1 (2018): 65–84.

Özyürek, Esra. "Commemorating the Coup in Turkey." *Jadaliyya*, August 18, 2016. https://www.jadaliyya.com/Details/33489/Commemorating-the-Failed-Coup-in-Turkey.

Pabst, Volker. " In Kars verschwimmen die Grenzen zwischen politischen, ethnischen und kriminellen Machtkämpfen." *Neue Zürcher Zeitung*, February 10, 2021. https://www.nzz.ch/international/tuerkei-im-konflikt-mit-den-kurden-mischt-auch-die-mafia-mit-ld.1598661.

Pamuk, Şevket. "Economic Change in Twentieth-Century Turkey: Is the Glass More Than Half Full?" In *Turkey in the Modern World*, edited by Reşat Kasaba, 266–300. Vol. 4 of *The Cambridge History of Turkey*. Cambridge: Cambridge University Press, 2008.

Parla, Ayşe. *Precarious Hope: Migration and the Limits of Belonging in Turkey*. Stanford, CA: Stanford University Press, 2019.

Patel, Kiran Klaus. *Projekt Europa. Eine kritische Geschichte*. Munich: C. H. Beck, 2018.

Paul, Axel T. "Arabellion. Vom Aufbruch zum Zerfall einer Region? Revolutionstheoretische Überlegungen." *Leviathan. Berliner Zeitschrift für Sozialwissenschaft* 31 (2017): 13–43.

Pekesen, Berna. *Nationalismus, Türkisierung und das Ende der jüdischen Gemeinden in Thrakien, 1918–1942*. Munich: Oldenbourg, 2012.

———, ed. *Turkey in Turmoil: Social Change and Political Radicalization During the 1960s*. Berlin: De Gruyter Oldenbourg, 2020.

Phillips, Christopher. "Eyes Bigger Than Stomachs: Turkey, Saudi Arabia and Qatar in Syria." *Middle East Policy* 24, no. 1 (2017): 36–47.

Picard, Elizabeth. "The Arab Military in Politics: From Revolutionary Plot to Authoritarian Regime." In *The Arab State*, edited by Giacomo Luciani, 189–219. London: Routledge, 1990.

Pink, Johanna. *Geschichte Ägyptens: Von der Spätantike bis zur Gegenwart*. Munich: C. H. Beck, 2014.

Pirjevec, Jože. *Tito: Die Biografie*. Munich: Kunstmann, 2016.
Plaggenborg, Stefan. *Ordnung und Gewalt. Kemalismus – Faschismus – Sozialismus*. Munich: Oldenbourg, 2012.
Pomiankowski, Joseph. *Der Zusammenbruch des Ottomanischen Reiches: Erinnerungen an die Türkei aus der Zeit des Weltkrieges*. Zürich: Amalthea-Verlag, 1928.
Power, Samantha. *A Problem from Hell. America and the Age of Genocide*. New York, NY: Basic Books, 2002.
Procházka, Stephan. *Die arabischen Dialekte der Çukurova (Südtürkei)*. Wiesbaden: Harrassowitz, 2002.
Procházka-Eisl, Gisela, and Stephan Procházka. *The Plain of Saints and Prophets: The Nusayri-Alawi Community of Cilicia (Southern Turkey) and Its Sacred Places*. Wiesbaden: Harrassowitz Verlag, 2010.
Provence, Michael. *The Last Ottoman Generation and the Making of the Modern Middle East*. Cambridge: Cambridge University Press, 2017.
Rafeq, Abdul-Karim. "The Arab States and the Ottoman Heritage." In *Die Staaten Südosteuropas und die Osmanen*, edited by Hans Georg Majer, 333–353. Munich: Südosteuropa-Gesellschaft, 1989.
Ramm, Christoph. "Die Türkei und ihre Politik der 'strategischen Tiefe.' Abkehr vom Westen, neuer Osmanismus oder nationale Großmachtphantasie?" In *Die Zukunft arabisch-türkischer Beziehungen. Nationales Interesse, nicht Religion als Basis der Kooperation*, edited by Sigrid Faath, 51–63. Baden-Baden: Nomos, 2011.
Reichmuth, Stefan. "Der Erste Weltkrieg und die muslimischen Republiken der Nachkriegszeit." *Geschichte und Gesellschaft* 40 (2014): 184–213.
Reilly, James A. *Fragile Nation, Shattered Land. The Modern History of Syria*. London: I. B. Tauris, 2019.
Reinkowski, Maurus. "Ein neuer Naher Osten? Zur realen Krise eines epistemischen Systems." *Leviathan. Berliner Zeitschrift für Sozialwissenschaft* 31 (2017): 95–113.
Richter, Heinz A. *Geschichte der Insel Zypern*. 4 vols. Mainz: Franz Philipp Rutzen, 2004–2009.
Roberts, John. "Hydrocarbon Resources in the Eastern Mediterranean: An Energy Perspective." *Südosteuropa Mitteilungen* 60, no. 6 (2020): 63–82.
Robinson, Richard D. *The First Turkish Republic. A Case Study in National Development*. Cambridge, MA: Harvard University Press, 1963.
Rodogno, Davide. *Against Massacre: Humanitarian Interventions in the Ottoman Empire, 1815–1914*. Princeton, NJ: Princeton University Press, 2012.

Rodrik, Dani. "Ergenekon and Sledgehammer: Building or Undermining the Rule of Law?" *Turkish Policy Quarterly* 10, no. 1 (2011): 99–109.

Rogan, Eugene L. *The Fall of the Ottomans. The Great War in the Middle East.* New York, NY: Basic Books, 2015.

———. *Frontiers of the State in the Late Ottoman Empire: Transjordan, 1850–1921.* Cambridge: Cambridge University Press, 1999.

Rogg, Inga. "Die Türkei verlegt den Kampf gegen die PKK immer stärker in den Irak." *Neue Zürcher Zeitung*, June 22, 2020. https://www.nzz.ch/international/die-tuerkei-fuehrt-den-kampf-gegen-die-pkk-immer-staerker-im-irak-ld.1562415.

———. *Türkei, die unfertige Nation. Erdoğans Traum vom Osmanischen Reich.* Zurich: Orell Füssli, 2017.

Rumpf, Christian. *Einführung in das türkische Recht.* 2nd ed. Munich: C. H. Beck, 2016.

———. "Die rechtliche Stellung der Minderheiten in der Türkei." In *Das Minderheitenrecht europäischer Staaten*, part 1, edited by Jochen A. Frowein, Rainer Hofmann, and Stefan Oeter, 448–500. Berlin: Springer, 1993.

———. *Das türkische Verfassungssystem: Einführung mit vollständigem Verfassungstext.* Wiesbaden: Harrassowitz, 1996.

Sayın, Ayşe. "'Yeni anayasa': CHP, Cumhurbaşkanı Erdoğan'la masaya oturmayacak." *BBC News Türkçe*, February 5, 2021. https://www.bbc.com/turkce/haberler-turkiye-55949720.

Sakwa, Richard. *The Putin Paradox.* London: I. B. Tauris, 2020.

Salamé, Ghassan. "Small is Pluralistic: Democracy as an Instrument of Civil Peace." In *Democracy Without Democrats? The Renewal of Politics in the Muslim World*, edited by Ghassan Salamé, 84–111. London, New York, NY: I. B. Tauris, 1994.

Savelsberg, Eva. "The Kurdish PYD and the Syrian Civil War." In *Routledge Handbook on the Kurds*, edited by Michael M. Gunter, 357–365. London: Routledge, 2019.

Sayarı, Sabri. "Political Parties." In *The Routledge Handbook of Modern Turkey*, edited by Metin Heper and Sabri Sayarı, 182–193. New York, NY: Routledge, 2012.

Schiffauer, Werner. *Die Gewalt der Ehre: Erklärungen zu einem deutsch-türkischen Sexualkonflikt.* Frankfurt a. M.: Suhrkamp, 1983.

———. *Die Gottesmänner: Türkische Islamisten in Deutschland. Eine Studie zur Herstellung religiöser Evidenz.* Frankfurt a. M.: Suhrkamp, 2000.

———. *Nach dem Islamismus. Eine Ethnographie der Islamischen Gemeinschaft Milli Görüş*. Berlin: Suhrkamp, 2010.
Schimmel, Annemarie. *Mystische Dimensionen des Islam. Die Geschichte des Sufismus*. Cologne: Diederichs, 1985.
———. *Sufismus: Eine Einführung in die islamische Mystik*. 3rd ed. Munich: C. H. Beck, 2005.
Schlumberger, Oliver. *Autoritarismus in der arabischen Welt: Ursachen, Trends und internationale Demokratieförderung*. Baden-Baden: Nomos, 2008.
Schmitt, Oliver Jens. "Introduction." In *The Ottoman Conquest of the Balkans. Interpretations and Research Debates*, edited by Oliver Jens Schmitt, 7–45. Wien: Verlag der Österreichischen Akademie der Wissenschaften, 2015.
———. *Levantiner. Lebenswelten und Identitäten einer ethnokonfessionellen Gruppe im osmanischen Reich im "langen 19. Jahrhundert."* Munich: Oldenbourg, 2005.
Schölch, Alexander. "Der arabische Osten im neunzehnten Jahrhundert (1800–1914)." In *Geschichte der arabischen Welt*, edited by Ulrich W. Haarmann, 365–430. Munich: C. H. Beck, 1987.
Schöllgen, Gregor. *Imperialismus und Gleichgewicht. Deutschland, England und die orientalische Frage 1871–1914*. 3rd ed. Munich: Oldenbourg, 2000.
Schonmann, Noa. "Back-Door Diplomacy: The Mistress Syndrome in Israel's Relations with Turkey, 1957–60." In *Israel's Clandestine Diplomacies*, edited by Clive T. Jones and Tore T. Petersen, 85–101. London: Hurst and Company, 2013.
Schulze, Reinhard. *Geschichte der islamischen Welt. Von 1900 bis zur Gegenwart*. Munich: C. H. Beck, 2016.
———. "Das islamische achtzehnte Jahrhundert. Versuch einer historiographischen Kritik." *Die Welt des Islams* 30 (1990): 140–159.
———. "Was ist die islamische Aufklärung?" *Die Welt des Islams* 36 (1996): 276–325.
Scott, James C. *Seeing Like a State. How Certain Schemes to Improve the Human Condition Have Failed*. New Haven, CT: Yale University Press, 1998.
Seufert, Günter. "Erdogans Lohn der Angst," *Le Monde diplomatique* [German-language ed.], November 2015. https://monde-diplomatique.de/artikel/!5247382.
———. "Die Kurden als zentraler Faktor der politischen Entwicklung in der Türkei: Wie weiter mit dem PKK-Verbot?" In *Der Aufschwung kurdischer Politik. Zur Lage der Kurden in Irak, Syrien und der Türkei*, edited by Günter

Seufert, 61–75. Berlin: Stiftung Wissenschaft und Politik, 2015. Accessed March 3, 2023. https://www.swp-berlin.org/fileadmin/contents/products/studien/2015_S10_srt.pdf.

———. "Resümee: Eine insgesamt ernüchternde Bilanz kurdischer Politik und westlichen Engagements im Nahen Osten." In *Die Kurden im Irak und in Syrien nach dem Ende der Territorialherrschaft des "Islamischen Staates": Die Grenzen kurdischer Politik*, edited by Günter Seufert, 79–86. Berlin: Stiftung Wissenschaft und Politik, 2018. Accessed March 3, 2023. https://www.swp-berlin.org/fileadmin/contents/products/studien/2018S11_srt.pdf.

———. "Von der 'Lösung der Kurdenfrage' zum Umgang mit 'Kurdistan'. Die Verhandlungen der türkischen Regierung mit der PKK." In *Der Aufschwung kurdischer Politik. Zur Lage der Kurden in Irak, Syrien und der Türkei*, edited by Günter Seufert, 47–60. Berlin: Stiftung Wissenschaft und Politik, 2015. Accessed March 3, 2023. https://www.swp-berlin.org/fileadmin/contents/products/studien/2015_S10_srt.pdf.

Shareef, Mohammed. *The United States, Iraq and the Kurds. Shock, Awe and Aftermath*. Abingdon: Routledge, 2014.

Shaw, Stanford J. *Between Old and New: The Ottoman Empire under Sultan Selim III, 1789–1807*. Cambridge, MA: Harvard University Press, 1971.

———. "The Nineteenth-Century Ottoman Tax Reforms and Revenue System." *International Journal of Middle East Studies* 6, no. 4 (1975): 421–459.

Sherif, Ashraf El-. *The Egyptian Muslim Brotherhood's Failures*. Washington, DC: Carnegie Endowment for International Peace, 2014. Accessed March 3, 2023. https://carnegieendowment.org/2014/07/01/egyptian-muslim-brotherhood-s-failures-pub-56046.

Şimşir, Bilal N. *Lozan Telegrafları*. Ankara: Atatürk Kültür Dil ve Tarih Yüksek Kurumu, 1990.

Sing, Manfred. "Against All Odds: How to Re-Inscribe Islam into European History." In *Housing Capital: Resource and Representation*, edited by Simone Derix and Margareth Lanzinger, 129–161. Berlin: De Gruyter Oldenbourg, 2017.

———. "The Tempestuous Affair Between Marxism and Islam: Attraction, Hostility, and Accommodation since 1917." In *Muslims and Capitalism. An Uneasy Relationship?*, edited by Béatrice Hendrich, 51–101. Würzburg: Ergon, 2018.

Skocpol, Theda. "Rentier State and Shi'a Islam in the Iranian Revolution." *Theory and Society* 11, no. 3 (1982): 265–283.
Solomonovich, Nadav. *The Korean War in Turkish Culture and Society*. Basingstoke: Palgrave Macmillan, 2021.
Spuler, Bertold. *Die Gegenwartslage der Ostkirchen in ihrer völkischen und staatlichen Umwelt*. Wiesbaden: Metopen, 1948.
Steinmeier, Frank Walter. "Der Westfälische Frieden als Denkmodell für den Mittleren Osten. Rede von Außenminister Frank-Walter Steinmeier bei den Osnabrücker Friedensgesprächen." Speech delivered on July 12, 2016. Accessed March 3, 2023. https://www.auswaertiges-amt.de/de/newsroom/160712-westfaelischer-frieden/282196.
Steuerwald, Karl. *Untersuchungen zur türkischen Sprache der Gegenwart*. Vol. 1: *Die türkische Sprachpolitik seit 1928*; vol. 2: *Zur Orthographie und Lautung des Türkischen*; vol. 3: *Zur Ablösung des arabischen und persischen Grammatikgutes*. Berlin: Langenscheidt, 1963, 1964, 1966.
Stieger, Cyrill. *Wir wissen nicht mehr, wer wir sind: Vergessene Minderheiten auf dem Balkan*. Wien: Paul Zsolnay Verlag, 2017.
Stoll, Georg. "Religion und Laizismus in der Türkei." *Konrad-Adenauer-Stiftung Auslandsinformationen* 5 (1998): 19–43.
Stone, David R. "The Balkan Pact and American Policy." *East European Quarterly* 28, no. 3 (1994): 393–407.
Strauss, Johann. "The Disintegration of Ottoman Rule in the Syrian Territories as Viewed by German Observers." In *The Syrian Land: Processes of Integration and Fragmentation. Bilād al-Shām from the 18th to the 20th Century*, edited by Thomas Philipp and Birgit Schäbler, 307–329. Stuttgart: Steiner, 1998.
Streeck, Wolfgang. *Gekaufte Zeit. Die vertagte Krise des demokratischen Kapitalismus*. 3rd ed. Berlin: Suhrkamp, 2018.
Strohmeier, Martin, and Lale Yalçın-Heckmann. *Die Kurden: Geschichte, Politik, Kultur*. Munich: C. H. Beck, 2000.
Suciyan, Talin. *The Armenians in Modern Turkey: Post-Genocide Society, Politics and History*. London: I. B. Tauris, 2016.
Sundhaussen, Holm. "Der Balkan: Ein Plädoyer für Differenz." *Geschichte und Gesellschaft. Zeitschrift für historische Sozialwissenschaft* 29 (2003): 608–624.
———. "Europa balcanica. Der Balkan als historischer Raum." *Geschichte und Gesellschaft. Zeitschrift für historische Sozialwissenschaft* 25 (1999): 626–653.

Suny, Ronald Grigor. *"They Can Live in the Desert But Nowhere Else:" A History of the Armenian Genocide*. Princeton, NJ: Princeton University Press, 2015.

Suter Reich, Virginia. *Zwischen Differenz, Solidarität und Ausgrenzung: Inkorporationspfade der alevitischen Bewegung in der Schweiz und im transnationalen Raum*. Zurich: Chronos, 2013.

Tamari, Salim. *Year of the Locust. A Soldier's Diary and the Erasure of Palestine's Ottoman Past*. Berkeley: University of California Press, 2011.

Tansel, Fevziye Abdullah, ed. *Ziya Gökalp Külliyatı*. Vol. 1, *Şiirler ve Halk Masalları*. Ankara: Türk Tarih Kurumu Basımevi, 1977.

Tapia, Stephane de. "Turkish Extreme Right-Wing Movements: Between Turkism, Islamism, Eurasianism and Pan-Turkism." In *The Extreme Right in Europe: Current Trends and Perspectives*, edited by Uwe Backes and Patrick Moreau, 297–321. Göttingen: Vandenhoeck and Ruprecht, 2011.

Tartanoğlu, Sinan. "Türkiye Ağır Yaralı." *Cumhuriyet*, July 17, 2018.

Taymaz, Erol, and Ebru Voyvoda. "Marching to the Beat of a Late Drummer: Turkey's Experience of Neoliberal Industrialization since 1980." *New Perspectives on Turkey* 47 (2012): 83–113.

Tee, Caroline. *The Gülen Movement in Turkey. The Politics of Islam and Modernity*. London, New York, NY: I. B. Tauris, 2016.

Tejel Gorgas, Jordi. "Making Borders from Below: The Emergence of the Turkish-Iraqi Frontier, 1918–1925." *Middle Eastern Studies* 54, no. 5 (2018): 811–826.

Tekeli, İlhan, and Selim İlkin. *Cumhuriyetin Harcı*, vol. 3: *Modernitenin Altyapısı Oluşurken*. 2nd ed. İstanbul: İstanbul Bilgi Üniversitesi Yayınları, 2010.

Tellal, Erel. "Relations with the Soviets." In *Turkish Foreign Policy, 1919–2006. Facts and Analyses with Documents*, edited by Baskın Oran, 88–101. Salt Lake City, UT: University of Utah Press, 2010.

Temelkuran, Ece. *Euphorie und Wehmut: Die Türkei auf der Suche nach sich selbst*. Hamburg: Hoffmann und Campe, 2015.

Testa, Ignace de. *Recueil des traités de la Porte ottoman avec les puissances étrangères depuis le premier traité conclu, en 1536, entre Suléyman I et François I jusqu'à nos jours*. 11 vols. Paris: Aymot, éditeur des archives diplomatiques, 1864–1911.

Tezcan, Baki. "The Second Empire: The Transformation of the Ottoman Polity in the Early Modern Era." *Comparative Studies of South Asia, Africa and the Middle East* 29, no. 3 (2009): 556–572.

Ther, Philipp. *Die neue Ordnung auf dem alten Kontinent. Eine Geschichte des neoliberalen Europa.* Berlin: Suhrkamp, 2014.

Thumann, Michael. "Die Geldmaschine der Armee." *Die Zeit*, July 28, 2016. Accessed March 18, 2023. https://www.zeit.de/2016/32/tuerkei-militaer-wirtschaft.

Todorova, Maria. *Imagining the Balkans.* New York, NY: Oxford University Press, 1997.

Toledano, Ehud R. "Forgetting Egypt's Ottoman Past." In *Cultural Horizons. A Festschrift in Honor of Talat S. Halman*, edited by Jayne L. Warner, 150–167. Syracuse, NY: Syracuse University Press, 2001.

———. "Social and Economic Change in the 'Long Nineteenth Century.'" In *Modern Egypt, from 1517 to the End of the Twentieth Century*, edited by Martin W. Daly, 252–284. Vol. 2 of *The Cambridge History of Egypt.* Cambridge: Cambridge University Press, 1998.

Topal, Alp Eren. "Against Influence: Ziya Gökalp in Context and Tradition." *Journal of Islamic Studies* 28, no. 3 (2017): 283–310.

Toprak, Zafer. *Türkiye'de "Millî İktisat."* Ankara: Yurt Yayınları, 1982.

Torbakov, Igor. "Neo-Ottomanism versus Neo-Eurasianism? Nationalism and Symbolic Geography in Postimperial Turkey and Russia." *Mediterranean Quarterly* 28, no. 2 (2017): 125–145.

Törne, Annika. *Dersim – Geographie der Erinnerungen. Eine Untersuchung von Narrativen über Verfolgung und Gewalt.* Berlin, Boston, MA: De Gruyter Oldenbourg, 2019.

Toynbee, Arnold. *The Western Question in Greece and Turkey.* New York, NY: Howard Fertig, 1970.

Trumpener, Ulrich. *Germany and the Ottoman Empire, 1914–1918.* Princeton, NJ: Princeton University Press, 1968.

Tuğal, Cihan. *The Fall of the Turkish Model: How the Arab Uprisings Brought Down Islamic Liberalism.* London: Verso, 2016.

———. "'Resistance Everywhere': The Gezi Revolt in Global Perspective." *New Perspectives on Turkey* 49 (2013): 147–162.

Tunaya, Tarık Zafer. *Türkiye'de Siyasal Partiler.* Vol. 1, *İkinci Meşrutiyet Dönemi 1908–1918.* 3rd ed. İstanbul: İletişim, 1998.

Tunçay, Mete. "Siyasal Tarih, 1908–1923." In *Çağdaş Türkiye, 1908–1980*, edited by Mete Tunçay et al., 25–81. Vol. 4 of *Türkiye Tarihi.* İstanbul: Cem Yayınevi, 1989.

Türk, H. Bahadır. *Muktedir. Türk Sağ Geleneği ve Recep Tayyip Erdoğan.* İstanbul: İletişim, 2014.

Türkeş, Mustafa. "The Balkan Pact and Its Immediate Implications for the Balkan States, 1930–34." *Middle Eastern Studies* 30, no. 1 (1994): 123–144.

Türkiye İstatistik Kurumu. *Milletvekili Genel Seçimleri 1923–2011*. Ankara: Türkiye İstatistik Kurumu, 2012.

Türköz, Meltem. *Naming and Nation-Building in Turkey: The 1934 Surname Law*. New York, NY: Palgrave Macmillan, 2018.

Tuysuz, Gul, and Sabrina Tavernise. "Top Generals Quit in Group, Stunning Turks." *New York Times*, July 29, 2011. Accessed April 22, 2019. https://www.nytimes.com/2011/07/30/world/europe/30turkey.html.

Ulgen, Fatma. "Sabiha Gökçen's 80-Year-Old Secret: Kemalist Nation Formation and the Ottoman Armenians." PhD. diss., University of California, 2010. Accessed March 18, 2023. https://escholarship.org/uc/item/2mh3z3k6.

Üngör, Uğur Ümit. *The Making of Modern Turkey: Nation and State in Eastern Anatolia, 1913–1950*. Oxford: Oxford University Press, 2011.

United Nations Children's Fund (UNICEF). *The State of the World's Children 2019: Children, Food and Nutrition. Growing Well in a Changing World*. New York, NY: UNICEF, 2019. Accessed March 3, 2023. https://www.unicef.org/media/63016/file/SOWC-2019.pdf.

United States Department of State, Bureau of Democracy, Human Rights, and Labor. *International Religious Freedom Report for 2018: Turkey*. Washington DC, 2019. Accessed March 3, 2023. https://www.state.gov/wp-content/uploads/2019/05/TURKEY-2018-INTERNATIONAL-RELIGIOUS-FREEDOM-REPORT.pdf.

Ünlü, Barış. "İsmail Beşikçi as a Discomforting Intellectual." *Borderlands* 11, no. 2 (2012): 2–21. Accessed March 18, 2023. https://webarchive.nla.gov.au/awa/20130514051100/http://www.borderlands.net.au/vol11no2_2012/unlu_intellectual.htm.

Uyar, Mesut. "Ottoman Arab Officers Between Nationalism and Loyalty." *War in History* 20, no. 4 (2013): 526–544.

Vocelka, Karl. *Glanz und Untergang der höfischen Welt. Repräsentation, Reform und Reaktion im habsburgischen Vielvölkerstaat*. Wien: Ueberreuter, 2001. (Simultaneously, Herwig, Wolfram, ed. *Österreichische Geschichte*, vol. 7. Wien: Ueberreuter 1994–2006.)

Volk, Thomas. "Turkey's Historical Involvement in Middle Eastern Alliances: Saadabad Pact, Baghdad Pact, and Phantom Pact." *L'Europe en formation* 367 (2013): 11–30.

Vömel, Jan-Markus. "Green was the Name of My Civilization: Turkish Islamism in the Late 1970s." *TRAFO—Blog for Transregional Research*, June 13, 2019. Accessed March 18, 2023. https://trafo.hypotheses.org/18818.

Vorhoff, Karin. *Zwischen Glaube, Nation und neuer Gemeinschaft: Alevitische Identität in der Türkei der Gegenwart*. Berlin: Klaus Schwarz, 1995.

Vryonis, Speros. *The Decline of Medieval Hellenism in Asia Minor and the Process of Islamization from the Eleventh through the Fifteenth Century*. Berkeley, CA: University of California Press, 1971.

———. *The Mechanism of Catastrophe: The Turkish Pogrom of September 6–7, 1955 and the Destruction of the Greek Community of Istanbul*. New York, NY: Greekworks.com, 2005.

Waal, Thomas de. *The Caucasus. An Introduction*. 2nd ed. New York, NY: Oxford University Press, 2019.

Wallach, Jehuda L. *Anatomie einer Militärhilfe. Die preußisch-deutschen Militärmissionen in der Türkei 1835–1919*. Düsseldorf: Droste Verlag, 1976.

Weber, Max. *Die protestantische Ethik und der Geist des Kapitalismus*. Introduction by Dirk Kaesler. 2nd ed. Munich: C. H. Beck, 2006.

Wedel, Heidi. "Alltagsleben und politische Partizipation: Gecekondu-Viertel als gesellschaftlicher Ort." *European Journal of Turkish Studies* 1 (2004): paragraphs 1–65.

Wehler, Hans-Ulrich. "Die türkische Frage. Europas Bürger müssen entscheiden." In *Die Türkei und Europa. Die Positionen*, edited by Claus Leggewie, 57–69. Frankfurt a. M.: Suhrkamp, 2004

Weiker, Walter F. *The Turkish Revolution 1960–1961: Aspects of Military Politics*. Washington, DC: Brookings Institution, 1963.

Weismann, Itzchak. *The Naqshbandiyya: Orthodoxy and Activism in a Worldwide Sufi Tradition*. London: Routledge, 2007.

Weitz, Eric D. "From the Vienna to the Paris System: International Politics and the Entangled Histories of Human Rights, Forced Deportations, and Civilizing Mission." *American Historical Review* 113, no. 5 (2008): 1313–1343.

Westad, Odd Arne. *The Cold War: A World History*. London: Penguin Books, 2018.

White, Jenny B. *Islamist Mobilization in Turkey: A Study in Vernacular Politics*. Seattle: University of Washington Press, 2002.

———. "Turkey in the 1970s: The Cultural Logic of Factionalism." In *Turkey in Turmoil: Social Change and Political Radicalization During the 1960s*, edited by Berna Pekesen, 305–323. Berlin: De Gruyter Oldenbourg, 2020.

Widmann, Horst. *Exil und Bildungshilfe. Die deutschsprachige akademische Emigration in die Türkei nach 1933*. Bern: Peter Lang, 1973.

Wild, Stefan. "Gott und Mensch im Libanon: Die Affäre Ṣādiq al-ʿAẓm." *Der Islam: Zeitschrift für Geschichte und Kultur des Islamischen Orients* 48, no. 2 (1971): 206–253.

Willis, Michael. *The Islamist Challenge in Algeria: A Political History*. New York, NY: New York University Press, 1996.

Winkler, Heinrich August. "Ehehindernisse. Gegen einen EU-Beitritt der Türkei." In *Die Türkei und Europa. Die Positionen*, edited by Claus Leggewie, 155–158. Frankfurt a. M.: Suhrkamp, 2004.

Winter, Stefan. *A History of the 'Alawis: From Medieval Aleppo to the Turkish Republic*. Princeton, NJ: Princeton University Press, 2016.

Yacoub, Joseph. *Year of the Sword: The Assyrian Christian Genocide*. London: Hurst, 2016.

Yapp, M.E. *The Making of the Modern Near East 1792–1923*. New York, NY: Longman, 1987.

Yasamee, F. A. K. "Colmar Freiherr von der Goltz and the Rebirth of the Ottoman Empire." *Diplomacy and Statecraft* 9, no. 2 (1998): 91–128.

Yavuz, M. Hakan. "How Credible Are Alternative Coup Scenarios?" In *Turkey's July 15 Coup: What Happened and Why*, edited by M. Hakan Yavuz and Bayram Balci, 309–317. Salt Lake City, UT: University of Utah Press, 2018.

———. *Secularism and Muslim Democracy in Turkey*. New York, NY: Cambridge University Press, 2009.

Yaycioglu, Ali. *Partners of the Empire: The Crisis of the Ottoman Order in the Age of Revolutions*. Stanford, CA: Stanford University Press, 2016.

Yegen, Mesut. "The Turkish Left and the Kurdish Question." *Journal of Balkan and Near Eastern Studies* 18, no. 2 (2016): 157–176.

Yelbaşı, Caner. *The Circassians of Turkey: War, Violence and Nationalism from the Ottomans to Atatürk*. London, New York, NY: I. B. Tauris, 2019.

Yenen, Alp. "Envisioning Turco-Arab Co-Existence between Empire and Nationalism." *Die Welt des Islams* (2020): 1–41.

———. *The Young Turk Aftermath: Making Sense of Transnational Contentious Politics at the End of the Ottoman Empire, 1918–1922*. Basel: Universitätsbiliothek Basel, 2019. Accessed March 18, 2023. https://edoc.unibas.ch/71692/1/Alp%20Yenen%20-%20Dissertation-%2020190805.pdf.

Yeşilbursa, Behçet. "Turkey's Participation in the Middle East Command and its Admission to NATO, 1950–52." In *Seventy-Five Years of the Turkish Republic*, edited by Sylvia Kedourie, 70–102. London: Frank Cass, 1999.

Zartman, I. William. "Conflict and Resolution: Contest, Cost and Change." *Annals of the American Academy of Political and Social Science* 518 (1991): 11–22.

Zorob, Anja. "Der Zusammenbruch des autoritären Gesellschaftsvertrags. Sozio-ökonomische Hintergründe der arabischen Proteste." In *Arabellions. Politik und Gesellschaft des Nahen Ostens*, edited by Annette Jünemann and Anja Zorob, 229–256. Wiesbaden: Springer VS, 2013.

Zürcher, Erik J. "Institution-Building in the Kemalist Republic: The Role of the People's Party." In *Men of Order: Authoritarian Modernization under Ataturk and Reza Shah*, edited by Touraj Atabaki and Erik J. Zürcher, 98–112. London: I. B. Tauris, 2004.

———. *Turkey. A Modern History*. London: I. B. Tauris, 2010.

———. "The Young Turks. Children of the Borderlands?" *International Journal of Turkish Studies* 9, nos. 1–2 (2003): 275–286.

———. *The Young Turk Legacy and Nation Building. From the Ottoman Empire to Atatürk's Turkey*. London: I. B. Tauris, 2010.

Turkey and its neighbors

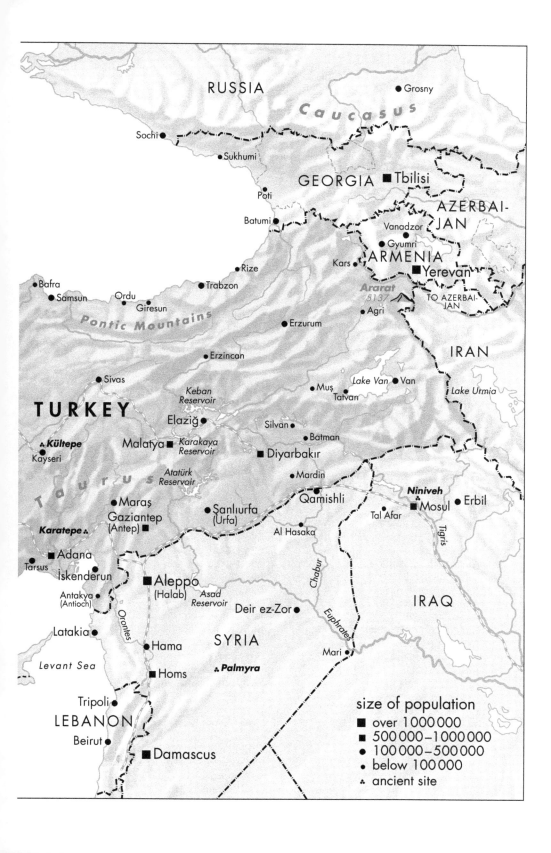

Index of Names

A
'Ali, Muhammad's nephew, 22
Abdülhak Adnan, 126, *see also* Adıvar 126
Abdülhamid II, Sultan, 41, 45–46, 49, 94, 222, 306
Abdullah Cevdet, 46, 102, 171
Abdülmecid I, Sultan, 35, 305, 306
Abdülmecid II, Sultan, 94
Adıvar 126, *see also* Abdülhak Adnan, 126
Aga Khan II, 94
Ağaoğlu, Ahmet, 196
Ağca, Mehmet Ali, 171
Ahmet Tevfik, 94, *see also* Okday
Akçura, Yusuf, 196
Aksoy, Muammer, 227
al-Asad, Bashar, 23, 254–255, 283, 288, 357
al-Asad, Hafiz, 23, 221, 255
Ali Fethi, 84, 87, 127, *see also* Okyar
Ali Fuat, 2, 84, 85, *see also* Cebesoy
Ali, Syed Ameer, 94
Alparslan, Sultan, 256
al-Qaddafi, Muammar, 250
Altan, Çetin, 166
Amanullah, Afghan King, 103
wife Soraya, 103
Anhegger, Robert, 105
Annan, Kofi, 149, 246
Arda, Orhan, 107
Arif Cemil, 64, *see also* Denker
Arınç, Bülent, 237–238Aronco, Raimondo d', 106
Arsal, Sadri Maksudi, 196
Atatürk, Mustafa Kemal, 2, 28, 31, 65, 69, 72, 78, 79, 83–85, 87, 90–97, 99–103, 107, 112, 114, 118, 126–127, 138, 176, 177, 267, 273, 306, 308, *see also* Mustafa Kemal
Atay, Falih Rıfkı, 53
Atsız, Nihal, 197–198
Auerbach, Erich, 105
Aybar, Mehmet Ali, 156
Aydemir, Şevket Süreyya, 44, 69, 72, 117, 121, 127, 218, 220

B
Babacan, Ali, 295, 301
Baghdadi, Abu Bakr al-, 95
Bahaeddin Şakir, 64
Bahçeli, Devlet, 239
Barzani, Mustafa, 281
Başbuğ, İlker, 241
Bayar, Celal, 80, 118–119, 126, 132, 134, 136–137, 153, 177, 201, 231, 251
Bayar, Cemal, 178
Baykal, Deniz, 209
Baykurt, Fakir, 166
Bele, 84, *see also* İbrahim Refet
Belling, Rudolf, 117
Ben Ali, Zine el-Abidine, 250, 252
Bendjedid, Chadli, 175
Ben-Gurion, David, 145
Berberoğlu, Enis, 280
Bethmann Hollweg, Theobald von, 61
Bir, Çevik, 240
Bismarck, Otto von, 42
Bitlis, Eşref, 225–226
Böckenförde, Ernst-Wolfgang, 248
Bonatz, Paul, 107
Bookchin, Murray, 282
Bora, Tanıl, 30, 147, 167, 169, 171, 174, 183, 184, 195, 197–198, 255
Bozbeyli, Ferruh, 164
Bronsart von Schellendorf, Friedrich, 54, 59, 61
Bruinessen, Pierre, 237
Bucak, Sedat Edip, 226
Büyükanıt, Yaşar, 238

C
Cafer Tayyar, 85, *see also* Eğilmez
Çakmak, 84, *see also* Fevzi
Can, Kemal, 198
Catherine II, (the Great), Russian Empress, 94
Çatlı, Abdullah, 226

Index of Names

Çavuşoğlu, Mevlüt, 285
Çayan, Mahir, 168–169
Cebesoy, 2, 84, 85, *see also* Ali Fuat
Cem, İsmail, 90, 207
Cemal Azmi, 64
Cemal Pasha, 62, 64
Cemal, 84, *see also* MersinliÇetin, Hikmet, 206
Chruschtschow, Nikita S., 145
Çiller, Tansu, 207–209, 212, 225

D

Damad İbrahim, Großwesir, 24
Davutoğlu, Ahmet, 255–257, 272, 295, 299, 301
Demirağ, Nuri, 126
Demirel, Süleyman, 151–153, 161, 164–165, 167–168, 181–183, 201–204, 208, 212, 226, 273, 275–276, 279, 292, 294, 309
Demirtaş, Selahattin, 265
Denker, 64, *see also* Arif Cemil
Denktaş, Rauf, 146
Derviş, Kemal, 229
Dink, Hrant, 236, 309
Dollfuss, Engelbert, 106

E

Ecevit, Bülent, 151–152, 154–155, 158, 161, 167–168, 181–182, 204, 208–209, 229, 233, 256, 273, 294, 309
Eğilmez, 85, *see also* Cafer Tayyar
Egli, Ernst, 106
Eldem, Sedat Hakkı, 44
Enver Pasha, 48, 55–56, 64
Erbakan, Necmettin, 151–152, 157, 181–182, 195, 211–214, 216, 228, 230, 235, 251, 257, 294, 309
Erdoğan, Emine, 272
Erdoğan, Recep Tayyip, 32, 91, 214, 228, 231, 233–236, 244, 256–257, 260–261, 264–267, 270–279, 286–288, 294, 297–298, 301–302, 309–310
Ergin, Muharrem, 195
Erim, Nihat, 154, 165, 170
Erol, Yarar, 211
Evren, Kenan, 172, 177, 180, 308

F

Falkenhayn, Erich von, 55, 93
Farisoğulları, Musa, 280
Feldmann, Otto von, 59

Fendoğlu, Hamid, 170–171
Fevzi, 84, *see also* Çakmak
Fidan, Hakan, 260Fourastié, Jean, 129
Franco, Francisco, 115
Fuchs, Traugott, 104–105

G

George, David Lloyd, 67
Georges-Picot, François, 75
Gezmiş, Deniz, 168–169
Gökçen, Sabiha, 88
Goltz, Wilhelm Leopold Colmar von der, 47, 55, 61, 70
Gül, Abdullah, 228, 238–239, 242, 244, 272–273, 309
Gül, Hayrünnisa, 238
Gülen, Fethullah, 189, 193–194, 261
Gümüşpala, Ragıp, 153, 160
Güney, Yılmaz, 90
Gürsel, Cemal, 135–136, 177, 194, 308
Güven, Leyla, 280

H

Hacı Bektaş Veli, 217
Halaçoğlu, Yusuf, 63
Hindemith, Paul, 105
Hitler, Adolf, 104, 106, 197
Holzmeister, Clemens, 106–107
Hoxha, Enver, 189
Humann, Hans, 59, 61
Hüseyin Rauf, 84, 126, *see also* Orbay
Hussein, Saddam, 221, 225

I

İbrahim Refet, 84–85, *see also* Bele
İmamoğlu, Ekrem, 267, 310
İnan, Abdülkadir, 196
İnönü, Erdal, 182, 224
İnönü, İsmet, 78, 80–81, 84, 87, 94, 113, 116–120, 125, 127–130, 132, 138, 154–155, 160, 177, 182, 198, 220, 268, *see also* İsmet Pasha
İpekçi, Abdi, 171
Isma'il I, Shah, 21
İsmet Pasha, 307, *see also* İnönü, İsmet

J

Jakob Baradai, 17
Jansen, Hermann, 104
Jasmund, August, 106
John Paul II, Pope, 171
Johnson, Lyndon B., 144

K
Kafesoğlu, İbrahim, 195
Kaplan, Cemaleddin, 95, 181, 286
Karabekir, Kâzım, 69, 84
Karimov, Islam, 206
Kavakçı, Merve, 191
Kavala, Osman, 280
Kaypakkaya, İbrahim, 168–169
Kazan, Şevket, 214, 226
Keçeciler, Mehmet, 182
Kemal, Yaşar, 166
Khomeini, Ruhollah, Ayatollah, 33, 213, 253
Kılıçdaroğlu, Kemal, 90, 262, 277, 301–302
Kışlalı, Ahmet Taner, 227
Kocadağ, Hüseyin, 226
Kohen, Moiz, 91, 184, *see also* Tekinalp
Köprülü, Fuat, 126
Koraltan, Refik, 126, 137
Korutürk, Fahri, 168, 177, 198
Koşaner, Işık, 241
Kotku, Mehmet Zahid, 194–195, 202
Kreß von Kressenstein, Friedrich, 55
Krippel, Heinrich, 107

L
Le Bon, Gustave, 47
Liman von Sanders, Otto, 54
Lossow, Otto von, 59

M
Macron, Emmanuel, 288
Madanoğlu, Cemal, 165
Mahmud II, Sultan, 40, 305
Makarios III, Archbishop of Cyprus, 147, 178
Mehmed (derwish), 114
Mehmed Ali Pasha, 41
Mehmed Cavit, 85
Mehmed V Reşad, Sultan, 46
Mehmed VI Vahdeddin, Sultan, 46, 65, 71, 94
Melen, Ferit, 165
Menderes, Adnan, 66, 126, 133–137, 145, 153, 203, 275–276
Menemencioğlu, Numan, 123
Mersinli, 84, *see also* Cemal
Metaxas, Ioannis, 115
Mimar Kemaleddin, 107
Molotov, Vyacheslav M., 130
Moltke, Helmuth von, 40–41

Mongeri, Giulio, 106
Mossadeq, Mohammad, 133
Mubarak, Husni, 250, 254, 310
Muhammad, Prophet, 13, 14, 112, 153
Mumcu, Uğur, 171, 227
Mustafa Fehmi Kubilay, 114
Mustafa Kemal, 2, 65, 69, 72, 78–79, 84–85, 87, 90–97, 99, 100–103, 107, 112, 114, 118, 126–127, 176, 273, 306, 308, *see also* Atatürk, Mustafa Kemal

N
Nazım Bey, 64
Nesin, Aziz, 216

O
Obama, Barack, 253
Öcalan, Abdullah, 155, 220–223, 226, 234, 282
Okday, 94, *see also* Ahmet Tevfik
Okyar, 84, 87, 127, *see also* Ali Fethi
Onat, Emin, 107
Orbay, 84, *see also* Hüseyin Rauf
Osman I, Sultan, 257, 305
Özal, Korkut, 202
Özal, Turgut, 19, 152–153, 179, 181–182, 195, 201–206, 208, 212, 222, 226, 231, 241, 255–256, 270, 277, 294, 308–309
Özdemir, Cem, 90
Özkök, Hilmi, 238

P
Padovese, Luigi, 237
Pamuk, Orhan, 90
Papandreou, Andreas, 207
Peker, Recep, 120, 127
Peres, Shimon, 244
Perinçek, Doğu, 169
Piłsudski, Józef Klemens, 115
Pir Sultan Abdal, 216–217, 309
Polatkan, Hasan, 137
Putin, Vladimir V., 253, 269, 273, 287–288

R
Reuter, Ernst, 105
Reza Pahlavi, Shah, 102
Ritter, Hellmut, 106
Romanos IV Diogenes, Emperor, 12
Röpke, Wilhelm, 105
Rushdie, Salman, 216

Index of Names

S
Safa, Peyami, 198
Said Nursî, 193–194
Salazar, António de Oliveira, 115
Saleh, Ali Abdullah, 250
Sançar, Nejdet, 197
Santoro, Andrea, 237
Saraçoğlu, Şükrü, 291
Sargsyan, Serzh, 244
Schäuble, Wolfgang, 290
Schuschnigg, Kurt, 106
Schütte, Wilhelm, 105
Schütte-Lihotzky, Margarete, 105
Schwartz, Philipp, 105
Seeckt, Hans von, 54
Selçuk, İlhan, 166
Selim I, Sultan, 22
Selim III, Sultan, 24, 305
Seyit Riza, 88
Sezer, Ahmet Necdet, 233, 237–238, 272
Soros, George, 280
Spitzer, Leo, 105
Sunalp, Turgut, 182
Sunay, Cevdet, 165, 177, 198, 308
Sykes, Mark, 75, 257

T
Talât, Pasha, 48, 56, 58–59, 64
Talu, Naim, 165
Tanyu, Hikmet, 198
Taut, Bruno, 106
Tehlirian, Soghomon, 64
Tek, Vedat, 107
Tekinalp, Munis, 91, 184, *see also* Kohen, Moiz
Thatcher, Margaret, 175
Tito, 267, 274
Togan, Zeki Velidi, 196–197

Truman, Harry S., 130–131
Trump, Donald, 281
Turan, Hüseyinzade Ali, 196
Turan, Osman, 164
Türk, Ahmet, 234
Türkeş, Alparslan, 136, 152, 155, 181, 197–198, 216, 276, 309
Türkkan, Reha Oğuz, 198
Türkler, Kemal, 170

U
Üçok, Bahriye, 227
Ulusu, Bülent, 179
Us, Gonca, 226

V
Valaury, Alexandre, 106
Verheugen, Günter, 246

W
Wehler, Hans-Ulrich, 248
Wilhelm II, Kaiser, 54, 61
Wilson, Woodrow, 62, 67
Winkler, Heinrich August, 248
Wolff-Metternich, Paul von, 61

Y
Yalman, Aytaç, 238
Yazıcıoğlu, Muhsin, 195
Yıldırım, Binali, 261, 272
Yılmaz, Mesut, 208–209, 212
Yücel, Deniz, 208, 280
Yüksekdağ, Figen, 265

Z
Ziya Gökalp, 97, 184, 196
Zorlu, Fatin Rüştü, 137
Zürcher, Erik Jan, 280

Index of Geographic Names

A
Aachen, 157
Adana, 15, 52, 60, 68, 139–140, 219, 357
Adıyaman, 21, 223
Adrianople, see also Edirne, 2, 25, 51–52
Aegean Sea, 52
Afghanistan, 12, 103, 123, 137, 171–172, 174–176, 242
Africa, 4, 50, 77, 242–243
Afyonkarahisar, 73
Akhisar, 66, 356
Akkuyu, 287, 298
Akrotiri, 148
al-Aqsa, Mosque, 20, 52, 56, 184, 213
Albania, 51, 78, 189, 246, 290
Alexandretta, Sanjak of, 6, 11, 15, 22, 78, 83, 221, see also Hatay, Province of
Alexandria, 52, 104
Alexandropol, 72, 357, see also Gyumri
Algeria, 175, 228
Algiers, Agreement of, 281
Al-Hasaka, 283, see also Haseke
Al-Qamishli, 283
Altai Mountains, 241
Amaseia, 8, 52, 69, 84, see also Amasya
Amasya, 8, 52, 69, 84, see also Amaseia
Anatolia, *passim*
Ani, 131
Ankara, 20, 25–26, 52, 60, 68, 70–73, 78–79, 83–85, 87, 93–95, 97, 100, 103–106, 110–111, 117, 122, 135, 139–140, 145–147, 149, 170, 172, 179, 204, 206, 209, 213, 219–220, 227, 260–261, 263, 267, 274–275, 279, 298
Antakya, 6, 15, 357
Antalya, 8, 16, 68, 356
Arabian Peninsula, 187
Ararat, Mount, 10, 60, 357
Ardahan, 56, 60, 71, 130
Armenia, 9–10, 16–18, 20, 62, 68, 72, 205, 244, 287, 311, 357
Arpaçay, 19

Asia, 4–5, 7–8, 11–12, 22, 27, 39, 60, 64, 77, 94, 100, 156, 189, 194, 196–198, 206, 211, 241, 244, 286–287
Aswan, 94
Atatürk Mausoleum, 107
Athens, 52, 122, 147–148, 204
Austria, 42, 66, 106, 289–290, see also Austria-Hungary
Austria-Hungary, 34, 43, 48, 51–54, see also Austria, Hungary
Ayasofya, 285, 310, see also Hagia Sophia
Aydın, 170
Ayvali, 66, see also Ayvalık
Ayvalık, 66, see also Ayvali
Azerbaijan, 9–11, 18, 72, 77, 196, 205–206, 244, 287, 311

B
Baghdad, 20, 52, 70, 74, 121, 144
Baku, 10
Balıkesir, 226, 276, 356
Balkan Pact, 122–123, 144–145
Balkan Wars, 25, 32, 39, 43, 46, 48–51, 53, 70, 73, 84, 92, 226, 306
Balkans, 9, 73, 76, see also Rumelia
Bangladesh, 212
Bashkiria, 77
Batman, 219, 223, 227
Batumi, 14, 56, 71, 357
Beirut, 52, 76, 221, 357
Bekaa Valley, 221
Belgium, 54, 78, 289
Belgrade, 52, 145
Bergama, 8, 356, see also Pergamum
Berlin, 61, 93, 200
Berlin, Congress of, 42, 50–51, 56, 306
Berlin, Treaty of, 14
Bingöl, 21, 170, 219
Bitlis, 52, 60, 63, 68, 92, 219
Bitola, 52, 92, see also Monastir
Black Sea, 7–9, 14, 16, 65, 77, 82, 157, 160, 163, 272, 275, 287, 297, 356

Bled, 145
Boğaziçi Üniversity, 208, 235, *see also* University of the Bosporus
Bosnia, 42, 257, *see also* Bosnia-Herzegovina,
Bosnia-Herzegovina, 48, 246, *see also* Bosnia
Bosporus, 7–8, 83, 106, 124, 130, 203, 291
Bozcaada, 82, *see also* Tenedos
Brazil, 259
Brest-Litovsk, Treaty of, 56
Brussels, 234
Bukhara, 77
Bulgaria, 9, 11, 23, 25, 42, 48, 50–52, 66, 74, 78, 122, 145, 206, 246, 356
Bursa, 52, 68, 356
Büyükada, 17
Byzantium, 12, 70

C
Caesareia, 8, 52, 70, 171, 200, 214, 231, 273, 357, *see also* Kayseri
Cairo, 20, 184
Çaldıran, 22, 305
Cappadocia, 8, *see also* Kapadokya
Çatalca Line, 51
Catalonia, 108
Caucasus, 10–11, 13–14, 27, 46, 61–62, 77, 108, 206, 218, 244, 287, 357
Central Asia, 11, 22, 27, 54, 77, 100, 194, 197–198, 206, 241, 244, 287
Ceyhan, 10, 283
China, 11, 258, 279, 286–287, 289, 300
Cizire, 282
Cologne, 95
Constantinople, 2, 16, 52, 118, 251, 278, 305, *see also* İstanbul
Copenhagen, 245
Çorum, 200
Crete, 48, 52, 68, 82, 356
Crimea, 14, 77, 287, 356
Cuban Missile Crisis, 144
Çukurova, 15, 22
Cyprus, 2, 9, 52, 68, 78, 108, 144, 146, 150, 155, 167, 206, 246, 293, 315, 356–357Czechoslovakia, 122–123

D
Dalmatia, 122
Damascus, 20, 52, 68, 70, 94, 221, 226, 283, 357
Danube, 52, 256

Dardanelles, 7–8, 16, 50, 55, 57, 65, 82–83, 291, 356
Davos, 244
Denizli, 200, 356
Dersim, 87–88, 277, *see also* Tunceli
Dhekelia, 148
Diyarbakır, 20, 26, 52, 58, 60, 68, 87, 219–220, 223, 257, 307–308
Dodecanese Islands, 123
Dolmabahçe Palace, 203
Drina, 257
Dumlupınar, 73

E
Edirne, 2, 25, 48, 51–52, 68, 257, *see also* Adrianople
Edremit, 66
Efrin, 282, 310, *see also* Rojava
Egypt, 8, 20, 36, 41, 44, 50, 52, 55, 76–77, 79, 145, 212, 250, 253–255, 292–293, 328
Elazığ, 21, 68, 86, 219, 357
England, 42, 61, *see also* Great Britain
Erzincan, 21, 218, 357
Erzurum, 20, 52, 60, 68–69, 170–171, 193, 306, 357
Eskişehir, 60, 72, 356
Ethiopia, 145
Euphrates, 7, 11, 20, 52, 59–60, 68, 207, 218, 221, 223, 281, 357
Eurasia, 196–197, 286
Europe, *passim*, *see also* European Community, European Union (EU)
European Community, 150, 233, *see also* Europe, European Union (EU)
European Union (EU), 4–5, 150, 200, 233–234, 237–238, 245–248, 250, 277, 284–285, 286, 289, *see also* Europe, European Community

F
Famagusta, 2, 149, *see also* Gazimağusa
Federal Republic of Germany, 108, 141–143, *see also* Germany
Fis, 220, 308
France, 4, 6, 42, 54, 67, 72, 74–75, 78, 83–84, 108, 145, 185, 251, 289

G
Gallipoli (Gelibolu) Peninsula, 55, 58, 306
Gaziantep, 71, 200, 223, 231, 357
Gazimağusa, 2, 149, *see also* Famagusta

Geneva, 83, 103, 148
Georgia, 9–10, 14, 18, 20, 68, 72, 357
German Democratic Republic, 141, *see also* Germany, Federal Republic of Germany
Germany, 4, 15, 53–56, 59, 64, 66, 80, 93, 104–106, 108, 115, 121–124, 141–143, 157, 176, 197, 217, 232, 236, 258, 289–290, 296, 306, 308, 313, *see also* Federal Republic of Germany, German Democratic Republic
Gezi Park Protests, 250–252, 257, 259, 280, 310
Gilan, 77
Girne, 148, *see also* Kyrenia
Gökçeada, 82, *see also* Imvros
Gölcük Earthquake, 228, 309
Golden Horn, 17, 272
Great Britain, 5–6, 41–43, 50, 54, 61, 67, 73, 75, 78–79, 123, 131, 144–145, 147–148, 247, 273, 281, 307, *see also* England
Greece, 9, 11, 16, 25, 41, 48, 50–52, 66–68, 72, 74, 78, 82, 115, 122, 124, 131, 145, 147–148, 150–151, 165, 204–205, 207, 246, 259, 285, 288, 308, 356
Greenland, 259
Gülhane, the Noble Restrict of the Rose Chamber, 54, 61
Güzelyurt, 149, *see also* Morphou
Gyumri, 72, 357, *see also* Alexandropol
Gyumri, Treaty of, 72

H

Hagia Sophia, 285, 310, *see also* Ayasofya
Hakkâri, 58, 219
Halabja, 225
Hamburg, 106
Haseke, 283, *see also* Al-Hasaka
Hatay, Province of, 6, 11, 15, 23, 78, 83, *see also* Alexandretta, Sanjak of
Helsinki, 245, 309
Heybeliada, 17
Hira, Mount, 197, 356
Hungary, 66, 69, 122, 246, 279, *see also* Austria-Hungary
Hünkâr İskelesi, Treaty of, 291

I

Iberian Peninsula, 8, 15, 91
Iconium, 8, *see also* Konya
Iğdır, 10, 15, 218

İmralı, 223
Imvros, 82, *see also* Gökçeada
Indonesia, 212
İnönü River, 72, 78, 112, 307
Ioannina, 51, 82
Iran, 7, 9–10, 12, 17–18, 21–22, 33, 38, 43, 52, 58, 60, 77, 95, 102–103, 111, 123, 144–145, 171, 174, 180, 183, 186, 196, 202–203, 212, 213, 218, 227, 243, 253, 264, 281, 284, 300, 357, *see also* Persia
Iraq, 9–11, 15, 17–18, 20, 38, 58, 70, 75, 123, 137, 144–145, 203, 205, 207, 218, 220–221, 223, 225, 243, 253, 279, 281–284, 300, 314, 357
İskender Paşa Convent, 195
İskenderun, 6–7, 15, 357
İslamköy, 153
Isparta, 153, 194, 356
Israel, 15–16, 22–23, 25, 110, 145–146, 184, 207–208, 221, 244, 260, 278, 310
İstanbul, 1–2, 6–8, 16–17, 20, 25–26, 41, 45, 48, 51–52, 55, 58, 64–66, 68, 70–71, 73–74, 76, 82, 86, 88, 92–94, 99, 102, 107, 117, 121–122, 124, 137, 139–140, 147–148, 164, 166, 170–171, 178–179, 195, 200, 209–210, 212, 216, 218–219, 226, 228, 240, 242, 244, 257–259, 263, 266–267, 271–272, 276, 280, 284, 286, 291, 294, 298, 301, 304, 306, 309–310, 356, *see also* Constantinople
Italy, 8, 50, 52, 67–68, 72, 78, 118, 122–124, 141
İzmir, 2, 8, 52, 66–67, 73, 85, 114, 127, 139, 193, 202, 219, 267, 307, 356, *see also* Smyrna
İzmit, Gulf of, 228, 356

J

Japan, 28, 189
Jeddah, 273
Jerusalem, 20, 52, 56, 184, 213, 227
Jordan, 14, 18, 20, 75, 207

K

Kahramanmaraş, 21, 71, 171, 200, 308
Kapadokya, 8, *see also* Cappadocia
Kars, 15, 19, 55–56, 60, 68, 71–72, 130, 357
Kasımpaşa, 272
Kastellorizo, 285
Kayseri, 8, 52, 70, 171, 200, 214, 231, 273, 357, *see also* Caesareia

Kazakhstan, 11, 196, 206
Kazan, 196
Kenya, 223
Kilis, 60, 233
Kızılırmak River, 7, 60, 356
Kobane, 282
Kocaeli, 164, 299
Kocatepe Mosque, 204
Konya, 8, *see also* Iconium
Korean War, 131, 293
Korucuk, 193
Kosovo, 51, 243, 246, 315
Kurdistan, 7, 19, 26, 46, 68, 72, 86, 155, 218, 220, 224, 227, 260, 281–283, 310, 313–314
Kut al-Amara, 55
Kuwait, 20
Kyrenia, 148, *see also* Girne
Kyrgyzstan, 11, 196, 206

L
Larnaka, 148
Latin America, 39, 164, 264
Lausanne, Treaty of, 6, 17, 34, 73, 77–83, 108–111, 122, 281, 307
Lebanon, 18, 20, 22–23, 38, 75–76, 83, 108, 213, 221, 357
Lefkoşa, 148, *see also* Nikosia
Lemnos, 56, 356
Lesbos, 48, 52, 68
Levant, 74–75, 357
Libya, 33, 50, 77, 250, 253, 255, 284, 297
Limassol, 148, 356
London, 41, 104, 148
Lydia, 8

M
Macedonia, 51, 91–92, 222, 246, *see also* North Macedonia
Maghrib States, 242
Malatya, 8, 21, 52, 171, 200–201, 237, 357, *see also* Melitene
Malaysia, 205, 211–212
Malazgirt, Battle of, 12, 251, 256, 305, *see also* Manzikert, Battle of
Manisa, 68, 170, 356
Manzikert, Battle of, 12, 251, 256, 305, *see also* Malazgirt, Battle of
Mardin, 60, 219, 223, 357
Marmara, Sea of, 7, 9, 73, 102, 137, 223, 356
Mecca, 14, 95, 112, 153, 197, 204
Medina, 14, 94, 112

Mediterranean Sea, 52, 68, 356
Melitene, 8, 21, 52, 171, 200–201, 237, 357, *see also* Malatya
Menemen, 114
Mersin, 15, 60, 68, 219, 298, 356
Mesopotamia, 18, 54–56, 61
Middle East, 4, 6, 27, 36–38, 67, 72, 74–80, 83, 119, 130–131, 133–134, 140, 144, 162–163, 173–174, 202–203, 216, 218, 223, 245, 252–254, 257–258
Midyat, 17
Misrata, 284
Mölln, 143
Monastir, 51, 92, *see also* Bitola
Montenegro, 25, 42, 50, 52, 74
Montreux, Straits Convention of, 83, 130
Morphou, 149, *see also* Güzelyurt
Moscow, 64, 72, 96, 130–131, 145, 147, 160, 198
Mostar Bridge, 52, 257
Mosul, 20, 52, 56, 60, 68, 70, 78, 83, 95, 108, 357
Mudanya, Armistice of, 68, 73, 307
Mudros, Armistice of, 25, 56, 71, 93, 306
Muş, 92, 219, 357
Mytilini, 48

N
Nagorno-Karabakh, 10, 244, 287, 311
Nakhchivan, 9–10, *see also* Naxçıvan,
Naxçıvan, 9–10, *see also* Nakhchivan
Neretva, Battle of, 267
Netherlands, 289
Neuchâtel, 98
Neuilly-sur-Seine, Treaty of, 66
New York, 104, 259
Nicaragua, 279, 297
Nigeria, 212
Nikosia, 148, *see also* Lefkoşa
Nile, 20, 94, 198, 241
North Africa, 50, 77
North Macedonia, 51, 92, 246, *see also* Macedonia

O
Of, 275
Oslo, 234
Ottoman Empire, *passim*

P
Pakistan, 144, 165, 212, 289, 293
Palestine, 41, 55–56, 75
Palu, 60, 86

Pamphylia, 8
Paris, 24, 66, 82, 224
Paris, Treaties of, 42, 66–67, 78, 82, 122, 306
Passarowitz, Treaty of, 24
Pergamum, 8, 356, *see also* Bergama
Persia, 10, 21, 52, 60, *see also* Iran
Persian Gulf, 20, 281
Poland, 80, 115, 246, 280
Pontic Mountains, 8, 356–357
Portugal, 8, 14, 78, 115, 141, 204
Prague, 237
Princes' Islands, 17
Prussia, 42

Q
Qandil Mountains, 283

R
Rhodes, 50, 52, 68, 285, 356
Rhodope Mountains, 9
Rif Mountains, 77
Romania, 42, 52, 122, 246, 356
Rome, 18
Rostock-Lichtenhagen, 143
Rumelia, 13–14, 70, 85, 109, *see also* Balkans
Russia (Russian Empire), 3, 11–14, 20, 24, 28, 33–34, 41–43, 51–52, 54, 56–57, 60, 62, 74, 76, 78, 94, 131, 196, 253, 279, 283, 286–289, 291, 296, 300, 357, *see also* Soviet Union (USSR)

S
Saadabad Pact, 122–123
Sabiha Gökçen Airport, 88
Saint-Germain-en-Laye, Treaty of, 66
Sakarya River, 60, 72, 85, 307, 356
Salihi, 66
Saloniki, 15, 91–92, 114, 147, *see also* Thessaloniki
Samsun, 52, 60, 65, 68, 84, 112, 237, 306, 357
San Remo, Conference of, 75
Şanlıurfa, 71, 194, 221, 223, 357, *see also* Urfa
Sarıkamış, 55, 57, 60
Saudi Arabia, 20, 38, 146, 205, 243, 253–254, 258, 290
Sebasteia, 8, 52, 60, 70, 216, 307, 309, 357, *see also* Sivas
Selimiye Mosque, 257
Serbia, 25, 42, 50–52, 57, 74, 243, 246

Sevastopol, 56, 356
Sèvres, Treaty of, 34, 66–69, 72–73, 81, 90, 108, 123, 281, 292, 307
Shatt al-Arab, 281
Shkodra, 51
Sicily, 96
Siirt, 219, 223, 271–272
Silifke, 287, 356
Simbirsk, 196
Sinai, 55–56
Sincan, 213
Singapore, 212
Sinop, 52, 157, 356
Şırnak, 219, 223
Sivas, 8, 52, 60, 70, 216, 307, 309, 357, *see also* Sebasteia
Slovenia, 145, 246
Smyrna, 2, 52, 66–67, 73, 307, *see also* İzmir
Sofia, 52, 92
Solingen, 143
South Korea, 162, 232, 293
South Sudan, 297
Southeastern Anatolia Project (GAP), 223
Southeast Asia, 211
Soviet Union (USSR), 9, 11, 72, 77, 88, 105, 115, 122–125, 130–131, 144, 145, 147, 176, 197, 205–206, 253, 281, 287–288, 291, *see also* Russia (Russian Empire)
Spain, 16, 115, 141, 204, 207
Sudan, 79
Suez Canal, 56, 131
Suez Crisis, 76, 145
Süleymaniye Mosque, 195, 202, 257
Susurluk, 226, 309
Switzerland, 105–106, 143, 289–290
Syria, 9–11, 14–15, 17–18, 20, 22–23, 33, 41, 48, 62–63, 67, 70, 75, 78, 83–84, 137, 145, 207, 218, 221–223, 252–255, 257–258, 281–284, 287–289, 298–300, 310, 314, 357

T
Taksim Square, 112, 170, 258–259
Tarabya, 106
Taurus Mountains, 8, 15, 356–357
Tbilisi, 60, 64, 357, *see also* Tiflis
Tehran, 122
Tekirdağ, 92
Temple Mount, 213
Tenedos, 82, *see also* Bozcaada
Thailand, 279

The Hague, 83
Thessaloniki, 91, *see also* Saloniki
Thrace, 8–9, 25, 32, 51, 67, 71, 78, 82, 92, 110–111, 124, 205–206
Tian Shan Mountains, 197
Tiflis, 60, *see also* Tbilisi
Tigris, 11, 20, 52, 60, 68, 207, 223, 256, 281, 357
Trabzon, 7, 16, 52, 60, 237, 275, *see also* Trebizond
Trebizond, 7, 16, 52, 60, 237, 275, *see also* Trabzon
Trianon, Treaty of, 66, 69
Tripolitania, 50, 77, 92
Tunceli, 21, 88, 219, *see also* Dersim
Tunesia, 250, 252, 255, 259
Tur Abdin, 17–18
Turkmenistan, 11, 18, 196, 206

U
Uganda, 279
United Arab Emirates, 258
United Arab Republic, 145
United States (United States of America, USA, US), 75, 78, 105, 125, 130–131, 135–136, 138, 144, 147, 149, 159, 162, 174, 183, 193, 199, 205, 242–243, 253, 276, 281, 288–289, 292, 299
University of the Bosporus, 208, 235, *see also* Boğaziçi Üniversity

Urfa, 52, 60, 71, 218, 357, *see also* Şanlıurfa
Urmia, 58
Uzbekistan, 11, 196, 206

V
Van Lake, 13, 20, 52, 356–357
Van, 52, 58, 60, 63, 68, 194, 219, 356–357
Versailles, Treaty of, 66, 80, 123
Vienna, 24, 82, 105
Višegrad, 257
Volga River, 196

W
Washington, D.C., 200, 202, 275, 289

X
Xanthi, 9

Y
Yassıada, 137
Yemen, 33, 113, 250, 253, 255
Yerevan, 60, 244, 357
Yugoslavia, 33, 122, 141, 145, 267

Z
Zaitoun Church, Cairo, 184
Zonguldak, 68, 163, 356
Zürich, 244

www.ingramcontent.com/pod-product-compliance
Ingram Content Group UK Ltd.
Pitfield, Milton Keynes, MK11 3LW, UK
UKHW040936300125
454403UK00006B/32